Affinities and Extremes

A PAPUA OR NEGRO
of the Indian Islands.

KATUT A NATIVE OF BALI
one of the Brown complexioned Race.

Engraved by W.H. Lizars

Affinities and Extremes

Crisscrossing the Bittersweet
Ethnology of East Indies History,
Hindu-Balinese Culture, and
Indo-European Allure

James A. Boon

The University of Chicago Press
Chicago and London

JAMES A. BOON is professor of anthropology at Princeton University and has previously taught at Cornell and Duke. He is the author of *Other Tribes, Other Scribes; The Anthropological Romance of Bali, 1597–1972;* and *From Symbolism to Structuralism.*

The University of Chicago Press, Chicago 60637
The University of Chicago Press, Ltd., London
© 1990 by The University of Chicago
All rights reserved. Published 1990
Printed in the United States of America

99 98 97 96 95 94 93 92 91 90   54321

Library of Congress Cataloging-in-Publication Data

Boon, James A.
    Affinities and extremes : crisscrossing the bittersweet ethnology
of East Indies history, Hindu-Balinese culture, and Indo-European
allure / James A. Boon.
        p.   cm.
    Includes bibliographical references.
    ISBN 0-226-06461-1 (cloth) — ISBN 0-226-06463-8 (paper)
    1. Bali Island (Indonesia)—Civilization.   2. Ethnology—
Indonesia—Bali Island.   I. Title.
DS647.B2B67   1990
959.8'6—dc20   89-20326
                                                            CIP

Affinities begin really to interest only when they bring about separations.
GOETHE, *Die Wahlverwandtschaften*

Every new ethnologist subdivides the nations which his
predecessor had connected.
J. C. PRICHARD, *Natural History of Man*

"In that land [the Siddhas' realm of Uttara Kurus], trees yield fruits at
pleasure, milk, and six kinds of food tasting like ambrosia; the trees bear
clothing, and in their fruits are ornaments. The men there are beautiful and
live ten thousand and ten hundred years; children are born as twins and
intermarry; at death birds called Bharundas come and carry away the dead,
throwing them into mountain caves."
A. B. KEITH, *Mythology of All Races*, VI,
citing myths that imagine marriages leading to burial
through air to earth, unmediated
by fire and unneedful of sanctifying water.

Contents

Prelude

The never neutral, seldom transparent evidence of Bali has been deposited over many centuries, abundant texts, lots of languages, and diverse disciplines. Needless to add, such evidence is also performed in the current lives and legacies of three million or so souls identified in the Indonesian nation as ethnically Balinese—by the first language they speak, the Hindu religion most practice, the wet-rice irrigation they craft, the status distinctions they agitate, the courtly past they presumably transmit, the distinctive colonialist aftermath they sustain, the lifeways and gender codes they articulate, and the tourist attractions their ceremonies and beaches now provide.

What has come to be called Balinese culture is a multiply authored invention, a historical formation, an enactment, a political construct, a shifting paradox, an ongoing translation, an emblem, a trademark, a nonconsensual negotiation of contrastive identity, and more. Its evidence is, to employ a bookish figure, well-thumbed. To make matters more layered still, practices and ideas associated with Bali—just one complex position in the so-called Malayo-Polynesian world—cut across different historical identities and classifications. They include for the foreseeable future "Indonesian" (*alias* Dutch East Indies, Indian Archipelago, etc.); from the fourteenth century onward "Hindu"; and in part (the Sanskritized part) what scholars call "Indo-European."

These facts open avenues of comparison: fundamental, unavoidable comparison. This book traverses several such avenues and a few detours . . . sometimes uncertain as to which is which. I am less concerned with any particular culture (even Bali), any isolable era (even now), or any religious or political persuasion per se, than with inevitably hybrid constructions in the history of differences. Interlaced chapters address contrasts and overlappings in discourses, rhetorics, rituals, and social regulations. I pursue motives that render either plausible or alluring representations of opposed religions, cultures, and polities. The pursuit leads away from abstraction toward more detailed readings of episodes, texts, and institutions selected for the multiple countertypes, contradictions, and even ironies they contain.

The book's contents flow quasichronologically from sixteenth-century transmitted sources to nineteenth-century narratives, contrastive histories, and Indology; to accumulated evidence of Balinese performances and semiotics; to social structures and myths of gender difference and marriage alliance, compared across Bali and Eastern Indonesia and back from Bali to Indo-European variations. Repeated concerns include ritual immolation, inequality and nicknames, ideological icons of degeneration, hierarchical codes of procreation/asceticism, the politics and aesthetics of courtly love, and continually (seemingly eternally) recurring ambivalence. History, textuality, and ethnology keep joining and separating throughout.

Taken together these chapters express misgivings about doctrinal approaches to ritual, religion, culture, politics, the history of ideas, and the construction of disciplines and isms. Doubting manifest creeds, even those enacted as practice, these readings explore diacritical dimensions of rival orthodoxies, suggest the salience of heterodoxies, ponder paradoxical aspects of text, and trace multiple dialectics of digression and indirection. It may help to bear in mind that even during detours Bali remains the culture "of reference"; Hinduism (versus Islam) remains the religion of reference, particularly in its Siwaic and Tantric aspects (Siwaic is the Dutch colonial romanized spelling for Sivaic); and Indo-European remains the *longue durée* of reference.

The "extremes" signaled in the book's title should become evident enough. The "affinities" refer both to structures of marriage alliance that loom large in several chapters and to values of magical attraction/repulsion. Similar values mark Balinese ritual forms, Hindu codes of society and polity, and Neoplatonist ideals found in certain European cultures and eras, or their heterodoxies. Themes of covert allure and cure, ideals of marriage, and companion topics of renunciation and asceticism or separation and divorce recall many texts-past, including Goethe's chemical-societal *Die Wahlverwandtschaften,* sometimes translated "Elective Affinities," sometimes "Family Relationships," sometimes otherwise.

My initial epigraph from Goethe could have been drawn instead from Max Weber citing Goethe or from others citing Goethe or citing Weber citing Goethe. The epigraph from Prichard (1843) suggests the theme of repeated divisionings in the history of ethnological classifications discussed in my opening chapters. This rhythm of subdividing predecessors' connections and constructions may not be discontinuous with contemporary ethnology, even postmodernist anthropology. The third epigraph, drawn from Indic sources, alludes to legendary affinities and extremes of marriage pursued in the concluding chapters. Together the epigraphs—one from a novel-sociology, one from an ethnologist subversive to "nations," one from myths that harbor theories of difference—prefigure this study's crisscrossings. No more than Hindu-Balinese culture or rituals of reversal (whether in Tantric or Western-hermetic variations) is the present author able to leave something behind or throw anything away. Pasts keep accumulating, often reverberating, and never quite adding up.

Topics and tactics can be outlined roughly as follows. Chapters 1 and 2 trace still-disturbing ideas in early modern European accounts of the East Indies and in British colonialist texts that established basic conventions for classifying the Indian Archipelago. These pages fly low along the horizon of the history of discourse, reserving more rarified points of theory and method for Chapter 3. I read against the grain of polar countertypes and doctrines of degeneracy in earlier ethnology, toward "heterologies" of multiple meanings that have been central to the inscription of differences. (Motives that entice readers through ethnological narratives will later be compared to magics enacted in places such as Bali.) These first chapters juxtapose disparate documents and oscillate between sixteenth- and nineteenth-century ambivalences; they are attuned to the history of reading about the East Indies and to intertextual relations among colonialist writings and illustrations.

Chapter 3 is devised as an interlude, a time to revisit, expand, and question issues in semiotics, history, interrelations of the arts, and styles of unsettling comparisons. These pages illustrate challenges presented by inherently ambiguous evidence—the stuff of anthropology, among other pursuits. Examples are chosen for their dramatic vividness that calls attention to itself. Chapter 3, intentionally delayed until the contents of Chapters 1 and 2 can serve as a point d'appui, names diverse theorists and concepts behind the book's array. They include notions of "destinations" and parallels between copious arts of rhetoric (of words) and copious arts of ritual (of objects). The book is composed in part as a catalogue of varieties of cross-cultural reading and representation produced from many sides of any encounter. My text offers an ensemble of modes.

Icons and captions provided at the outset of each chapter—some visual emblems, some verbal emblems—should complement and disperse the positions taken in the interlude. Critical concepts are favored when they parallel properties of the forms under investigation. I discount any pat distinction between emic/etic and try to see every subject or document interpreted as in turn an agent interpreting. Chapter 3 also provides yet another overture to Bali geared to performances and their contexts.

Chapter 4's desituations assemble a small host of data and arguments about Hinduized rituals, narratives, and cosmologies. This chapter's studied fragmentariness matches the fragmentariness of method and theory advanced in Chapter 3. It suggests that the more thoroughly evidence of any culture is interpreted, the less integral it may become. Ever-ravelling, coherence materializes only relationally, processually, and discontinuously. Saturated with evidence from Bali, Chapter 4 also broaches Western frameworks corrosive of bounded time and space—examples include conventions of Menippean satire and Bakhtin's idea of "chronotopes." Occasionally this chapter and the others mime in prose (!) the cross-cultural, polylingual, and intertemporal phenomena being read. Not to aspire to paradoxical pastiche would strike my own culture (after all, *ça existe*) as discourteous to others, in a seriously playful sort of way—imitation, praise, and all that. Nevertheless, I have resisted the temptation to apotheosize Bali as PolyBali, and I have avoided promoting the rereading of Indology toward its Indonesianizations and Europeanizations (these extreme destinations) into the ultimate experiment in cross-cultural expansiveness. Possibly, ironically and comically, this resistance and avoidance have failed. Time will tell.

Chapters 5 and 6 place Balinese social divisions in a fluid typology between configurations of Eastern Indonesia and Indo-European hierarchies. In this analysis of marriage alliance, social structure, and gender codes, emphasis falls on ritual reversals—inversions enacted, as the saying goes, in practice and "texts" (themselves, it is vital to remember, results of and programs for practice, and vice versa). During fieldwork in 1971, 1972, and 1981, I emphasized practitioners' vantages in Balinese marriage networks, status-caste movements, and commercialization of cremation and ritual commodities. Here library research turns such topics toward comparative institutions, transforming mythologies, histories of ethnological countertypes, and ideas about ritual, rhetoric, and reading-interpretation.

Chapters 5 and 6 have had several incarnations, or rather avatars. They bowed in around 1982 as a composite paper distributed for conferences on ritual and performance, on feminism and kinship theory, and on gender in island Southeast Asia. The analytic model of rivalrous "houses" with a panoply of refined/earthy arts and performances links Chapters 5 and 6—one on Indonesian and Indo-European marriage ideals, the other on cross-cultural chivalry and courtly etiquette and transgressions. Drawing on many comparative historians, the arguments in Chapter 6 about ritual-rhetorics of "love" pertain to Max Weber's typologies and to what R. H. Bloch has called exactingly the "literary anthropology" of medieval France.

While emerging, these sections have been divided and separated, extended, rejoined, redisassembled, and so forth. "It shows," critics may retort. Yet I labored to present convoluted patterns of cross/parallel cousins and cross-sex/parallel-sex twins plainly. The more demonstrations were ironed out, however, the stranger things seemed. I have elsewhere argued that, in disciplines like anthropology, "the straight is crooked too," and so is the crooked (Boon 1986: 244). What becomes standardized in cultures (for example, a style of marriage) and what becomes standardized in disciplines (for example, a style of description or a criterion of coherence) strike me as all the more bizarre for being elevated to the status of norm (Boon 1982a: chap. 1). Because of this fact, it seems unrewarding simply to overthrow the old standards, and more timely to reveal their strangeness and usher them onto the plane of contingency.

Chapters 6 and 7 and the book's Conclusions pull issues of heterodoxy, Tantrisms, and reformism/resistances into concerted discussions of a few provocative works. My interest in so-called Tantrism pertains to methodology as well as contents: Tantric values are propagated through polymorphous rites, texts, and tactics that are not doctrinal, seldom corporate, not coherent or even necessarily cultic, and possibly contrary to several orthodoxies. If there is one moral to this book, it is that to a significant extent history happens through and as dispersals similar to Tantrism's; so do cultures.

Chapter 7 inserts Hindu-Bali as a third extreme between the Sivaic and Puranic myths and tales outlined in the work of Wendy Doniger O'Flaherty and a Hindu-Javanese social formation described by Robert Hefner. Here, after systematic contrasts of marriage structures and expansive comparisons across Indo-European history, we shift back to styles of text and practice and concrete details of ritual usage. I occasionally call even these more immediate and contemporary varieties of differences "Hindoo," to keep flagging colonialist constructions as one component of their history which now includes nationalism and internationalism too.

The book's conclusions plump for disciplinary heterodoxy; I invite nations and critical theorists alike to multiply their sense of various isms, including totemisms, Tantrisms, and themselves. "Baliology," among its Indo-European, Indonesian, and Malayo-Polynesian extremes, reemerges at the end, diverse enough in its own right, as the works/texts of Balinese and Balinists affirm.

A Note on Style

This book's writing contains alliterative rubrics and mnemonic slogans—entexted ethnology, hybrid history, bittersweet Baliology. Like some ritual, my style at such points obviously calls attention to itself, a tactic I would sharply distinguish from myself calling attention to me. The author of these chapters could not write consistently nonalliteratively if he tried (and I have tried). Regardless, coinages that display themselves (and, I trust, much else as well) admit their own nature as one rhetoric among others from diverse texts and times. These chapters have, I hope, their muted moments and reserved episodes; they may sometimes read like the true-blue kinship analysis they sometimes are. What they are not is an interdisciplinary sales pitch. Still, it seems that the titles and subtitles ought not conceal the fact that the prose will now and then assert (some would say intrude, some indulge) itself. So, I alliterated right off the bat.

The study's rhetorical and reflexive turn is quite different from a "deconstructive" task. It retains hope in fleeting *pitié* with plights from the past, the present, and doubtless, alas, the future. I also regret tendencies among poststructuralist friends to confuse, anxiously and reductively, any empathy—even figurative empathy—with either juvenile nostalgia or preemptive patronizing. Cannot interpretation simultaneously and ironically play child to the parent and parent to the child (whichever the genders), neither of them confidently outgrowing or preceding either?

Toward a Weberian end of *Mitleid,* these essays crisscross disciplines, languages, cultures, and each other. And their devices draw inspiration from those of their sources. "Crisscrossed," for example, echoes English language constructions (although it isn't one) that convey intensification, multiplication, and repetition through reduplicated consonants (crss-crss) plus a vowel shift (i/o). English speakers are most familiar with similar devices from arenas of childspeech and intimate conversation: splish-splash, lovey-dovey, itty-bitty, kichie-koochie-koo. . . . The grammatical and rhetorical potential of reduplication is immeasurably more fully realized in such Austronesian languages as Balinese and Indonesian. (These tongues, together with similarly reduplicative Indo-Pacific languages like Hawaiian, used to be called Malayo-Polynesian). A favorite Indonesian example of mine is *sungsang*, which means topsy-turvy, and is tempting to write as *sang-sung* (turvy-topsy). This example appeals because it is, by chance, mutually so nicely translatable, and because topsy-turvydom is a playful-sounding term that resonates with immense historical issues of hierarchy and politics, as well as domestic rituals and human intimacies. So, every time these essays crosscriss, readers are encouraged to think reduplicatively, as a Balinese puppeteer (*dalang*) or *topeng* dancer might (see Chapter 4).

Modes of rhetoric-minded writing (written to be rhetoric-mindedly read) are a venerable heterodoxy in anthropology, comparative studies, and many translation-conscious endeavors (see sources in Boon 1972, 1977, 1982a). This odd, disjointed tradition seems worth sustaining. That this book is part of even a quasilegacy means that none of its ingredients coincides with anything new, including so-called postmodernism. Nor does this study wholly embrace that routinized "Other-consciousness"—intent on the scapegoating of presumed scapegoaters—that is fast becoming orthodox. What follows is certainly reflexive, not (I hope) uncritical, and involved with issues of power and knowledge. Yet it is wary of slaying predecessors (belatedly), wounding contemporaries (with a few part-exceptions), or desecrating ancestors. The latter, as anthropology attests and the cliché has it, are dead anyway; sure, they erred, but many deserve commemorating, even when they do not happen to be Marx or Freud (Boon 1986, 1989b).

Hoping to sound neither too wizened nor a bit fusty, I should say that proclamations of epistemological emancipation (which I fundamentally distinguish from political emancipation) impress me as eerily repetitious of long-rehearsed texts. Encountering sentences like these—"Post-modern ethnography foregoes the tale of the past as error and denies the myth of the future as utopia. No one believes anymore in the unconditioned future" (Tyler 1986: 138)—I read quickly on, waiting for the other shoe, the self-ironic one, to drop. In this instance it doesn't. Although I profess being a non-Utopian who anticipates no unconditioned future, I nevertheless (or therefore) feel that the claim just cited commits the very sin against which it testifies. It begins to essentialize the difference between postmodern and pre-postmodern ethnography by charging modernism with Judeo-Christian-like capitulation to values of redemption-hoping postponement. It thus emits a classic "past as error" tale, unforegone, and declares the new unbelief Utopia-now. Following Lyotard, perhaps Jameson, and other *frères* and *soeurs semblables,* Tyler adds many salutary reminders under the rubric of the postmodern; he even resurrects analytic metaphors of polyphony (see Boon 1972). But, as he might agree, any *hoffnung* of a new synthesis is itself a position worth preserving a difference from, perhaps an ironic and historical one.

Would-be clean slates, untradition, pastlessness, antihistory, neo-this-and-that, and postwhatnot are invented too—out of the relics and self-disrupting legacies that the containers construed as cultures, replete with rituals and reformisms, contain. Postmodernism is sometimes presented as a polar alternative, one that escapes nostalgia and idealization of the whole, one reconciled to partiality and unending dislocation. My die-hard irony disputes nothing here but the false dichotomy and the characteristic "theorized" recourse to doctrinal -isms preserved in formulations by prefix (including "de-"). That same irony, demonic no doubt, instantly trips to prior Romantic works (F. Schlegel's *Lucinde*), or to canonical modernist texts that doubted the integral, the at-home, and the synthetic in as wholly fragmentary a fashion as I can imagine. If, for example, postmodernism is what it is claimed to be, what is this:

> These fragments I have shored against my ruins.
> . . . .
> Datta. Dayadhvam. Damyatta . . .
> (Eliot 1965)

What that is is *The Waste Land*'s subjectivity citing Sanskrit's gift, sympathy, and control in a French Symbolist-inspired poem resinging Wagner's *Tristan* to *Parsifal,* or Chrétien's *Perceval* before. "These fragments I have shored . . ." (Boon 1972, 1989b). Pasts keep accumulating, including previous moments attuned to the fragmentary, moments not yet nostalgic for something against which to declare themselves "post."

This study is, while different, counter-neo. Un-new indeed it is to crisscross hierarchies and histories of Malayo-Polynesia and medieval France with intense reflexivity and self-consciousness of rhetorical devices. One bold predecessor eschewed closure, championed displacement, advocated "suspension" rather than resolution, and resisted what America was becoming and had become. Henry Adams's *Mont-Saint-Michel and Chartres* (1904) was preceded by his history of Tahiti (1893–1901)—and, oh yes, of these United States (1889–91). Adams's figure of Chartres' "Virgin" was foreshadowed by the voice his prose gave Tahiti's queen Tamaii—following those mysterious field interviews he conducted with Marau, daughter of Tamaii, and "an English Jew named Salmon," the same Marau whose "two sisters had married out of their race" (Spiller 1947: iv). From such intricacies of comparative circumstance (even leaving aside the fact that Henry Adams had also received instruction about Buddhism/Hinduism in Ceylon's Temple of the Tooth) emerged the first consolidated history—European style—of Tahiti, whose royalty had faced dilemmas that possibly reminded Adams of the history of his own distinguished lineage with its presidential forebears. Such is democracy.

The transgressions of cross-cultural history-hearing, history-writing, and history-reading may be almost too twisted to pursue, or endure. But persist we must. (Was, by the way, Henry Adams simultaneously historian, fabulist, and even ethnologist in each and all of his odd assemblage of chronicles, novels, essays, and poems?—*Jawohl.*) Now, unlike Tahiti (or the likes of Tahiti elsewhere in Polynesia), Bali's connections with Europe are not just direct and colonialist. Rather, Balinese and European courtly traditions are *also* indirect, greatly removed historical cognates: two cases among many, many others of Indo-European inventions. This study seeks interpretive advantages from this additional layer of affinities separating Hindu-Indonesian Bali and Indo-European Europe.

Finally, a prefaced word about the postlude. All my books have interwoven mythic or literary correspondences and sociopolitical affinities and affinity in both evidence and theory, in arguments and epigraphs, in commentary and quotation. They occasionally turn allegorical, although still empirical (see Clifford 1986). The postlude is a prose-place (*locus, topos*) organized by issues of affinity/separation. It was composed to broken-mirror the similar forces that orchestrated Margaret Mead's life-narrative and those protagonists attracted/repelled to/by it as she anticipated Bali.

Most of all I include the postlude—whose every syllable, like Gregory Bateson's *Naven,* is hyper*recherché*—to help what has preceded appear by contrast perfectly conventional, indeed almost routine. Two related pieces have been published (Boon 1986, 1989a), hestitantly and with trepidation, since a version (1985b) of this revised postlude first appeared. Had either been offered here as a Postpostlude, a similar contrastive light might have "normalized" the postlude itself, making even its final twist toward Melville (another Malayo-Polynesian comparatist) seem tame. The book would then have continued attesting the rhythm and mystery of recurrent distinctions between unfamiliar and routine discourse, culture, and practice, remembering that what is regarded at one time as one becomes at another time the other. Systems keep reopening; intrigues proliferate. Hindu-Bali testifies to this fact. The defamiliared becomes conventional, the conventional defamiliared; fragments turn aphoristic, aphorisms fragmental, but not so neatly or in such polar fashion. Heterodoxy, dispersal, and multiplied dialectics, even digressions, intervene . . . or sometimes flirt.

Acknowledgments

This book was written largely at Cornell University; I thank colleagues and students there in the Department of Anthropology, Southeast Asia Program, and Department of Comparative Literature. It was completed at Princeton University with encouragement from members of the Department of Anthropology and colleagues in European Cultural Studies.

Portions of the work were tried out at conferences in many locations: Leiden, Canberra, New York, Washington, Bellagio, Fez, Salzburg, Ithaca, Princeton, Research Triangle. I am particularly grateful to those who spearheaded these events: H. Schulte Nordholt, H. Hinzler, H. Geertz, A. Milner, L. Osmundsen, R. Schechner, the late V. Turner, E. Bruner, the late M. Rosaldo, S. Yanagisako, J. Collier, E. Oniko-Tierney, D. LaCapra, A. Arthurs, J. Scott, J. Culler, W. Cohen, S. Errington, J. Atkinson, J. Hagstrom, S. Kaplan, B. Lee, and many more.

Additional colleagues, friends, and family whose responses or example have been invaluable include: O. Boon, R. Smith, C. Geertz, J. Peacock, D. Schneider, M. Singer, I. Brady, S. Lindenbaum, S. Gilman, M. Strathern, I. Karp, C. Chase, and others too numerous to mention.

For kindnesses ranging from invitations and hospitality to encouraging words and constructive queries and quips, people to thank include: P. Worsley, A. Vickers, B. Lovric, A. Day, R. Blair, J. Gordon, P. Stang, G. Dening, M. Dening, I. Donaldson, A. Forge, J. Fox, R. Darnton, N. Davis, E. Showalter, K. Blu, W. Peck, H. Meyer, A. Sweeney; the list goes on.

Three chapters of this book appear in shorter, similar form elsewhere: Much of Chapter I in *Degeneration: The Dark Side of Progress*, ed. J. Chamberlin and S. Gilman (Columbia University Press); most of Chapter 5 in *Power and Difference: Gender in Island Southeast Asia*, ed. S. Errington and J. Atkinson (Stanford University Press); part of the Postlude in *Semiotic Mediations*, ed. R. Mertz and R. Parmentier (© 1985, Academic Press). Excerpts from *Blackberry Winter* by Margaret Mead, copyright © 1972 by Margaret Mead, are used by permission of William Morrow and Co.

Particular thanks to E. Bruner for editing collections (Bruner 1984; Turner and Bruner 1986) whose scope and formats allowed me to try out preliminary materials since woven into several of these chapters; and to S. Lindenbaum for permission to quote her unpublished paper (n.d.). Among many Balinese friends acknowledged in Boon (1977), I remain especially grateful to I Gde Made Ardika, who helped me assess changes in Bali in the 1980s.

For the spelling of Balinese and Indonesian terms used in this study, see Boon (1977: x). In work on the history of ethnological ideas, colonialist discourse, and comparative Indo-European expanses, I hesitate to erase all variations of names, nomenclatures, and spellings that enter hybrid evidence. Thus, I have sometimes standardized; but where fluctuation is part of the interpretive and empirical point, I have not.

These efforts are dedicated with admiration, affection, and a play of similarities and difference to "Tuan Clip."

Affinities And Extremes

Chapter One
Early Indonesian Studies:
Birds, Words, and Orangutans; or
Divinity, Degeneracy, and Discourse

A 1978 issue of the interdisciplinary journal *Archipel* cites recent examples of the Western habit of representing Indonesia by simplified extremes: whether images of its most famous tourists' paradise or reports about its most notorious hellhole for political prisoners. In the stereotypes of the French media, Indonesia thus becomes "a distant world, at once attractive because of its exotic landscapes and repellant because of the rigors of its regime: a simplified vision that could be expressed schematically with the *binôme* 'Bali-Buru' "(*Archipel* 1978: 3–5; my trans.). This sensational conjunction of the presumable "isle of the gods" (*pulau dewata* in Indonesia's domestic tourism slogans for Bali) and the actual isle of inhuman incarceration is a *vision simplifiée* that the Indonesian nation now provides as a representation of itself.

Archipel's contemporary polar image (half of which the government would wish to conceal) comes at the end of a long history of formulations by outsiders that schematized Indonesian peoples, obscured their complexities, and made them appear both alluring and repelling. *Archipel* adds a word of qualification to today's popular French idea of "Bali-Buru": "between these two extremes, that there is no question of avoiding, there exists the entire history and the density of everyday life of a population numbering some 130 million." Similar observations apply to past representations of Indonesia, both popular and scholarly ones, including those enduring ethnological stereotypes this chapter surveys and samples. Even when past observers managed somewhat to penetrate the *epaisseur* of a people's everyday life, they repeatedly reinsinuated polar schemes, as if to excuse themselves to their readers for having lingered too long over drier details. In ethnology, as in mythology, the appeal has proved often to stem from the enticing extremes.[1]

Regenerative Degeneracies

Because of its very pervasiveness, the concept of degeneracy is difficult to isolate in the intellectual and textual history of anthropology. In her influential *Early Anthropology in the Sixteenth and Seventeenth Centuries* (1964), Margaret Hodgen considers such Renaissance and Reformation figures as Johann Boemus, the German Hebraist whose *Omnium Gentium Mores* (1520), translated into English as the *Fardle of facions* (1555), syncretized the Bible and ethnological information from travelers, missionaries, and traders. Works by Sebastian Muenster (*Cosmographica,* 1544), Thomas More (*Utopia,* 1516), and the French jurist Jean Bodin (best known as a forerunner of environmental determinism)—representatives of diverse religious factions during the sixteenth century—shared Boemus's dilemma of restoring authority after confidence in the accuracy of Scripture had been shaken (see Skinner 1978). Boemus's notion of degeneracy tied to human diversity helped consolidate issues in ethnological interpretation for centuries to come. While mankind suffered the Fall in Genesis, evil became manifest as diversity only with the flood:

According to his reworking of the scriptural narrative, it was Ham, a
son of Noah, not Cain, who severed the Adamic bond. It was he who
vanished into Arabia. . . . During these migrations, even the language was altered, "and knowledge of the true God and all godlie
worshippe vanished out of mind"; so that in the end those who went
to Egypt founded the worship of the sun and moon, while many others became so uncivil and barbarous "as hardly any difference be
discerned between them and brute beasts." . . . distance, weakening
the slender threads of memory and the process of transmission "of
minde to minde without Letters," led to the decline of ancient institutions. With this process of degeneration, a state of barbarism descended upon the sons of Ham. (Hodgen 1964: 234)

Hodgen indicates that this "theory of the degeneration of savagery"
stemmed from "the ancient and medieval belief, still viable during the Renaissance, that the world and man were subject to inevitable and progressive decay" (p. 378). But the Renaissance equation of degeneracy and diversity led
observers increasingly to refine and elaborate the symbols of corruption; later,
various Enlightenment figures would project the stigmas onto lower categories
of their taxonomies of mankind, rather than onto doctrinal opponents in sectarian disputes.

I use Hodgen's study as a point of departure because of its historical sweep
and its attention to the sixteenth and seventeenth centuries, the time when first
Portuguese and then Dutch images of the East Indies were consolidated. I
have elsewhere criticized Hodgen's assumptions about objectivity and spotty
sense of "early anthropology's" political and discursive complexity, even during the era of representing diversity in "fardles of fashions," collections of
curiosities, and wonder-cabinets that was her primary concern (Boon 1982a:
chap. 2). More recent interpretations of early modern and Renaissance representations have sharpened into a new historicism of rhetoric, including the
rhetoric of ethnology (see the essays in Greenblatt 1988, particularly Mullaney). Hodgen's book tends to dismiss as merely credulous and superstitious
earlier rhetorics and representations, often using the designation "medieval"
as a stigmatic epithet. Still, no work in the history of anthropology has surpassed Hodgen's breadth of reference.

A professed faith in "unencumbered objectivity" kept Hodgen from adequately assessing medieval "etymologies," although Isidore's *Etymologies* be-
token anthropology between the sixth and fifteenth centuries. Scholars recently have read more deeply into Isidore and the works he drew on and
engendered. Aiming to reverse history's unfolding into diverse tongues and
vernaculars, they intertwined linguistic, political, and religious assumptions:
that language *breeds* into different varieties; that procedures of etymology
echo the workings of genealogy; that naming may effect a return to "holistic
grammar"; that topics (*topoi*) of rhetoric are the very places of memory; and
that world chronology may be replaced by eschatology (R. H. Bloch 1983).

Such principles underlay what Michel Foucault (1970) has called the "pre-Classical episteme"—a hermeneutics of tracing resemblances, contrasted to later baroque and Enlightenment styles of order. Specialist scholars in medieval semiology, including its equivalent to ethnology, have revealed a fundamental "descent trope" in these views of language, history, and culture:

> The initial fixing in language of the properties of things . . . was, in turn, passed on, inherited, along linguistic lines that are also family lines. . . . language seems to function in a family way . . . the basic conceptual framework for the evolution of language is one of biological reproduction. (R. H. Bloch 1983: 41)

Medieval models of multiplying diversity, incorporating portions of Greek and Roman theories of rhetoric, accentuated the importance of *topoi*, a position that became marginalized later when emphasis on rhetoric gave way to visualized logics of taxonomy (see Ong 1983). Bloch summarizes intricate matters of *topoi* as follows:

> The notion of topic (*topos*), which Cicero inherited from Aristotle, denotes a proper place from which to speak, or a place from which arguments can be made. Rhetoric is the topology of the various arguments which found or ground speech. The *topos* defines the final product of the etymological process. End point of the attempt to reverse linguistic chronology—the loss of the proper and dispersion of meaning, it implies a place where arguments end, where sound gives way to silence, motion to rest, and where words begin to border on meaning and meaning on things. (1983: 54)

The attitude in question interweaves diverse strands of what today are considered different domains:

> The positing of a place at which words and things both meet and come to a standstill serves to transform etymology—the history of words through time—into geography, a series of spatially defined relations between fixed meanings. . . .
> What is remarkable in Isidore's concept of etymology [drawing on Cicero, Aristotle, Varo, etc.] is, in fact, the equation of the qualities of things and their origin, the conflation of logical and chronological categories. . . . Relations assumed to exist in nature (e.g., that man springs from earth) become the equivalent of those which are a function of language (e.g., the derivation of *prudens* from *prudentia*), and even of language's lowest common denominator, sound (e.g., an etymology *ex vocibus*). (1983: 55–56)

Bloch reminds us that this mixture is "the product neither of a confused mind nor of inattention to traditionally important categories of thought"; rather, Isidore does not distinguish speech and referent or the arts of language and of physical science because "his ontology is essentially an ontology of words" (Bloch 1983: 56; see also Burke 1970; and see below, Chapter 6).

This "essentially lexical" view of knowledge and consciousness, including knowledge of differences, was underestimated by Hodgen, intent on medieval ideas only as a prelude to notions of degeneracy from the sixteenth century on. Her study also ignores traces of *topoi* during the very period when visualized codes of taxonomy supplanted rhetorical schemes (see Chapter 2). Like Enlightenment scholars themselves, Hodgen sees *topoi* as an uncritical aping of sources rather than a complex argumentation related to ideas of authority. Yet, despite its weaknesses, Hodgen's book illuminates a Western idea of degeneracy in striking fashion, failing only to notice that part of its tenacity stemmed from its fragmentary quality.

Although Hodgen lodges doctrines of degeneracy in Renaissance-Reformation pessimism reinforced by the Age of Discoveries, her evidence shows that such ideas range beyond any particular era or areal demarcation. (Her own catalogue of ethnological catalogues demonstrates this fact without specifically "theorizing" the issue of victimized Others as many histories of ethnology do today—e.g., Todorov 1984). From the German Boemus in 1520 Hodgen moves through many examples to the remarkable study on degradation in the tongues of men by the Britisher B. Brerewood in 1614; she later jumps to the renowned Lafitau (*Moeurs des sauvages ameriquains,* 1724) for whom, says Hodgen, "the problem of variation in religion remained orthodox and unchanged. . . . The religion of the Indians of North America was thus the result of decay" (p. 268). Eventually nineteenth-century American proslavery agitators, such as J. C. Nolt and G. R. Glidden, "reiterated the old story that the blacks failed to belong to the same creation as the whites, that their organization doomed them to slavery and precluded their improvement." Hodgen adds that American Indians were likewise branded unimprovable by means of particularly convoluted reasoning: "Indian archaeological monuments were interpreted as the work of people greatly superior to the rude tribes found by Europeans in these regions, and were taken, therefore, as indications of degeneration" (p. 381).

This representative selection, which can look like a simple series of influences, actually conceals crucial transformations in the notion of degeneracy itself (if indeed it is an isolable concept): from the bottom human rung in an all-enfolding, plenitudinous Great Chain of Being (largely a model of morality) to a qualitative sectioning of humanity into disparate species (largely a model of physicality). Although these variations are a central concern for Hodgen, as a historian she was determined to disclose a strict development. She imagined that the history of ideas unfolds as standard historiographic conventions imply the history of events unfolds: abruptly and in bold periodizations. Her task, then, is to spotlight its substantive eras. Having once evoked the vague, lingering, gloomy ancient and medieval doctrine of corruption in which "the savage was only a little more corrupt than anybody else" (p. 278), she outlines sharp discontinuities, creating two more stages. One she locates in works at the end of the seventeenth century:

The break came . . . with Sir William Petty's abortive essay entitled *The Scale of creatures* (1676–77), Sir William Tyson's *Orang-outang, sive homo silvestris; or, the anatomy of a pygmie* (1708), and Carl Linnaeus' *System of nature* (1735). After the publication of these books mankind was no longer considered a perfect whole, standing alone and indivisible in an unassailable central position in the hierarchy, with the animals classified and ranked below him and the angels classified and ranked above. In both biological and ethnological inquiry the discovery of "missing links" became the order of the day. It became the task of the naturalist to effect a rapprochement between man and the ape and of the student of man to compose an acceptable social or cultural hierarchy as an extension of the biological. (p. 418)

The next stage she overdramatizes as a muted revolution in ideas, without explaining how this "event" could have been so clear-cut, given the earlier dawn of "missing link" ideas. In Hodgen's portrayal of the emergence of evolutionism in the 1860s, readers almost hear a Zeitgeist go "Bang":

Overnight, as it were, and in the almost uncanny silence of unquestioning agreement, the hierarchical concept of nature, which once was taken to be an orderly arrangement of forms in space, became a progressive sequence in time. The savage, who in the context of the medieval schematization of the universe had been given a merely logical and spatial antecedence to European man, was now endowed with temporal or historical priority. Meanwhile, the doctrine of degeneration, which had so long darkened the human spirit, seemed to give way quite suddenly to its opposite, the doctrine of progress. For the zoological world the temporalized hierarchy became natural history, or the evolutionary series; and for the cultural world it became culture history, or the developmental or evolutionary cultural series. (p. 451)

Hodgen here underestimates the complexity of nineteenth-century attitudes by assuming that the rise of a doctrine of progress automatically implies cancellation of degeneracy. (Indeed, below we find a kind of bifocal view of Europe as both extremes in no less an evolutionist than A. R. Wallace.) In her account, the history of ethnological ideas seems devoid of internal contradictions, and the rhythm of its movement appears cataclysmic. One might say that Hodgen's march of the idea of degeneracy itself conforms to a model of degeneracy.

I doubt that intellectual history happens this way. And certainly historians of ethnological ideas should not unquestioningly depict things this way. It may prove more accurate to think of shifting matrices and varied dispersals rather than doctrines: divinity/degeneracy distinctions (or even divinity/degeneracy/decadence distinctions), each side capable of elaboration and transformation, but always in implicit reference to the other. The West's so-called doctrine of degeneracy has possibly been applied to exotic cultures in a fashion more prismatic than cataclysmic. In its indirect manifestations no stage—Great Chain of Being, implicit missing links, separable species, evolutionary se- quence—need ever be left behind, just as none is altogether absent from the start.[2]

It is this more dialectic, evasive, even surreptitious rhythm that character- izes ideals of degeneracy/divinity dispersed through Western texts on Indone- sia. To demonstrate this point, I shall highlight two moments from the history of a knotty ethnological discourse. I first glance at early sixteenth-century records of Western contact with Malay speakers. I then leap to a nineteenth- century genre: the first-person travel narrative, represented by A. R. Wallace's meandering natural history, *The Malay Archipelago*. This bizarre book of cul- tures and nature drew on "descriptive histories" (an important variety of com- parative study considered in Chapter 2, below). Yet the genre aimed to please with adventure tales, and adventure required personal contact with signs of divinity/degeneracy. Wallace's text demonstrates that even a tome dedicated "to Charles Darwin, author of *The Origin of Species*," transgressed the bound- aries of the evolutionary school's doctrines as depicted by Hodgen. Indeed, Wallace's popular book restored rumors of Renaissance-style divinity/degen- eracy; where evidence for the rumors was sparse in ethnography, certain ani- mal species from nature could be used to implicate cultures, as it were, by contamination.

A Prologue of Pigafetta

We owe so many names the world over to Antonio Pigafetta, from "Pata- gonians" to the antipodal "Ave de paraiso," from the "Big-footed" devil wor- shipers of Tierra del Fuego to the feathery divines of the "odorous Moluccas." The last-named creatures appear repeatedly over four and a half centuries of Western texts on East Indies lands and peoples, particularly their clove- producing islands: "Tarenatte, Tadore, Mutin, Machian and Bachian."[3] One vivid example of such accounts, which looks back to Pigafetta's *Prima Viag- gio* (1525), appears in John Crawfurd's lively and influential *Descriptive Dic- tionary of the Indian Islands* (1856):

> PARADISE, (BIRDS OF).The first mention of these remarkable birds is by Pigafetta, who informs us that the king of Bachian, one of the true Moluccas, gave the companions of Magellan a pair of them, along with a slave, and two bahars, or near 1000 pounds weight of cloves, as a gift to the emperor Charles the Fifth. "He gave us besides," says he, "two most beautiful dead birds. These are about the size of a thrush, have small heads, long bills, legs a palm in length, and as slender as a writing quill. In lieu of proper wings they have long feathers of different colors, like great ornamental plumes. Their tail resembles that of a thrush. All the other feathers, except those of the

wings, are of a dark color. They never fly, except when the wind blows. They informed us that these birds came from the terrestrial paradise, and they called them Bolondinata, that is 'birds of God'."
. . . The name of the bird as given by Pigafetta in this account of it, is properly burungdewata; and I have no doubt was correctly enough written by the author but corrupted in transcription. It is the Malay name, and signifies "bird of the gods"; that is, of the Hindu deutas or deities. . . . Before the arrival of the Europeans, the Malay and Javanese traders seem to have brought the birds of Paradise to the western emporia of the Archipelago from the Spice Islands, most probably for sale to the Chinese, for such an article would not have been in demand either by Hindu or Mahommedan consumers. (1856: 32)

Consider, then, these birds of paradise, undesired by Hindus and Muslims, sought after by Chinese and Europeans, but doubtless for different reasons. Pigafetta seems to connect the birds intimately with the evidence of kingship he enthusiastically reports from these actual fortunate isles. His accounts suggest that nature itself turns divine in this peculiar locale—"that entire province where cloves grow . . . called Malucho." In this topsy-turvy climate the cloves are gathered twice a year, "once at the nativity of our Savior, . . . and the other at the nativity of St. John the Baptist" (1906, 2: 87). In the scheme of Renaissance similitudes possibly tucked into Pigafetta's text, nature joins society in testimony to the divinity of this unique place: heavenly birds coincide with cloves and stand in affinity with kings rather than cannibals. In the very paragraph cited by Crawfurd, Pigafetta proceeds to associate the omen of the birds (of a singular deity!) with a proper alliance of kings: "they call them bolon diuata, that is to say, 'birds of God.' On that day each one of the kings of Maluco wrote to the king of Spagnia [to say] that they desired to be always his true subjects" (p. 105). Crawfurd's *Dictionary,* of course, does not perpetuate Pigafetta's Renaissance interpretation; yet those fragmentary signs and symbols within the names Pigafetta bestowed remain; and Crawfurd's summary anticipates the culmination of tales Pigafetta initiated in Wallace's *Malay Archipelago* (1869), by which time bagging a bird of paradise was an adventure de rigueur for explorers of the exotic East Indies. Alas, nature, and the Indonesian cultures that again in nineteenth-century narratives appear to echo its various modes, will reveal other faces as well, including degenerate ones.

The subtle situation of degeneracy in stereotypes of Indonesia is part of the story I have to tell. But first we should consider how from the beginning, although the Moluccas seemed divinely endowed, the diabolical lurked off-stage.

Pigafetta had arrived with Ferdinand Magellan off Ternate and Tidor in 1521. Throughout the three-year voyage (1519–22) it was Pigafetta's task to write. By 1525 he published an account that included the first extensive Malay word list in a European language. While he possibly compiled it to further

Western trade contacts, no one really knows quite why or exactly how Pigafetta wrote (see below, Chapter 3). We are not even sure when the vocabulary
was inscribed, although the "most prudent opinion is that he composed it after
his return to Europe, utilizing miscellaneous notes taken in different places."[4]
We know even less about his sources: how much did he rely on Magellan's
slave Enrique, a Malay-speaking Sumatran? Does the "Vocaboli de Questi
Popoli More" conceal under its "Moorish" label a Molluken-Maleisch, or is it
a trade-language Malay tinged with Filipino? Asianist linguists, philologists,
and lexicographers today scrutinize Pigafetta's 426 entries to guess what the
words spoken in 1521 must actually have been. (To my knowledge no modern
dragoman has been warned off by the coincidence that Pigafetta's term #331,
which poses *girobaza—juru bahasa* in contemporary Malay spelling—as
"interpreter," is immediately preceded by the Malay *gila, al mato* or "mad-
man"!)

I want to raise questions about Pigafetta's list by sifting its words through
four categories outlined by Kenneth Burke in his *Rhetoric of Religion* (1970).
Burke's work accentuates "logology," devoted to words about things and
gods, rather than to things and gods themselves. His provocative approach to
reading rhetorics directs us to "polar" or dialectic definitions in the realms of
society, polity, and theology—precisely the province of ethnological discourse. Now, most of Pigafetta's entries are "words for the natural," including
things, material operations, body parts, flora, fauna, items of material culture.
Among these are terms for the eight winds and for fifty-four numbers from
one to one million. Pigafetta includes scattered adjectives (tired, angry), verbs
(to trade), and assorted simple expressions from "Don't be afraid" to "Oh,
how it stinks!" A few entries cover what Burke calls "words about words": for
example, *berapa bahasa tahu?*, "How many languages do you know?"
(*Quanti lingagi sai?*). "Words for the socio-political realm," primarily reciprocal social relationships, are better represented. We find unmarried/married
(*bujang/sudah berbini*) and friend/enemy (*saudara/sobat*). Earlier, starting
with item eleven, there is a list of kinship terms: father, mother, child, brother,
cousin (*saudara sepupu*), grandfather, father-in-law, son-in-law.

This brings us to Burke's final category, "words for the supernatural." And
oddly enough, it brings us as well to the beginning of Pigafetta's list. Here are
the initial entries:

God (al suo Ydio)	Allah
Christian	nasrani (naceran)
Turk	rumi
Muslim Moor	islam
Heathen	Kafir (Caphre)
Mosques	mesdjid
Priests	maulana, katib, modin
Wise Men	orang pendeta (horin pandita)

| Devout Men | (mossai) |
| Their Ceremonie | sembahyang didalam mesdjid |

Contrary to the desire of modern scholars (see Lach 1965: 596–97), we know little about this list, save the list itself. We do, however, know something about Renaissance arts of interpretation, whereby scriveners considered the world, and the life and language in it, a closed book. We can surmise that Pigafetta wrote as Magellan voyaged: circularly. In crossing from the Old World to the New and on back to the Old, he probably saw and heard according to conventions less like linguistic empiricism and more like great chains of being. Certainly it is according to the latter conventions that he organized his word lists.

Next comes something we do know about Pigafetta, although little has been made of the fact. He compiled four word-lists: besides the 426 Malay items, 160 Philippine terms from a "heathen" (*gentili*) people of Zubu; 8 words from a Brazilian tribal language (millet, flour, fishhook, knife, comb, scissors, good/better), and 90 words from the Patagonians of Tierra del Fuego. In terms of simple information, taking the Brazilian list as our standard, we know eleven times as much about the Patagonians, twenty times about the Philippine population, and fifty-two times about the Malays, who by comparison appear alluringly copious. But any quantification of information obscures, indeed belies, critical dimensions of Pigafetta's lists. Because modern scholarship segments itself into geographical areas, Asianists have ignored Pigafetta's New World words, just as Americanists have passed by his insular Asian vocabularies. But I suspect that the lists have as much to do with each other as with what they purport to report.

Certain items are standard; even the brief Brazilian list includes fishhook (in Malay, *mata kail*), and the longer lists reveal strings of terms in standard order: after Patagonian armpit and Malay heart, both have nearly identical runs—in Malay, teat, stomach (here Patagonian has bosom), body, penis (Patagonian adds testicles), vagina, communication with women, buttocks (Patagonian lacks this entry), thighs, etc. Our concern, however, is with nonstandard items. Some entries—"wood eaten by beavers" on the Malay list, for example—seem too specific to recur. Other nonstandard aspects of the list may be more meaningful. Recall that the Malay words commence with Allah and the text on the Moluccas presents elaborate courts full of splendors and intrigues: tales of designing queens, pretenders to thrones, processions of praus with 120 oarsmen in tiers, rowing to the sound of gongs beneath banners of parrot feathers, "filled with girls to present them to [a king's] betrothed" (1:80). (Even the heathen Philippine list includes before its numerals the term raja [*raia*] "for a king or captain-general.") Then compare at once Pigafetta's "Words of the Patagonian giants." It opens with body parts and, a few verbs aside, restricts itself to simple objects; until the last two items that resound down the history of ethnological imagery: *Setebos* "for their big Devil" (*al diauolo grande*); *cheleule* "for their small ones" (*ali picoli*).

That the Malay list commenced with Allah, sectarian divisions, and names of religious specialists does more than identify the Moluccans as "Moorish people." Joined with the formulaic text on kingship, it suggests legitimate monarchs, some of them distinctly "Moro," such as the king of Giailolo; others less so. But the religion is ordered in proper alliances of kings: "That king told us that since we were friends of the king of Tadore, we were also his friends, for he loved that king as one of his own sons" (2:85). As soon as the account leaves the Moluccas, Pigafetta's narrative grows less grandiose, more *pizzicato*. Just after the word list, we pass into fragmented tales of realms antithetical to kingship: an island inhabited by a race "as small as dwarfs"; Sulach, whose heathen inhabitants "have no king, and eat human flesh"; another lofty island whose "savage and bestial" inhabitants "eat human flesh . . . have no king, and go naked"; and alas, Buru, "inhabited by Moros and heathens. The Moros live near the sea, and the heathens in the interior. The latter eat human flesh."

The conventions in Pigafetta opposing bedeviled heathens to divinely ordained kings are clear (indeed, they are *topoi*—see Chapters 2–3). The Moluccan monarchs are now in league with the king of Spagnia rather than the ruler of Portagalo. Again: "Each one of the kings of Maluco wrote to the king of Spagnia [to say] that they desired to be always his true subjects" (2: 105). It was these same kings who presumably kept at bay the degenerate forces of nearby islands and thwarted such forces within their own lands. In Pigafetta's entire account, however, the ultimate contrast to the kings of Ternate and Tidor is the group of diabolical, antipodal Patagonians half a world away. Not that the New World is altogether devoid of kingly signs: the text on Brazil includes a word for their king (*cacich*). But like the degeneracy imagery in the East Indies, these hints of divinity in the Americas remain scattered, if not invisible. New World ethnological stereotypes are centralized around the imagined degeneracy of Patagonians. Thus, Pigafetta, particularly in the order and contrasts of his word lists, inscribed Indonesia and Patagonia as ethnological antitheses, rhetorically perfect extremes.[5]

In short, these early accounts epitomized the Indian Archipelago according to its favored locale: scene of cloves, mace, paradise birds, and proper kingship. In this part of the globe, the marks of degeneracy—cannibalism and nakedness—remained dispersed or unseen. But in future accounts, produced under different historical circumstances, attributions of degeneracy would encroach once more on the ethnology of Malay-speaking lands.

Between Wallace's Lines

Indonesian studies as we know them today became routine in late eighteenth- and early nineteenth-century English-language "descriptive histories." Fundamental books by William Marsden on Sumatra, Stamford Raffles on Java, and John Crawfurd on the archipelago at large flirted with various ideas of decay; but even these three connected works by near-contemporary officials fracture Hodgen's stages-of-degeneracy theory and raise doubts about any possibility of an integral doctrine (see Chapter 2). Compendia by philologist-historians prepared the way for other genres, including first-person, ethnological narratives. The connections between such genres are subtle and diverse. Important indirect "influences" are attested (or invented) in a peculiar preface by Sir Arthur Keith (M.D., D.Sc., LL.D., F.R.S.) to the final work (1927) by Charles Hose (Hon. Fellow, Jesus College, Cambridge; member of the Sarawak [Borneo] State Advisory Council; formerly Divisional Resident, and member of the Supreme Council of Sarawak). I cite this revealing passage merely to suggest the motives connecting scientists like A. R. Wallace to previous scholar-administrators like Stamford Raffles and to apologize in part for the transgression against historicity this chapter commits in leaping from sixteenth-century Pigafetta to nineteenth-century Wallace. (My transgression will be placed under the justifying sign of "destinations" in Chapter 3.)

Herewith Sir Arthur Keith, introducing Charles Hose's *Fifty Years of Romance and Research, or a Jungle Wallah at Large:*

> Nature has given [Charles Hose] an endowment she bestows on few—the power of remaining young in heart and in outlook as years mount up. It is because he has retained his boyish spirit of adventure and his freshness of vision that he has been able to give zest to his narrative. There is in it something of Robinson Crusoe, something of *Treasure Island,* something of White's *Selborne,* something he caught in his boyhood from the romances of Walter Scott, something he drank in as a youth from Stamford Raffles, from the Rajahs Brooke, and from another who remained a boy at the age of ninety-one—Russel Wallace. That spirit of boyish adventure and youthful outlook he carried with him to Borneo, and it abode with him there. It was because he had the power of becoming a child again that it was possible for him to enter into the native mind and see the world as Nature's savages see it—minds which swarm with spirits of all kinds—spirits which have to be obeyed or propitiated. How stupid we white men often are! We have to know each other very intimately for many years to discover the motives of conduct, and yet we can persuade ourselves that in half an hour, by a few questions, framed in imperfectly understood words, we can fathom the secrets of a native people whom we wish to rule. Charles Hose never made this mistake; he approached the tribes as one boy approaches another, and in the course of time came an exchange of secrets, and this exchange gave Dr. Hose the key to successful government. (Keith, in Hose 1927: xx)[6]

Thus, the history of *reading* texts ties Daniel Defoe, to Stamford Raffles, to Walter Scott, to Alfred Russel Wallace, to Charles Hose . . . , producing a discourse intermittently tinged with such stereotypes as we have traced to Pigafetta. Their destinations include first-person "scientific" narratives as well. What was pervasive in sixteenth-century accounts perhaps became digressive in nineteenth-century ones; yet dispersal, like concentration, has a force of its own.

A crowning nineteenth-century first-person narrative is Wallace's *Malay Archipelago* (1869)—odd hybrid of a book, part natural history, part ethnology. Strangely enough, although listed by such officials as Charles Hose with tomes by Walter Scott, among others, Wallace's bizarre text has been conventionally construed as empirical. I seek instead to return it to an intertextual chain of reading. Perhaps a blinding light from Wallace's dedication to Darwin has caused scholars to "conventionalize" the work. Perhaps tales of the origins of the theory of natural selection have been substituted for actual experience of (really reading) the volume. Did, the standard queries run, Wallace achieve *his* creative paradigm-shift on Ternate or on Gilolo (one scene of Pigafetta's cannibals!)? Did Wallace mysteriously converge with his rival's ideas by reflecting on the Moluccas just as Darwin had reflected on the Galapagos?

I wish to redress this imbalanced reading, or not-reading, of Wallace's tome in favor of its peculiarities. I am not proposing that the entire study coheres around the degeneracy/divinity imagery that seasons it from the outset. I merely recommend reconsidering pat assumptions concerning *The Malay Archipelago*'s messages and suggest that to regard the work as a routine natural history is to ignore eerie undercurrents.[7]

Standard summaries of Wallace's book begin with his opening apology for the lapse of time between its publication in 1869 and his actual travels ending in 1862. This apology, however, does not begin the book. The first U. S. edition (1869), for example, begins on its cover's spine, upon which perches a gilded bird of paradise, its plumage trailing toward the Harper and Brother's imprint. On the front is embossed a winsome, doe-eyed *mias* (orangutan), whose tresses overflow the circular frame (which truncates a fuller illustration from the text); its gaze confronts in innocent benevolence the reader about to commence his voyage. Two frontispieces follow, both now famous ethnological icons (see p. 2). The first depicts a struggle labeled "Orang-utang attacked by Dyaks." One of the five muscular, near-nude hunters falls back as the enraged prey tears flesh and tendons from his biceps; comrades sprint to his aid, wielding spears and axe. The second picture reveals lolling "Natives of Aru shooting the great bird of paradise." Two youthful archers cradled in the crux of branching trees effortlessly fell their abundant victims being fetched by a helper below. One last feathered marvel graces the title page:

The Malay Archipelago
The Land of the Orang-utan and the Bird of Paradise
A Narrative of Travel with Studies of Man and Nature

Wallace confesses himself to be a writer of the most strategic kind: "The chapter on Natural History, as well as many passages in other parts of the work, have been written in the hope of exciting an interest in the various questions connected with the origin of species and their geographical distribution" (p. vii). It is the variety of interest Wallace hoped to excite with the opening illustrations, and the extended moments deep into his text referring back to them, that I wish to open as a question. The puzzling theme I shall trace is the hinted affinity between man and nature, or more precisely between certain excesses in each.

The boundary between man and nature is just one of the lines at issue in *The Malay Archipelago*. Wallace, of course, is best known as codiscoverer of natural selection and as sole discoverer of Wallace's Line, the profound geological rift dividing insular Southeast Asia into two natural worlds: Indic on the one hand and Australia-like on the other:

> The great contrast between the two divisions of the Archipelago is nowhere so abruptly exhibited as on passing from the island of Bali to that of Lombock, where the two regions are in closest proximity. In Bali we have barbets, fruit-thrushes, and woodpeckers; on passing over to Lombock, these are seen no more, but we have abundance of cockatoos, honeysuckers, and brush-turkeys, which are equally unknown in Bali, or any island further west. (p. 25)

Anything that smudges the lines is untidy. Wallace regrets reports of "a few cockatoos at one spot on the west of Bali, showing that the intermingling of the productions of these islands is now going on." Needless to say, cultures mingle even more. It seems a discourtesy to nature's regions that the Balinese have established themselves in Lombok as well. Not just for this most spectacular line, but for all sorts of lesser lines, Wallace notes the failure of distributions of flora, fauna, races, and cultures to respect boundaries nature seemingly intended. Wallace resists hybridization in all forms, apparently. His text illustrates with peculiar intensity that half hope by natural historians that things would divide neatly, coupled with repeated confirmations that— whether in matters of geological divisions and species, race, and region, or physical form and moral character—"the same line does not limit both" (p. 30).

The border between Bali and Lombok is a striking point in Wallace's text as well as in his geography. He inserts an anecdotal account (pp. 186–95) of a (Hindu-Balinese) raja in Eastern Lombok who outfoxed his subjects when they proved reluctant to pay their taxes and tried to deceive their ruler's census takers. In the Dutch translation of Wallace, *Insulinde: Het Land van den Orang-Oetan en den Paradijsvogel* (1870), this tricky tale is called "eene volkstelling," although not labeled "folktale" in the English original. The tale reads like the moral reverse of similar episodes in Multatuli's *Max Havelaar* (1967), the great parody of 1860 (aimed against Dutch colonialism) that Wallace pointedly derided. Wallace finds that this work by Multatuli (*alias* Edward Douwes Dekker) "has been excessively praised . . . for its supposed crushing exposure of the inequities of the Dutch government of Java. Greatly to my surprise I found it a very tedious and long-winded story, full of rambling digressions, and whose only point is to show that the Dutch Residents and Assistant Residents wink at the extortions of the native princes" (p. 107). Whether to counteract Multatuli's case or no, Wallace includes his story of a raja on Lombok, suggestive of a benevolent authority rather than the harsh oppression depicted by Multatuli, whose work is digression and nothing but digression, precisely in accord with its genre of Menippean satire (see Chapter 4).

The theme of man and nature in Wallace extends beyond issues of natural selection and vagaries in distribution and diffusion. He depicts more than simple contradictions (or discourtesies) between natural regions and the dispersal of cultures. In special moments we shall savor, Wallace suggests an affinity between human and animal groups, but at the point where the latter transforms into nature's most wondrous extremes.

Wallace penned many natural history articles for the scientific community, but he stitched together *The Malay Archipelago* for popular consumption. When citing Stamford Raffles's earlier, stately tomes, he remarks that "few Englishmen are aware of architectural remains in Java because they have never been popularly illustrated" (p. 114). This deficiency he hopes to remedy; throughout he writes for "the ordinary Englishman" for whom "this is perhaps the least known part of the globe" (p. 13). Events are not set out in strictly chronological order, and an occasional standardized essay is tucked into his text. Wallace, nevertheless, organizes the whole as a first-person travel narrative. One obvious advantage to this format is its fluidity and ease of digression. Even outright chronicles by strategy-minded historians—such as Horace St. John's mid-century *Indian Archipelago*—occasionally indulged in paeans to the birds of paradise: "All the birds are beautiful enough. . . . More beautiful than any are the birds of paradise—*disclorés maximes et inenarrabiles*—fabled to be the messengers of God, who fly toward the sun, but overpowered by the fragrance of the isles over which they pass, sink to the earth and fall into the hands of man" (1853). The same scholar who decried "despotic, decrepid native governments" could thus pause to reinject notes of Linnaeus and Pliny in his discourse. But first-person narrative, freed from an artifice of historiography, managed better than chronicles like St. John's to build suspense and surprise.

An irresistibly extreme example is *Travels in the East Indian Archipelago* (1869) by shell-collector A. S. Bickmore, a work contemporary with Wallace's but lacking its scientific pretensions. Bickmore accumulates information on customs and usages from circumcision to polygamy. He adorns his readable account with opium smokers, deer hunts, the inevitable birds of paradise, and several episodes about the cannibal Battak (see Chapter 2), one drawn from Marsden's account of a native from Nias whose murder of a Battak was revenged by his being "cut in pieces with the utmost eagerness while yet alive, and eaten upon the spot, partly broiled, but mostly raw." The study laces select items from past accounts with details from Bickmore's own travels. He includes a "page of romance" about a young officer's amorous adventures. Later we are spirited into the scene of a "mazy waltz" on a brilliantly lighted portico with a festoon of flowers at a wedding festival in Palembang: "I prepared to meet the Resident in full dress. He . . . at once commenced introducing me to the host and hostess, the bride and bridegroom, and all the assembled guests. The chills and burning fever, from which I had been suffering, vanished, and in a moment I found myself transferred from a real purgatory into a perfect paradise" (p. 530).

The book's final pages contain one last glimpse of purgatory in a daring "struggle for life," with an illustration labeled "killing the python" plus three pages of caption, worth reading with a theatrically Southern accent:

> In the bottom of the boat, aft . . . I espied, to my horror, the great python closely coiled away. . . . Suffering the acutest agony from the deep wound I had already given him, he raised his head high out of the midst of his huge coil, his red jaws wide open, and his eyes flashing fire like live coals. I felt the blood chill in my veins as, for an instant, we glanced into each other's eyes, and both instinctively realized that one of us two must die on that spot. . . . The next time he darted at me I gave him a heavy cut about fifteen inches behind his head, severing the body completely off, except about an inch on the under side, and, as he coiled up, this part fell over, and he fasted his teeth into his own coils. . . . The long trail of his blood on the deck assured me that I was indeed safe, and, drawing a long breath of relief, I thanked the Giver of all our blessings.
>
> This was my last experience in the tropical East. (1869: 539–42)

Although Wallace included his own "python" adventure, complete with sensational illustration (pp. 304ff.), his narrative devices are mercifully less blatant than Bickmore's. Occasionally he seasons portraits of cultures with the kind of vivid simile usually reserved for natural species, as in an uncharacteristically circumstantial description of a Javanese ritual:

> The next morning . . . the two lads, who were about 14 years old, were brought out, clothed in a sarong from the waist downward, and having the whole body covered with a yellow powder, and profusely decked with white blossoms in wreaths, necklaces, and armlets, looking at first like savage brides. They were conducted by two priests to a bench placed in front of the house in the open air, and the ceremony of circumcision was then performed before the assembled crowd. (p. 114)

But most of Wallace's discursive flair is reserved for orangutans and paradise birds. The orangutan chapter, first of three dealing with Dyaks, concludes
with striking features of the creature's distribution: "It is very remarkable that
an animal so large, so peculiar, and of such a high type of form as the orang-
utan, should be confined to so limited a district—two islands [Borneo and
Sumatra], and those almost the last inhabited by the higher Mammalia" (p.
72). More lines. The chapter is primarily devoted to a sequence of episodes
during his stay in Sarawak, whose renowned ruler, Sir James Brooke, abetted
the indefatigable Wallace (on twenty-six nights he once managed to collect
1,386 moths) in his "search of shells, insects, birds, and the orang-utan" (p.
46). The intensive narrative highlights differences in each encounter. I select
several excerpts on the "great man-like ape of Borneo" to demonstrate the
circuitous route to standardized information in Wallace:

> On April 26th . . . we found another. . . . It fell at the first shot, but
> did not seem much hurt, and immediately climbed up the nearest
> tree, when I fired, and it again fell, with a broken arm and a wound
> in the body. The two Dyaks now ran up to it, and each seized hold of
> a hand, telling me to cut a pole and they would secure it. But al-
> though one arm was broken, and it was only a half-grown animal, it
> was too strong for these young savages, drawing them up toward its
> mouth notwithstanding all their efforts. . . . It now began climbing
> up the tree again, and, to avoid trouble, I shot it through the heart.
> (pp. 51–52)

Later:

> This little creature was only about a foot long, and had evidently
> been hanging to its mother when she first fell. . . . I fitted up a little
> box for a cradle. . . . It enjoyed the wiping and rubbing amazingly,
> and when I brushed its hair seemed to be perfectly happy. . . . Find-
> ing it so fond of hair, I endeavored to make an artificial mother, by
> wrapping up a piece of buffalo-skin into a bundle. . . . The poor
> little thing would lick its lips, draw in its cheeks, and turn up its eyes
> with an expression of the most supreme satisfaction when it had a
> mouthful particularly to its taste. . . . If [not sufficiently palatable]
> food was continued, it would set up a scream and kick about vio-
> lently exactly like a baby in a passion. . . . after lingering for a week
> a most pitiable object, [it] died, after being in my possession nearly
> three months. (pp. 53–57)

Later still:

> Very soon, however, one of the Dyaks called me and pointed upward,
> and on looking I saw a great red hairy body and a huge black face
> gazing down from a great height, as if wanting to know what was
> making such a disturbance below. I instantly fired, and he made off

at once, so that I could not then tell whether I had hit him. . . . Running, climbing, and creeping among these, we came up with the creature on the top of a high tree near the road, where the Chinamen had discovered him, and were shouting their astonishment with open mouth: "Ya, ya, Tuan; Orang-utan, Tuan." [A full page of repeated shots later:] . . . we all began pulling at the creepers . . . down he came with a thud like the fall of a giant. And he was a giant, his head and body being full as large as a man's. . . . His outstretched arms measured seven feet three inches across. . . . On examination we found he had been dreadfully wounded. Both legs were broken, one hip-joint and the root of the spine completely shattered, and two bullets were found in his neck and jaws! Yet he was still alive when he fell. The two Chinamen carried him home tied to a pole, and I was occupied with Charley the whole of the next day, preparing the skin and boiling the bones to make a perfect skeleton, which are now preserved in the Museum at Derby. (pp. 58–60)

Each episode is many times longer than these abbreviated versions; they are filled out with some comments on ethnozoology and corrections of measurements estimated in earlier sources. But by and large they celebrate the extraordinary strength of the manlike *mias*. Even Wallace's regretted infant specimen, when skinned and preserved after finally passing away, turned out to have broken an arm and leg when clinging to its mother, shot dead in her sheltered treetop (p. 57). Symbol of unimaginable endurance and touching tenacity, the *orang* turns truculent only when threatened. The beast, concealed in nature, becomes manifest when disturbed.

It is worth following the cue from Wallace's title and frontispieces by juxtaposing this image from Borneo with counterpart adventures in Aru.[8] (The "connected form" of descriptions of birds of paradise is in the more conventional natural history of chapter 38, where information from the adventure stories is repeated with less climactic commentary; the work thus contains multiple—two—versions of the same "data".) Aru itself presents those mingled racial, linguistic, and cultural characteristics of the kind that both disturb and somehow attract Wallace. He observes that the complicated mixture of races would "utterly confound an ethnologist," and he puzzles over the combination of Papuan physiognomy with delicate European features but dark skin and hair that argue against Dutch intermixture. He then detects some Portuguese words—*jafui, porco*—in their language and concludes that early Portuguese traders had deposited "the visible characteristics of their race. . . . If to this we add the occasional mixture of Malay, Dutch and Chinese with the indigenous Papuans, we have no reason to wonder at the curious varieties of form and feature occasionally to be met with in Aru" (pp. 453–54).

It is the lines of contrast and evidence of intermixtures in both physical traits and linguistic features that interest the natural historian, not the inhabitants or languages themselves. Unlike their predecessors in comparative philology, scientists like Wallace plotted lexical distributions with little accompanying interest in translation: "And the [Aru people] certainly do talk! Every evening there is a little Babel around me: but as I understand not a word of it, I go on with my book or work undisturbed" (p. 453).

Even in the alloyed isles of Aru, Wallace seeks "nicely-balanced relations of organic and inorganic nature." While he seems to desire the same balance in the orders of human nature, without the confusion of diffusions and mixtures, an unsettled ambivalence enters the picture. Consider first Aru's nature. The island habitat presents a perfected form hitherto seldom witnessed by Europeans. Wallace encounters first the *burung raja*—in which his Aru hosts saw nothing more "than we do in the robin or the goldfinch"—and then the great paradise birds. He evokes a naturalist's epiphany, moving from sound to vision:

> At early morn, before the sun has risen, we hear a loud cry of "Wawk-wawk-wawk, wok-wok-wok," which resounds through the forest, changing its direction continually. This is the Great Bird of Paradise going to seek his breakfast. Others soon follow his example; lories and parroquets cry shrilly, cockatoos scream, king-hunters croak and bark, and the various smaller birds chirp and whistle their morning song. As I lie listening to these interesting sounds, I realize my position as the first European who has ever lived for months together in the Aru islands, a place which I had hoped rather than expected ever to visit. I think how many besides myself have longed to reach these almost fairy realms, and to see with their own eyes the many wonderful and beautiful things which I am daily encountering. (pp. 449–50)

At this charmed moment Wallace seems still to subscribe to his newfound conviction that "surely all living things were not made for man. Many of them have no relation to him" (p. 449). This insight accompanied his sense of the inevitable doom that civilization spelled for the "nicely balanced organic relations" he was privileged to glimpse. Ironically, civilization would extinguish "these very beings whose wonderful structure and beauty [civilized intellect] alone is fitted to appreciate and enjoy" (pp. 448–49). But Wallace's conviction is short-lived; with the heavenly, early-morning medley ringing in his ears, the routine reemerges: "But now Ali and Baderoon are up and getting ready their guns and ammunition, and little Baso has his fire lighted and is boiling my coffee, and I remember that I had a black cockatoo brought in late last night, which I must skin immediately, and so I jump up and begin my day's work very happily" (p. 450).

Wallace summarizes paradoxes of distribution in Aru and New Guinea in chapter 38, where he offers a mercantilist view of organic species that recalls sixteenth-century observations on mace, cloves, and other natural rarities: "it seems as if Nature had taken precautions that these her choicest treasures should not be made too common, and thus be undervalued" (p. 574). Back in the narrative proper matters remain more ambivalent. Again, although civilization portends the birds' demise, it seems wantonly wasteful for nature to manifest its perfection in creatures existing only in a place "with no intelligent eye to gaze upon their loveliness." Later readers learn that something special is manifest in Aru's human inhabitants as well. Wallace's adventure culminates neither in his personal epiphany nor in documentation of the many specimens collected, but in a slightly ecstatic passage providing an elaborate caption to that second frontispiece (explained in much abridged fashion in chapter 38). The Aru archery technique is designed to avoid bloodstains on the plumage. (We see portrayed a kind of "herbal" hunting in stark contrast to Dyak methods, as ferocious as that enraged orang the natives hack and spear.) But the Aru illustration implies more than techniques of preserving valuable skins:

> The birds had now commenced what the people here call their "sacaleli," or dancing-parties, in certain trees in the forest, which are not fruit trees, as I at first imagined, but which have an immense head of spreading branches and large but scattered leaves, giving a clear space for the birds to play and exhibit their plumes. On one of these trees a dozen or twenty full-plumage male birds assemble together, raise up their wings, stretch out their necks, and elevate their exquisite plumes, keeping them in a continual vibration. Between whiles they fly across from branch to branch in great excitement, so that the whole tree is filled with waving plumes in every variety of attitude and motion [see chapter illustration]. . . . The bird itself is nearly as large as a crow. . . . At the time of its excitement, however, the wings are raised vertically over the back. . . . The whole bird is then overshadowed by them, the crouching body, yellow head, and emerald-green throat forming but the foundation and setting to the golden glory which waves above. When seen in this attitude, the bird of paradise really deserves its name, and must be ranked as one of the most beautiful and most wonderful of living things. (pp. 466–67)

This magnificent sacaleli scene is not the whole climax. After a comment about his specimens and a blank line suggesting a change of topic, Wallace proffers yet another epiphany, this time over a human correspondence to Aru's perfected nature:

> Here, as among most savage people I have dwelt among, I was delighted with the beauty of the human form—a beauty of which stay-at-home civilized people can scarcely have any conception. What are the finest Grecian statues to the living, moving breathing men I saw daily around me? The unrestrained grace of the naked savage, as he goes about his daily occupations, or lounges at his ease, must be seen to be understood; and a youth bending his bow is the perfection of manly beauty. (p. 467)

Thus, an apparently anecdotal picture of hunting routines conceals a conjunction of aesthetic ideals: nature's paradise birds and culture's Aru bowsmen, both caught in the act and at the moment of their respective perfections. This natural species with its divine resonance elevates alloyed Aru toward a similar state of beauty. And Wallace's narrative offers this apex of man and nature boundless homage.

From this explicit point in Wallace we might crisscross back to Borneo: does a similar correspondence infuse the Dyak picture? Are there affinities joining these iconic extremes, which themselves suggestively invent a correspondence of creatures and cultures? The Dyaks (by which term Wallace includes the Iban) fair relatively well in his ethnological generalizations. They appear superior in both mental capacity and moral character to the Malays who plunder them. Although their "half-savage state" makes them apathetic and dilatory, they have shown the good sense to back the late, lamented Rajah Brooke:

> In forming a proper estimate of Sir James Brooke's government, it must ever be remembered that he held Sarawak solely by the good-will of the native inhabitants. He had to deal with two races, one of whom, the Mohammedan Malays, looked upon the other race, the Dyaks, as savages and slaves, only fit to be robbed and plundered. He has effectually protected the Dyaks, and has invariably treated them as, in his sight, equal to the Malays, and yet he has secured the affection and good-will of both. Notwithstanding the religious prejudices of Mohammedans, he has induced them to modify many of their worst laws and customs, and to assimilate their criminal code to that of the civilized world. That his government still continues, after twenty-seven years—notwithstanding his frequent absences from ill-health, notwithstanding conspiracies of Malay chiefs, and insurrections of Chinese gold-diggers, all of which have been overcome by the support of the native populations, and notwithstanding financial, political, and domestic troubles—is due, I believe, solely to the many admirable qualities which Sir James Brooke possessed. (p. 104; on the history of the Brookes in Sarawak, see Pringle 1970)

Yet the stability achieved remains fragile. Wallace's narrative links the potential ferocity of a roused orang and the physical power of the half savages that share its habitat. It would seem that neither the Aru nor the Dyak emblem simply identifies a population with its animal neighbors. Rather, each fauna pulls its human counterpart toward its extreme characteristic: lyrical divinity on the one hand, bestial might (beneath apparent docility) on the other: avian grace versus animal urge. It is difficult to know whether Borneo, like Aru, suggests the possibility of a culture becoming nature's simulacrum, but certainly the murmur is there in Wallace's text.

Wallace's work concludes with a socialist complaint about the "deficient morality" that is the "great blot of modern civilization, and the greatest hindrance to true progress" (p. 597). He deems many savages inferior intellectually but superior morally, and he finds Europe's urban masses "worse off than the savage in the midst of his tribe" (p. 598). Moreover, "thickly-populated England," full of proprietors, is still in a "state of social barbarism . . . as regards true social science" (p. 599). Wallace's socialist stance makes England itself a barbarian-civilized mixture; even in his homeland, dividing lines are shaky. And again he seems most concerned with the interstices of his own categories, what Mary Douglas (1970) calls, in the realm of symbolic classifications, "dirt." The plea for Europe's masses is tucked into Wallace's final chapter on archipelago races where he strictly and conventionally contrasts Malays and Papuans. Ideally, again, the lines seem clear:

> It appears, therefore, that whether we consider their physical conformation, their moral characteristics, or their intellectual capacities, the Malay and Papuan races offer remarkable differences and striking contrasts. The Malay is of short stature, brown-skinned, straight-haired, beardless, and smooth-bodied. The Papuan is taller, is black-skinned, frizzy-haired, bearded, and hairy-bodied. The former is broad-faced, has a small nose, and flat eyebrows; the latter is long-faced, has a large and prominent nose, and projecting eyebrows. The Malay is bashful, cold, undemonstrative, and quiet; the Papuan is bold, impetuous, excitable, and noisy. The former is grave and seldom laughs; the latter is joyous and laughter-loving—the one conceals his emotions, the other displays them. (p. 590)

But these crisp distinctions smudge; these lines too blur. Recall again the "savage Malays" of orangutan land and elsewhere: "The savage Malays are the Dyaks of Borneo; the Battaks and other wild tribes of Sumatra; the Jakuns of the Malay peninsula; the aborigines of Northern Celebes, of the Sula Islands, and a part of Bouru" (p. 585).

Wallace's narrative concludes as it has proceeded: in a continual tension between desired orderly divisions and their enticing chinks. Moreover, we have seen how notions of divinity/degeneracy emerge where nature seems to transcend itself. Thus Wallace both resists and celebrates transgressed boundaries; his story moves less within the confines he would establish than between them, finally concluding with the social barbarism of the civilizing West. He assumes that a popular readership would be more readily lured across different Indonesian and Malay cultures if transfixed by a polar image. Where the image was lacking in cultures, it could always be borrowed from nature. He thus restores some of the flavor (but not, of course, the world view) of Pigafetta's sixteenth-century account from the heyday of the Great Chain of Being. The extreme symbols for typifying Malay-speaking cultures arise from Wallace's selective schematization of the area's exotic fauna. We may as well designate the device what it was: a *totemism*, i.e., the semiotic use of select natural species to signify select social divisions (Lévi-Strauss 1963).[9] In comparing the difference between Dyak and Aru to the difference between *mias* and *burung*, Wallace propounded, or rather committed, a *totemism* in Western ethnological discourse under the sign of evolutionist science.

Ramifications

Just as peculiar activities become normative in every culture, so strange sorts of texts become standard in ethnological pursuits. Nothing is less empiricist, more convention-laden, than certain components of "natural histories" that once assumed responsibility for representing East Indies cultures. By seizing such works not at their hearts but at their somewhat obsessive digressions, we can better assess the source of their appeal, the oddness of their format, the complexity of their discourse, and the mythic categories they trail. Tracing circuitous hints of degeneracy/divinity in such texts helps expose hidden continuities among different ethnological genres. Even a too-confident sense of disjunction between pre-Enlightenment varieties of description (Pigafetta, for example) and scientific ones (Wallace, for example) grows bothered. From the earliest Western sources Indonesia was spared the encompassing stigma of degeneracy (as diabolicalness) that became associated with certain New World populations. The divinity of Indonesian kings outshone suggestions of cannibalism. Yet with the West's double lens of divinity/degeneracy already in place, even where kingship reigned, symbols of decay slithered about, sure to reemerge.

Unsettling moments in ethnological discourse point to the advisability of enriching Margaret Hodgen's model of the history of anthropological ideas while maintaining her sense of variations in any doctrine of degeneracy. The texts reread in this chapter suggest how various are the discursive modes in which cultural or racial decay can be imputed. It may even be the fact that rumors of degeneracy last longest where the doctrine is most fragmentary. Fleeting transitions are more difficult to purge than bold declarations. A concluding remark in Hodgen's study helps clarify what is striking about the Indonesian case:

> The main difficulty . . . for all social evolutionists was to hit upon that nonliterate people which was demonstrably the lowest, nearest the beast, and hence oldest. On this matter agreement has never been achieved. In an earlier period of ethnological controversy, now beginning to be forgotten, Cook, Fitzroy, and Wallis were said to be in favor of the Fuegians, as was true also for Karl Marx and Charles Darwin; "Burchell maintained that the Bushmen [were] the lowest. D'Urville voted for the Australians and Tasmanians; . . . one French writer even [suggested] that monkeys were more human than Laplanders." (1971: 510)

Neither Indonesian peoples themselves nor the history of their documentation cooperated very well with this negative quest. Earlier "missing link" formulations tended to usher the famous orangutan (*orang hutan* = forest dweller or wild man) toward the human as much as to push human groups down. Reputed cannibalism cropped up in the literate Battak of Sumatra; headhunting was hard to isolate (see Brady 1982; Rosaldo 1984). And notorious amok-running and ritual suicide (as in the courts of Bali and Java) occurred at every level of civilization and "savagery." As Crawfurd's *Dictionary* took pains to explain:

> AMUCK. The muck of the writers of Queen Anne's time; who introduced the word into our language. In Malay it means a furious and reckless onset, whether of many in battle, or of an individual in private. The word and the practice are not confined to the Malays, but extend to all the people and languages of the Archipelago that have attained a certain amount of civilization. Running a-muck with private parties is often the result of a restless determination to exact revenge for some injury or insult; but it also results, not less frequently, from a monomania taking this particular form, and originating in disorders of the digestive organs (1856: 12).

No two criteria of degeneracy—physiological, psychological, cultural—pointed precisely in the same direction. No nonliterate people perfectly filled the bill of the Renaissance's "diabolical," the Enlightenment's taxonomic "missing link," or the social evolutionist's "beastliest and oldest." Over the centuries Indonesian cultures refracted charges of degeneracy whose symptoms proved difficult to "fix," because their symbols kept dispersing.

Rumors of decay persisted at the peripheries: between the seams of arguments and at points where ethnological texts might otherwise have altogether frayed. During that peculiar set of historical circumstances we call the nineteenth century, from its place in the margins degeneracy continually reinfiltrated assessments of Indonesia's cultures, including the reputations of Bali/ Java/Sumatra to be scrutinized below. Categories like divinity/degeneracy, which do not exactly develop, can nevertheless permute. In a way Indonesia has remained perceived as a land of extremes—up to and including "Bali-Buru"—because ethnological ideas often operate like myth: exhibiting "a 'slated' structure, which comes to the surface, so to speak, through the process of repetition." (Lévi-Strauss 1963: 226)

An Envoi of Verne

Traces of Western responses to Indonesian cultures and nature appeared in works devoted to lands well beyond the realm of Malay-speakers. A lingering note of degeneracy imagery—appropriate finale for our disturbing story—was sounded in a famous fiction of 1874. Did this winning work draw inspiration from Borneo and Sumatra's manlike orangs, or did it merely adapt ideas from Linnaeus's tantalizing tales of troglodytes, those "missing links" in a comfortable Enlightenment taxonomy who "have a language of their own which they speak in a whistle, so difficult, that scarce any one can learn it except by long association with them . . . In many places of the East Indies they are caught and made use of in houses as servants" (J. Burke 1972: 268).

From either source or both of them, Jules Verne's enchanting robinsonnade
introduced its own *homo sylvestris,* duly domesticated:

> The settlers then approached the ape and gazed at it attentively. He
> belonged to the family of anthropoid apes, of which the facial angle
> is not much inferior to that of the Australian and Hottentots. It was
> an orang-outang [one of the anthropoid apes] . . . possessed of al-
> most human intelligence. Employed in houses they can wait at table,
> sweep rooms, brush clothes, clean boots, handle a knife, fork, and
> spoon properly, and even drink wine. . . . Buffon possessed one of
> these apes, who served him for a long time as a faithful and zealous
> servant. . . .
> "A handsome fellow!" said Pencroft; "if we only knew his lan-
> guage, we could talk to him."
> "But master," said Neb, "are you serious? Are we going to take
> him as a servant?"
> "Yes Neb," replied the engineer, smiling. "But you must not be
> jealous." (Verne 1957: 280–81)

In a book about a *Mysterious Island* in the Pacific (eventually called by its
castaways "Lincoln," complete with a lake named "Grant"), four enlightened
Yankees and a freed slave—escaped by balloon from their capture in Rich-
mond during the siege of 1865—set about to build a world from scratch. In
Verne's story no Eve intrudes; yet his narrative voice, renowned today for its
forward vision and technological prophecies, cannot resist seasoning the tale
with a nostalgic *topos* from the desultory history of ideas of degeneracy.
Again, whether Verne developed these passages from reading about Borneo,
about troglodytes, or about both is unclear; nor would it matter. The orang is
"Jup," the ex-slave is "Neb":

> By this time the intelligent Jup was raised to the duty of valet. He
> had been dressed in a jacket, white linen breeches, and an apron, the
> pockets of which were his delight. The clever orang had been mar-
> velously trained by Neb, and any one would have said that the Negro
> and the ape understood each other when they talked together. Jup had
> besides a real affection for Neb, and Neb returned it . . . he endea-
> vored to imitate Neb in all that he saw him do. The black showed the
> greatest patience and even extreme zeal in instructing his pupil, and
> the pupil exhibited remarkable intelligence in profiting by the lessons
> he received from his master. (p. 297)

Neb is loyal to Jup, and Jup to Neb. Verne shored up a chain of being by
evoking subtle affinities between two creatures that certain classifications declared marginal. Thus an Indonesian orang exported to a Pacific atoll served
once more to foster hints of cultural or racial degeneracy, in an adventure
destined to become a children's classic. Such are the odd and oozy twists

characteristic of nineteenth-century ethnological discourse, and its ongoing aftermath.

What an unlikely cast of characters emerges when we hold fast to the tail of "degeneracy," as one episode leads to another across discovery literature, descriptive histories, naturalists' quests, and fantastic voyages. We have on the brighter side Pigafetta's "Ave de Paraiso," but also Wallace's giant *mias* carcass he informs us he called "Charley," and Verne's orang "Jup" (short for Jupiter) in some kind of similitude with manumitted Nebuchadnezzar (who "only answered to the familiar abbreviation of Neb"—p. 24). Representatives of exotic extremes often find themselves bestowed with proper names; and in the case of Charley, Neb, and Jup with nicknames: special kinds of words coined in ethnological narratives to label, or rather to subjugate, the unknown.

Chapter Two
Colonialist Countertypes:
Emblazoning Bali versus Rejang and Java,
or Representations and Ambivalence

L ate eighteenth- and early nineteenth-century English-language histories devoted to "the Indian Archipelago" helped consolidate a British colonialist format for portraying peoples of Sumatra, Java, and Bali. In this style of demarcating cultures, Balinese sources were eventually represented solely by Kawi texts (an esoteric, Sanskritized literary language), and Balinese usages in general were characterized by courtly rites of widow immolation (*satia*). The process of inscribing different East Indies civilizations has entailed selective exaggeration as much as detailed description—two aspects of ethnology that may indeed be inseparable. This chapter's subject is a highly compressed episode in this still-unfolding discourse.

Just thirty-seven years separated three intimately connected works to be considered: William Marsden's *History of Sumatra* (1783), Stamford Raffles' *History of Java* (1817), and John Crawfurd's *History of the Indian Archipelago* (1820).[1] It is partly in contrast to Marsden's descriptions of Rejang in Sumatra and Raffles' description of Javanese that Crawfurd constructs a composite local and historical account of Balinese "religion" that decisively situates the island's practices under the sign of *satia:*

> The Raja of Blelling stated to me that, when the body of his father, the chief of the family *Karangasem,* was burnt, seventy-four women sacrificed themselves along with it. In the year 1813 twenty women sacrificed themselves on the funeral pile of *Wayahan Jalanteg,* another prince of the same family. I am satisfied, from the conversations which I held on this subject with some Mohamedans of Bali, whom I met in Java, that no compulsion is used on these occasions, but abundance of over-persuasion and delusion. (Crawfurd 1820, 241–42)

If we are to understand how wrenching passages like this one relate to other texts of their time, it is insufficient to restrict ourselves to manifest political doctrines, possible causes, or direct consequences. Rather, a serious reading must consider rhetorical devices in the images and blazons of Sumatra, Java, and Bali in Marsden, Raffles, and Crawfurd respectively. In the case at hand, the formulaic commonplaces—what historians of literary rhetoric call *topoi*—proved more durable than the British administrations whose interest they manifestly served.[2] This plain historical fact relates in turn to a more general issue: Although histories of discourse and systems of controlling local cultures are linked, they are not simply coordinate. The rhetoric accompanying political strategies is irreducible to direct instrumental motives; its exaggerations—some of them harmful, others beneficial, most both—continually exceed and outlive them. To trace the continuities and breaks in colonialist ethnology (indeed, in any ethnology) requires attending to both central arguments and digressions. In the digressions lapsed stigmas may linger and suggestions of glorification emerge. In the digressions creeds of control trail hints of ambivalence, occasionally even of self doubt. In the digressions unsettling reputations of different cultures become rumored, whether or not the reputations are ever confirmed. This play of rumor and insinuation has a power, sometimes a force, of its own.

Our three colonialist texts advance successive peoples as preferred subjects: the Rejang are commended as improvable; the Javanese are commended as monumentalized; the Balinese are commended as "Kawified." Moreover, each of these exemplary subjects is elevated relative to others who are patently denigrated: Rejang over Batak; Java over Malay, Bali over Papuan. Subtle shifts occur among seemingly similar representations, some of them insidious. The "countertyping" that runs within and beneath overt stereotypes and emblems of East Indies peoples and cultures involves multiple victims and multiple culprits as well, in a play of contradictions displaced from any straightforward policy of domination. Such contradictions recall that dispersed "murmur" in Foucault's (1970) work on fluctuating discursive formations, or those "heterologies" revealed by De Certeau (1986) in his histories of ethnological and historical ideas.[3] There, and here, lines of contrast keep multiplying, and they overlap.

Marsden's Rejang: "An Eligible Standard of Description"

The Irishman William Marsden, the Englishman Stamford Raffles, and the Scotsman John Crawfurd were all functionaries in the East Indies, trained to different degrees in "Asiatic Researches." Crawfurd's career was played out in Raffles' shadow; both Raffles and Crawfurd followed a trail blazed by Marsden, "the first literary and scientific Englishman who, with the advantages of local experience, treated of the Malaya countries" (Crawfurd 1856: 271). Marsden's detailed descriptions and relatively cautious generalizations helped establish the "basic assumption that the people of the Indian Archipelago, their manners, customs, arts, science, and agriculture are worthy of scientific study" (Harrison 1961: 247; De Casparis 1962).

Certain contrasts among the three scholars are conspicuous. Much more than Marsden, Raffles made outright categorical proclamations attuned to administrative ends. Although Crawfurd's *History* exuded a certain "imperialist spirit" and could lapse into "Toynbee-like generalizations" (Harrison 1961), he condemned European tactics in the East, with the exception of Spain's relatively liberal economic policies in the Philippines. Moreover, Crawfurd's nose for contradictions bespeaks a less doctrinaire side to his observations; for example: "There can be no doubt that the Malayan nations were first made acquainted with opium directly or indirectly, by the Arabs, the same people that made them acquainted with ardent spirits, and gave them a religion that denounces the use of both" (1856: 312). Raffles' discursive proclamations and Crawfurd's textual and iconographic ambivalences will reenter our story directly.

William Marsden's *History of Sumatra* commences by isolating the Rejang and drawing from them what John Crawfurd later calls in his *Descriptive Dictionary of the Indian Archipelago* a "general character of the native of Sumatra" (1856: 366). Marsden deems the Rejang less influenced than their Minangkabau neighbors by Malays from the north or Javanese from the south. Those converted to "Mahometanism" he argues, "have lost . . . the genuine Sumatran character" (1783: 41). The Rejang are designated by Marsden a pure type and a representative one. Their government and law are said to characterize the part of Sumatra amenable to British influence; moreover, they manifest "a proper language and a perfect written character."[4]

Marsden's description has a more "modern" ring than many earlier accounts of Sumatra. By promoting a Rejang standard, Marsden avoids sensational signifiers, extravagant emblems, or vivid oxymorons that once betokened Sumatra. His list of peoples—Minangkabau, Malays, Achinese, Batak, Rejang, and Lampong—displaces an earlier device that organized ethnology around one provocative anomaly in particular: the "strange civilization" of the Batak, those "lettered cannibals." This style of emblem remains catalogued in Crawfurd's *Dictionary,* which labels Batak "one of the advanced nations of Sumatra" yet the "lowest in the scale of civilization":

> The Bataks are of the same brown-complexioned, lank-haired race as the rest of the inhabitants of Sumatra. They are divided into many independent states. . . . They understand the smelting and forging of iron, the growth of rice by irrigation, the culture, the weaving and the dyeing of cotton, and have domesticated the ox, buffalo, horse, and hog. But they have gone much beyond all this, for they have invented alphabetic writing, having a peculiar character of their own, and a rude literature written on palm leaves or slips of bamboo. Thus advanced, the most remarkable circumstance connected with the manners of the Bataks is their undoubted practice of cannibalism, a fact now as well ascertained as it is of the New Zealanders. The victims are enemies, criminals, and now and then a slave. . . . says Mr. Anderson, ". . . it is not for the sake of food that the natives devour human flesh, but to gratify their malignant and demon-like feelings of animosity against their enemies." (1856: 41–42)

That such classifications can underpin elaborate, evidence-laden interpretations is clear from Crawfurd's ironic observations on Batak religion:

> The Bataks have no consistent system of religious belief, but an abundance of superstitions, such as belief in evil spirits, omens and the like. Slight traces of Hinduism are discernible in their language. Thus their astrologers are called *guru,* the Sanscrit for a "spiritual guide". . . . The burning, instead of interring the dead, concremation, division of castes, prominent practices of Hinduism are unknown to the Bataks. It is indeed obvious that no form of the religion of the civilized Hindus which has existed since the days of Menu, could ever have existed among a people systematically cannibals. It

is not a little remarkable of the Bataks, that while all the other natives of Sumatra, possessed of a knowledge of letters, have adopted the Mahommedan religion, they have sturdily rejected it for centuries, although surrounded by those who profess it. (1856: 42–43)

In 1783, then, Marsden consolidates an alternative style of ethnology with the earlier variety still catalogued in 1856 by Crawfurd. But the point I wish to stress is that Marsden's device of *describing* Sumatra by standardizing Rejang is no less selective than *inscribing* Sumatra as "land of the lettered cannibals." An averaged epitome, no less than a sensational anomaly, is a mode of exaggeration, a rhetorical gesture (Boon 1977: 33–34; 1982a; chaps. 1–2).

Marsden's text actually manages to have things both ways. It establishes the fiction of Rejang as the normative Sumatran and retains sensational commonplaces for other peoples. Conventions about isolated aborigines, the so-called Orang Kubu and Orang Gugu, are echoed. Marsden repeats speculations about similarities between "species of people dispersed in the woods" and lesser primates, although he questions their reliability. The Orang Kubu, occasionally entrapped "just like the carpenter in Pilpay's Fables caught the monkey," are said to have a language

> quite peculiar to themselves and . . . eat promiscuously whatever the woods afford, as deer, elephant, rhinoceros, wild hog, snakes, or monkeys. The Gugu are much scarcer than these, differing in little but the use of speech from the Orang Utan of Borneo; their bodies being covered with long hair (1783: 41).

Nor does the eclipse of the Batak image by the standard Rejang altogether eliminate "cannibals" from Marsden's account. He seasons several pages with reports of local lore about cannibal episodes, the kind of tale inevitably enmeshed in exchanges of accusations and stigmata across indigenous political and religious factions and between upland and lowland groups.

Marsden's simultaneous dispelling and recharging of sensational representations is most evident in his "comparative state of Sumatrans in society," 204 pages into the *History,* just before the extensive ethnography of Rejang titles, government, and powerful groups. This digression in the form of an exordium gathers remnants from a "Great Chain of Being" of fixed civilizational ranks. With polished Europe and ancient Greece and Rome (and perhaps China) at the top, second rank goes to the Persian, Moghul, and Turkish empires. Superior Sumatrans win third place, along with North Africans and some Arabs. Less civilized Sumatrans join the South Seas, Mexico and Peru, and the Tartar horde along with all who at least possess property. At the bottom fall "the Caribs, the New Hollanders, the Laplanders, and the Hottentots, who exhibit a picture of mankind in its rudest and most humiliating aspect" (p. 205).[5]

That stipulated, Marsden turns to the promotion of the Rejang (and defamation of Malays), offering copious data on social divisions, authority, marriage, and brideprice. Advocating a diplomacy of pomp and display, the only kind of "improvement" he feels Sumatrans can respond to, he argues, intricately, as follows:

> Their senses, not their reason, should be acted on, to rouse them from their lethargy; their imaginations must be warmed; a spirit of enthusiasm must pervade and animate them, before they will exchange the pleasures of indolence for those of industry. The philosophical influence that prevails, and characterizes the present age, in the western world, is unfavorable to producing these effects. A modern man of sense and manners despises, or endeavors to despise, ceremony, parade, attendance, superfluous and splendid ornaments in his dress or furniture. . . . Even our religious worship partakes of the same simplicity. . . . Probably, in proportion as the prejudices of sense are dissipated by the light of reason, we advance towards the highest degree of perfection our natures are capable of. . . . but certainly all this refinement is utterly incomprehensible to an uncivilized mind, which cannot discriminate the ideas of humility and meanness. We appear to the Sumatrans to have degenerated from the more splendid virtues of our predecessors. Even the richness of their laced suits, and the gravity of their perukes, attracted a degree of admiration; and I have heard the disuse of the large hoops worn by the ladies, pathetically lamented. (pp. 205–6)

This dense passage repays careful scrutiny. It foreshadows the renewal of pageantry in British (and Dutch) colonialism; it portends that variety of archaizing display later prominent in Victorian administration and paternalism.

At the same time that Marsden discloses indigenous assessments of Europeans' decline into unsplendid fashion, he extols Rejang usages over their Malay neighbors, whose "appearance of degeneracy" reflects the "sinking into obscurity, though with opportunities of improvement, [rather] than emerging from hence to a state of civil or political importance" (p. 207). This nexus in Marsden's *History* thus reveals a field of rival forces on both sides of a colonial encounter. Sumatrans are construed as "uncivilized" or insufficiently rational insofar as they remain bedazzled by display and nostalgic for the West's past of hoops and perukes. (Rejang themselves reputedly find reformed European costume a decline from its showier antecedents.) Yet the more thorough decline is attributed to Malays, less susceptible of improvements than Rejang.

Politically, of course, hardly a word of Marsden's text fails to legitimate British interests in Sumatra. Marsden's vision of pomp and ceremony for subjugating Sumatran societies is an early case of guidelines for "the invention of tradition" soon to be standard (Hobsbawm and Ranger 1985). The ideas at work, however, are more than a matter of polar prejudice. If improvements are to occur, it is the Rejang (not their neighbors) who are amenable and the British (not the Dutch) who can effect them—hence, the new standard Sumatran. The convolutions in Marsden's argumentation imply multiple factions, both Indonesian and European. For British Marsden, Sumatrans are declined or degenerate in principle, but Rejang less so than Malay. The implicit slogan of his history heralds an emergent colonial strategy: the way to reverse decay is with display. The intricate inflections articulated by this "policy" include not just contrasts among Sumatrans "divided and conquered" but also contrasts between contemporary Britain and its showier past (now to be reinvented) plus contrasts (now to be accentuated) between British administrative style and the still-plain Dutch, among other rivals. Multiple contrasts thicken, but, as I shall now show, they also shift, even when policy appears continuous.

Raffles' Java: What Might Have Been

The direct link between Marsden and Raffles' *History of Java* has been often noted: The *History of Sumatra* "obviously served as Raffles' model" (Bastin 1965b: 87). Yet the different strains of countertyping in Raffles' work kink this chain of colonial influence.

If Marsden seeks by way of Rejang to claim Sumatra for British improvements, Raffles means to enoble Java in splendid tomes portraying the island as worthy of a caliber of administration only he could sustain:

> Undoubtedly one of the main reasons for writing the *History* had been the desire to publicize the benevolence and wisdom of his own measures compared with the "tyrannical and rapacious" policies of the Dutch colonial regime; he also wished however to inform the public of the loss sustained by the nation through the restitution of Java and its dependencies to the Netherlands. In essence, therefore, the *History of Java* was a work of propaganda; in other respects it was a distinguished contribution to oriental studies. (Bastin 1965: 83)

(By the time of the work's *publication,* the Dutch had regained control of Java—see below.) Raffles' *History* is an opus of glory. Its discourse and lavish illustrations make everything in Java outsized: princes and commoners, courts, the animal kingdom, dress, handicrafts, heirlooms, arts, script, mystical language, literary language, architecture, antiquities, pomp. Cataloguing other islands, it celebrates the Javanese:

> it may be noticed, that of the three chief nations in these islands, occupying respectively Java, Sumatra, and Celebes, the first has especially by its moral habits, by its superior civilization and improvements, obtained a broader and more marked characteristic than the others. Both the Malayan and Bugis nations are maritime and commercial, devoted to speculations of gain, animated by a spirit of adventure, and accustomed to distant and hazardous enterprises; while the Javans, on the contrary, are an agricultural race attached to the soil, of quiet habits and contented dispositions, almost entirely un-

acquainted with navigation and foreign trade, and little inclined to
engage in either. (1: 57)

Raffles heads his *History* with a portrait of Raden Rada Dipura in noble profile
(see p. 28). Attributing the superior Javanese character to an excellent soil,
Raffles itemizes agricultural products and what little native trade he acknowledges exists. He then proposes benevolent "improvements," ultimately "ar-
chaeologizing" Java's past as a "history," with his own work perhaps representing a literal improvement over indigenous chronicles. Raffles' book is
designed to convey in print and illustration a concrete model of his policies'
ideals, a portrait of the wonder that Java promised, had his administration
endured.

In Raffles' text properly speaking, sensational stigmas are few. His opening
notes do repeat the commonplaces from early Portuguese reports that savage,
cannibalistic "gunos" inhabited Java's mountains and that Javanese run amok
at the slightest provocation. But no formulaic anomaly comparable to Sumatra's "literate cannibals" lingers even in the margins of Raffles' consolidated
view of the Javanese. Remnants of Hindu ritual among the remote Tenggcrese
are said to grace their "interesting singularity and simplicity of character." The
customs of these *dewa* worshipers with their *Panglawu* book are placed in
quiet contrast with standard Javanese usages, particularly burial practices (1:
331). Javanese customs that might prove offensive, such as the ritual washing
of corpses, are set in worthy parallel to Old and New Testament traditions and
to Virgil's Romans, who "likewise were in the habit of washing the dead body
several times before interment with water, which in their case was warm" (1:
321). Even in Raffles' few pages on Borneo, the "wild men" commonplace is
not developed.

Yet, disquieting signs of degeneracy punctuate Raffles' comments on slavery or, rather, slaves. Raffles had declared manumission in Java so to create
adequate civil, criminal, and commercial laws to thwart "this abomination"
permitted by "Mahometan laws." He blamed slavery and piracy on the dete-
rioration of Malayan tribes, which he felt the British were qualified to reverse;
he stipulates in particular:

> the constant wars between petty chieftains and heads of villages; the
> ill-defined succession to the throne . . . ; the system of domestic
> slavery, and all its concomitant evils, as wars for the purpose of pro-
> curing slaves. . . . Had Java remained permanently annexed to the
> British Crown, the redress of these evils would have been, in a great
> measure, in the power of the English nation (1: 232).

Although principally concerned with those guilty of practicing slavery, Raffles
seems also to implicate those guilty of being reduced to it. Suggestions of
cultural (and by the work's end racial) degeneracy of the "class of slaves" stain
the edges of his policy. In some ways this stems from his pro-Java stance and
from certain features of local practice. Raffles carefully distinguishes the

"condition of slaves on Java," where they serve as domestics, from that of the plantation slavery found in the West Indies. Early in his work he reports: "The native Javans are never reduced to this condition; or if they should happen to be seized and sold by pirates, a satisfactory proof of their origin would be sufficient to procure their enfranchisement" (1: 75). Prejudices at work among local populations are later made apparent from the list of peoples that Muslims regularly reduce to servitude: "The Pagan tribes in the vicinity of the Mahometans, such as those on Bali and some of the tribes of Celebes . . . and other easterly nations, are in a great measure the victims of the kidnapping system, and being infidels are considered as fair booty" (1: 234).[6]

The theme of "slavery" submerges when Raffles addresses details of Javanese justice, customs, literature, and a tally of antiquities in his section on history proper. But slaves resurface at the work's conclusion in a brief but vivid appendix on Bali, viewed by Raffles as a living archeology of Java's pre-Muslim past. In Raffles both the Balinese and their rulers show up poorly against the Javanese:

> The natives of Bali, although of the same original stock with the Javans, exhibit several striking differences, not only in their manners and the degrees of civilization they have attained, but in their features and bodily appearance. . . . though living under the rod of despotism which they have put into the hands of their chiefs, they still possess much of the original boldness and self-willed hardihood of the savage state (2: ccxxxi).

Raffles lists Bali's principal exports, which had included slaves, and notes the disinclination to engage in sea trade. Because he helped eliminate interisland slave traffic, he hopes that in Bali slavery "will soon be entirely annihilated":

> While it existed in its full vigor, all prisoners taken in war, all who attempted to evade the laws by emigration, all insolvent debtors, and a certain class of thieves, were subjected to the sad condition of slavery. These laws still subsist, and are enforced, as formerly, for the purpose of procuring the home supply; but the diminution of the foreign demand must limit exceedingly their exercise, and in a short time ameliorate the state of the unhappy individuals who had suffered by them (2: ccxxxv).

Then in an unexpected footnote there suddenly appears the unhappiest such individual of all, this one more "savage" than the Balinese. The accompanying color illustration labeled "A Papuan or Native of New Guinea, 10 years old" and the information the picture was doubtless contrived to represent, provide perhaps the strangest moment in the entire *History*.[7] Certainly it is a bizarre *lapsus* in a study that has been credited with helping undercut the imperialist idea that certain peoples or classes are rightly or naturally reducible to servitude. In his note Raffles expatiates:

Having repeatedly had occasion, in the course of this work, to advert to the slave trade, and the sources whence the supplies of slaves were obtained, it may not be uninteresting to introduce to the reader a native of Papua, or New Guinea, stolen from his country in the course of this traffic. The lad represented in the annexed plate came into my service at Bali under very peculiar circumstances, and has accompanied me to England. Since his arrival he has excited some curiosity, as being the first individual of the wooly haired race of Eastern Asia who has been brought to this country. . . . The following remarks upon the individual now in England, whom we sometimes call Papua, and sometimes (more to his satisfaction) Dick, were obligingly communicated to me by Sir Everard Home, Bart. "The Papuan differs from the African negro in the following particulars. His skin is of a lighter color, the wooly hair grows in small tufts and each hair has a spiral twist. The forehead rises higher, and the hind head is not so much cut off. The nose projects more from the face. The upper lip is longer and more prominent. The lower lip projects from the lower jaw to such an extent that the chin forms no part of the face, the lower part of which is formed by the mouth. The buttocks are so much lower than in the negro as to form a striking mark of distinction, but the calf of the leg is as high as in the negro" (2: ccxxxv).

It is difficult to know just what the Papuan is doing here in Raffles' digression. But the effect is to end the *History* with an image antithetical to its major thrust. The cartoon for Sir Everard's caption was almost certainly made to match the schematic outline rather than any actual native. Readers gaze upon a picture not of an unfortunate individual but of the projection into a set of extremes of a typology of physiognomies (see p. 28). Moreover this final illustration seems perfectly opposed to the work's initial set of portraits, beginning with the noble profile of Raden Rada Dipura, who embodies the heights of Javanese civilization—heights that Raffles' administration sought to harness. And at the work's tail end, facing the opposite direction, stands the caricature of an unprognathous Papuan, the first such servant brought back to England who would sooner, readers are assured, be called "Dick."

Crawfurd's Bali: A Culture for Kawi

Raffles' icon of the Papuan made an encore appearance in Plate 2 of John Crawfurd's *History of the Indian Archipelago* (1820). This time, however, the figure is lifted from his dramatic, tinted landscape, about-faced, and juxtaposed to a relatively outsized "Katut a Native of Bali." No longer an implicit polar opposition to Java's nobility, "Dick" now stands in explicit contrast to "the brown complexioned Balinese." Across such shifts in the history of ethnology, the semiotics of prejudice remain intertwined with the semiotics of praise.

Crawfurd's composite illustration (reproduced as this book's frontispiece) is suggestive of a certain prominence given Bali in his study. His four chapters on religion make Java the locus for historical work and Bali the source for contemporary evidence of Hinduism, leaving Islam and Christianity to be treated as expanding movements. The framework is presented as follows:

> The first [chapter] will contain an account of the ancient religion of the people; the second of their modern Hinduism; the third of the Mahomedan religion; and the fourth of the progress and character of Christianity among these islanders. Java is, to my knowledge, the only country of the Archipelago that affords materials for the discussion of the first subject; and, therefore, my references are constantly made to that country; and Bali affords, so exclusively, the materials of the second, that the chapter on this topic is expressly denominated an account of the religion of Bali. (2: intro.)

Crawfurd thus views Hindu forms as something with a past (Java) and a present (Bali) yet lacking dimensions of historical process associated with Islam, Christianity, or other developing "isms." This moment in comparative Indonesian studies portends a dehistorization of Bali that would endure. To insist on the peculiarities of Crawfurd's influential construction, I would formulate it as follows: Bali is the *locus* of the living Hindu *topos,* Java is the *locus* of its past.

Crawfurd was more the Indologist than Raffles; his elaborate constructions for Bali possibly pertain to their rivalry, most evident in Crawfurd's criticisms of Raffles' *History* in an 1819 *Edinburgh Review* and Raffles' severe criticisms of Crawfurd's *History* in an 1822 *Quarterly Review* (Collis 1970: 180). The feelings linger on in Crawfurd's *Dictionary* entry commemorating Raffles: "He was not, perhaps, an original thinker, but readily adopted the notions of others—not always with adequate discrimination" (1856: 364).

In an earlier address given to the Bataviaasch Genootschap on September 11, 1815, and published in its *Verhandelingen* (1816), Raffles discusses his recent tour of eastern districts:

> I visited the Teng'gar mountains, on which it had been represented to me that some remains of the former worship of Java were still to be found, and accident threw me on the shores of Bali, while attempting to reach Bauyuwangi. (1816: 50)

Declaring his knowledge of Tenggar and Bali imperfect, he seasons a dry outline of Bali's social ranks, priests, *Kawi* and common language, slavery, marriage, and law with just one anecdote, brief but vivid:

> The bodies of the deceased are invariably burnt, and the wives and concubines of the higher classes perform the sacrifice of *Satia*. A few days previous to my landing on Bali, nineteen young women, the

wives and concubines of the younger Rajah, who was lately put to death, sacrificed themselves in this manner. (1816: 62)

In the same speech Raffles reports on Kawi inscriptions and ancient historical compositions to which "a paraphrase of the whole in Javanese is annexed." He suggests that Kawi versions of the *Mahabharata* and *Ramayana* are poems "held by the Javanese of the present day in about the same estimation as the *Iliad* and *Odyssey* of Homer are by Europeans" (1816: 45). He advances his call for translations by including in the *Verhandelingen* a sample Kawi inscription translated into modern Javanese by Nata Kusuma and thence into English by John Crawfurd. Raffles' *History* (1817) also includes the list of Kawi texts he obtained in Bali after Crawfurd's more extensive stay; there his appendix on Hinduism concludes with a paraphrase of the account by "an intelligent Mahomoten" in Bali.

Crawfurd joined Raffles in Batavia after serving in India (see Ricklefs 1971); in 1814 he was sent on the reconnaissance mission to Bali and Celebes. His 1820 opus contains a lengthy chronological table of principal events— both endogenous and exogenous—from 1160 to 1816 (2: 481–563); the final four entries suggest how quickly Crawfurd's *History* itself had been relegated to a past:

> Christian 1813. Java 1740. Hegira 1226.
> The British government of Java, under the direction of Sir Stamford Raffles, in a spirit of great liberality, effects a number of beneficial changes, commercial, fiscal, and judicial.
> C. 1814. J. 1739 H. 1227
> A brother of the Hindu Raja of Blelling in Bali, having insulated the post of Blambangan in Java, a British expedition, proceeding to Celebes, stops at Bali, and receives the submission of the Raja. The king of Boni in Celebes, refusing to acknowledge the European supremacy, is attacked by a large force sent from Java and defeated, but escapes and carries on a predatory warfare, until the surrender of the island to the Dutch.
> C. 1815. J. 1742 H. 1228.
> Mangkubuwono the Third, sultan of Java, dies, and is succeeded by his son, the reigning prince, the fourth of the same name.
> C. 1816. J. 1743 H. 1229.
> August 19—Java is ceded by treaty to the Dutch and taken possession of. The British authorities quit Celebes, and surrender it to the Dutch. The Spice Islands are surrendered to the Dutch.

Crawfurd's mission to Bali politically passé, his *History* (1820) salvages a way to emblazon the island. His chapter on the "Religion of Bali" reads like an extension of the prevalent imagery in his early translation where now-familiar episodes of courtly cycles predominate.[8] The particular story of glory/downfall and creation/destruction, etched upon a stone in Surabaya at the behest of Raja Kunakua, contains the formulaic hope that "men might behold what was inscribed, which is replete with wisdom, and that they might improve thereby" (Crawfurd 1816: 9). I cite an upswing phase in this spotty saga, secondarily translated by Crawfurd:

> Let the story of the destruction of the conquered country be related. He replaced the nobles in their stations as before. His wisdom sought the good of the country. . . .
>   The body of the king's son was decked out and prayers offered up for it according to the practice observed for the dead. His wives, all of exquisite beauty, wished to follow him in death. They bowed and kissed his feet. They seemed determined to follow his fortune, to make it their own, and not to survive him.
>   Alas! exclaimed they, do not forget the expression of our sincerity. We are fatherless; we will serve thee; we are pleased that you take us along with thee. You are our Guru. For you were skilled in the arts of love, and knew how to give joy to the heart. Such were the words of the afflicted. We will wed no more; we will acknowledge the authority of no other lord. We will not make a second marriage, for you alone knew the arts of love. We dread the thoughts of being subjected to another's authority. We are inexperienced and ignorant of the most approved conduct.—The times were changed. Let a spectacle complete in every respect be related describing a narrative of excellence. . . . (Crawfurd 1816: 12–13)

Crawfurd's *History* (1820) mentions actual Kawi texts only briefly. While he approves the "vigor of fancy and force of intellect" in Kawi epics, he declares Kawi literature in general and particularly modern Javanese literature puerile: "the very stammering of infancy without its interest or amusement" (2: 21). These now-notorious remarks by an "ever scornful Crawfurd" (H. Meyer 1985) do not prevent his praising a pervasive "air of Romance" emanating from Kawi traditions evident in the tendency of Javanese to make "a tale of it":

> A common-place conversation, for these are most circumstantially narrated, is delivered in solemn and labored measure; and the petty action of a Javanese chief with the Dutch East India Company, becomes an ambitious imitation of one of the battles of the *Mahabarata,* or of the combats of the god or hero Rama with the giant Rawana." (2: 27)

Although Crawfurd offers several discriminating extracts to illustrate occasionally shapely Kawi narratives or more edifying tales, he conveys little of the complex courtly imagery involved. This topic is reserved for his chapter on the "Religion of Bali," which treats not Kawi texts but royal cremations and widow immolation.

The chapter opens by divorcing Bali's Hinduism, including Brahmana priests, from the familiar excesses of India. Bali lacks the most elaborate food restrictions, the extremes of celibacy, and the fullest "perpetual and tiresome routines of ceremonies." In Bali he has discovered no religious mendicants; moreover, "those whimsical and extravagant acts of self-mortification which have made the Hindu devotee so famous, are unknown to the Ascetics of Bali" (2: 240). Immediately thereupon, as if to compensate for Bali's inadequate notoriety, Crawfurd turns to widow sacrifice—a practice "carried to an excess unknown even to India itself," and the only Hindu custom "of which the certainty has been long ascertained among foreigners":

> When a wife offers herself, the sacrifice is termed *Satya;* when a concubine, slave, or other domestic, *Bela,* or retaliation. A woman of any caste may sacrifice herself in this manner, but it is most frequent with those of the military and mercantile classes [*Satriya, Wisiya*]. It very seldom happens that a woman of the service class thus sacrifices herself; and, what is more extraordinary, one of the sacred order *never* does. The sacrifice is confined, as far as I could learn, to the occasion of the death of princes and persons of high rank. (2: 241)

Crawfurd presents an assemblage of previous explorers' accounts of widow immolation, and not just in Bali. He mentions the Natchez in America and Pigafetta's paragraphs published in 1523 on Zebu equivalents in the Philippines plus his brief mention of Java (2: 243, 254). Before adding Purchas's editions in 1625 of Cavendish's evidence from Java (see Boon 1982: chap. 5), Crawfurd quotes at length Prevost's translation of the extensive 1633 Dutch account of Bali. Here are a few characteristic extracts:

> The queen's body was burnt without the city, with two and twenty of her female slaves . . . these unhappy victims of the most direful idolatry are thus carried in triumph, to the sound of different instruments, to the place where they are to be poignarded and consumed by fire. . . .
> Some of the most courageous demanded the poignard themselves . . . respectfully kissing the weapon. . . . As soon as the horrors of death were visible in the countenance . . . they were left in a state of perfect nakedness.
> When a prince or a princess of the royal family dies, their women or slaves . . . eagerly solicit to die for their master or mistress. . . . The king . . . makes choice . . . they are considered as consecrated. The young women, little skilled in these religious exercises, are instructed in them by the aged women, who . . . confirm them in their resolution.
> On such occasions the princesses of royal blood leap themselves at once into the flames. . . . As soon as they feel the heat, they precipitate themselves into the burning pit, which is surrounded by a palisade of coco-nut stems. In case their firmness should abandon

them at the appalling sight, a brother, or other near relative, is at
hand to push them in, and render them, out of affection, that cruel
office. (2: 244–53)

To these vivid images of widow and slave devotion and sacrifice, ultimate
tokens of courtly authority, Crawfurd adds several sentences of evidence about
corpse preservation and status differentials that mark allowable intervals before cremation. That the connection between Crawfurd's own data and what
the 1633 account reported to have "eye-witnessed" is left so vague only further seals the reputation of Bali:

> I had written my account of the funeral rites, of narrative of the
> Dutch envoys, or the above passage in Purchas, and I have since
> made no alteration, that the reader may have an opportunity of com-
> paring it with those earlier accounts, and drawing his own conclu-
> sions. (2: 255)

Crawfurd's text proceeds no further; it leaves the composite blazon of Bali
suspended, invoking a reader's authority that could not then, and cannot now,
exist. Evidence of the frequency and extent of actual *satia* and *bela* across
periods of Balinese history is obscure by its very nature. Political, social, and
mythic meanings of widow immolation possibly attached to refractory ways
of making the past answerable to the future (Geertz 1980; Boon 1982a; chap.
6). Was the pulse of sacrifices regular, or were sacrifices "critical" responses
to pressures perceived as external? In either case Balinese may have fixated
on *doing* sacrifices for reasons connected to those that make Europeans fixate
on *describing* them. Did incentives develop for courts to "play to" this intense
ritual image, as forces in local rivalries, colonialist encroachments, Islamization, and trade continued unfolding? Even assuming that these questions
could be answered and issues resolved, the kind of "conclusions" that Crawfurd's imagined reader might have drawn remain in doubt and open-ended.

A recent article by A. van der Kraan (1985) leads me to reinforce this point
at some length. Van der Kraan assembles all major outsider testimony about
Balinese *satia* and *bela*. He translates the Dutch account by Oosterwijck
(1633; the source for Prevost's translation used by Crawfurd) and three other
sources that postdate Crawfurd: an 1829 French account by Dubois, an 1846
account in Dutch by the Swiss biologist Zollinger, and one in 1847 in Dutch
by the German Sanskritist Friederich. Van der Kraan also includes an English
account by the Danish adventurer Helms (1847), but makes no reference to
the commentary on Helms in Geertz (1980: chap. 4). Van der Kraan's interesting compilation echoes Crawfurd (and indeed, Covarrubias 1937: chap.
11); yet he neither situates his own compilation in the history of such compi-
lations nor credits Crawfurd with stipulating the very aspects of *satia* and *bela*
that his own survey underscores: "The texts will show, among other things,
that *mesatia* was not practiced by all Balinese, that it did not equal 'widow-
burning,' and that the sacrifices were not genuinely voluntary" (1985: 91). I

have shown Crawfurd making these points without, however, claiming to be able to judge what kind of persuasion characterized these ritualized deaths.

Now, van der Kraan's sources are really no more authorizable than Crawfurd's; they are simply more elaborate and numerous. Although the five sources are multiply translated texts charged with countertypes and repeated *topoi*, van der Kraan's article ends by making them sound nearly "descriptive," indeed documentary. Toward achieving something like reliable witnessing, he hastens to discount the blinkered views he calls "religion":

> And, according to Oosterwijck, Dubois, Helms, and Friederich, religion played a vital role also in sustaining the victims in their decision. All these observers testify that in their final moments the Belas were accompanied by female priests who, apart from carrying out certain rituals, *no doubt* sought to strengthen the victims in their resolve by reminding them of the happiness which awaited them in the hereafter. . . . They were regarded as holy beings, their feet were no longer allowed to touch the ground. . . . the women, and especially *of course* the slaves among them, enjoyed more honor, prestige, and status than they had ever experienced before. *It goes without saying* that all this public adulation made it extremely difficult for the women to retract their decision. . . . The families of the victims clearly wanted the sacrifices to take place, and they encouraged the women to persevere. Again, *it goes without saying,* that this family pressure made it very difficult indeed for the women to retract their decision even if they had wished to do so. . . . But why did the families of the victims behave in this way?. . . . According to Dubois . . . religious beliefs. . . . Friederich, however . . . material motives . . . rewards from the courts, like a rice field (*sawah*), an appointment as *pambekel.* . . . *It seems highly probable* that both these factors influenced the Bela families. (1985: 120–21; emphases added)

This flurry of rhetorical "no doubts," "of courses," "going without sayings," and "highly probables" seeks to demystify insider knowledge but instead disguises real difficulties in adducing possibly multiple motives.

Van der Kraan's commentary offers a materialist reading (actually just the flip side of a "religious" one) and in doing so revitalizes old blazons of courtly Bali as "women sacrificers," or of "a land where women were property." ("Despotic rajas" and "the plight of women" were commonplace justifications for colonial takeover—see Boon 1977, 1). He reasons as follows: Because the partners who were sometimes immolated along with the raja's corpse included not just high-status wives but low-status *bela,* "the only thing they had in common was their sex: the victims were invariably women" (1985: 120). But as concubines, or servants, or lesser wives associated with the palace sector of concubines, *bela* shared with *satia* another feature: both were tied sexually, and often reproductively, to the deceased. In Indic rituals for expanding polities that accentuated cremation, such female victims were keyed to a celebrated style of male victim: the hero who dies in battle. South Asian militarist ideals included female equivalents to knightly valor-in-death; they have been traced through texts that venerate immolated heroines in tandem with war heroes and through archaeological remains of commemorative "suttee stones."[9] Such models for auspicious death have figured in royal ceremonies of Indicized polities including Bali, where *satia* and *bela* possibly formed part of a repertoire of extreme practices to ensure renewed progeny and a heightened ancestry of noble houses.

To isolate, as van der Kraan does, an issue of "women's sacrifice" overlooks possible parallels with "death in battle" themes. Moreover, to separate concubines from wives sidesteps the complicated ways such categories are embedded in alliance networks of different kinds, particularly at the level of secondary wives (see Boon 1977; Geertz and Geertz 1975). Accentuating *bela,* van der Kraan assumes that sacrifices were addressed to the deceased, rather than to the rituals' witnesses or to the realm, and that their end was destruction; from here he leaps to "property":

> From the point of view of the courts, sacrificing a number of women who, as slaves or as subordinate members of the family, had "belonged" to the deceased, was not essentially different from sacrificing some of his/her personal possessions; . . . the chair and the couch . . . the mirrors and utensils destroyed at the cremation . . . were also intended to make life more pleasant for the deceased in the hereafter. In the final analysis, the practice of *mesatia* shows quite clearly that at the Balinese courts women, especially of course those of slave status, were regarded simply as property. (1985: 121)

These entangled issues strike me as less clear. Were the chairs and couches and mirrors and utensils "personal possessions" or "potlatch valuables" cyclically destroyed? Might the "meaning" of the destruction of these women pertain to ways courts were sometimes made memorable or narratable? We can deplore human sacrifice and still speculate that these women, like these objects, were perhaps not "simply property" but more intricately *pusaka:* human heirlooms (see below, chaps. 5–6). Both blazons—"women as property" and "women as *pusaka*"—are tragic, but tragic in different ways for different reasons. (Van der Kraan's commentary forecloses this kind of conflictually cultural question.) Valuables in ritual cycles of human immolation may represent the contrary of "property": "gifts" (whether willing or unwilling) of sacrifice. History is, lamentably, replete with these victims too.[10]

The episode in colonial discourse from Marsden, through Raffles, to Crawfurd has many ramifications. Perhaps most consequential to Balinese studies was Crawfurd's idea of Balinese religion as an analogue of its Kawi writings. This sort of analogy conforms to doctrinal models of "religion" that prevailed in nineteenth-century ethnology and influenced various comparative approaches (see Boon 1987). Crawfurd's attitude anticipates later works about Bali that only partly qualify it, including modern philological researches (e.g., Hooykaas 1973a, 1980a). Moreover, emblazoning Bali as virtually "the Kawi culture" portends many other near-sobriquets in colonial and postcolonial accounts, indigenous narratives, nationalist ideology, internationalist tourism, and all manner of ethnographic, philological, and aesthetic images for Bali. The copious list includes: "the land of temples without number," "the island of peasant aesthetes," "the Rangda-Barong culture," "the cockfight culture," "an allegory of antithesis to Islam," "the exemplary Hindu-Dharma faith," "the Eka Dasa Rudra culture," "the Kecak culture," and so on. An intricate history of "appreciating" Bali has accumulated interpretive orientations, political slogans, select hybrid performances, photogenic standards, reformist programs, scholarly appropriations, and touristic trademarks geared to the merchandizing of domesticated difference. In the elaborate production of such devices and inventions—some of which will be explored further in the following chapters—we Balinists and Balinese, including Balinese Balinists, have repeatedly and inescapably conspired.[11]

It bears reiterating that the representations produced in this many-sided discourse take shape in a dense field of contrasts harnessed, rhetoric unleashed, ambivalences repeated, and ambiguity sustained. Hence the strange string of types and countertypes raveled in the present reading:

> Balinese (versus Papuans)-not-Javanese (versus Balinese)-not-Rejang (versus Malays), inscribed by British-not-Dutch (or even Scots-not-English-or-Irish), or later again Dutch-not-British ("Dutch" too being divisible), etc.

It is tangles of political interests and intermingled cultural contrasts alone that remain "standard" in the unaverageable history of Indonesian ethnology, Balinese studies, and anthropology overall.

Afterword: A Note on Additional Layers of Comparative Indic Discourse

To frame a striking sequence of British colonialist texts leading to a blazon of Bali, I introduced Marsden without addressing overlapping countertypes already in place. The "descriptive history" of Marsden contrasts with an alternate genre of "mythic history" that patently exaggerated civilizations' excesses. This other rhetoric, itself a countertype of sorts found in comparative panoramas of India, was implicitly resisted by Marsden but reentered Indonesian studies through the back door, so to speak, of "Hindu Bali."

In 1786 renowned Orientalist William Jones (1746–94) launched comparative Indo-European studies with his "Aryan thesis" that Sanskrit, Greek,

Latin, and perhaps Gothic and Celtic are so formed "that no philologer could examine all the three without believing them to have sprung from some common source which, perhaps, no longer exists."[12] This major motive of comparative philology and mythology would fuel the enthusiasm of early German Romantics, British Christian apologists, and world philosophers alike. The late eighteenth century thus produced various motives *for* "histories" of non-European civilizations. In 1783 William Marsden had helped organize East Indies studies around leveled description and later direct translations (in his *Dictionary and Grammar of the Malayan Language,* begun in 1786). Jones did as much for India but also steered Indo-European scholarship into a quest for origins and diffusionist debates on the relative antiquity of Indian, Judeo-Christian, and Egyptian traditions. (Perhaps only Pierre Bayle's *Dictionnaire historique et critique* of 1697 had proved so threatening to orthodox theology cum historiography.) In such pursuits translation becomes not a direct and confidently controllable enterprise but a potentially subversive, disturbingly comparative one that pitts scholars arguing a greater antiquity of exotic sources against theologians defending Scripture as nonderivative. Many recent scholars have stressed the intense ambivalence in the period "from the mastering of Sanskrit by Sir Charles Wilkins and Sir William Jones in the 1780s to just before Sir James Frazer began to displace astronomical gods in favor of vegetation gods in 1890," none more cogently than H. B. Franklin:

> As Western Europe began to question its own God, the philosophical, etymological, polemic games it played with the other gods became increasingly serious. . . . Only after the war to preserve Scripture as literal Revelation was lost did the battles of mythology become again mere alarms and skirmishes. . . . The new discoveries in India, brought about by the Asiatic Society's pioneering work in Sanskrit, threatened to turn diffusionism itself against the apologists. For many of the Hindu vedas seemed to be at least as old as the Old Testament and embarrassingly similar to the New. . . . The diffusionist barricades built by the apologists were gradually taken over by the skeptics and heretics. (1963: 11)

One mode of making Western "histories" of India themselves "mythic" can be illustrated by Thomas Maurice, a Christian apologist who adopted Jones's own view that spurious gospels had circulated in India. In 1795 Maurice published his overwhelmingly nonlinear

The History of Hindostan;
Its Arts, and its Sciences, As connected with The History of the Other Great Empires of Asia, During the Most Ancient Periods of the World, With Numerous Illustrative Engravings. Discussing the Indian Cosmogony; the Four Yugs, or Grand Cosmological Periods; the Longevity of the Primitive Race; and other Interesting subjects of Ante-Diluvian History: Containing also, in very ample detail, The

Indian and Other Oriental Accounts of the GENERAL DELUGE; Extensive Inquiries Relative to the Exaggerated Chronology of Eastern Empires; the Rise and Gradual Growth of Astronomy, The Origin of the Sphere; and the formation of the Solar and Lunar Zodiacs of Asia.

Maurice's impossibly intricate work orders history in chapter-avatars of Visnoo, with syncretic portraits of such compounded deities as "The Isis Omnia of Egypt, the Indian Isa, and Grecian Ceres." He concludes with "The Calci, or Tenth Avatar," an "evident allusion to the Destroying Angel and White Horse of the Apocalypse."

Maurice's sensational cycles respond to apprehensions that Indian and Egyptian texts and traditions might undermine Christian authority. But Maurice documents non-Western sources and images so thoroughly that a "heretical" edge develops. The Hindu, Egyptian, and European civilizations brought into coordination wind up mutually sensationalized. Although Maurice sought to confirm Christian supremacy, in the eyes of certain readers his tomes could end only by relativizing everything, Scripture included.[13]

I recall Maurice's style of comparative history and description to throw Marsden's contemporaneous style into sharp contrast. Against Maurice's blend of myth and history and his anxiety over supremacy, stands Marsden's leveled description and rhetoric of control. I might simply juxtapose to Maurice's title (cited above) Marsden's:

The History of Sumatra
Containing an Account of the Government, Laws, Customs, and Manners of the Native Inhabitants, with a Description of the Natural Production, and a relation of the Ancient Political State of that Island.

The comparison with Maurice shows that Marsden's "descriptive history" was distinctive even in its own day. Yet I again caution against mistaking the kind of contrast separating Marsden and Maurice as an absolute distinction between sound empiricism versus fantastical speculation or between an account of actual usages versus one of the imagination. (Maurice, after all, was perfectly capable of continuing William Jones's practical goals of codifying and translating Indic laws; indeed, Jones's will to become the subcontinent's "Justinian" anticipated Raffles' ambitions in Java). Nor can the descriptive/mythic distinction be explained away by respective subjects of study in Marsden versus Maurice.

Whether a comparative ethnology of averaged standards or one of extremes better suits Sumatra, India, or other civilization depends on the aspects selected for emphasis. Unlike Marsden's, Maurice's history accentuates the most disturbing images, not the most typical ones. He compares not ordinary Hindustan to ordinary England, but Kalki to the Apocalypse; the exaggeration was abundantly reciprocal. We saw above, moreover, that even Marsden does

not eliminate all traces of exaggerated countertypes in those emblems he preserves in digressions and asides to set off the Rejang as preferred subjects.
Marsden's normative discourse imagines the Rejang to be amenable to subju-
gation and displays them as such. His "descriptive history" is no breakthrough
into empirical neutrality but another form of rhetoric—inevitably. The
"mythic" dimension Marsden accordingly suppresses or marginalizes re-
emerged in the texts of professed disciples: Raffles' monumentalizations for
noble Java and Crawfurd's catalogues and composites for Hindu-Bali. Insofar
as ethnological discourse operates "heterologically," anything suppressed is
by that very token tacitly invited eventually to return in the chain of successive
texts (De Certeau 1986: chap. 1).

My reading has implied limits to the effectiveness of standardized averaging
for rendering descriptions compelling or convincing, not to mention alluring
or accurate (see Boon 1986b). The standard-average is itself an exaggeration
with questionable variants: the too-average case, the lowest common cross-
cultural denominator, the wished-for normal-universal, the pipe dream of future "differencelessness" or other ideological fantasy. In the ongoing history
of ethnology, including Indonesian studies and interdisciplinary "Baliology,"
this stereotype too—a utopian one amongst other impossible ideals and sad
stigmas—requires countering. Toward that end, comparative readings of rhetorical texts inscribing ambivalent islands sustain a countertyping that would
also countertype countertyping itself.

Chapter Three
Alliterative Interlude:
Entexted Ethnology, Hybrid History,
Basics of Baliology, Ritual-cum-Rhetoric

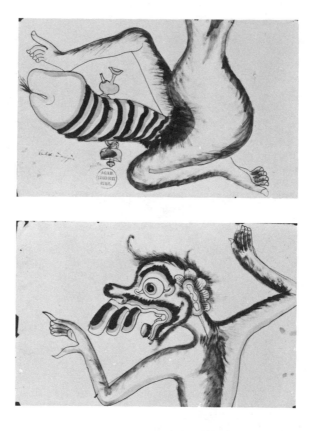

A Balinese drawing on English paper commissioned around 1881 by H. N. Van der Tuuk, philologist extraordinaire and compiler of the *Kawi-Balineesch-Nederlandsch Woordenboek*. Such iconography remains prevalent today in Balinese charms for cures. This image may parody the attributes of Siwaic priests, whose ritual regalia include lingams and bells. Parodic and demonic tokens have been routinely expurgated from representations of Balinese culture by forces of colonialist domestication, nationalist piety, and internationalist propriety.

I thank Dr. Hedi Hinzler of Leiden University for providing this file photograph (Bibliotheek der Rijksuniversiteit te Leiden; Cod. Or. 3390–10, rect.), emblematic of ambiguities in comparative Balinese studies. The image here has been split and inverted along the original's crease.

Parallels between cultural and historical processes and properties of rhetoric and discourse pertain to institutions and practical life as much as rituals and performative events. Interpretive metaphors of "the text" illuminate pervasive human agonies and conflicts along with occasional harmonies and consensus. Like the "texts" of languages, the "cultures" of history (and the "histories" of culture) establish paradoxical equivalences and contrasts in diverse sectors of experience—sometimes routinely, sometimes through struggle, usually mixed. Cultures, then, or the signs and symbols contrastively constituting them, are neither pat nor static. Harnessing contradictions, cultures persist through, not despite, the passage of the past. The fact that evidence of cultures results in or from time—itself experienced through variable cultural constructions—makes these truisms all the more true. This chapter's interludes address these difficulties of time, text, and culture, hoping through tactics of fragmentary play to read more seriously evidence of all three. It will become increasingly apparent that the spirit reigning here is Erasmian:

> For what merry pranks will not the ramshackle god, Priapus, afford?
> What games will not Mercury play . . . ? And is it not the custom
> for Vulcan to act as jester . . . and partly by his lameness . . . to
> enliven . . . ? The half-goat satyrs act our interludes. (1941:22)[1]

Entexted Ethnology

Discourses of cultural difference rely on many demarcations and composite formulations: particular cultures ("Bali"); qualified cultures ("Hindu-Bali"); religiously, politically, or economically related expanses ("Hindu," "Indianized," "Indonesian," "Third World"); sweeping historical-ethnological complexes ("Indo-Europe," "Polynesia"). As chapters 1 and 2 revealed, such discourses themselves are pushed and pulled historically, politically, and cross-culturally. Each culture they imperfectly inscribe—through its speech, kinship, ritual, writing, economy, mythology, polity, and art—constructs a sense of present-past-future or alternative code of time, timely or timeless: eternal, cyclic, cycles within cycles, contrasting paces, pulses, and rates.

The notion of "text" employed in this study has an equivalent Indic term in *tantra;* this parallel will loom large later on. "Text" has several additional advantages over other influential models and metaphors. Unlike "machines," texts keep raveling even as they are woven. Unlike "organisms," texts invite reading and rereading rather than diagnosing or inspecting. Many theorists—recent, not-so-recent, even ancient—have shown things textlike to be in a state of continual production. A discontinuous chorus of philosophers, anthropologists, literary critics, historians, social theorists, political thinkers, theologians, and tricksters (both subversive and conservative ones) have professed that texts do not re-produce or re-present something outside themselves. Texts are no dutiful and subservient reference to "external" life, event, or context. Moreover, a culture (I mean a text) is never experienced immediately, but always interpreted, with interruptions and bumps—both by the different parties living it and (more obviously) by different observers observing it (Boon 1982a: chaps. 3–4). "Living" and "observing" can be understood as two modes of "reading" whose respective alienations pertain to what Durkheim called *conscience* and to what Gadamer called "horizons" (see Jay 1982).

Metaphors of text and of reading applied to anthropological fieldwork strike some critics as fancy devices to silence or disempower the interlocutor. I would reply that "read texts," radically construed, certainly speak back; they may, moreover, change their mind's message on each rereading. Listening to someone local in the way one rereads intricate texts may give the subject more autonomy than would the interactive pressure of a friendship, a coauthorship, a sisterhood or fraternity, or a conspiracy. "Doing" metaphors have their limitations too.

One not-so-recent reexamination of the nature of the text came when Roland Barthes opposed *le texte* to *l'oeuvre*. Repeating a gesture from an earlier study (Boon 1982a: 151), let me amplify Barthes' position:

> The difference is this: the work is a fragment of substance, occupying a part of the space of books (in a library for example), the Text is a methodological field. . . . The Text tries to place itself very exactly behind the limit of the doxa. . . . Taking the word literally, it may be said that the Text is always *paradoxical*. . . . The work—in the best of cases—is *moderately* symbolic (its symbolic runs out, comes to a halt); the Text is *radically* symbolic: *a work conceived, perceived and received in its integrally symbolic nature is a text.* Thus is the Text restored to language; like language, it is structured but off-centered, without closure. . . . The Text is plural. Which is not simply to say that it has several meanings, but that it accomplishes the very plural of meaning; an *irreducible* (and not merely an acceptable plural). (Barthes 1977: 156–59)

For Barthes, the work, reduced to a fragment of substance, has characteristically been explained by tracing a filiation back from its proprietor-author. Barthes contrasts this task of excavating sources and influences with the interpretive reading of a text, "itself the text-between of another text" (1977: 160). Texts reveal a "paradoxical ideal of structure: a system with neither close nor center" (1977: 159). If I may couch his method in an interrupted aphorism: A text's unity lies not in its origin (back along a filiation) but in its destination. From this vantage the onus and opportunity of interpretation shifts to the "text's" language, its translations and transpositions, its reception and readership, or really the cumulative yet dispersing history of readings. Neither final praise nor blame devolves upon a presumable author; credits and culpabilities multiply.

Throughout his career Barthes remained in many ways Saussurian, with any "sign" defined as the connection between a signifier and a signified, each in turn a position in a fuller field of signifiers and signifieds. In the analytically designated total set of signs making up "language," meaning operates by contrast. Any signifier signifies a particular signified by being *not* those other signifiers that could occupy its position (this paradigmatic set of signifiers is implicitly complete at the level of *langue*). Simultaneously, any signified is the relationship of difference from those other signifieds held in reserve at the level of *langue* that could conceivably occupy its position.

This kind of oppositional meaning can be illustrated by devices like musical "scales" that demarcate a continuum of sound into such arbitrary contrasts as "do-re-mi-fa-sol-la-ti. . . ." Similarly, color categories involve relational contrasts. In a three-category system, "black" designates not "red" or "white," "red" not "white" or "black," and "white" not "black" or "red"; four categories, or seven, or more shift the points of discontinuity. To make matters of signification more arbitrary still, colors need not be ordered as a variously differential spectrum (nor musical sounds as a scale); other devices abound. Although Saussure's semiology is famous for neutralizing the factor of time in order to analyze systematic aspects of communication as a synchronic *langue,* he knew that the activities of signification, including speech, were always changing, or at least in flux (Saussure 1966; Culler 1981; Boon 1972: chap. 2). Barthes placed the sign's temporal destinations under the sign of "text."

Barthes' own readings accentuated paradox, irreducible plurality, decentering, text-betweenness, systems without closure, radical symbolics, and related properties. Many scholars in semiotics and semiology, hermeneutics, cultural and literary history, and comparative institutions have stressed related issues in different ways. A partial list of such figures important to these chapters includes: H. Adams, E. Auerbach, J. J. Bachofen (vis-à-vis Nietzsche and Burkhardt), M. Bakhtin, R. Barthes, R. Benedict, G. Bateson, W. Benjamin, K. Burke (his corpus), M. de Certeau, E. Curtius, G. Davenport, just a dash of Derrida, M. Detienne, L. Dumont, U. Eco, L. Febvre, M. Foucault, N.Frye, C. Geertz (his combination), H. Kenner, C. Lévi-Strauss (his *oeuvre*), M. Mauss, M. Merleau-Ponty, F. Nietzsche (vis-à-vis and versus Wagner), W. O'Flaherty, W. Ong, P. Ricoeur, D. Schneider, M. Singer, V. Turner, M. Weber, F. Yates. This doubtless idiosyncratic list is expanded in the book's bibliography.[2]

Writings by such scholars have shown that signs empower and symbols often victimize. Both signs and symbols, moreover, conceal even as they communicate. Cross-cultural histories accordingly convey resonances of resignation, sadness, tragedy, resilience, wit, and polyform laughter. If we read back far enough, of course, all the actors have disappeared into the discourse deposited, including those human symbols literally sacrificed. Luminaries as different as W. Benjamin, P. Ricoeur, and M. de Certeau have incorporated history's lamentation into their allegories of knowing the past. The multivalent rituals "read" by anthropologists remind us, too, that regeneration entails death as well as intercourse. Rituals display any society's production of sub-sistence, offspring, alienations, corpses, and, along the way, meanings.

To concentrate on meaning and/or signification is hardly to overlook "plain" facts that politics, for example, can be ugly. Few theorists of any per-suasion would deny that ethnographers and litterateurs alike, as well as their critics, can be naive. This, then, is the way the world is: children and adults may be naughty, cruel, or kind; states encroach, colonialism is hard to bury; genders conflict and/or complement; hierarchy makes "us egalitarians" un-comfortable; Utopians have no answers; religions agonistically and/or rou-tinely perdure; the defeated may rebound or may not; war recurs. It may be for these very reasons that rituals remain indirect and contradictory, as do "cultures" and "histories," along with the semiotics and hermeneutics of inter-preting them. These basic—yet not unentexted—facts enter into ambiguous discourse of cultural differences across opaque representations, imperfect in-scriptions, certain suffering, and exaggerated or muted contrasts.

Barthes' criteria of textuality and K. Burke's sense of rhetoric have implic-itly guided our opening chapters across histories, narratives, social forma-tions, and ideological constructions. They will lead us on to Balinese semio-tics and parodies, and further—from "destinations" of Indonesian diversity, colonialist tomes, and European desires toward Hinduisms, Tantrisms, and what has been occulted in various Indo-European traditions. Each of my read-ings remains tethered to the place that has come to be called "Bali," versus other *loci,* or *topoi,* or islands, or histories, or cultures . . . beaches all (see Dening 1980, 1988).

In the case of Bali, properly speaking, rhetoric affects not just the wordy side of life: the shaped, selected speaking and writing continually emitted, often with music, as ingredients of ritual and practice. Hindu-Bali's "aspect of text" extends to matters some observers would consider text-external: insti-tutions, social arrangements, political strategies, and infringed taboos. Yet these components, too, I shall argue, are irreducibly plural, decentered, para-doxical, and systematically without closure—just like mantras, conversa-tions, and narratives. In short, there is more to the *text* of Balinese culture (indeed, of any culture) than the culture's manifest texts. Evidence of histori-cal influence, philologically attested filiations, and political control, happens in and as ritual panoplies and heterodox convergences. These strange connec-tions and overlappings are what is there to compare.

Hybrid History (and Ultra-hybrid Myth)

Myth, Marcel Detienne (1979) reminds us in the wake of Lévi-Strauss, commences with rumor. The same may be said of comparative discourse, which mingles facts and desires in a historical dialectics sometimes scandal-ous. To display how hybrid ethnology's past may be, I shall reintroduce Antonio Pigafetta's *Prima Viaggio,* a text already encountered in Chapter 2. Even to designate the tomes associated with Magellan's scribe by their Italian title underestimates indeterminacies at work when multilingual, transcontinental, diversely promoted, cross-cultural evidence is translated; although the noble Pigafetta "himself" hailed from Vicenza.

The name "Pigafetta" covers a Renaissance tangle of political patronage that has been tugged at by many fine scholars, among them Donald Lach (1965). Rumors of Rosicrucian associations persist concerning this knight of Rhodes who was approved by Charles V to accompany Magellan. Once returned, Pigafetta was possibly snubbed by Portugal's John III, attentively received by France's queen mother, and promised backing by Mantua's Isabella d'Este upon consulting a Venetian papal nuncio assigned to Spain. Courted by doge, pope, Spanish royalty, and grand master of the Knights of Rhodes, Pigafetta apparently kept talking and telling even while writing/concealing the promised report, one possibly never published in full.

An extensive version of the fragments is in French; three earlier shorter versions survive (I omit dates). Now, why only smatterings of whatever Pigafetta wrote were transmitted pertains to fundamental motives of exploration, economy, and ethnology, particularly in the sixteenth century. These motives include: partial secrecy, describing to entice but conceal, reporting to mislead, publishing to attract sponsors yet guard any advantage. Everything Renaissance was cryptic, dis-covery above all.

"There is no question," Donald Lach reminds us, "that the Portuguese jealously guarded every scrap of information which might have led potential competitors to the sources of the spice trade" (1967, 3: 453). Portugal's rivals, too, infused accounts with discrepancies of expansionist ballyhoo and furtive misinformation, among other rhetorical devices. And they peppered accounts with gaps. Pigafetta, for example, omitted reference to a rival report of Magellan's storied voyage by that non-eyewitness, Maximilian of Transylvania (a bastard by the archbishop of Salzburg), who had been tutored by Peter Martyr, chronicler of Spain's New World wonders. Like England's Samuel Purchas a century later (Boon 1982a: chap. 5), Maximilian interviewed voyagers, in this case Captain Juan Sebastian del Cano and the crew of Magellan's only surviving ship, "Victoria." Maximilian's account, *De Molucco insulis,* was published in Latin at Cologne and Rome (Lach 1967: 172–76). More hybrid languages, texts, and times. Perhaps such omissions in Pigafetta will be illuminated by New Historians of Renaissance fashioning, disguising, and "erasure" of hybrid selves, performances, and chronicles, even when encountering remotest others to produce their representations. For now all we know is that "Pigafetta seems to have kept a diary during the entire years of his absence from Europe" (Lach 1967: 193). But the diary, too, is absent.

In Chapter 1 I addressed issues of the composite tongues, "local" languages, and doubtless tricky informants that Pigafetta heard and diary-jotted from between 1519 and 1522, while voyaging, before publishing. By way of interlude, I wish to acknowledge here the multiple languages and doubtless tricky patrons Pigafetta published in, for, and against, when cataloguing monarchs of different religions, always contrasting them to neighbors deemed monstrous. More than the contexts of Pigafetta's collecting and publishing were intricate, contradictory, and dialectic; the text itself, or moments within it, are radically enmeshed. In one plenitudinous paragraph, for example, an image of Javanese courtly rites (when they presumably still resembled what Hindu-Bali would longer remain) is compressed into a contrastive array of exotic bonds between the sexes. I necessarily cite J. A. Robertson's translation published in 1906, because earlier English translations of Pigafetta— including one by Lord Stanley Alderly (1874) still used in standard historical summaries—expurgate component 3 of what follows. Herewith a restored fragment of paragraph from early modern history and ethnology; I offer it as emblematic for the reading and the weeping:

> 1) . . . We were told also that when one of the chief men of Java Major dies, his body is burned. His principal wife adorns herself with garlands of flowers and has herself carried on a chair through the entire village by three or four men. Smiling and consoling her relatives who are weeping, she says: "Do not weep, for I am going to sup with my dear husband this evening, and to sleep with him this night." Then she is carried to the fire, where her husband is being burned. Did she not do that, she would not be considered an honorable woman or a true wife to her dead husband. . . .
>
> 2) . . . Our oldest pilot told us that in an island called Acoloro, which lies below Java Major, there are found no persons but women, and that they become pregnant from the wind. When they bring forth, if the offspring is a male, they kill it, but if it is a female they rear it. If men go to that island of theirs, they kill them if they are able to do so. . . .
>
> 3) . . . When the young men of Java are in love with any gentlewoman, they fasten certain little bells between their penis and the foreskin. They take a position under their sweetheart's window, and making a pretense of urinating, and shaking their penis, they make the little bells ring, and continue to ring them until their sweetheart hears the sound. The sweetheart descends immediately, and they take their pleasure; always with those little bells, for their women take great pleasure in hearing those bells ring from the inside. Those bells are all covered and the more they are covered the louder they sound. . . . (Pigafetta, 2: 169)

Confession: as dialectically involved in contemporary issues as Pigafetta, I have been unable to resist rearranging the source to make extreme what was once in-between. This *bricolage* now juxtaposes as #1 and #2 the first and third representations from the "original," one an ethnographic and historical tragic fact (widow immolation), the other a mythological fact (female autoprocreation). These opposites today (1989) attract, given agendas of feminist readings ("affinities and extremes"). To us the Javanese nobility (#1) sounds misogynist, to put the *topos* of suppliant *suttee* or *satia* mildly; and Acolorese women (#2) sound ultrafeminist, to put the *topos* of aggressive Amazons mildly. Yet, current interests in gender, while vital and important, may make less headway into those now extreme-sounding Javanese gentlecouples disarmingly satisfied with sexual dimorphism, to put the *topos* of the ringing-bells-heard-from-inside mildly.

Many are the multiplicities, precedents, and destinations toward which Pigafetta's passage might be read: (1) Tragic practices of widow sacrifice and the militant ideal of female equivalents for heroic death-in-battle that characterized expanding Hinduism from Brahmanical India to at least the second decade of our century in Bali (see Chapter 2); (2) The *isle-des-femmes* motive winding through classical and medieval *topoi,* subsequently invoked at diverse moments of political assertion; (3) Ritualized "arts of love" hitching either satisfied or renounced sexuality to etiquette, hierarchy, and propriety (see Chapters 5–6).

Important critical questions gather around these possibilities. Can we assume that any of them draws us nearer sixteenth-century understandings of this passage, if indeed it originated then? It is difficult to believe (but also to "unbelieve") so. Lucien Febvre's celebrated formulation for the 1500s—"the century that wanted to believe" (so like or perhaps unlike us, or at least like Febvre) remains as pertinent now as in 1942, when Febvre's *Belief and Unbelief in the Sixteenth Century* was published. No more than sixteenth-century poetry or Rabelaisian parodies was the era's ethnology made to add-up or to give a consistent picture:

> As for never throwing out anything they wrote. . . . Sometimes everything was printed just as it was, indiscriminantly: exclamations of admiration, cries of hatred, protestations of tenderness, explosions of fury—nothing got lost. . . . On page three of the collection the reader would see a dithyrambic eulogy of a man whom he found treated on page thirty as a sodomite, a murderer, or at the very least an atheist. (Febvre 1982: 21)

Still, and still following Febvre, a historicist desire to draw nearer "then" must be retained in a fresh range of reading-destinations to and from the past.[3]

Another question: Can we escape doubts that enlightened issues of gender, class, power, hermeneutics, or deconstruction possibly themselves blind or blinker? No escaping these unabsolutes either, so far as I can see. Indeed, the three destinations just enumerated to and from Pigafetta's text (including high critical ones) may bypass important meanings, some of them possibly nearer sixteenth-century beliefs and/or unbeliefs. What other signs might have seethed, what underimages lurked, in those caparisoned foreskins ringing inside Javanese sweethearts? A speculation beckons.

Nineteenth-century scholars deleted Pigafetta's Javanese bells. Readers today are apt to be outraged by the victim wives and either exhilarated or dumbfounded by the restored figure of bells-heard-from inside—a dazzlingly carnivalized emblem of gynocentrism. But given certain schemes of religious difference that punctuated early modern or Renaissance history, I begin worrying about other details, including where the bells hang before ringing inside: between the young man's penis (Italian *il membro*) and his foreskin (Italian *la pelessina?*). Something seems paradoxical, even wrong, about this text's picture or representation. What kind of *topos* is this locus of ringing?

By the early 1500s, after two centuries of Islamization, first of coastal cities, then of courts and gradually peasants, Javanese youths were doubtless circumcised. Why, then, the foreskin? (The prevalence of pre-Islamic circumcision in Java outside its Hindu courts, which of course would not circumcise, is still unclear [Boon 1977: 211]; the complicated facts of female circumcision in Java, possibly increasing again today [Carpenter 1987], is separate from the ceremonies of state at issue here.) Islamic courts of the time staged the circumcision of a sultan's sons (plus loyal followers) as their principal ceremony of state. This style of rite was substituted for those ceremonies of noncircumcising Hindu predecessors devoted to cremations of raja's corpses (plus loyal followers). That contrast continued to mark the difference between Islamic Sasak versus Hindu-Balinese courts in nineteenth-century Lombok, the island neighboring Bali. Such cases show that circumcision/noncircumcision, much more than a logical opposition, could be made to represent rhetorical, religious, and political antitheses. One might dramatize the polarity in this way: circumcision-plus-eventual-burial-of-body-minus-foreskins (Islam) versus and vis-à-vis eventual-cremation-of-entire-body whose rituals and iconography bedizened the intact *lingam* (Hindu). Those historians, philologists, and anthropologists who are inclined to domesticate the past and render its texts and rituals decorous neglect such invented extremes (Boon 1977: chap. 9; 1982a). Yet archaeological remains from Java (O'Connor 1985) and motifs documented from Pegu and elsewhere (Lach 1965: 553) reveal that bell-jingling penises were a Siwaic *topos:* one kind of insistent phallus, among others (see this chapter's opening illustration, p. 50).[4]

Such details heighten the anomaly of Pigafetta's text. The present-foreskins and bells sound Siwaic, as does idealizing widow-burning as an analogue of death in battle. (The latter value precludes calling the ritual icon Tantric, because Tantric persuasions have traditionally opposed Brahmanical values on immolation and countered associated caste hierarchies—see Conclusions below.) But it is already 1520 or so, well into Java's Islamic "era." Perhaps Pigafetta, writing what he had heard told about Java's courts and gentlecouples, caught traces of contradictions then being worked out in Javanese tellings, or belatedly in practice. This possibility is difficult to confirm, because the politics of transmitting/censoring indigenous court chronicles make them refractive of local ritual practices (see Wolters 1982, Vickers 1987, C. Geertz 1980, Boon 1977, chap. 9). Of course, external ethnological accounts may be no less refractive; but their respective angles differ. It is this multiplication of angles and these displacements of what becomes hidden or suppressed that enrich semiotic evidence and further the possibilities of interpretation.

Several destinations of Pigafetta's text became clearer later on. Subsequent sixteenth and seventeenth century European ethnology would strikingly confirm that Javanese courtiers were by then showily circumcised in composite ceremonies displaying many texts and multiple languages (Boon 1982a: chap. 5). Moreover, as Chapter 2 reviewed, by the early seventeenth century Europeans reported that East Indies practices of *suttee* had retreated to Bali.

These destinations, however, are only half the hybrid story of historical encounter. What about the other side of this ethnology: Europe? What about similar differences dividing Western religions and proto-nations and inscribing European "eras"? Similitudes of circumcision/uncircumcision were altering for "us Europeans" before, during, and after Pigafetta wrote about having heard things told him in Java when it was Bali-like. Innumerable scholars have traced the West's centuries of relevant commentaries. Old Testamental covenants of circumcision shifted to New Testamental Pauline sublimations into baptism. The typological contrast of actual circumcision versus "circumcision of the heart" led to patristic paradoxes of Christ as exemplar. These venerable concerns have been neatly paraphrased by Leo Steinberg: "It is because Christ was circumcised that the Christian no longer needs circumcision" (1983: 50). (Note, by the way, that although circumcision is not Koranic, Islam has remained unburdened by hitches in whether followers of the prophet should resemble him in this respect: by convention Islamic prophets and followers alike must be *sine praeputio*—Boon 1977: 210.)

Steinberg's controversial excurses in *The Sexuality of Christ in Renaissance Art and Modern Oblivion* review iconography and sermons that aggravated disputed ideas of circumcision. Previously New Testamental noncircumcision had crisply distinguished Christian (but not Christ) from Muslim or Jew. But Renaissance theologians and Vatican sermons, seeking to thwart the heresies of Manichaeus, Apollinarius, and Valentinus, began professing concrete, literal incarnation. The new heresies were deemed oblivious to Christ's true carnality tokened by the first relic: a blooded foreskin anticipating the passion. Late Quattrocento preachments glorifying Christ's carnality, sexuality, and circumcision conceivably may have undermined—I'm growing more speculative—any simple diacritical value of circumcision signifying non-Christians, including Muslims and Jews.[5]

Regardless, sixteenth-century texts eventually extended similitudes of circumcision versus "anticircumcision" (compare "antimasque" or "Antichrist," or later Nietzsche's "antichristus" paralleling "antisemite"). After Luther branded as "sodomists" not just Jews, Muslims, and Turks but certain Christians (namely Catholics,or rather Papists), the Feast of the Circumcision (January 1) was increasingly associated with Jesuits and Counter-Reformation policies. So was "sodomy," in Protestant (particularly Huguenot) invective.

Accusations of sodomy were aimed at Jesuits, various fraternal orders, and the regions they contacted, China in particular (Spence 1985). I have elsewhere reviewed Protestant interpretations of circumcision as both: (1) punishment for sodomy, a degradation associated with once-innocent cultures experiencing a "fall" into contact with the antichrist pope, *and* (2) a proper ritual for authoritative monarchs and patriarchs free of papal taint, including Muslim and Old Testamental ones (Boon 1982a: pt. 3). Thus, destinations of circumcision, uncircumcision, and anticircumcision included both multiply ambivalent and dramatically antithetical open-ended readings.

The comparative point may be stated briefly and pungently: In the sixteenth century, circumcision at times separated Christian/Muslim in Europe and Muslim/Hindu in Indonesia. At these ritual junctures and collisions discourses gathered and kept unfurling. Although Pigafetta's paragraph explicitly refers to anything but circumcision (namely, self-sacrificed widows, Amazons, and bedizened foreskins), it may, mythlike, trail traces of this absence. (Readers are reminded of those hints of Pigafetta's own possible Rosicrucian heterodoxy.)

By broaching extreme possibilities in reading Pigafetta, I have hazarded a studiously exaggerated retrospect on a source we routinely and more tamely encountered in Chapter 1. This fragment of "Interlude" is offered, then, as a rehearsal-in-excess of some collisions in subsequent chapters, rhetorically displaying how hybrid history-becoming-ethnology can be, and possibly was. Against such heterodox potential, *any* agenda in reading across cultures and histories—whether colonialist, nationalist, internationalist, feminist, or postmodernist—must proceed by inhibiting the seizing of all differences. This understandable limitation guarantees an absence of totalized appropriation; and it means that readings should intensify and continue on to other futures, other destinations, preserving a sense of copiousness that must nevertheless be restrained.

Some Basics of Baliology[6]

Hindu-Balinese practices—including copious performances, a millennium of writing, and the absence of circumcision—are concentrated in Bali, western Lombok, and parts of East Java, Sumatra, and Sulawesi recently converted to Balinese "religion" (*agama*) or settled by Balinese transmigrants under Indonesia's national program to relocate population. The designation "Hindu-Buddhist" refers to the occurrence of both "Siwa" and "Boda" persuasions among Brahmana priests (Hooykaas 1964, 1973b).

Many sourcebooks for regulating Balinese social, legal, and ritual arts stem from pre-Islamic Java. Beginning in the fourteenth century, Java's own unautochthonous Indicized courts encountered first Islamic and then European forces (Catholic Portuguese/Spanish, then Protestant Dutch/English). They all had distinctive strategies of trade, political authority, and religious instruction; Majapahit Javanese statecraft, ritual, and dramatic performances apparently altered accordingly; components of Majapahit courtlife persisted, with transformations, in neighboring Bali.

Removed from developing Islam and later from the more conspicuously intrusive forms of Dutch colonialism,Bali experienced a cultivation of scribal and performing arts tied to rites of ancestor commemoration; wet-rice technology (*subak*) and production cycles; cults of kingship (*raja*) and priests (*pedanda*); and intricate temple systems that organized agriculture, civic units, domestic space, and funerary areas into overlapping networks of shrines tended by ritual practitioners. Here Hindu gods, tutelary deities, and local ancestors still make periodic visitations, to be entertained and propitiated. Demonic agents deemed to upset the social and cosmic equilibrium require regular and sometimes "critical" appeasing at places vulnerable to their influence, such as the ground, the sea, and all crossroads.

Hindu-Balinese cremation is the second funerary rite after provisional burial (immediate cremation is a mark of highest privilege). This practice and Bali's emphasis on dance in popular ceremonies are just two traditions that contrast vividly with Indonesia's Islamic mainstream, itself diverse. Although most courtly Balinese writings derived from Indic Sanskrit sources, temples contrast sharply with South Asian varieties. Bali's temples seem more Polynesian than Indic, as do certain features of subsistence and spatial arrangements. Many Balinese rituals have counterparts among non-Hindu Indonesians—including Christians and Muslims (however "nominal")—particularly wet-rice growers with rival centers of authority marked by displays during rites of passage. Bali-Hinduism's recognition as a legitimate doctrine by the national Ministry of Religions set a precedent of interest to other regions. Religious and ethnic identities remain intricately politicized in Indonesia, despite governmental efforts to neutralize partisan differences and convert them into bureaucratized "functional groups."

The sponsorship and practice of Balinese arts have been involved in rivalries among rajas, ancestor groups, localities, and now national and commercial agencies. The manufacture of sacred objects ("sacred" in Durkheim's sense of set-apart)—gongs, masks, daggers, written texts, and so on—and expertise in the ritual ways of maintaining, cleansing, and reconsecrating them impinge on status and prestige. Narratives and dramas may contain stories of their own origins; different sectors, dynasties, or ancestors are credited with instituting distinct performances. Contrary claims in these matters still animate Balinese political processes and social arrangements; they also introduce complications into the historiography of Balinese arts and ritual.

At a more formalized level, Hindu philosophies of interrelated visual, verbal, spatial, and sonic arts correlate action, word, and thought by orchestrating ritual deed, spoken syllables, and mental images. Any object can become magically charged by means of drawings, inscriptions, incantations, or spells (Weck 1937; Hooykaas 1980a). Some Balinese experts make fine distinctions between trance and "inspiration" (*taksu*) among other types of augmented awareness. Trancers frequently experience divine or demonic possession; the more spectacular varieties of trance include prepubescent trance dances (*Sanghyang Dedari*) and exorcist enactments of the Tantric tale of *Calonarang*. In the latter case the famous witch *Rangda,* whose dread masks often belong to village-area temples, engages friendlier forces of the lionlike *Barong,* whose costumes are often owned by hamlets; the end is regularly a stand-off.

Esoteric ideas have become popularized through both court-based and village-centered transmission to novices of aesthetic skills; masters shape students into musically cycled muscular coordination of postures plus pulsations of eyes, limbs, feet, and fingers. Performers achieve desired concentration and effacement; their poise seems suspended in dynamic tension with the risk of demonic abandon—as a host of observers has attested.[7]

Balinese temple celebrations require gongs and metallophones (*gamelan*), ritual processions, and dances. They may include puppet theater (*wayang*), masked dance-drama (*topeng*), or many unmasked dance-dramas. Such performances upgrade weddings, tooth-filings (where still practiced), and so on. Specific orchestral ensembles accompany each variety of performance. Rituals thus mobilize an array of specialists, some restricted by title-caste or social position, some not. Brahmana priests (*pedanda*) study Sanskritized manuals and rituals of purifying water (*tirtha*) required by clients for certain ceremonies. Puppeteers (*dalang*) are highly respected virtuosi; not restricted by title-caste, they may be concentrated in certain ancestral groups. A dalang becomes the actors, propmen, screenwriter, director, and conductor rolled into one. Dancers activate choreography that betokens in gestures codes that a dalang depicts through puppets. Temple celebrations, weddings, and cremations may become bustling events, with diverse clusters of performances and onlookers, including a priest intoning mantras, a reading club (*sekaha mebasan*) reciting select texts, a *wayang* (cremations excepted), phases of the ritual itself, several accompanying gamelan, and side attractions.

Historically, genres of dance and drama have recombined different channels of refined versus agitated form: sound (in phased periodicities of percussion), voice (in chant and prayer, individual and choral song, and spoken dialogues), styles of movement, levels of gesture, and above all languages ("Archipelago Sanskrit," Old Javanese or Kawi, High Balinese, vernacular Balinese, Indonesian, etc.) Genres have included: (1) *Gambuh,* unmasked court dramas dating back at least four hundred years, whose orchestra adds haunting flutes to percussion; tales derive from indigenous cycles of love and political intrigue called *Malat,* or *Panji* in Java. (2) Masked *Topeng,* performed by a soloist or by multiple actor-dancers staging narratives from dynastic chronicles. (3) *Parwa,* probably originating around 1885, resembles *Wayang Wong,* whose masked dancers replace the leather puppets of *Wayang Kulit; Parwa* contents, however, are limited to episodes from the *Mahabharata.* Bali's versions of the

Ramayana are the major source for *wayang* stories, both the nighttime variety that projects puppet shadows by lamplight onto screens, and the daytime shadowless variety, regarded as the more potent message to ancestral shades. This is just a sample of myriad, transforming genres (De Zoete and Spies 1939).

Narratives portray stock characters, placed in ritually opposed categories of right-hand (mountainward) versus left-hand (seaward). The panoply from Hindu myth and epic includes gods, heroes, adventurous knights, ladies, prime ministers, ladies-in-waiting, servants, ogres, demons, animals (some anthropomorphic), and the popular clowns, marked by specifically Balinese characteristics. A concept of "audience" encompasses ordinarily removed deities, lured to their "seats" by offerings; partisan ancestors whose descendants have "promised in their hearts" a particular performance; human spectators of all social ranks; and outsiders as well, including non-Balinese Indonesians and foreigner tourists. Indeed commoners, construed as "outsiders" (*jaba*) to high title-caste courts (*puri*), have been essential witnesses to their ceremonies. Despite Bali's exclusivistic statuses, performances were seldom designed for a closed audience. This fact may explain the lasting resilience of semiprofessionalized dance and drama organizations: whether talented peasants moonlighting in troops for hire, or office-workers, factory laborers, or service-industry employees (particularly in tourism) earning after-hours income.

Stage layouts and situations in and around temples echo cosmological distinctions of refined/crude and godly/demonic implicit in spatial arrangements, interaction, and punctuations of temporal flow. Styles of offerings and ceremonies activate complementary cycles of patterned sound, gesture, story, and regalia: esoteric mantras and hand postures (*mudra*) of high priests of the right-hand powers (*pedanda*) and high priests of the left-hand powers (*sengguhu*); plus charms, tokens, and homey icons of diverse curers (*balian*) dealing in sorcery and love magic. Hindu-Balinese realms of health and disease, activities of allure and cure, and values of aesthetics and exorcism remain semiotically intertwined, with any separation of theatrical, political, or religious aspects difficult to sustain (Lovric 1987a).

Recent studies of Balinese performances have adopted rationalized schemes advanced by I. G. Sugriwa, R. Moerdowo, and other Indonesian scholars (see Bandem and DeBoer 1981; Lansing 1983). They distinguish: (1) rites by the deities' female attendants and male guardians indispensable to sacred sacrifice; (2) optional performances in a temple's middle-courtyard with masks and costumes that are ritually consecrated; (3) "secular" dances outside the walls performed along with cockfights, games of chance, and so forth; (4) commercial dances with unconsecrated masks, a prime example being the picturesque monkey dance (*Cak*)—partly concocted by Walter Spies for a commercial movie in the 1930s—that has become the trademark of Balinese tourism during Indonesia's Suharto regime.

Balinese performance traditions straddle rivalrous courts, village-based rules riddling status restrictions, and governmental management and promotion by commercial agencies selling tickets. Balinese arts have undergone the transformation from sumptuary motives to motives of consumption and consumerism, from tributary mediations to a cash nexus. Several modern institutes and schools for the preservation and advancement of Balinese arts now promote experiments in training and standardization, including notation systems.

Indonesian national agencies with their own imaginative legitimations may regulate aspects of Balinese ritual. As we shall see in Chapter 7, cremation practices were brought into greater conformity during Eka Dasa Rudra in 1979, Bali-wide exorcist ceremonies with traditional justifications. In 1981 cockfight betting was again officially banned. The Parisada Hindu Dharma organization is committed to propagating unified Hindu-Balinese doctrine and practice. But the rationalization of ritual has hardly developed uniformly. Proletarian themes, paralleling aspects of Javanese popular drama (Peacock 1968), appear only here and there. Hindu-Balinese "theatricality" sustains an array of variations, a murmur of heterodox positions to be stressed in subsequent chapters.

The rituals and performances of Bali, obviously in flux today, may long have been "traditionally" unsettled between hierarchy and locality. They have flowered at the intersection of diverse languages, historical forces, and transforming constructions of rival authorities. This fact has led observers of Balinese life and art to weave performance metaphors into our own metaphors of and for Balinese performance. De Zoete and Spies, for example, likened Balinese ritual sequences to reversible combinations of evenings in Wagner's *Ring;* C. Geertz (1980) has compared Balinese subjects of temporarily "suasive" lords to the spear-bearing extras in an operatic extravaganza. An intricate tissue of captioned images from hybrid arts has thus become a mainstay not just in the semiotics of Bali but in the semiotics of Balinese studies. The culture so represented begins to resemble a Peircean profusion of symbolic activities in historical fact.

Ritual-cum-Rhetoric

In the influential terms of Charles Peirce's semiotics, a "symbol" is something that replaces something for someone. Peirce pondered how things can be regarded as replaceable or substitutable: one word for another, words for something else, one language for another. Anthropologists building on Peirce designate full sets of conventional replaceables a "culture," and highly concentrated activities that accelerate semiotic activity have been called "cultural performances" (M. Singer 1972, 1984; Boon 1973). Special occasions for substituting interrelated arts, languages, institutions, narratives, moods, and motivations intensify general cultural and historical processes (Geertz 1973).

Social arts involve role-playing, typing, casting, and framing, as Erving Goffman long insisted. Concentrated into formal performances, the channels of everyday presentation become selectively recombined. Voice may be converted to gesture, to music, to script, to score in all directions. Narrative flow and set postures may interrupt each other. Oral, aural, visual, tactile, and olfactory codes and channels, including print and images, are counterposed, transposed, and transformed. These activities isolate, distend, mesh, cancel, transfigure, or otherwise exaggerate (hyperbole/litotes) semiotic connections and narrative sequences; semiotics thus implies rhetoric. Kenneth Burke's rhetorical "dramatism" of human motives indicates that social actors commit these figures anyway, but certain texts and activities may heighten multiple tropes.

Studies in the semiotics, rhetoric, and dialectics of cultural performances challenge functionalist assumptions of reinforcement and replication. Ethnographic evidence from societies lacking specialist theater show that ritual, too, plays with structure and questions moral standards. For example, in Bateson's celebrated *Naven* New Guinea's Iatmuls control awareness by reversing, contradicting, exaggerating, and parodying regular norms (see Postlude below). Even without writing, ritual forms—always historical—may be both inside and outside society's proprieties. This transgressiveness recalls subversive aspects of Greek cults countering the *polis*—a resistance that possibly led Greek drama toward the West's destination of theatrical critique/compliance (Detienne 1979).

Recent studies joining anthropology and theater dispute whether "ritual" can be patently integrated or "drama" can become comfortably *either* conservative *or* dissenting (Blau 1982; Schechner 1986). Semioticians of cultural performances argue similar points (Singer 1984, Bruner 1984). In distinct historical circumstances professionalized performances may be institutionally separated from periodic rituals. But boundaries remain flexible, negotiable, and often controversial. Distinctions between drama and worship, liturgy and theater, ceremony and burlesque, may shift and reverse; the same event becomes simultaneously "liturgy" to one sector of its actors and audience, burlesque to another. Indeed, when distinctions between religion/theater or ritual/drama begin calcifying, convictions about "theater" may turn religious, or nearly so. "Secularists" grow cultic, theater-buffs sound like believers.

Investigations of cultural performances attend not just to heightened replaceables and transposables but to absences as well. An absence may underpin a stylization. Mime, for example, is language minus speech; and masks faces minus movement, or full movement. As masks stand to faces, puppets may stand to bodies (Napier 1986). In the Balinese shadow theater already mentioned, the performative moments minus the percussive sounds of gamelan contrast to the moments minus the silence. Any such variations gain performative power by the felt absences their conventions activate/eliminate; they may orchestrate a sense of "history" of performance styles. Western drama's classical unities of place, time, and action, for example, invite subversive shifts in dramatic proprieties to "new theaters" that stage extra locales, previous and subsequent events, and off-stage implications.

Through semiotic multiplicities and dialectical absences, codes and genres of performance allude each to each, constructively and deconstructively. Construed and enacted as performances, cultures too remain in complicated conversation with their pasts; they may even defer (on this issue, readers might defer to the Postlude). Let me mention another example from our "culture of reference," which I fear may be starting to feel upstaged by semiotic technicalities. Balinese dance styles possibly developed from combat techniques, battle gestures, and flirtatious activities of court life. Although this history is iconographically inscribed here and there, its past presence defies retrieving. To deem, say, Baris dance sublimated battle, overlooks the fact that precolonial Balinese warfare, judged by later standards, may have been fairly sublimated in its own right. Nevertheless, the very convictions of connections between Baris dance and actual battles—a commonplace in Bali—have semiotic salience.

Like Saussurian semiology discussed above, Peirce's semiotics underscores complexity, open systematics, and difference in the comparative study of languages, histories, and cultures (Eco 1979). Signs conceived as contrastive and symbols viewed as replaceables are not incompatible approaches (Boon 1982a; chap. 4). Yet Saussurian emphasis on the differential remove of meaning and Peircean stress on its performative layers can be distinguished. Moreover, both approaches require, and deserve, being saturated with multiplicity and turned toward the historical poignance of victims and martyrs as well as those inspiring or deluding them. Symbols may be phallocentric, gynocentric, or otherwise, all requiring resistance. Signs include corpses and blood and foreskins (present/absent) and the messages—disseminations, flows—that they contradictorily disperse and cycle. These dispersals and cycles happen at those hybrid places we call cultures, colliding in those intertextual histories we call time.

Balinese rituals in practice are as hybrid as the historical evidence "entexting" their past. They are intermedia, multilingual, and polyscriptive: high/low Balinese, Kawi, Sanskrit mantras, Indonesian, pastiches and parodies of foreign tongues, including touristspeak, Arabic, etc. Ritual cyclically accelerates the circulation of production in every sensory realm and material medium. *Pedanda*-backed Siwaic ceremonies are in the business of cremating corpses (not, we recall, circumcising sons, among a plenitude of other possibilities, including circumcising daughters, as "they" do next door in Java [Carpenter 1987: 72]). Local rites adjust attributes of social life to presumably ancestor-pleasing dimensions and malady-preventing ones. An on-going process across time and languages, rituals assert, sometimes obliquely, contrastive identities in a field of meanings always political, of course, but not only that.

I call these properties "ritual-cum-rhetoric," a kind of pastiche mantra to evoke a history (provided it be multiplied) of "complex polyglossia" underscored in the works of Mikhail Bakhtin. At one point Bakhtin extended his concerns to "the Orient" (a construction that we are in a better position than he to ironize):

> But the Orient, which was itself always a place of many languages and many cultures, *crisscrossed* with the intersecting boundary lines of ancient cultures and languages, was anything but a naive monoglotic world, passive in its relationship to Greek culture. The Orient was itself bearer of an ancient and complex polyglossia. Scattered throughout the entire Hellenistic world were centers, cities, settlements where several cultures and languages directly cohabited, interweaving with one another in distinctive patterns. Such, for instance, was Samosata, Lucian's native city, which has played such an immense role in the history of the European novel [i.e., as the source of Menippean Satire]. (Bakhtin 1981: 64; emphasis added)

By "hybridization" Bakhtin alludes to the "crucible of the utterance:" any language act emerges from polyglossia, a fact obscured by the politics of standardizing normalized language. Bakhtin credits a deliberate hybridized resistance only to that genre he calls the "novel" (Bakhtin 1981: 358–66). Yet, it is to this reflexive, "intentional double-voiced and internally dialogized" discourse that Chapter 4 compares Balinese ritual with its rhetorics, plus any "history" that manages to leave traces thereof.

Fully interpreted, then, ritual is more than something that simply happens in society or in history, a mere contained in these more substantive containers. Ritual is also more than a disguise and ought never be reduced to a compensation. Instead, ritual is profoundly languagelike, provided we remember that language includes rhetorics as well as grammar. Rhetorics entail more than words, and they (along with words) produce help or harm. Ritual attaches diverse social distinctions and political differences, insistently and often contentiously, to the circulation of whatever society produces and reproduces over and by means of time—including corpses. And however they are made, corpses are one of the many things that social actors inevitably become.

The "suasion" side of ritual has been repeatedly flagged in anthropology by C. Geertz in all phases of his corpus, including *Religion of Java* (1960), "cultural systems" (1973), *Negara* (1980), and various interims and aftermaths. The circulation of values component recalls formulations of Marcel Mauss, Lévi-Strauss, and others who refined Durkheim's approach in *L'Année sociologique*. As I have argued in previous works (1977, 1982a), such views of ritual and rhetoric are themselves in motion, circulating through time. Time and space are moved and framed by ritual-cum-rhetoric that counterarticulates multiple languages and motives (in Kenneth Burke's sense), including those that allow ritual-cum-rhetoric to be so construed. Recently it has become customary to call such constructions "chronotopes", for better or for worse. This usage, again, follows Bakhtin, who happens to have been born in Russia the same year (1895) as Walter Spies, four years before Vladimir Nabokov (Boon 1986), and nine years before Lévi-Strauss was born in Belgium, among other births. Yet Bakhtin has been made, happily, to seem new: more *topoi*, or *antitopoi*, that fracture time and frazzle sequence. How strange is the history of discourse (and births), how resistant to a chronology of decline or enlightenment. "Chrono*topes*," then, help explain why matters of interpretation remain complicated, meta-, poly-, partially repetitive, and preferably reflexive, but not only that.

Discourse parallels ritual parallels discourse, dialectically. . . . Hence I once suggested that Bali's enacted discourse (this ritual) and anthropology's inscribed ritual (this discourse) share provocative features (1982a). Read across relevant cultural history, institutional complexities, and comparative religion and mythology, both "Bali" as a text-between-texts and "comparative anthropology" as a text-between-texts represent open-ended counters to standardized practices, reformist doctrines, and negotiated uniformities. A token list of many relevant features of the Menardian-Menippean "library" called ethnology might include:

1. The outlandish, globe-circling, multilanguaged contents of the "GN" category in the stacks.

2. The clownish, trickstering (Radin 1972) impact of cultural relativity, which obliterates, or at least rib-tickles, absolutes.

3. The peculiar assemblage that counts as an anthropological document: displaced reportage, citations, paraphrases, folk etymologies, interlinear translations, polyglot glossaries, and odd appendices (see D. Tedlock 1983). The so-called "monograph" is more a grotesque, or *polylogue* (Kristeva 1980), or partly disguised collage (Clifford 1981)—Menippean all (see Chapter 4).

4. Anthropology's "authority" (Clifford 1988), like area studies' (Boon 1977), bridges many dimensions: "native point(s) of view," always multiple and contradictory; fieldwork expertises, not necessarily mutually reinforcing; comparativist dislocation; the arts of exaggeration and contrastive typologies that no ethnographic account can avoid or escape.

5. Anthropologists convert "cultures" (as historians often do "eras") into packages of print; a fact theory does well to acknowledge (Ong 1982; Kenner 1962).

Whether countercanonical play serves the political left or the right (if either) remains a continually reopening question. I might mention Allon White who, following Natalie Davis, juxtaposes two views of the "politics of transgression": Bakhtin's and Kristeva's (1980) assumption that subversive overplay is radical; and anthropological demonstrations by Balandier that the same kind of play may serve to restore or conserve (Turner 1974, Turner and Bruner 1986). White poses the question rhetorically: "How far does carnival-esque transgression remain complicit with the rules and structures which it infringes, and how far does it really subvert and radically interrogate those rules and structures?" (1982: 60; see also Stallybrass and White 1986). Rhetorical questions can be left that way.

Resemblances between the heterodoxy of anthropological discourse and similar properties of Hindu-Balinese ritual-cum-rhetoric suggest that the would-be subversive and the wished-for conservative may be complicit in each other; yet they need not compromise. Extreme messages mingle because of the multiple nature of any "audience." Balinese rites both argue auspices of a hierarchical status quo *and* oppose varieties of Islamic and/or Indonesian nationalist centralization (whether right or left). As we shall see, genres and situations of performances may simultaneously implement subtler shifts and contestings across different statuses, roles, and systems.

Similar fluctuations characterize the history of comparative interpretations: that cross-cultural discourse of the *longue durée* that investigates, questions, advances, and occasionally trumpets humanity's polyglot circumstances, not necessarily totalizingly. Difficult questions proliferate that deflect standard polarizations of relativism/certainty, literature/science, or culture/politics. Can multiple languages sustain epistemologies of dispersal and voices of irony, while also ensuring that any such voice, including irony's (ironies'), will be only one among others? Can entities like "Hindu-Bali," Hinduisms, Tantrisms, and anthropologies, encounter across their chronotopes and join forces, now and then, disinterestedly to doubt their own boundaries?

"Discourse" (to employ Bakhtin's "cheerfully irreverent quotation marks"—1981: 55) inscribed, enacted, and performed may be as hermeneutic as a requiem, as cryptic as a fairy tale, as meta- as myth, as jargonized as a joke, and as poly- as a pop tune. Subplots, counterpoints, condensations, brackets, quotation marks, intertextualities, and "winks upon winks" are hardly the exclusive property of high culture or scholarly alienation (Geertz 1973: chap. 1). Popular ritual-cum-rhetorics inflect hardship and duress, and pain and violence, with *jouissance* too. Balinese marriage, for example, includes rituals that make stylized abduction into a wink, and not just the man's wink (Boon 1982b). Moreover, following Siwa's (Siva's) cue, this chapter momentarily regarded castration (rather, circumcision) with a serious wink, and not just Isis's (or the ethnographer's) wink. Like sacrifice, none of these extremes or dismemberments is funny; but none of them is morally simple either. Bakhtin champions laughter (as did Foucault—1970:xv). It is the laughter conveyed textually by Rabelais (the same figure used by Febvre as a pretext to explore the sixteenth century). If this kind of laughter alone dramatizes the impoverishment of ethical rectitude, then ritual-cum-rhetoric may be—from a world that is only partly literary, or even literate—the fullest revelation by history's cultures of their many causes for tears of all motives.

Chapter Four
Siwaic Semiotics:
Allegorical Machineries,
Spatial Desituations,
Polycosmology, Parodic Performance

This snapshot from the midst of a peripheral ritual in Bali's Tabanan district was taken by the author in 1981; participants unrelated to the shrine's deceased founder draw livelihood from arid lands he converted to coconut groves (Boon 1977: chaps. 4–9).

Any fuzziness and malcomposition of this slide—here decolorized for economy's sake and archaizing pleasure—may help counteract the glossy legacy of picture-books of Bali.

Manifest copiousness (this ritual array is minimal by Balinese standards) can make dispersed components seem like compositions, even without benefit of an outsider's framing.

The black rectangle at lower center contains (invisible in the photo) a cassette. This substitute for a gamelan is acceptable for these folk in this context: one unartful case of ingredients desituated along conventional lines of Hindu destinations.

D isciplinary depictions of Hindu-Balinese life and art have become festooned not just with commonplaces and countertypes sampled in Chapter 2, but with tokens of what "Balinese say" or "Balinese believe." According to Miguel Covarrubias, for example, "The Balinese say that a house, like a human being, has a head—the family shrine; arms—the sleeping-quarters and the social parlor; a navel—the courtyard; sexual organs—the gate; legs and feet—the kitchen and the granary; the anus—the pit in the backyard where the refuse is disposed of" (1937: 88). Balinese, at least select ones, do indeed say (and write) such things, as do other Indonesians who like to liken domiciles to crocodiles, ships, macrocosms, intercourse, and so on. Yet these tropes are just that—tropes—and are not to be generalized as a culture's tacit creed or central doctrine (Turner and Bruner 1986).

"Tropic" as well is the scholarly privileging of evidence that reinforces such metaphors and rounds off a consolidated world view. (Practitioners, too, engage in this interpretive activity when circumstances favor visualizing a consensual cosmology.) Again, I cite Covarrubias, whose *Island of Bali* provides a vivid case of a book that would be an island that would be a coherent culture; his work, difficult to resist, has influenced the general course of Balinese studies:

> Like a continual undersea ballet, the pulse of life in Bali moves with a measured rhythm reminiscent of the sway of marine plants and the flowing motion of octopus and jellyfish under the sweep of a submarine current. There is a similar correlation of the elegant and decorative people with the clear-cut extravagant vegetation; of their simple and sensitive temperament with the fertile land. (1937: 11)

When simile-makers make similes from the makings of simile-makers, everything starts to sound suspiciously figurative.

Other sorts of scholar may amalgamate into a domain of "religion" what Covarrubias reports the Balinese as saying or writing, particularly when the sayings or writings are inscribed in esoteric manuscripts. C. Hooykaas, for example, longtime doyen of Balinese philology, produced vast, indispensable translations of and commentaries on Balinese writings. Although these sources had never been thoroughly standardized by monastics or centralized by a dominant court, Hooykaas projected ideals of a regimented canon and an established liturgy in his prescriptions for codifying a library of Balinese materials (Hooykaas 1970).

I wish to take nothing away from Covarrubias's account of Balinese "saying" or "believing," or from Hooykaas's documentations of what he once titled *Religion in Bali* (1973a). However, these domains—if they are domains—should not be essentialized, elevated above other expressions, or declared integral. Rather, their signs and symbols join the "text" of Balinese culture: a decentering, dialectical field of reopening values of the kind discussed in Chapter 3.

Allegorical Machineries

In order to counter representations of Balinese values as a synthetic consensus, I propose to designate the abundant bits of allegory and well-turned sayings—compiled by such figures as Covarrubias and Hooykaas, indeed by all us Balinists—with an unlofty label pinched from Alexander Pope:

> The Machinery, Madam, is a term invented by the Critics to signify that Part which the Deities, Angels, or Daemons are made to act in a Poem: For the ancient Poets are in one Respect like many modern Ladies: Let an Action be never so trivial in itself, they always make it appear of the utmost Importance. These Machines I determined to raise on a very new and odd Foundation, the Rosicrucian Doctrine of Spirits. (1960 [1712]: xi)

Through his Augustan winks Pope thus explicated the apparatus of Gnomes, Sylphs, Nymphs, and Salamanders from Earth, Air, Water, and Fire that he hitched to the superficially inconsequential event of the "rape" of Arabella Fermor's lock of hair by Lord Petre. Any machinery is an intricate set of similes and metaphoric images woven through a semantic fabric (like this one). It is a conspicuous level of personification, deification, or "demonization" situated, allegory-like, within, over, or underneath the action itself. Machineries project into mirrored realms the here and now. Pope lampooned elaborate machineries prevalent in masques, dramas, and metaphysical poetic conventions of an earlier day. For each trivial act and banal sentiment, he devised a puffed-up concomitant in a mocking throwback to humoral affinities:

> The Peer now spreads the glitt'ring Forfex wide,
> T'inclose the Lock; now joins it, to divide.
> Ev'n then, before the fatal Engine clos'd,
> A wretched Sylph too fondly interpos'd;
> Fate urg'd the Sheers, and cut the Sylph in twain,
> (But Airy Substance soon unites again)
> The meeting Points the sacred Hair dissever
> From the fair Head, for ever and ever!
>   Then flashed the living Lightnings from her Eyes,
> And Screams of Horror rend th'affrighted Skies. . . .
>   (Canto III, 2.147–56).

> For, that sad moment, when the Sylphs withdrew,
> And Ariel weeping from Belinda flew,
> Umbriel, a dusky, melancholy Sprite,
> As ever sully'd the fair Face of Light,
> Down to the Central Earth, his Proper Scene,
> Repair'd to search the gloomy Cave of Spleen
>   (Canto IV, 2.11–16).

Few true-blue anthropologists would endorse Pope's mockery; our discipline rejects aloof, moralistic, belletristic disparagements of any semiotic conventions. Nevertheless, Pope's exaggerated sense of machineries in the parodic *Rape of the Lock* may raise our consciousness about such "literary" devices and conceits. Invoking Pope can help question, or carnivalize, uncritical assumptions that allegorical apparatuses convey the meaning of meanings, the basis of belief, the essence of "being," or the foundation of symbolic systems. Now for the semiotic substitution: If an analogy is drawn between Pope's poem and Balinese culture, what might be said of its machinery?

The machinery, Madam (and Sir), is abundant. Bali's undersea ballet virtually bubbles over with allegory, even unaided by "Covarrubiasian" commentary or Hooykaasian consolidation. Like Majapahit Java, "ancient" Polynesia, "traditional" India, Tantric heterodoxies, and other ritual hierarchies, Bali's deities, *dedari,* and demons bedazzle. A marriage may be staged as a reunification of Siwa-Parvati; at burial, cremation, and re-cremation, a corpse may be divine king-for-several-days. Basic activities—from wet-rice irrigation to human birth-through-burial—revolve around bespirited temple ceremonies. Local rituals and islandwide politics coordinate regional and national issues with Indic mythology, permutational and lunar calendrical systems, ancestor commemorations, exorcisms, and esoteric-exoteric principles of the vitality of ironsmiths and other magically charged tasks. Social processes echo narrative episodes from genres whose very writing or reciting may also embody socioliturgical codes.

Chapter 3 mentioned Hindu-Balinese myths, epics, courtly legends, and folktales keyed to geography, speech, script, drama, or icon in cycles of percussion and song of gamelan orchestras. But episodes *also* materialize as social and political forces: ascendant ancestor groups, auspicious marriages, nonstop rivalries of competitive houses (including commoners), and compartmentalizations of bureaucratic activities and administrative policies. These forces have helped shape Bali's precolonial Negaras, its response to the Dutch colonial presence in North Bali after 1849 and throughout Bali after 1906, and its adjustment to the national regime since 1949. Bali's cross-cultural collisions and accommodations stretch over the mercantilist sixteenth century, subsequent "world systems," the touristic twentieth century, and today's commercialized cassette-culture whose newer performance substitutes may not seem degraded to insiders. In these arenas and times, ritual has provided an arsenal of not just legitimation (the functionalist view) but rhetorically effective argumentation (Boon 1977).

Like a thousand "Popish" parodies, Balinese institutions, rites, ceremonies, dramatic arts, iconographies, scribal productions, and popular performances have alluded back and forth, unsettlingly, in a process that C. Geertz has termed metacommentary, with the apt reminder that Balinese forms are "dialectical in an ordinary, quite unHegelian way" (1973: chap. 15). Yet Balinese machineries may, like Bateson's *Naven,* retain even "a dash of Hegelian dialectics" (1958:266). Indeed, interpretations of Bali can ill afford to leave any dialectic—Hegelian or unHegelian—behind or to omit any ingredient from the recipe.

Many colonial scholars assumed that Balinese indices of rank had once added up to a stratificational scheme (Boon 1977: pt. 1; a recent study that reverts to this view is Robinson 1988). Nineteenth-century military envoys and missionaries and twentieth-century administrators overestimated one or another status machinery: (1) Indic *warna* categories—Brahmana, Satria, Wesia, Sudra; (2) historical legends heroizing noble ancestors and tying select commoner houses to distinguished origin-points as well; (3) titles that convey the status of partly endogamous groups, which may hold rights to special administrative or ritual tasks with purity/pollution overtones; (4) heraldic privileges and sumptuary restrictions on temple heights and associated ritual regalia—such regulations could be governed locally by residential hamlet (*banjar*) or irrigation society (*subak*), by court officials, or by priests perform- ing ceremonies for clients. These devices complicate the question of whether Bali's history conceals the story of a singular mode of dominance, even status- dominance (Geertz 1980; see also Schulte Nordholdt 1980, Vickers 1984, Hanna 1978).[1]

Contemporary Balinese sanctions of privilege and display, although in- creasingly mediated by cash payments and commercial transactions, still ani- mate competitive factions of temple memberships. An example documented in 1972 neatly suggests the crisscrossed criteria of status and respect: "Pesaji" is the name of a group residing in western Bali; their title is "I Gusti," although some neighbors refuse them this honorific. They lack any prestigious legacy of courtly responsibility, but they tell a tale tracing predecessors to a northern district where they are recognized as Wesia. Rights to attend specific temples sporting twice-born components in architectural style and ceremonial practice would confirm these claims in their area of origin.

Rank in Bali codes various distinctions: male/female, elder/younger, wife receivers/wife providers (see Chapter 5). Yet related status machineries do not simply stack up in mutual reinforcement; nor need one assume that they ever did or some day might. Contradictory constructions satisfy different parties, each construing plausibility to its own advantage. What rivals share are fluc- tuating hierarchical assumptions, ground rules for an ongoing cultural argu- ment. Geertz and Geertz (1975) have countered conventional functionalist as- sumptions that status indices are "normally" congruent either in action or in ideal. I have compared issues in Balinese status to mythic contradictions, po- etic oxymoron, dramatic tension, social dialectics, and religious or literary paradox (Boon 1977, 1982abc).

In the matter of Bali's *warna* schemes and twice-born (*triwangsa*) rank, for example, ritual purity and political power are mutually irreducible. As in cer- tain Indic codes of hierarchy, priestly purity encompasses the courtly political prowess upon which it is dependent for protection (Dumont 1980). In Bali the political "function" (*artha*) may fall to either Satria or Wesia (titled Dewa or Gusti), depending on the kingdom-district and its legends of connections to other kingdoms. Balinese caste-titles reflect no fixed or faulty confirmation of privilege by power; rather they keep reopening venerable paradoxes of earned versus endowed status. They have been the subject of both accommodation and conflict, but in either case work dialectically: "If the titles simply offered a redundant index of political power, they would ring hollow. . . . Balinese titles, like Hindu varna categories, perpetuate a contradiction that would not be there unless they were" (Boon 1977: 184).

Precolonial rank was unlikely as rigid as colonialist and nationalist representations have made it appear. Nevertheless, certain machineries—for example, the *warna* scheme and principles of hypergamy—code a fixity of social strata; they provide advocates (both indigenous and outsider) of this view with materials for arguing their case. Standard histories of presumably traditional civilizations have conventionally stressed machineries of stasis. However dynamic such pasts might have been, they retrospectively appear inflexible when read from a strategically centralized "top" down. Yet Balinese status need never have conformed to any uniform standard or a single dimension of interest. Neither prestige, nor power, nor wealth necessarily replicate each other; nor would ritual space lead us to believe that they could.

Spatial Desituations

Just as status machineries "mystify" nothing truly uniform underneath, so ritual cosmographies are not a distorted nature, a hit-or-miss geography, or a quaintly ceremonial *topographia*. Hindu-Bali's spatial machineries interrelate irreducible orientations, attributes of landscape, and ideas of directionality. A celebrated example should clarify the "textness" of ritualized space.

Like many classifications of Indonesian and Pacific peoples, Balinese categories distinguish sunrise/sunset orientations (*kangin/kauh*) and mountainward/seaward directions (*kaja/kelod*). These contrasts should not be taken to represent compass points *manqués* (although geometric cardinality can occur as an additional code). Rather, the categories resonate with distinct properties of orientation and direction. Through the year the *kangin/kauh* dimension slowly shifts with respect to geography. Similarly, *kaja/kelod* alters perpetually as one moves across territory. Western accounts have frequently repeated a virtual "etic topos" of Balinese studies: in South Bali "north" (seaward) is south. This commonplace manufactures an apparent disparity by implicitly silhouetting ritual space against uniform cardinal standards, as if they were natural or a logical given.

Other machineries standardize Balinese space by mapping an unfluctuating radial order around a single sacred mountain. Both Hindu mandalas and idealized chronicles configure Bali into a lotuslike "rose of the winds." Balinese practitioners and many foreign scholars who advocate symbolic redundancy represent space concentrically. Yet vantages across Bali's regions unhinge concentrism; to keep in play the *kaja/kelod* distinction requires shifting actual mountains of reference, and indeed across the east-west axis different kingdoms did just that. Linking cardinal directions to cosmological complements (e.g., northeast/southwest = sacred/demonic) further desituates concentrism. The necessary shifts, region to region, contradict a singular coordinate scheme of the maharaja (Dewa Agung), located in a capital sited toward Gunung Agung. Taken together, the machineries suggest that no center is constant or consistent.

This textlike space stabilizes no synthesis. The semiotics of *kaja/kelod, kangin/kauh,* ritual location, and cardinalized attributes show that exceptionally (ideally) everything can mesh and that inherently everything does not. Recalling Barthes (1977), the symbolic does not "run out" at topography, or geography, or actual cardinality. Rather, machineries render topography, geography, cardinality, and the like partially convertible. This "radical symbolic" poses a relative center-mountain/periphery-sea; but every point on any periphery becomes in turn a conceivable "center," if that's what we should call it. These relations and transformations continually extend and encompass the "ever receding peripheries of Hinduized time and space" (Boon 1977: 158).

Pragmatic spatial machineries associated with this process can be reduced to neither materialist nor utilitarian explanations. This much is clear from C. Geertz's (1980) work on ritual, political, judicial, commercial, and irrigation components of the precolonial Balinese state (*negara*). Over several centuries court centers gravitated (almost literally) toward optimal points between sea-drainage and mountain-springs. Their positions possibly facilitated arbitration of conflicts along an entire watershed area irrigated from the same source, with lower-lying broader reaches of paddy vulnerable to uplanders' interference with the water supply.

Now, the pragmatics of strategic location may coincide with other machineries: for example, the capital court between upper (mountainward) and lower (seaward) becomes in another register highest (as center versus periphery). But culturally, pragmatics are never pure and simple. Geertz demonstrates that rituals of *negara* established a politics that was noncentralized, although idealizing centers, and nonterritorial, although geared to ritual attributes of locality. Balinese statecraft managed competitive loyalties. Although Geertz's interpretation challenges models of conspiratorial despotism, it hardly makes rank or power a pretty picture. Rather, it shows how dispersed (yet undiluted) cultural and historical forms of aggression, retrenchment, victimage and virtuosity can be. In this regard I would accentuate Bali's active ancestor groups who have shifted location or title-caste affiliation; the plethora of machineries facilitate preserving select relations with past temples, even as they gain fresh advantages. Such groups help explain Bali's appearance of cultural conservatism despite a history of local mobility, irrigation expansion, and dynamics of ancestor commemoration, across precolonial, colonial, and national eras (Boon 1977: 107–15; chap. 4, pt. 2; see Chapter 7 below).

To underscore the importance of multiple spatial machineries in domestic routines, let me both salute and question an account by M. Hobart who commendably rejects static dualistic schemes when tracing "interesting connections between ritual purity and the flow of water" (1978: 5, 6). Hobart mentions coordinated contrasts in Balinese symbolic formulations: "Appropriately, the burial site for the three high castes, *triwangsa*, lies slightly to the north-east of the commoners' graveyard, to the south of which a small group of Chinese tombs faces open ricefields. (Apparently, this satisfies both Balinese ritual and Chinese geomantic requirements simultaneously!)" (1978: 10). (For evidence of such simultaneous satisfaction even between Balinese social segments, see Boon 1977: 134–40, 220.) Hobart reviews and expands material on an east/west axis and mountainward/seaward tied to "the socially recognized stages of human life." He diagrams movement between passage-rite sites, including the nine-vector choreography linking death temples to houseyards:

> The proper place for birth, the rebirth of an ancestral spirit, and its attendant ceremony of *pekumel* is in the *meten*, even if this is not always practicable. As the descent group deities are worshipped from the *sanggah*, this implies a movement of the soul downwards and to the west, as divine essence is incarnated in humble and perishable human form. . . . The site for the subsequent rituals—*lepas aon*, held on the fall of the umbilical cord; *ngerorasin*, the twelfth-day naming ceremony; and *kambuhan* on the forty-second day, which terminates the mother's impurity—is moved due south and down again, as the pollution of birth sets in. From the 105th day onwards, the location is shifted yet again to the *bale dangin*. This coincides with the child's release from *kumel*. Only at this stage may a village priest, *pemangku*, officiate, for previous ritual is the duty of the less pure birth-specialist, *balian manakan*. The remaining ceremonies in life occur here, to ensure individual welfare and the reproduction of the group, through birthdays, *oton*, tooth-filing, *mesangih* and marriage, *mesakapan*. The more subtle distinctions of status are expressed in the secular [sic] use of living space mentioned. Death should also take place in the *bale dangin*. (1978: 16)

Having clarified an orderly sequence couched in ideal ground plans, Hobart's analysis takes a peculiar turn. He acknowledges that radial *kaja/kelod* bears "little relation to the compass points" (1978: 7), yet he calls the island's extremities (e.g., due north where *kaja* is "south") problems that must be "suppressed" for the system to work. He mentions "difficulties in interpreting movement and relative position" as if these difficulties were not the point of codes that shift positions relationally and multiply. When he plots upstream/

downstream, inflow/outflow, purity/pollution, and male/female, Hobart still seems to expect convergence, neglecting machineries that produce their own contradictions: for example, locales with lowly, noncremating "Bali Aga," who reside upstream, construed in special sacred-dangerous ties with headwaters.

Hobart even suggests that coordinations between upstream/downstream and purity/pollution may escape arbitrariness: "Nor is this selection apparently arbitrary in a society which practices irrigated rice agriculture and is dependent upon water and sunshine for the successful harvests of its staple crop" (1978: 13). His remark both overlooks sunny isles that lack "upstream" purity and implies a use-function theory of symbols, as if they could be "good to" produce subsistence. Here he brushes us back toward old disputes between materialists and idealists, the former accentuating surplus, the latter noting Bali's traditional reluctance to fish the surrounding sea because this sacred-dangerous receptacle of corpse ashes is deemed off-bounds for utility (see, for example, Covarrubias 1937).

My quarrel with Hobart (Boon 1986b) concerns his eventual elimination of oxymoron from a sense of "natural symbols" borrowed from Mary Douglas (1970). (Douglas's own subsequent work also sometimes dodged cultural contradiction—Boon 1983b). Hobart declares:

> Nature may provide convenient objects by which to represent social values, or society itself (Douglas 1970), but its symbolic significance may stem also from the fact that certain aspects are in no way dependent on society. Water, after all, does not flow downhill because some collective representation states that it must (1978: 21).

Now, water merely flowing downhill is really neither the cultural nor the political issue. Balinese irrigation water indeed flows downhill, but through channels routing it indirectly—mediatedly—between paddies through waterworks not individually owned. And this deviated flow occurs precisely because some collective representation states that it must. For similar reasons women bathe downstream relative to men. Nor does this fact escape cultural contradiction, even for the upstream men, because the "purer" water they are deemed to merit is in actuality the downstream outflow of a relatively upstream village area, complete with female bathers.

Water, no one disputes, keeps flowing downhill; but the symbolic fact (that never runs out) is that purity/pollution relations shift, to be reapplied at different points, *despite* Bali's absolute slope. Moreover, that ultimate downstream, the sea, is charged by ritual death pollution, but it is also marked by the "purer" index of ocean temples (*pura segara*). Thus, while the repeatable distinction of upstream/downstream may be paralleled with other cultural distinctions, if there is one thing that even relational upstream/downstream is meaningfully not like, it is nature's own flow.

Hobart offers other insights into water-types and social-types by paraphrasing a Balinese just-so saying about hypergamy: "Just as water cannot flow uphill, semen cannot flow up-caste" (1978: 21). No question here of a "natural fact," only of a simile borrowed from nature. But these machineries too are part of a textual field more radically symbolic than he implies. Connections between Bali's complex typology of water and semen (the latter is also ritually typed) may relate to myths of transfiguring husband's ashes into brother's sperm. Such ideas align with court rituals that retrospectively converted high-caste wives into sisters, according to positive values of incest equated with nearest endogamy (Boon 1982a: chap. 5; 1977: chap. 6; see below, chaps. 5–7). To point even passingly to facts of gravity as, "after all," a presumable base obfuscated by symbols recalls comments by the inveterately practical-minded clowns of shadow theater (*wayang*), who also like to expose cultural facts as disguised natural facts. But this is just one wink in wayang's repertoire.

Hobart observes that high castes are carried on to "the conspicuous display of wealth and support" (1978:18). Few foreign or native observers of Bali would, I imagine, quarrel with this claim. But do low castes differ by more than degree? And at what point does Balinese ritual display become "conspicuous" versus "productive," if that is the contrast being implied? Citing theoretical views of Maurice Bloch, Hobart attributes a vaguely false consciousness to high castes and perhaps to "natural symbols" in general.[2] He alludes to "obfuscations" in which "purity and pollution are presented as realities of the same order as life and death, with a legitimacy conferred by appearing as natural" (1978: 21). Seemingly reluctant quite to name what culprit undermines authenticity, Hobart couches quasi-accusatory charges in the passive mode: "emphasis is shifted . . . , discrepancies are hidden . . . , through this formalization a synthesis is produced . . ." (1978: 21).

Against suggestions that Balinese symbols disguise discrepancies by conferring a deceptive "semblance of naturalness," I have argued that the welter of machineries usher "nature" along with everything else into a discourse of irreducibly discrepant codes, posed and counterposed in contests of advantages and rivalry, vanquishings and victimage. That particular machineries may advance ideologies serving particular interests should really not be news. Bali's "masses," however—divided, shaded, and conflictual—have themselves helped author this cultural-historical text.

Polycosmology

Thus far this chapter has questioned construing cultural sayings or beliefs in either essentialist or consensual terms. It has also criticized a tendency to explain semiotic devices as "works" that obscure some natural referent or that camouflage true relations of production. Even hackneyed machineries do more than disguise brute power, pure prestige, just productivity and redistribution, or the natural flow of water from mountain-high to ocean-low. They are not smoke screens but masks upon masks, whose "symbolic" never runs out. I would extend this argument even to the most familiar cosmology that supports the interest of an elite. These allegories, too, are dialectical, partially heterodox, and potentially self-contesting.[3]

Siwaic cosmology has been a central concern of Balinese studies since the Dutch began promoting canonical standards in philology and archaeology, after regaining the East Indies from the British following the Napoleonic wars. Scholars from the mid-nineteenth century to our day have documented ritual cosmography, geomantic and tellurian codes, ceremonial choreography, and overall "worldview." A summary Hindu-Balinese cosmography coordinates divinity in a rich set of transformations: (1) self-inclusive panoply of distinctions as "center" (Siwa); (2) two-around-a-center (tripartite Brahma/Wisnu/Siwa); (3) four-around-a-center (Iswara/Rudra/Brahma/Maheshwara/Mahadewa/Sangkara/Wisnu/-Sambu/Siwa). "Center" is a spatial metaphor for the shifting Siwa factor, the logical middle of the triad, the conjunction of cardinal east, south, west, and north; the heart of the rose of the winds.

Color equivalents for the cardinal scheme (fivefold) and the lotus scheme (ninefold) make Siwa polychrome: all distinctions are simultaneous but not blended. The Brahma/Wisnu/Siwa triad echoes a complete sacred A/U/M syllable; Siwa becoming white versus Brahma-red and Wisnu-black. The shift in color underscores Siwa's recurrence in each projection. Thus, the difference between tripartite Siwa (versus Brahma/Wisnu) and four-around-the-center Siwa (versus Iswara/Brahma/Mahadewa/Wisnu) is like the difference between white (versus red/black) and polychrome (versus white/red/yellow/black). Much as Lévi-Strauss (1963a) once suggested for totemic representations, it is not the resemblances but the differences that resemble each other.

Swellengrebel's important overview of Balinese cosmology made Siwa less central than synthesizing: "the third element is less the linking, intermediary member than it is the higher, synthesizing unity of which the other two are individual aspects" (1960: 46). I would go further: Siwa is really less a synthesis than a generic differential. Siwa both embodies creative/destructive polarities and generates shifts across varying degrees of opposition. While the Siwa factor implies all distinctions, it can be manifest only in a specific instance or set of them, never wholly. That is a vital aspect of Siwa's own semiotics. Each set of differences resonates towards another. This interpretation of Siwa differs from conventional philological summaries like this one: "Siwa is the all-encompassing unity. Brahma, Wisnu and Iswara are individual aspects of his creative power" (Ramseyer 1977: 108). Indeed, it is a fractious unity that can never be wholly unabsent, a decentering "center" that implies its own displacement.

Bali's Hindu codes of divinities and colors extend to metals, demons, descent lines, musical tones, numbers, days, weekly and monthly cycles, and heraldic attributes (thunderbolt, snake snare, discus, lotus, etc.). Reformed, rationalized representations of cosmology, whether by Western or Indonesian scholars, often construe a given machinery as a means to consolidate such components: Brahma is red is *paing* is nine is seaward is copper. . . . I think the codes are more accurately seen as keys to inherently fluctuating affinities: all-difference, to threefold, to fivefold, to ninefold—operated by Siwa's shifts. No machinery, moreover, can be redundant because each throws the other slightly out of cog or into a different degree of categorical contrast.

Consider just one example of this dance of categories: There cannot quite be a center (even a vanishing one) of colors; nor can there be a polychrome of space. At the level of tripartite contrasts in color, white is the ultimate negative (not-red, not-black); transformed to fivefold, white becomes one among the other negatives (not red, black, or yellow), allowing polychrome to become ultimate negative. Color, then, works in an inverse fashion to deity, where Siwa remains the ultimate position in both the tripartite and fivefold (four-around-the-center) schemes. The difference between color and deity—as fields of differentials—may be represented as follows: It takes two colors (white and polychrome) to fill the role of one deity (Siwa). In fivefold schemes Siwa can remain "center" because Iswara substitutes for him in the "cardinal" deities. White, however, slips down to the cardinal colors to be replaced by polychrome at the "center." Meaning, again, operates as not redundancy but interrelated irreducibles. Machineries articulate categories relationally, not substantively; in Kenneth Burke's terms, their symbols are polar (I would add, repetitively polar) rather than positive (1970: 24n).

Important issues pertain to these semiotics. Again, in the Brahma/Wisnu/Siwa tripartition, Siwa can be made central (Brahma/Siwa/Wisnu), but that does not make even Siwa the substantive middle, consolidated compromise, or sum and unity. If I am correct, unreformed Hindu-Balinese machineries pose first, second, and third each as an in-between of the other two. This pattern of mutual extremes extends to distinctions of demonic/human/divine in cosmographies of underworld/earth/heaven. The "middle" human world is neither a blend of heaven and hell nor some Manichaean composite; rather each category stands doubly opposed in two directions. This theme is pronounced in values of *kama/artha/dharma* that separate and interrelate demonic passion, political prowess, and ancestral duty, and as will become clear later, Tantric tonalities (Boon 1982b: chap. 6).

Scholars of Bali alert to polar codes may still slip back into substantivist, even "territorial" assumptions about cosmology and space. An example is Tan's (1960) stimulating analysis of Balinese architecture—priestly, noble, and common. Tan plots demonic/worldly/heavenly cosmology and the ninefold plan laid out as squares, which may be read simultaneously as three rows across by three rows down *and* as eight boxes around the central one. Any box in this division can itself be so divided, in an infinite regression of ninefolds. The squares may be actual walled-off courts in fully elaborated palaces (*puri*) or remain implicit in the placement of shrines and facilities for the nine components of domestic life: ancestor commemoration, conjugal beds (and sometimes unmarried daughters' beds), passage-rite site, guest quarters, kitchen and granary, and so on (such domestic activities as bachelor sleeping and ingestion remain uncoordinated in this ninefold ideal). Although Tan does not make the point, the groundplan cannot precisely coincide with codes of, say, color. The ninefold squares are both three threes and eight-around-a-center; polychrome in and of itself cannot doubly totalize; it must be juxtaposed with deity or an alternative code.

Again, Siwa generates a panoply of codes. Siwa is cosmographically the middle square (or its vanishing center). Yet situated as the northeast temple square, Siwa relates the ninefold lotus form to ritual direction. With Siwa in mind we can see that left/right, up/down, and even male/female are implicitly tripartite (squared into threes) as well; this paramount fact relates cosmography to social structure. For example, Tan comments on the *kamulan* shrine where Siwa appears as Iswara, his "East" avatar:

> The *sanggah kamulan* is divided into three compartments, each with a little door, dedicated to the deified ancestors, who are sometimes identified with the *trimurti,* the trinity Brahma-Ishvara-Vishnu. Brahma is associated with the male ancestors, Vishnu with the female. This is the shrine a man builds himself when he marries. (1960: 449)

Here Ishvara is not a middle between male/female but a spatial embodiment (in the sometimes humble material of the *kamulan*) of male/female ancestral distinction, activated as Brahma on the one side, Vishnu (Wisnu) on the other.

Tan later describes a palace's literal substantiation of the squares:

> The first attempt at a description of a typical *puri* was made by Moojen, amended by Van Romondt, and further revised for our present use. The ground plan is divided into nine courts, in this case not imaginary, but substantiated by high solid walls. We recognize again the well-known triadic division into sacred, intermediate, and profane parts. (1960: 457)

But this comment is insufficiently relational; it makes the central term seem like a blend rather than a mutual extreme. (Durkheim's own sacred/profane formulation was converted to more relational oppositions by his successors, including M. Mauss). Tan's gloss of space and cosmology fails to keep the intermediate position (site of the king's *ukiran* pavilion) in the counterplay implied in nine squares. Cosmologically the lowest row is categorically demonic, in polar distinction to both ancestral duty (upper row) and political prowess (middle row). The "central" *ukiran* pavilion of the king, hardly intermediate, enters a tripartite-polar set of propinquities and juxtapositions. Positions are stretched across three extremes, not along a continuum graduated from profane to sacred through some compromised middle-ground.

Chapter 6 will consider the comparative history of polities attuned to extreme tripartition. Here let me just indicate relevant features of the famous three-temple clusters (*kahyangan tiga*) of Bali. The full complement of local temples consists of *pura puseh* dedicated to origin-point, *pura dalem* dedicated to death, and *pura bale agung* often translated awkwardly as "meeting house temple." Rationalist assumptions that political and civic activities are "secular" rather than "ritual" have prevented many observers from seeing the *pura bale agung* as another extreme, a "liturgy," so to speak, in its own right. The three extremes of origin/death/civic maintenance instill in localities the differences of ancestral/demonic/political (*dharma/kama/artha*).

These few remarks about patent machineries supporting royal privilege are meant to show that even the hierarchical establishment's own symbols do not quite stack up; they partly off-set themselves in meaningful ways. A textual quality of para-dox obtains not just between two sides of a court/popular distinction (or a class or caste conflict) but *within* priestly forms and within folk narratives. Machineries play upon contradictions other than class, caste, or sect, yet upon those as well. Machineries, moreover, are grasped in different ways by various parties, and never purely disinterestedly. Multiplied *partis pris* preclude adducing an overall allegory of unified belief or "saying." These diverse dialectics and subtle shifts of "Siwaic semiotics" become most conspicuous in the genres now to be invoked.

Parodic Performances

Bali is part of the Southeast Asian region, where many societies have institutionalized monasticism; it is also one destination in that history of Indicized expansion often marked by sharp sectarian divisions and caste-competition. Yet compared to the monks and specialist scribes of either Southeast Asia or "Further India", Balinese priests have not emphasized the arts of formal exegetical argument. The proclivity of even literati ritually *to do* rather than exegetically to indoctrinate once prompted C. Geertz to characterize Bali as an orthopractice rather than an orthodoxy. Although this comment by an eminent anthropologist incurred the wrath of an eminent philologist (see C. Hooykaas 1976a, C. Geertz 1976), the claim is easily confirmed. Frustrated investigators of Balinese meanings have commonly reported anecdotes like one by J. Hooykaas in her enthralling study of changeling children. She emphasized folklore and such life-crisis rites as the three-month birth anniversary:

> There also a bajang cholong is used. The word cholong means something like "stealthy;" bajang cholong is, therefore, fairly well translated by "changeling" since it conveys the idea of the child exchange being done with stealth.
>
> The treatment of the changeling in Bali is exactly the same as that which obtained for it in Europe. In Bali the changeling is regarded as unclean and is treated as such. A Brahmin lady, well known as a maker of offerings, was shocked when I asked her for details of the

bajang cholong. "We leave that to sudras," she said scornfully. (J.
Hooykaas 1960a: 426)

Any Sudras, we can rest assured, would have deferred as well, although for
different ostensible reasons. The exegetical buck passes ultimately back to the
ancestors who make known their desires, without explanation, to performers
in trance. Balinese shades, like many others, conventionally answer imperti-
nent "Whys" with a silently sacrosanct, uninterpreted "Because."

Outside reformist circles, Balinese textual practices minimize neutralized
commentary. Reading groups (*sekaha mebasan*) may discuss distinct episodes
from favored narratives; but their busywork is ideally another ingredient of
ritual celebrations. To enact, cite, or even refer to a text may unleash its
power. Exegesis in any strict sense does not number among the functions of
traditional textual and ritual experts—whether a high caste or commoner,
heavenly or netherly, lettered or less lettered (including *pedanda Siva* and
Bauddha, sengguhu, pemangku, dalang, and obscure *dukuh,* possibly connected to the social status of Pasek). Moreover, as C. Hooykaas stated, low-
caste temple priests, exorcists, and puppet masters alike "have some share in
the brahman's panoply of magic weapons" (1980a: 20).

Hindu-Balinese ideals include options of ascetic withdrawal after complet-
ing social duties of procreation and maintenance. Yet neither monasticism,
liberation from ritual cycles, nor ultimate extinction of social ties became a
dominant "confession" (in Weber's comparative sense). Bali has not accentuated renunciation as a counter to dense regulations perpetuating life's divisions and cycles. Moreover, Balinese formats of textual knowledge and transmission contrast with ascetic-charged styles of literariness. Just as Bali has
institutionalized little ascetic remove from life-in-society, so it demonstrates
little interpretive remove from texts that would make them partly alienated
objects of exegetical reflection. In Bali's "interpretive scene" the restricted
role of exegesis proper facilitates a play of affinities, analogies, and contradictions across social forms, performance genres, and ritual registers.

Bali's "many-sided literature" has been attributed to its "thousand years of
familiarity with the art of writing" (C. Hooykaas 1973a: 12). Writings range
over Indic mythology and epic; assorted indigenous, Hindu, Islamic, and Chinese sources; chronicles of courtly expansion and collapse; and manuals for
the ritual regulation of etiquette and of cures in the event of etiquette's dangerous lapse. Now, these materials may not be primarily "about" their contents.
They sometimes seem more like performance in the medium of script, just as
wayang is performance in the medium of puppets and *topeng* is performance
in the medium of persons (actor-dancers).

The importance of literature and ritual in Bali may pertain to the island's
position vis-à-vis Islam: the Islam that displaced antecedents of Hindu-
Buddhism in Java, the Islam practiced in the part of Lombok never subjugated
by Hindu-Balinese (van der Kraan 1980), the Islam of enclaves in North and

West Bali. Indonesian Islam itself contains manifold strains, including so-called mystical, rationalist, and strictly reformist ones. Issues about the historical process of Islamization in Indonesia remain controversial (see J. Peacock 1973, 1978; Boon 1977: 205–14; Day 1983; Vickers 1987). Many varieties and phases of Islam discount theatrical allegory, ambiguous myth, and reversible microcosmic/macrocosmic categories of divine/demonic polarities and tripartitions. In the interconnected histories of religion, literature, philosophy, and method, any reformist development tends to restrict ritual and rhetoric by narrowing the range of acceptable narrative sequence, doctrines, prayer, and sermon. Like Calvinism and like Augustan movements in literature, Islam prefers the pure "letter," the direct moralistic word. Viewed historically, then, Bali's multiple performances, low on exegesis, may have intensified partly as a kind of allegory of antithesis to Islam.

Insofar as exegetical measures question the whys and wherefores of ritual and belief at a remove, they also entail centralized standards for glossing meaning; this much, exegesis shares with any reform movement. Exegesis, however, requires no thoroughgoing rationalization, no enforced univocality of referents, moralistic monotheism, or universalistic ethic for "true believers." The Dutch developed routinized exegesis for Bali, and subsequent nationalist developments have propagated reforms. Nevertheless Hindu-Bali's ongoing propensity to "comment" on one performance by producing another has remained a kind of resistance. This complex context of literary production recalls features of other "manuscript cultures" in the history of writing and print (Eisenstein 1979; Ong 1982; McLuhan 1962).

Issues of exponential performances have been a keynote in A. L. Becker's work on Javanese shadow theater (*wayang*). He has snatched *wayang*'s meanings and recensions from the clutches of somber-minded philologists and propounded an epistemology of text-building, one transferred to Balinese versions by M. Zurbuchen (1987). They seek a refreshed philology-linguistics-anthropology attuned to contextualized performance.

Becker presents *wayang* as a theatrical world of paradigmatic, associational links—shaped cycles and nested structures that place description, dialogue, and action in varying paces, tonalities, and hierarchies. Many commentators have stressed realms of sensual demons, dignified ancestors, distant deities, and pragmatic clowns who coexist and bring the timeless and the timely into conversation. An aesthetics of plural voices and multiple languages is advanced by the clowns and, of course, the *dalang* puppeteer:

> A wayang includes within it, in each performance, the entire history of the literary language, from Old Javanese, pre-Hindu incantation and mythology to the era of the Sanskrit gods and their language, blending with Javanese in the works of ancient poets (the suluks), adding Arabic and Colonial elements, changing with the power of Java to new locations and dialects, up to the present Bahasa Indonesia and even a bit of American English (in which one clown often

instructs another): I do not just mean here vocabulary, syntax, and phonological variation. That is also true of modern Javanese. The difference is that in the shadow play, the language of each of these different eras is separate in function from the others; certain voices speak only one or the other of these languages and dialects, and they are continually kept almost entirely separate from each other. One could even say that the content of the wayang is the languages of the past and the present, a means for contextualizing the past in the present, and the present in the past, hence preserving the expanding text that is the culture. (Becker 1979:232)

Wayang, then, is performatively poly-: polythematic, polystylistic, polycyclic. James Brandon's *On Thrones of Gold* outlines fractured epics cobbled into distinct episodes: "In the *Reincarnation of Rama* the god Guru explicitly commends the incarnation of Wisnu's authority and truth to Kresna and Ardjuna, thus passing on to the Pandawas the rights of kingship previously held by Rama and Leksmana [an idea not found in the Indian epics]" (1970: 16). In *wayang* the frameworks of the *Ramayana* and the *Mahabharata* (plus *Panji* and other cycles) jostle and juggle each other, as they have done in the actual literary and political history of Java and Bali. Such episodes are not to be understood through easy polarities of good versus evil (see Rassers 1959; Held 1935). Rather, everything moves around. For example, a fundamental contrast between the Kosala/Videha factions is repeated in heroes/Rakshasas. Bhima suggests something like a clown-factor projected onto the Pandawa brothers; similarly Panji suggests an "Indonesianization" of the heroic cycle, just as Menak represents an Islamization. More generally, the *Ramayana* echoes principles of creation myths where "clowns" are integral mediators bridging divinity and nobility; on the other hand the *Mahabharata* remains more a chronicle, with clowns providing a foil to divinity and nobility (Boon 1977: 190–205; 1982a: 191–200). That these shifts and variations keep accumulating in *wayang* precludes reading any episode as a melodrama of right versus wrong.

Wayang's epistemology resembles Western examples of so-called Menippean satire, a form of parodic rhetoric that multiplies voices and viewpoints, tongues, citations, pastiches, and etymologies. This literary language conjoins hoity-toity high tones and popular blather in a celebration of bazaar-life or "commercial" culture rather than the proprieties of centralized, territorial control. F. A. Payne (1981) has called the serious play of Menippean satire a "medley": interwoven genres, oscillating between prosody and prose; collages of narrative and artifact that avoid reliably authorial "authority," obliterate absolutes, and disturb boundaries of dialects and rectitude. Menippean satire is in a sense the original "blurred genre" (Geertz 1980), or rather the copious possibilities out of which distinct genres are precipitated or sedimented. An astonishing number of works slip into this pervasive poly-genre named for one of Lucian's satires.[4] These texts occupy the margins between drama, romance, history, ethnology, or autobiography and the book as a self-conscious material production. They resemble plays that weave stage directions, multiple authors, many actors, several levels of commentary, and the physical and "spiritual" conditions of possibility of their own manufacture into a package of pages.

One critic who has underscored Menippean rhetoric in the history of literary and political writing is Northrop Frye. His *Anatomy of Criticism* (echoing Burton's *Anatomy*) salutes parody, comedy, and the ironic use of erudition, eventually isolating Menippean satire itself, in whose image his book is cast:

> Most fantasy is pulled back into satire by a powerful undertow often called allegory, which may be described as the implicit reference to experience in the perception of the incongruous. . . .

> This type of fantasy breaks down customary associations, reduces sense experience to one of many possible categories, and brings out the tentative *als ob* basis of all our thinking. Emerson says that such shifts of perspective afford "a low degree of the sublime," but actually they afford something of far greater artistic importance, a high degree of the ridiculous. And, consistently with the general basis of satire as parody-romance, they are usually adaptations of romance themes: the fairyland of little people, the land of giants, the world of enchanted animals, the wonderlands parodied in Lucian's *True History*. (1957: 225, 234–35).

He eventually isolates Menippean satire itself:

> [It] deals less with people as such than with mental attitudes. Pedants, bigots, cranks, parvenus, virtuosi, enthusiasts, rapacious and incompetent professional men of all kinds, are handled in terms of their occupational approach to life as distinct from their social behavior. The Menippean satire thus resembles the confession in its ability to handle abstract ideas and theories, and differs from the novel in its characterization, which is stylized rather than naturalistic, and presents people as mouthpieces of the ideas they represent. (1957:309)

Like *wayang*, Menippean works (rather, texts) open distinctions between written and oral renditions; they strain toward plenitudes rather than routines; their generators (authors, actors, readers) share the *dalang*'s penchant for "motivating" proper names and etymologizing everything. No more than the *dalang* can Menippean punsters—whether More and Erasmus, Melville and Twain, or Joyce and his re-joycer, Hugh Kenner—leave anything arbitrary. Thus, strategies of "expanding the text that is the culture" (and the history) that Becker discloses in *wayang* are well known westward.

Nevertheless, outside of Menippean books, European examples of this text-building are seldom performed in those noncompulsive settings—"more like a Western sports event than serious theater" (Becker 1979: 230; he names not rock concerts)—that characterize Indonesian shadow theater. Compulsive "audiencehood" versus free-for-all spectatorship is, of course, relatively recent in Europe's history of bourgeois proprieties. Still, bookish Western genres resonant with *wayang* are ironic rather than either pious or reformist; they too manage, in Northrop Frye's sense, "to incorporate the demonic."

Becker's own rhetorical strategy artfully poses *wayang* against everything it isn't: sequential; decorous; unified in space, time, or authorial vantage; monolingual. His approach helps heighten the question: If that's what *wayang* isn't, what is it? To attempt to ponder this question from within remultiplies questions of vantage: the *dalang?* one audience member? a different audience member? the puppets? different puppets? a camera and tape recorder (see Keeler 1987)? To attempt to ponder this question from without again invites broaching anti-Aristotelian instances of nonsequential, nondecorous texts and contexts attuned to counterunities. Such heterodox dimensions of Western discourse (largely Menippean) have been called by M. Bakhtin "the grotesque," "carnivalization," and "languages of the Marketplace" (1968). Here laughter—whether hilarious, nervous, teary, or tragicomic—is the key to text-building (Bakhtin 1981).

I incline to doubt patently moralistic interpretations of Menippean forms, including *wayang,* whose protagonists (whether heroes, gods, demons, or clowns) may be designed to transgress conventions and make proprieties problematic. Exemplary characters or apt "role models" are as elusive here as they are in, say, *Hausmärchen.* In the case of *wayang,* ethicized and ethicizing commentaries may come from the domestic right (e.g., Mulyono 1978a, 1978b, 1979a, 1979b) or from the foreign left (e.g., Anderson 1965). Ironically, these two sides of the political spectrum tend to read internally contradictory epistemologies of play as disguised codes for conduct. Against both extremes, I propose a third position, not a compromise. Might such codes for conduct be what the forms themselves subvert, and not necessarily toward politically assessed ethical betterment? Do "Third World" performances, too, keep multiplicities moving, para-doxically? Can they be read radically without being automatically reduced to manifest or camouflaged political allegiance (which, of course, they certainly can and do contain—see McVey 1986)? Do their many voices sustain each other by canceling themselves out, yielding a field of motives (in Kenneth Burke's sense) saturated with positions, and divorced from particular moralized ends, including use-value?

Many observers have applauded the servant-clowns in *wayang* whose controlled disruptiveness creates insulated satire from the margins. Geertz's (1973:139–40) influential portrait of Semar, for example, touts his conjunction of spiritual refinement plus rough-hewn comportment, his blend of god-clown opposites, and his championing of nonabsolutism:

> Like Falstaff, Semar is a symbolic father to the play's heroes. Like Falstaff, he is fat, funny, and worldly-wise; and like Falstaff, he

seems to provide in his vigorous amoralism a general criticism of the
very values the drama affirms. . . . Semar reminds the noble and refined Pendawas of their own humble, animal origins. He resists any
attempt to turn human beings into gods and to end the world of natural contingency by a flight to the divine world of absolute order, a
final stilling of the eternal psychological-metaphysical struggle.

Other scholars have assessed the social and political uses of satire, topsy-
turvydom, and ritual reversal, as in James Peacock's (1968) analysis of the
functions of the ludic in *ludruk* (Javanese proletarian dramas). Recent Western
performers have apprenticed themselves to Balinese clowns, enriching their
own repertoire through participant empathy (Jenkins 1980). Indeed, Becker
himself trained as a dalang to advance his linguistics and life. But I am asking
an additional question: Might the subversiveness of such clowning genres as
wayang be an end and not a means?

Whether or not *wayang* is a kind of Menippean satire performed, certainly
Balinese *topeng* is. J. Emigh's stimulating account of contemporary *topeng
pajegan* highlights relevant dimensions (1982). Unlike *wayang, topeng* is appropriate at cremations (because, I suspect, *topeng* "plays" to ancestors and
clowns rather than to Hindu deities and heroes). Like satirical danse macabre,
topeng embeds the grandiose and sublime in the actual and earthy. Emigh
observes that during theatricalized visitations the past is ushered into current
contexts. The *topeng* virtuoso's dancing, masking, and vocalizing matches a
dalang's puppetry. A sole performer becomes king, beast, hero, rogue, and
buffoon, blending martial arts and magical *mantras*. All is set to the multiple
musical pulse of gamelan, achieving a synesthetic experience, as the dancer
"plays with the dynamics of the performance situation" to enact proud *patihs*
and their "antic opposites" (Emigh 1982:25–29; see also Young 1982).

Topeng parodies court life and the ingredients of quasi-historic chronicles
(*babad*). But *babad* values themselves materialize one way on palm-leaf manuscripts (*lontar*), another way in social action, and yet another way in open-
air theater (see Boon 1977:70–92, 145–64). Script, institutions, and dance
"ironize" each other. Emigh outlines comedic structures of *topeng* as follows:

> As with any good comedy team, the "brothers" have contrasting
> styles. The Penasar Kelihan is the straight man, full of self-
> importance and bound to the world of the past by word and gesture.
> The Penasar Cenikan, on the other hand, has the freedom from con-
> straints of a comic innocent. . . . His speech is almost in contempo-
> rary Balinese. When he does sing a *kidung* selection or quote *keka-
> win* poetry, the result is often parody. In his light, nasal voice, he
> often makes light of the pretentiousness of his older sibling. . . .
> (1982:26)

He adds the important point that "the Penasar Cenikan does not mock the
heroic values espoused by the Penasar Kelihan—he speaks as an outsider to

the heroic world that supports those values." It may be more accurate still to
say that all the worlds of *topeng* are made outside, vis-à-vis each other. The
audience at large most readily identifies with the low-popular, or low-
mimetic, components. But the tone is less interestedly satirical in the Swiftian
sense than disinterestedly parodic—"satiric" in the Menippean sense.

Topeng parallels Menippean rhetoric in its antitheses between heroic, high-
caste eloquence and everyday colloquial talk. The particular play Emigh summarizes progresses toward the values of Si Mata Mata, a Sganarelle-like
jokester who sneezes when he should compliment and who debunks all status
puffery. But just when the vernacular, human, and contemporary have gained
ascendancy, the stage-space reverts to Sidha Karya, the high-caste Brahmana
personage whom legend credits with establishing proper cooperation between
raja and priest (*bagawanta*) and with creating the authority of pedandas in
many areas of Balinese ritual and performance. Thus, in the very act of un-
dercutting vainglorious language and comportment (recalling the braggado-
cious stock types of comedy), *topeng* preserves a sampler of the gamut of
language and etiquette. *By subverting, it catalogs.*

An aspect of *topeng*'s context Emigh calls a "bewildering and intriguing
paradox," also fits the Menippean mold:

> Kakul can only take on the role of priestly mediator because of his
> skills as a dancer and storyteller. A priest cannot perform the Sidha
> Karya ceremony himself and Kakul would not perform it without
> previously doing the rest of the performance. . . . The village of
> Tusan, with a large Brahmana population, must bring in an outside
> performer, a Sudra, in order to complete successfully a ceremony
> attending the cremation of a high priest. (1982:35)

Topeng, then, pertains to Bali's general "division of labor." The performing
arts join various priesthoods and local temples in networks of crosscutting
specialization at the local and island-wide levels. Locales engage in exchanges of respective talents, tasks, and often trancers (Boon 1977: 100–102;
Lansing 1983). In such circumstances performers and priests become semiotic
substitutions. These Balinese conventions call to mind histories of festival
forms addressed by scholars from Mauss to Bakhtin (Boon 1982a: 175, 278–
79). Their insights into relevant social, ritual, and textual forms lead me to
surmise that genres resembling Menippean satire are produced in contexts
where sacrament and dramaturgy become conceivable replaceables for each
other. One might even consider Hindu-Bali "itself"—as represented, counter-
typed, and performed over an altogether hybrid history—a prolonged case of
such parodic possibilities, a cumulative activity of rhetoric that, by subverting, catalogs.

Having posed that overbold assertion, let me "suspend" it by taking refuge
in certain lower brow, laughter-provoking items from the long tradition of
documenting Balinese performances. No methodological device seems less

appropriate than Margaret Mead's routine of stopwatch timing to plot sequences and coincidences of trances, dances, and everything else (splitting seconds in the land of *jam karet*—rubber time! [see Belo 1960]). Other analytic techniques—no less arbitrary, even gimmicky—have proved more productive: Colin McPhee's (1966) confinement of Balinese music in Western notation, for example; or Becker's phrase diagrams of text-building (1979). Indeed, the collection and translation of priority-manuscripts is a descriptive device on the grand scale (C. Hooykaas 1970), although this accomplishment has seldom been reviewed with suitable irony by philologists. To acknowledge the artificiality of routinized translation is not to deny benefits from transcribing and regulating manuscripts. Still, many aspects of Balinese texts and performances have slipped through the net of an established philology that is unmindful of the politics of canonizing standards, contents, and glosses.

Now, crisscrossing Bali and Menippean satire is also a gimmick, and conspicuously so, yet one possibly pertinent to certain spirits of Balinese genres. Several fresh devices have graced recent studies of how Bali's performances happen. In a translation of *topeng*, J. Emigh and I Made Bandem (1982) employ eight (count them, 8) different typefaces for voices sounding in Sanskrit, Kawi, Middle Javanese, High Balinese, "medium Balinese," Low Balinese, and modern Indonesian, plus one for stage directions. This delightful device is infinitely more helpful than a stopwatch; a sense of Menippean satire begins to emerge in and as translation. Elsewhere Zurbuchen (1987) details the *dalang*'s languages and their context. Citing W. Ong's concept of "noetic," she accentuates Bali's "multiple code situation." *Wayang* is internally reflexive; its cosmologies turn back on themselves in classifications of *wayang lemah, wayang sudamala,* and *wayang sapuleger* that match Heaven/World/Underworld criteria of completeness outlined above. Zurbuchen stresses script activated as sound; relevant rhetorical figures include poets who liken their own works to both architectural split-gates (*candi*) and voluntary associations (*sekaha*) of words, rather than workers.

The material quality and crafted sense of heard-syllables suggests that manuscripts are utilized not as playbooks or illusionistic narratives so much as script-scores. They strike me as lettered notations in the musical sense, inscribed for the sounding. Becker and Zurbuchen help us wonder whether *wayang* forms world in the way that gamelan forms sound; within *wayang* (with its gamelan orchestra accompanying), world may be shaped like or as sound, recalling the Menippean theme of the world shaped like or as book. It is vital to recall that languages of *wayang* are not languages *by* or *of* so much as languages *to*. Languages key less to speaker or reference than to receiver: Sanskrit is language not *of* or *about* the gods but *to* the gods; Kawi is language *to* the ancestor heroes; High Balinese is language *to* the raja or *pedanda* priest; and so on. Everything remains, in the parlance of recent Western critical discourse, "de-centered," or perhaps, as we saw with Siwa, continually shiftable.

Speculations and research about *wayang* can themselves adapt a Panjiesque epistemology and direct it across cultures and performances as well. If, for example, we compare Javanese *wayang* and Balinese *wayang,* or Javanese *wayang* and Bali, striking contrasts in context appear. Unsurprisingly, *wayang* is desired at a Balinese temple and forbidden in a Javanese mosque; yet in Balinese cremation *wayang* has been generally disallowed (although exceptionally permitted, thus conceivable); while at Javanese burials *wayang* has been inconceivable. Although *wayang* enjoyed court favor and patronage in both islands, Hindu-Bali and Javanese Islam shifted the contrast of allowed/disallowed *wayang* to different rituals. Considered in light of such variations, Balinese cremation festivities suggest an implicit parody of Islamic circumcision (whether in Java or in the Sasak courts of neighboring Lombok), and vice versa. The rituals themselves, very serious indeed, begin almost to resonate parodically (*wayang*ishly), particularly when we recall that each served as the principal ceremony of state for neighboring styles of courts that in other respects were organized similarly. Once performances and institutions are opened to comparative, parodic possibilities, their interpreters can both pursue Barthes' radicalized readings of "the text" and reinstate Bateson's leavening analyses of ritual "with a little Hegelian dialectic" (1958: 266). To investigate Balinese (not-Sasak) culture as serious parody (including laughter as a source of tears) invites us not just to broach the island's life *as lived* across and among all its native differences, but to appreciate its historical situation in Indonesia and its distinctive place in the variations of Southeast Asian and Indo-European configurations stretching across the more immediate colonialist past and the most gradual *longue durée.* The latter destinations occupy the following chapters.

Chapter Five
Twice-Born Twins Times Two:
Legendary Marriage Structures and
Gender in Hierarchic
versus Asymmetric Houses

In those days [the beginning of the first *ara* of the *avasarpini* era] the land was level, men were good and extremely tall and strong, and lived for long periods of time, receiving from wish-trees whatever they needed. This was the *yugalin* ("pair") period, for sons and daughters were born as pairs and intermarried, but there was no pressure on the means of subsistence, and contentment reigned, a picture of society and life obviously similar to that of the Uttara Kurus in the epic. As time went on the people increased, and at length the Kulakaras, the first lawgivers, appeared, the last of whom was Nabhi. To his wife was born a son called Rsabha . . . who taught, for the benefit of the people, the seventy-two sciences, of which writing is the first, arithmetic the most important, and the knowledge of omens the last; the sixty-four accomplishments of women; the hundred arts, including such as those of the potter, blacksmith, painter, weaver, and barber; and the three occupations. To him tradition also attributes the discontinuance of the *yugalin* system of intermarriage. In due course he bestowed kingdoms on his sons and passed into the ascetic life.

—A. Keith, *Mythology of All Races* (1917); comparing the Jain story of Rsabha to the Puranic hero Krishna accompanied by Baladeva or sometimes, outside the ordinary mythology, by Rama.

Only a comparative study can explain.
—A. M. Hocart

T he history of Balinese culture has been shaped in part by rivalrous
ancestor groups whose leaders may favor endogamous unions for their
members, among other varieties of marriage.[1] In islands east of Bali,
corresponding social units have been, ideally, exogamous. I hope to illuminate this empirical, historical, and cultural difference by examining aspects of
gender both within and beyond the realm of social organization. Balinese evidence—particularly the prevalence of optionally endogamous, quasicorporate
ancestral houses—throws into relief other Indonesian social and ritual complexes: this is our first frame of comparison. Simultaneously, Balinese ideas
and activities adapted from India open toward that other massive cultural and
historical sphere: Indo-Europe, our second frame of comparison. Because
Balinese institutions and texts have straddled Indonesian and Indo-European
systems of values, so should Balinese, Indonesian, and Indo-European studies
straddle each other.

These pages address two types of social tie, taking a cue from Balinese
myth and marriage: collaterals distinguished as either parallel (same-sex) or
cross (opposite-sex), especially in the realm of cousin marriage; siblings distinguished as either same-sex or opposite-sex, especially in realms of twin
births and legendary incestuous unions. By "gender" I refer to a culturally
construed difference: male/female. In anthropology's technical parlance, a
"cross" link includes this difference, a "parallel" link does not. Thus, "cross"
indicates the presence of gender (this difference), while "parallel" indicates
the absence of gender. By opposing gender codes in twinship to gender codes
in collaterality, we can pass from Bali's logic and ethic of optional endogamy
to neighboring Indonesian systems of exogamy at comparable levels of cultural constructions.[2]

To recall the terms of Chapter 3, the symbolics of gender do not "run out"
at actual sex roles or relations between men and women. Gender codes multiply vantages and reverse hierarchies, rather than consolidate a singular
"man's" or "woman's" viewpoint. Nor can gender be isolated from other
codes of difference: birth order, location, and so on. This fact makes the politics of gender in "places such as Bali" complicated. For example, long-
documented qualms expressed by Balinese brides about virilocality cannot be
taken as the female view. Opinions of marriageable daughters differ depending
on the variety of marriage, and daughters do not necessarily represent the
opinions of mothers. Moreover, conventional formulas against virilocality
may be repeated even when residence is taken up at the familiar hearth of a
patriparallel cousin. Issues of division of labor and ritual work (karya) along
male/female lines are enmeshed in hierarchical aspirations of successful
houses to release their members—daughters foremost—from unrefined tasks.

Balinese images of women and men do not simply complement a stratified rank of male over female. Stereotypes of demonesses from folktales and ritual coexist with those of female deities; while Balinese exorcisms celebrate demonic Durga, rice rituals are devoted to divine Dewi Sri. Many ills, particularly in the realm of marriage, are attributed to male Rakshasas and other goblins. We shall consider later Tantric-Siwaic reversals of purity/pollution coded by male/female prevalent in both esoteric courtly circles and ongoing vernacular rituals of cure. Finally, in marriage institutions and rituals that concern us here, the category "female" will be shown to remain symbolically double, even where wives do not necessarily link opposable social units. Wives in their various resonances and valences represent an encompassing mediator not just in exogamous kinship systems but in what we might call endogamous "twinship systems" too. Their accent falls not just on wives or wives-become-mothers but on sister-brides-become-ancestresses, and superior ones.

Preliminaries

Bilateral or cognatic values characterize Southeast Asian societies, even where certain rights, obligations, or statuses may be transmitted unilineally. Nevertheless, to designate Southeast Asia "nonunilineal" retains, by default, unilineality as the touchstone order. Moreover, the labels "bilateral" and "cognatic" seem too diluted to evoke the social, ritual, political, and symbolic forces that animate the region, Indonesia in particular. Comparative typologies geared to a lowest common denominator of social organization often neglect evidence of how "cultures" are made mutually extreme during their continual transformation (see Boon 1983a: chaps. 1,3–5).

Bali as a *"Société à Maisons"*

In 1979 Lévi-Strauss published a brief article winkingly titled *"Nobles sauvages"* devoted to rethinking F. Boas's and A. L. Kroeber's long efforts to understand anomalies in Kwakiutl and Yurok societies respectively. Lévi-Strauss delineates a structural type found in Northwest Coast, Californian, and other Amerindian groups; perhaps Africa and Japan; certainly medieval Europe and Melanesia; and most expansively and notably Polynesia and Indonesia (1983a: 170). A recent English translation renders this sociopolitical complex "house societies"; but we shall retain the original *"sociétés à maisons"* for its important plural form. With convincing brio Lévi-Strauss proposes a unit missing in the ethnology of Boas's and Kroeber's day, "whose institutional arsenal did not offer the concept of house in addition to that of tribe, village, clan, and lineage" (1983a: 174).

A *maison* reveals features familiar to Indonesianists; they include:

> A corporate body holding an estate made up of both material and immaterial wealth [land, heirlooms, relics, stories, names, etc.],

which perpetuates itself through the transmission of its name, its goods, and its titles down a real or imaginary line considered legitimate as long as this continuity can express itself in the language of kinship or of affinity and, most often, of both. (1983a: 174; brackets added)

House "wealth," then, is both material and immaterial. House continuity is sometimes thought to pulse either irregularly or cyclically (Lévi-Strauss cites Tsimshian notions of reincarnation of grandfathers as grandsons; one thinks immediately of similar Balinese ideas about transmigration of souls within a house, coded in naming devices, views of same-sex twins, etc.) Principles of exogamy in *sociétés à maisons* are not necessarily exclusive. Characteristic functions of exogamy-plus-endogamy can be illustrated by the Kwakiutl who used exogamous marriage to capture titles and endogamous marriage "to prevent their leaving the house once they have been acquired" (Lévi-Strauss 1983a: 183). Although specific practices and institutional arrangements vary across cases, the possibility of nonexclusive exogamy-plus-endogamy remains central.

Any *société à maisons,* hardly static, accentuates tensions in social processes, such as "the dialectic of filiation and residence":

In the Philippines, as well as in some regions of Indonesia, and also in several parts of Melanesia and Polynesia, observers have for a long time now indicated the conflicting obligations that result from a dual membership in a group with bilateral descent and in a residential unit: village, hamlet, or what in our administrative terminology we would call ward or neighborhood. (Lévi-Strauss 1983a: 180)

Such dialectics intensify in Bali, which manifests: (1) "bilateral" descent groups (inflected, however, by agnatic emphases and by efforts to retain own-women as spouses and eventual ancestresses); (2) simultaneous village-area (*desa*) and hamlet (*banjar*) residence (neither of these social frames coincides with rice-production cooperatives). Here, then, filiation and residence are indeed bifurcated; but there is an additional bifurcation of "residence" itself. This fact underscores the importance of relating modes of residence to ritual space and locality (Boon 1977: chap. 5).

As Lévi-Strauss notes, the role of "houses" can seem transitory; hence Boas's suspicion that the Kwakiutl were evolving toward more matrilineal (less "housey") arrangements found among the Haida and Tlingit. Other examples however, including medieval European ones, suggest that the type can endure for centuries. Lévi-Strauss offers "possible combinatorials" of *sociétés à maisons,* an "institutional creation that permits compounding forces which everywhere else seem only destined to mutual exclusion because of their contradictory bents"; this itemization of varieties of dialectic is vintage Lévi-Strauss:

> Patrilineal descent and matrilineal descent, filiation and residence, hypergamy and hypogamy, close marriage and distant marriage, heredity and election: all these notions, which usually allow anthropologists to distinguish the various known types of society, are reunited in the house, as if, in the last analysis, the spirit (in the eighteenth-century sense) of this institution expressed an effort to transcend, in all spheres of collective life, theoretically incompatible principles. By putting, so to speak, "two in one," the house accomplishes a sort of inside-out topological reversal, it replaces an internal duality with an external unity. Even women, who are the sensitive point of the whole system, are defined by integrating two parameters: their social status and their physical attraction, one always being capable of counterbalancing the other. (1983a: 185)

(Chapter 6 will discuss Balinese spouses enhanced by make-up—particularly costumed brides on the verge of wifehood and outfitted corpses soon to be ancestors).

Lévi-Strauss locates the *maison* in general "at the intersection of antithetical perspectives of wife-taker and wife-giver." It is this point which may help us compare Balinese ancestor groups to strictly exogamous houses elsewhere. Possible viewpoints from which to conceptualize any *maison* from the inside can be permuted as follows: "The father, as wife-taker, sees in his son a privileged member of his lineage, just as the maternal grandfather, as wife-giver, sees in his grandson a full member of his own" (Lévi-Strauss 1983a: 186). This complementary conceptualization from the two sides may help explain why so-called nonunilineal systems equate the daughter's son and either the son or the uterine nephew. Regardless, the paramount point for our purposes is this: whether strictly exogamous or partly endogamous (as in Bali), houses are ranked both internally and externally by birth order, by anisogamy, and by other indices of differential transmissions of estates, heirlooms, titles, prerogatives, and renown.[3]

Finally, Lévi-Strauss's comments on early European houses (before intensified agrarian capitalism and centralized power over territories) apply equally well to Bali and many other societies and polities of Indonesia and Indo-Europe.

> When the basic units of the social structure are strictly hierarchic, and when this hierarchy further distinguishes the individual members of each unit according to both the order of birth and the proximity to the common ancestor, it is clear that matrimonial alliances contracted internally or externally can only be made between spouses of unequal status. In such societies, marriage is therefore unavoidably anisogamic. Their only choice being between hypogamy and hypergamy, in this respect, too, these societies must compound two principles. (1983a: 181)

To facilitate later discussions it may be worth mentioning here a near-antithesis of "unavoidable anisogamy": incestuous siblings, real or imagined. *Sociétés à maisons,* moreover, often accentuate female-mediated bonds; houses remain "female" in key categorical ways. Below we sample Siwaic and Tantric schemes of value in Bali that preclude our glossing "centers" (whether of power or of productivity) as "male."[4]

Balinese Ancestor Groups Incline Toward "Household"

In previous publications based on fieldwork in 1971, 1972, and 1981, and on the history of Balinese studies, I emphasized Bali's optional ancestor groupings and the ideology and ritual surrounding them, beyond the royal courts (*puri*) and Brahmana compounds (*griya*). Nonnoble "houses" were underestimated in much Dutch colonial ethnography; their importance could be better appreciated after J. Belo's (1936) study of Balinese endogamy and subsequent fieldwork (1957–58) by H. and C. Geertz in a village area dominated by competitive metalsmith houses (see Geertz and Geertz 1975). Over the history of Balinese studies pertinent social and political principles came to light only gradually. By correcting an overemphasis on *warna* schemes, divine kingship (presumably permanent), priestly texts and ceremonies, Java-derived arts, or local cooperatives in irrigation and civil codes, we discover in Bali a "basic unit of social and cultural process: the optional ancestor group" (Boon 1977: pt. I, 63–66, 221). Many contemporary developments in title-caste mobility, marriage alliances, political allegiances, economic entrepreneurship, and interlocal temple networks, including recent success stories of Balinese who capitalize on the expanding tourist industry, are harnessed to these forces (see Chapter 7).

Rival houseyards have competed for prominence throughout the precolonial, colonial, and postcolonial eras of Balinese history. Characteristically a house or cluster of houseyards begins to outstrip other members sharing hamlet and/or village-area duties and obligations (Geertz and Geertz 1975). Rising houses in a given locality "activate wider kinship and marriage networks and concomitant temple affiliations," often producing internal factions as ambitious members gain superior jobs or temple custodianships; disputes, often muted, arise concerning succession to leadership, marriage strategies, political maneuvers, and temple affiliations. Balinese ancestor groups recall Oceanic "status lineages" (including, if we reverse the status associated with endogamy, Maori *hapu*); their legendary narratives of perpetuators' worthy achievements join what J. Fox has called "the common form of historiography throughout the Malayo-Polynesian world" (see Boon 1974; 1977: 118, 221, 229).

Ascendant houses, regardless of title-caste, aspire to:

1. Ancestor temples that direct ritual concerns of supporters away from village-area temples.

2. Gifted founders and legendary forebears whose special virtues (cf. Machiavelli's *virtù*) reappear in select descendants.
3. Varied marriages: endogamous unions between patrilateral parallel cousins, favorable alliances with other houses, and individual unions, sometimes upgraded to an active alliance.
4. Grades of descendants, based on mother's rank and, arguably, talent and achievement.
5. Exclusive occupations in the temple system, courtly arts, local administration, and various tasks with ritual overtones (Boon 1977: 95, passim).

Marriage policies, including possibilities of both dowering and title adjustments, and death rituals enable a house to extend relations regionally while still declaring itself a self-contained ritual and social universe.

Lévi-Strauss made explicit reference to Balinese houses in his College de France lectures collected in *Paroles données,* which briefly reviewed the older Dutch works and more recent observations of Belo, Bateson, Mead, H. and C. Geertz, and Boon:

> Particularly revealing was the quandry of H. and C. Geertz [1975] when confronted by the institutions called *dadia* in Bali. When they observe it in a noble context, the word "house" occurs spontaneously and rightly in their account; but in the village context they do not know what definition to choose, and hesitate without deciding among lineage, caste, cultural association, and faction. "A little of all those, and sometimes even a political party," nicely observes Boon [1977]. Isn't the distinctive quality [*le propre*] of the house— as historians of ancient Europe describe it—to bring together all these aspects? And do not houses emerge and are they not extinguished? (1984: 198; my trans.)

Such has indeed been the case in Bali, where houses, rising and falling over the course of time, have displayed their relative standings through many devices: estates comprising houseland, ancestor temple land, and ricelands owned by members who stock their rice bins directly; ranked titles that differentiate status both internally and externally; heirlooms (including the famous *pusaka* of weapons, clothstuffs, and texts); sumptuary privileges or their recent commercial equivalents; copious ritual, architectural, and narrative adornments; spouses drawn from both inside and outside (the latter including brides from prearranged marriages, mock-captured wives, and borrowed sons); fluctuating networks with other houses, manifest in mutual temple attendance. We thus see before us living, breathing *maisons* in action, a social form that is negotiable, flexible at both the center and the margins, more effective in its potentiality than its actuality, more "cultural" than corporate.[5]

Excursus I: Between Bali and Outer Indonesia

Even if . . . the search for the atom of kinship may encounter obstacles, it facilitates analysis in depth of rules of conduct. It establishes correlations among rules and demonstrates that they acquire significance only as integrated in a greater ensemble, including attitudes, kinship nomenclatures, and marriage rules, plus the dialectic relations that together unite all these components [*les relations dialectiques qui unissent entre eux tous ces éléments*]. (Lévi-Strauss 1983b: 104; my trans.)

In famous exchange systems east of Bali, exogamous units engage in the transfer of spouses. The most auspicious legitimate sexual intercourse occurs between social categories (the cross-relation): economic, political, and religious activities, both cooperative ones and competitive ones, beat to the rhythm of ideal mother's brother's daughter (MBD) marriage, called "circulating connubium" by Dutch ethnographers. In the classic hypogamous configuration relative rank is intransitive: if unit A provides brides to unit B, B to C, and C to A, A is superior to B, B to C, *and,* yes, C to A. Rank, coded at the level of each exchange relation, does not project into an overall hierarchy. Eastern Lesser Sunda examples of such exchanges between "houses" include the *uma* in Sumba, the *luma* in Seram, the *amu* in Savu, the *ume* in Atoni, and the *fada* in Mambai (Fox 1980a: 10–12).

Although ethnographic details of "asymmetric systems" differ, their structural features can be generalized crisply; here, for example, Rodney Needham relates such societies to ideological dualism of the sort stressed in Dumézil's work on Mitra-Varuna:

A society of this kind is ordered by an absolute classification in which descent lines and categories are articulated by a constant relation; women, goods, and services are conveyed in only one direction (whence the designation "asymmetric"), proper to each class of valuable, and never in the reverse sense. Affines stand to one another in enduring relations as wife-givers and wife-takers, and this opposition is crucial to the constitution of the society. It is characteristic of asymmetric systems that sovereignty is partitioned between the line of reference (for example, one's own agnates) and one or other of the two categories of affines. Jural power rests with lineal kin, and mystical influence is ascribed to one party of affines, but systems vary as to whether the latter will be wife-givers or wife-takers. Among the Karo of Sumatra, Indonesia, it is the wife-givers who are the sources of mystical benefits; they are "visible gods." Among the Purum of Manipur, on the Indo-Burma border, it is on the contrary the wife-takers who are in charge of all rituals in which their wife-givers are the principals. . . .

The variation in the side (wife-giving or wife-taking) that is as-

cribed mystical influence emphasizes the importance of the partition
in itself; what counts is not which party does what, but that there is a
constant relationship of complementary governance in agreement
with the Mitra-Varuna scheme. (1985: 182–83)

One might want to qualify Needham's assertion of "absolute classification";
yet, his summary has the merit of underscoring that "variation in the side"
ascribed ritual priority to be discussed below.

Sharp contrast to asymmetric configurations appears in cases where auspicious coitus may occur within the ancestral house. Bali, for example, shares
features of ritual, myth, and spatial and temporal codes (including some components of house ideology) with societies that range from Sumbawa and
Sumba to Seram. Yet Balinese endogamy and hypergamy (bride-providers inferior) seem designed to transfer both wives and status to a center, or to one
among rival centers. Such endogamy-hypergamy formulations are often associated with hierarchies, in contrast with decentralized exchange systems articulated by MBD marriage. We should recall that exogamous exchanges constitute social divisions in and as a gender distinction: gender plus generation
(mother's brother-sister's son) mark the locus of social division; they "operate" the affective charge of "social division" itself. Ideals of MBD marriage
simultaneously divide and repair society; that is, the values constitute "society" as reparably divided. From this vantage a society that even optionally
allows house endogamy appears bizarre, indeed nonsensical, in social organizational terms (Boon 1978).

To help Bali and exchange societies seem less bizarre, each to each, we
might reconsider the gender codes implicit in basic cross/parallel formulations. Again, any parallel tie (female-female or male-male) indicates the absence of gender difference; any cross-bond indicates its presence. Thus, cross/
parallel can be formulated as presence/absence of gender. This fact helps explain Lévi-Strauss's (1969) dialectical view: To activate a parallel-valence is
to suppress a cross-valence; and vice versa.[6]

In this regard some succinct definitions in Robert Lowie's 1920 classic
Primitive Society are worth recalling:

> the children of siblings of the same sex are parallel cousins and are
> usually themselves called siblings in primitive languages; the chil-
> dren of siblings of unlike sex are cross-cousins and are generally des-
> ignated by a term expressing greater remoteness of kinship. Cross-
> cousin marriage may theoretically be of two types: a man may marry
> either the daughter of a mother's brother or of a father's sister. Prac-
> tically these two forms may coincide through the fact that the moth-
> er's brother by tribal custom usually espouses the father's sister. So
> far as this is not the case, marriage of a man with the maternal uncle's
> daughter is decidedly the more common variety." (1961: 26–27)

Lowie wished to demonstrate "diverse motives" behind cross-cousin marriage; he accordingly reviewed: (1) Tylor's elaboration of Fison's idea that

rules favoring cross-cousin marriages and prohibiting parallel-cousin marriages stemmed from exogamous moieties; (2) Rivers's evidence of preferred *first* cross-cousin marriage where dual organization is lacking. Lowie then queried: "Why does one tribe permit cross-cousin marriage, while the institution is anathema to its next-door neighbors? Why do some communities under no conditions allow the other variety of cross-cousin marriage" (1961:29). Lowie cautiously inclined toward suggestions that such rules help preserve ownership and rank: "The cross-cousins would thus remain as the next of kin whose marriage, being permissible by customary law, could at the same time preserve the property and the social prestige within the family" (1961:31).

Lévi-Strauss's *Elementary Structures of Kinship* was in part a monumental salute to *Primitive Society* (see Boon 1983a: 94, 98). Yet, building on Durkheim and on Mauss, Lévi-Strauss advanced as axiomatic the fact that base social units forbid self-provisioning of spouses; society's reciprocal nature revolves around exchange and "communication" of spouses. Still, Lévi-Strauss echoed Lowie's central formulations: "In an exogamous system [cross-cousins] are the first collaterals with whom marriage is possible" (Lévi-Strauss 1969: 98). Rather than explaining associated rules exclusively "functionally," he proceeded to plot the variational logic and ethic of marrying the nearest "other" that prohibitions permit or positive rules enjoin. Lévi-Strauss thus converted Lowie's caveats and hesitations to the ground or foundation of comparative dialectics.

In an influential "domestication" of Lévi-Strauss's more dialectical formulations, J. P. B. de Josselin de Jong in 1952 emphasized the matrilateral variant of "that fundamental exchange mechanism resulting in the dichotomy of cousins." Josselin de Jong summarized his own tilt toward matrilateral cross-cousin marriage systems (informed by Indonesian evidence):

> cross-cousin marriage is not simply one of many types of preferential marriages, as most anthropologists are inclined to consider it. For it is the only type which, normally and exclusively, enables every man to find a spouse whenever kinship terminology divides all individuals of the same generation into (real and classificatory) cross-cousins and (real and classificatory) siblings (real siblings and parallel-cousins). Other types, such as levirate, sororate, avuncular marriage, are never exclusive or primary, being always based on and added to pre-existing other types. They should not be called "preferential" but "prerogative" marriages (*"unions privilégiées"*). (1977: 286, 265)

For Lévi-Strauss, he argued, "not the nuclear family, but a group of at least two men and their women, allied by rules of exchange, is the really primary unit" (1977: 287). Josselin de Jong thus pared down Lévi-Strauss's "atom of kinship," to an irreducible complex of consanguinity and affinity, minus descent.

The famous "atom of kinship" formulation proposed, revisited, and revised by Lévi-Strauss (1963b, 1973b, 1983b) has one major drawback: despite the author's warnings, it allows readers to infer substantive social relations rather than dialectical fields of structural differences. (Readers led partly around Lévi-Strauss by Josselin de Jong's commentary sometimes mistook the "atom of kinship" for an "elementary structure," whereas the "atom" is the minimal set of contrasts for generating the range of elementary structures.) Moreover, in Josselin de Jong, and in parts of Lévi-Strauss's original *Elementary Structures* as well, the locus of social organization was made to appear constant across cultures. Josselin de Jong thus reinforced a residue of functionalism in Lévi-Strauss's own formulations of bilateral, matrilateral, and patrilateral cross-cousin variants; this functionalism eliminates from the outset meaningful comparisons with patriparallel cousin marriage systems, even neighboring ones (see Boon and Schneider 1974; Boon 1982d).

Today the importance of escaping a strictly social organizational framework is clear from evidence of variations even within a particular elementary type, such as hypogamous mother's brother's daughter marriage. Consider, for example, the contrasting indigenous models of MBD marriage in Sumba and Seram. Following Adams (1980), in Sumba wife-givers are classified as female and givers of textiles. In Seram, however, wife-givers are classified as male and superior, because, if I understand Valeri (1980), indirect marriage exchange is seen from the vantage of brother-sister rather than husband-wife. This cultural shift in conceptualizing the exchange system reverses indicators of gender and status, thereby dislocating so-called hypogamy. Culture thus separates two cases that look equivalent from the perspective of social organization. Might such play in the combinations of gender and status symbols open comparisons to ancestor groups that allow or accentuate endogamy?

First Transitional Thought-Experiment

To attain a cultural fulcrum for comparing *sociétés à maisons,* we should look beyond features that some cases lack—such as systematic exogamy—to features that all cases have—such as sets of siblings distinguished by gender and birth-order categories. James Fox's characterization of MBD marriage in Indonesia's Lesser Sundas helps set the stage: "If relative age distinctions . . . between siblings of the same sex form the categorical basis for differentiating groups of the same kind, then relationships between siblings of the opposite sex serve to categorize their alliance" (1980: 13). Citing Valeri's evidence from Seram, Fox suggests that in cross-cousin exchange ideologies, the transmission of blood in the female line may relate to "the idea of a return or reunion of life: the 'life' that a brother and a sister share can be restored only by the marriage of their children or the descendants of their children" (1980a: 12–13). (The "idea of a return" becomes emphatic in narratives of reunited children of a brother and sister that mark Balinese endogamy.)

Fox's treatment of this issue should not lead us to isolate anew societies that practice "circulating connubium." Indeed, his "categorical bases" can smooth this study's opening toward Balinese variations, provided we revise his relative age distinction (elder/younger) to one of relative birth-order (see also Berthe 1972). Toward this end, let us hazard a thought experiment.

Imagine a social classification made up exclusively of gender and birth-order. Heuristically, forget collaterality (and therefore "descent"); ignore siblingship. Restrict the imagination to combinations of the gender difference (M/F) plus birth-order as categorical bases. The logical possibilities are few: M-M-F, M-F-F, F-M-M, F-F-M, F-M-F, M-F-M. Next, constrict the categorical field one step further: the "parallel" component becomes male-male, resulting in concentrated categories of M-M-F, F-M-M, M-F-M. At this level, then, that is all the "difference" there is.

Now, imagine that similar thought experiments underlie various narratives and ritualized ideals of some Indonesian societies. Permutations of male-female/male-male plus relative birth-order may be manifest in diverse cultural projections: *genealogically* as three siblings, even triplets; *narratively* as brother-sister and brother-brother protagonists; *cosmologically* as pairs of deities, such as Siwa/Buddha construed as elder/younger brother in the *Bubukshah* traditions of sectarian relations (see Rassers 1959: 65–91). I suggest that such projections imply a basic gender/birth-order "grammar," also figured in and as two sets of twins (male/female, male/male): twins times two.

Back to reality. As Fox states, in societies ordered by marriage exchange, differentiation *within* a social unit is marked by positional contrast in the parallel bond (birth-order); differentiation *across* social units is marked by the cross-bond, or rather *is* the cross-bond. The dialectical point underlying my comparison may be phrased dramatically: in Bali this within/across distinction is ablated whenever the "house" portrays itself as coterminous with "society." In these circumstances values attached both to the parallel relationship and to twinship become salient. In twinship a birth-order and perhaps also a gender difference occur *where none was anticipated*. Out of what might have been a single birth-position can emerge both birth-order and gender. Twinship "itself" is an empirical event suggestive of the categorical bases outlined above. In Balinese house ideology an irregularity of nature is selectively converted to a model of and for culture, and rituals are enacted accordingly.

Some Elementary Structures of Twinship

Notions of divine, perhaps incestuous, twins occur worldwide, including Indonesia, Indo-Europe, and Oceania. However isolable they might appear, neither "twinship" nor "incest" are things in themselves, even symbolically (see Schneider 1976, Boon 1982b,c). Eschewing the dubious topic of what twinship and/or incest might mean substantively and generally, we can still pursue diverse domains their conjunction interrelates. What, variably, might twinship-plus-incest signify?[7]

In a survey of Indo-European twinship imagery, Donald Ward emphasizes twins of parallel-sex, usually brothers: "The mythologies of peoples who speak languages related to Indo-European include traditions of both cross twins and parallel twins. The tradition of cross twins, however, is not nearly so complete and well-defined as that of parallel twins, and as a result, does not lend itself readily to comparative investigation" (Ward 1968: 3). Parallel twins, of course, may code differences (Ward 1968: 4): for example, aggressive/docile, hunter/shepherd, hunter/agriculturalist, foolish/clever, fair/dark, or, it should be stressed, male/female (again, I distinguish the gender differences from sexual dimorphism). Cross twins may loom larger in covert Indo-European traditions than Ward acknowledges, ideas of their power having possibly been suppressed by historical forces of orthodoxy: European undercurrents of Gnostic heresies and Osiris cults; Tantric and Sivaic mythologies reasserted during India's "Hindu renaissance" over and against ethical-reformist movements of Buddhism. Cross-sex twins possibly clustered at the margins of Indo-European orthodoxies. Construed broadly, such margins can include both Europe's hermeticisms and Bali's Hindu-Buddhism, replete with Tantric tonalities.

Practices prompted by incestuous images of twinship are a classic topic in Balinese ethnology (De Zwann 1919, Belo 1935, Bhadra 1969, H. Geertz 1959: 31). Ambivalent cultural values link parallel-cousin marriage, legendary sibling marriage, and incestlike unions; actual practices of FBD marriage are likened to stepped-back incest, less dangerous or "hot," but still highly charged. Influential narratives and reworked "histories" resolve fretful love matches into reunions of forgotten twins separated at birth into rival kingdoms. A sister-spouse protagonist may simultaneously attract an ostensibly unrelated suitor, effect an alliance of "houses," and achieve incestuous marriage when her partner is revealed as her brother, perhaps her twin (Boon 1977: 136–41; 199–204; 234–39). The rituals, texts, and contexts associated with these themes suggest less a "socio-logic" than a socio-poetics, an imagined perfectibility unavailable in any combination of actualities. It is even possible, although difficult conclusively to prove, that past widow immolations were meant to redefine wives, and perhaps concubines, as sisters, with the cremated husband's unions ritually reconstrued as "incestuous," the nearest endogamy (Boon 1983a: chap. 6). Despite such sensational extremes, the associated values cannot be dismissed as a "mystification" imposed by an elite. Rather, ideas of twins and incest inform different impulses of marriage; these include sensual allure and the magical arts of attraction/repulsion in courtship, battle, and cure; strategic alliance producing political advantage; and ancestral interests cultivated by ascendant houses who favor endogamy.

The ideology of an ascendant Balinese "house" accentuates the ancestors' viewpoint in social values. Ancestors are imagined to envision a world of descendants, divided by gender, birth-order, and generations alone. House rituals even manage to treat outsider spouses (married-in women or borrowed sons) as if they were insiders. In this ancestor-centered outlook (one position in a panoply of ideological vantages implied in full ritual cycles), endogamy is an encompassing value. Parallel collateral bonds thus become more or less "functional equivalents" of cross bonds in exogamous exchange societies (Boon 1978; 1982d). In Bali's houses, opposite-sex parallel-cousins (children of brothers) may be favored spouses, although "hot." Together with opposite-sex twins and opposite-sex siblings, such cousins (whatever the degree) are the main opposite-sex relations germane to ancestral interests. Upon occasion, then, Balinese imagine that their ancestors imagine their "house" as a self-sufficient social and ritual entity.

We turn now to narratives that complement unions between opposite-sex twins, siblings, or parallel-cousins in a striking way: they add another brother. Episodes joining a brother-sister (perhaps twins, perhaps incestuous) to a second brother-protagonist include: (1) *Malat* tales (called *Panji* in Java); (2) Tantrism-tinged accounts of excessive sexuality and wayward intercourse; (3) above all, the *Ramayana,* a dominant sourcebook for Balinese ritual and performance (see Worsley 1984: 99–100). How might one "read" this bifurcated brother-function coupled with a doubled sister-spouse? Do such texts—central to Bali's emphatic ancestral ideology among both nobles and commoners—preserve a sense of their radical departure from values of social exchange?

Second Transitional Thought-Experiment

Alert to Balinese endogamy, which contracts the "elementary function" into the parallel bond, I recall again Lévi-Strauss's "atom of kinship." This analytic model makes an affinal tie generic. "Society" irreducibly entails both a sibling link and a spouse link: cross-sex siblings with a spouse parallel-sex to one of them. Again assuming that the parallel bond is male, we next reduce the atom to its relational core by canceling any "descent" projection; that is, by collapsing the temporal dimension whereby categories reproduce themselves. So "synchronized," the atom contains two male valences and one female valence. One "male" stands to the female as "brother" (they are *like*); the other male stands to female as "spouse" (they are *other*). Tales filled out by "another brother" seem almost to personify this slightly expanded field of distinctions: a model of social totality constricted into a bundle of cross/parallel-sex possibilities. This reading must resist construing the narratives "genealogically," much less "historically." Rather we provisionally consider the two male positions as parallel-sex pure and simple: on the cross-sex axis one male valence is *like* the female (routinely glossed in standardized genealogical conventions as "sibling"); the second male valence is *other than* the female (conventionally glossed as "spouse"). This rarified categorical reading may be called "mythic," to distinguish it from fuller narrative dimensions simultaneously at work in any actual tale.

In actual narratives additional contrasts may accrue. The two male valences, portrayed as born-protagonists, must also contrast by birth-order. In genealogical projections the male valences become "men" and the female "woman." At this level kinds of contrast called paradox come into play. Such narrative dimensions may be construed as interwoven riddles (Lévi-Strauss 1963b; Boon 1985a). How, for example, can a woman's brother and her "not-brother" (her spouse) themselves be brothers? A "genealogical" answer to the rhetorical riddle is "incest." However, at the rarified mythic level abstracted above, where categories are restricted to gender/birth-order, "incest" properly speaking cannot enter in. Its relevant valences do not obtain.

Mention of incest helps underscore the advantage of carefully distinguishing *mythic* (in this case, gender/birth-order) from *narrative* dimensions (here implying more genealogical projections). Again, sibling incest is a *valued* transgression in Balinese ideology. Here incest, I suspect, is analogous to twinship *as twinship pertains to the sphere of birth-order* (and *not* genealogy). Twinship is a valued infraction of birth-order: a godlike instance of two births where one was expected. In twinship what should, mundanely, remain separated in time—birth positions—nearly coincide (a situation sometimes deemed auspicious for the highborn, but catastrophic for commoners). Analogously, sibling incest is a valued infraction of coital order, a godlike coupling of what, mundanely, remains separated. Both twinship and incest represent transgressions against proper distance, one of birth-order positions, the other of sexual relations. In Hindu-Balinese terms both thus connote deity-rivaling status, a risky affair for all but the worthiest humans. Previous commentators have stressed the standard just-so stories linking twinship to incest because twins share the same womb; this native construction is itself based on a metonymic association. I recommend instead a fuller metaphoric (and analogical) interpretation of the link between incest and twinship more pertinent to the ideology of Balinese houses: *twinship is the incest of birth-order.* In images of incestuous brother-sister twins, his side may be bifurcated into another brother, her side remains duple: the sister-spouse. Certain narratives echoed in marriage practices also envision retained daughter-sister components balanced by a male-side split into brother/husband. The sole female is pivotal; her ideal disequilibrium sustains paradoxes of shifting power and authority, in episodic motives of renewal and lapse, deflective of centralized standards.

Excursus II: Toward Inner Indo-Europe

Rama and Laksmana depart to enter meditation [*ke pertapaan*]. . . . Afterwards Rama is ordered to Mitila kingdom, because raja Janaka is conducting a marriage-contest [*sayembara*] for his child named Dewi Sita. Rama wins that *sayembara* and marries Dewi Sita. Rama, Sita and Laksmana are sent away into the forest [*diasingkan kehutan*]. (*Lilaracana-Ramayana*, Santoso 1973; my trans.)

To recapitulate: Balinese mythic twins condense gender/birth-order categorical distinctions into a single birth-slot. We may construe even the apparent "triplets" of any narratives as twins times two: cross twins and parallel twins. This reading opens paths from Balinese twinship motifs to gender and marriage ideologies associated with Indo-Europe.

One path of speculation returns us to those Indo-European codes surveyed by Ward (1968). Parallel-sex twins appear in both the *Vedas* and the *Mahabharata;* in the *Rig Veda* the twins' sister is Surya, the pervasive female component complementary to male Soma. The *Mahabharata* proclaims its Asvin-like twins Sudras from birth, perhaps implying an intervention of divinity in the lower social orders (on counter*varna* themes, see Boon 1977: 196). Matters are more explicit in some versions of the *Ramayana*. Ward reviews dioscuric aspects of the abduction and liberation of Sita, the contrasting characteristics of Rama/Laksmana (handsome/plain, errant/faithful, etc.), the banishment of Rama, and the exile of all three. He adds: "In some of the popular oral tales that treat this theme, Sita is reported to be the sister of the heroic brothers . . . ; one can assume that a mythological incestuous element is involved . . . parallel to the Vedic tradition" (Ward 1968: 63).

To speculate further: Sita is sister-spouse to Rama and Laksmana's distilled parallel-sex. The *Ramayana,* moreover, seems to accentuate marriage and collaterality (the combined forces of Rama, Sita, and Laksmana). This basic "alliance" orientation contrasts to the Mahabharata's emphasis on dynasty and "descent." The *Ramayana* patently questions all direct evidence of legitimate dynasty when Rama manages, through Sita, to regain his chariot (in some versions).

Balinese performances of episodes from the *Ramayana* amplify implications of twinship codes. Echoes of dioscuric features in the monkey realm imply additional valued transgressions that pose rules and boundaries through images of their infraction. The complex of Rama/Laksmana/Sita in the heroic world is repeated by Sugriwa/Subali/Hanuman in the animal world. Indeed, Sita and Hanuman (her theriomorphic counterpart) both suggest trickster-style symbols: Hanuman in the realm of battle, Sita in the realm of marriage, two intimately related spheres of courtly values. Moreover, the conjunction of marriage, ordeal by fire, and twinship embodied in Sita resonates with multiple attributes of alliance and endogamy in Balinese houses. Here rival valences of displaced exchange, exclusivistic hierarchy, and even asceticism meet. Ancestor-pleasing endogamy is nuanced vis-à-vis incest (Sita-Rama as twins) *and* asceticism (the trio of Sita-Rama-Laksmana removed in contemplative *tapas*). Incest and asceticism alike represent variants of the antisocial (incest marginally less so, because it at least requires two). Such negative forces are harnessed in Bali's ancestral houses, where retained brides may become heirlooms, along with weapons and preserved texts. This constellation of values perhaps implies, at one level, the eclipse of exchange conceptualized in categories of social divisions.[8]

Another path leads, tantalizingly, to still more distant Indo-European variations. Ward notes a "significant difference" between Indic and Germanic dioscuric myths: "In the Indo-European tradition the liberators are the brothers and joint husbands of the maiden in distress. In the German epic one of the liberators is the fiancé, while the other is her brother. Such a change is not only possible, but necessary" (Ward 1968:68). Contrary to Ward's suggestion, Balinese evidence reveals a "brother-fiancé" component in Indic-style variants. Moreover, the brother-fiancé is tucked into the combined cross (brother-sister) and parallel (brother-brother) protagonists; and *the fiancé is incestuous.* This point helps tie Indic legendary transgressions to Germanic themes of domestic incest, such as Siegmund/Sieglinde (note also the many parallels between *Lohengrin* and the *Ramayana*). Chapter 6 will relate such legends to diverse house ideologies, including medieval and Renaissance European ones, both during their prime and in subsequent revitalizations.

These possible ramifications of the *Ramayana,* inadequately sketched here, point beyond previous readings of Balinese and Javanese marriage factions as polarized contests between right/left and good/evil, as in W. H. Rassers's classic effort:

> In Guru, with his quickly inflammable heart and with his train of divine gods, one . . . recognize[s] the representative of the right phratry; he falls passionately in love with the beautiful Lady from the other half of the tribe, who is engaged in initiating herself in world-shattering asceticism. Dewi Tenaga is indeed destined to be his wife, but the exogamous division and the fact that her initiation test must first be completed oblige her to refuse his offer of marriage, and to fly from his pursuit. But this does not prevent Guru's passionate desire from having any result: from his "evil seed" [*kama salah* = spilled sperm] a son is born to him with the appearance of a monstrous giant, who is given the name of Batara Kala. (Rassers 1960: 49)

Sita's significance in Bali would seem to lie in bridging opposable spheres that Rassers felt compelled to construe as archaic, polar phratries. Sita herself (situated within twins-times-two) suggests rather a condition of generic ambiguities, doubled valences, and nonstop paradoxes of reversal. As she professes to Rama, before she is obliged to enter the Oblation-eater: "Tiger among men, by giving way to anger like a trivial man, you have made womankind preferable" (O'Flaherty 1975: 201).

Thus, destinations of twinship tied to an ideal of marriage and marked by a feminine valence link Sita, her trials, and the *Ramayana* to that Indic realm of Uttara Kurus evoked in this chapter's (and this book's) epigraphs, where *yugalin* pairs perfectly reproduce their gendered difference. Moreover, the doubled figure of a sister twin plus twin brothers characterizes Indo-European texts that pose contrasting advantages of consanguineal and alliance bonds. J.

Oosten's study of the Indo-European social code persuasively summarizes relevant transformations across myths, epics, and folktales. Oosten poses not an urhistory but structural ambiguities that animate contrasts of loyalty to brothers versus loyalty to husbands, loyalty to kinsmen versus loyalty to kings, and problems of "the opposition between allochthonous rulers and autochthonous subjects" (1985: 166). For example, Greek myths encode Helena as sister of the Dioskuroi Kastor and Polydeukes; but the *Iliad* "substitutes a husband and his brother, who are unequal in rank, for two brothers of a woman who are equal in rank but different in nature (one human, one divine)" (p. 155). Oosten surmises that similar transformations "occurred in most Indo-European cultures during the process of state formation and the development of the great epics" (p. 155). Regardless, he clarifies concrete tensions at play in what I have called "twins-times-two," shifted into different projections of myth, epic, and "genealogy," with an eye toward the fuller extent of Euro-Indic variations:

> The responsibility of a husband for the wife, rather than of the brothers for their sister, has become the central issue in the *Iliad,* just as loyalty to the husband is substituted for loyalty to the brothers in the later versions of the tale of the *Nibelungen* [see Boon 1989b]. One wonders whether a similar development determined the form of the Indian *Ramayana* that relates how the brothers Rama and Balarama recaptured Rama's wife Sita from the demon Ravana. (p. 155)

I have simply extended this question to a further destination of the *Ramayana* itself: Hindu-Bali. Finally, Oosten later suggests:

> Since Indo-European kinship organization was not based on lineages or corporate groups, but on an ego-centered kindred, different groups of gods . . . should not be considered as representatives of lineages or corporate groups. Conflicts between these groups of gods are rather to be interpreted in terms of structural conflicts between different principles of kinship in the social organization of Indo-European society: descent versus alliance, succession through the mother versus through the father, etc. (p. 164)

Here I would caution only that the contrast between corporate lineage versus kindred is not exhaustive. Indeed, self-heralding "houses" may be a social form particularly suited to rekindle fragments of mythic, epic, and legendary argumentation that revolve around the very tensions Oosten reviews. Neither corporate lineage nor ego-centered kindred, the hierarchical house—certainly, at least, the Balinese ancestral house—is a different con*text*ual possibility.

Three Conclusions

Cross-twins concentrate not just gender but birth-order into a single birth-slot. They seem to symbolize a veritable "atom" of house ideology, which allows marriage within a sphere imagined to be society's equivalent: the fictively autonomous house. Just as different symbolics of exchange shift the frames for conceptualizing wife-giver/wife-taker formulations, so in-marrying ancestral units imply a cultural shift in the function of cross/parallel distinctions. This kind of ideological transformation manifest in Balinese culture helps explain why Bali appears ambiguous, indeed anomalous, when viewed through typologies based on social organization.

Methodological Conclusion

If Balinese "twinship" ties valences of cross/parallel (gender-present/gender-absent) to birth-order, then investigators err when they restrict the referent of twin tales to actual birth. (It seems especially unwise to infer from images of triplets a history of polyandrous incest!). Although actual births may trigger reflections upon twinship, myths of twins do not simply gloss natural facts of multiple births (however "awed" *they, we,* or anyone else might be by them). Rather, myths enmesh such facts in cultural paradoxes that biological actualities alone (even rare ones) cannot comprehend. Whether or not multiple births actually happened, they could be imagined. My argument against reductionist naturalist fallacies can be phrased in a Lévi-Straussian chiasmus: That twins in fact *do* happen implies not that cultural images mimic nature but that nature "herself," particularly in her exceptional cases, has an imagination.

Interpretive Conclusion

Incestuous twinship conveys a doubled transgression: against routine births (properly separated), and against routine coitus (sufficiently distant). The ambivalent desirability of the transgression characterizes aspects of the ideology of Balinese houses. Perhaps significantly, this ambivalence straddles a historical and cultural intersection of contrasting social orders conventionally abstracted in comparative kinship studies: exchange/hierarchy. In classic examples of exchange systems, the gender difference coincides with social difference (e.g., clan to clan); hence wives, or more accurately spouse relationships, are "signs" that constitute opposable parties through their mediation. In contrast, hierarchical "house societies" gear social difference more exclusively to birth-order: rivals compete to become primary centers rather than mutual exchangers. Spouses, then, are not inevitably "signs" mediating social divisions (per Lévi-Strauss's "elementary structures"). Nor, however, are spouses (wives in particular) therefore inevitably "property" (per scholarly convictions that History has proceeded as an utterly expropriating patriarchy). Wives may also be, or become, *pusaka:* valuables originating from exchange, subsequently conserved and cultivated to restore to descendants loyalties that might otherwise be forgotten. Daughters—like the weapons and regalia received from metalsmiths by courts, and then preserved—may be retained as wives by the house, which ritually converts even outsiders into insiders in order to counteract forgetfulness. Here "history" of a different sort enters in, to be championed.[9]

House hierarchies may also celebrate *épreuves*, familiar from *Swayamvara* episodes of Indic epics, from manifold Indonesian tales with plots like that of *Jayaprana* (Boon 1977:193), and from parallel European traditions. These love-tests eventually legitimate an ostensible *mésalliance;* to celebrate them is to qualify certain marriage values. The arch bride is neither exchanged nor simply retained; rather she is superficially lost, although profoundly restored: the female-*pusaka* is renewed by an outsider champion. How do the exogamous/endogamous transformations evidenced across *sociétés à maisons* compare to such "histories"? A related question: Does a promise of incest remain, even where *Swayamvara* (or *sayembara*) marriage (suggestive of individualized unions) is ritually indicated? Such questions would return us, with qualifications, to the concluding chapters of Lévi-Strauss's *Elementary Structures*—pages devoted, as were the works of Mauss and Durkheim, to the philosophy of social forms and processes, and their dialectical contraries. He ponders "why the relations between the sexes have preserved that affective richness, ardor, and mystery which doubtless originally permeated the entire universe of human communications" (Lévi-Strauss 1969: 469). We need only add that ardor can be either positive or hostile (just as, for Durkheim, solidarity could be negative), but never neutral, never safe. And we must add as well that because "origins" are inachievable, our knowledge of the destinations of communication is limited to substitute-dispersals.

Concluding Conclusion

This chapter has tried to cultivate Lévi-Strauss's sweepingly comparative sense of *sociétés à maisons:*

> The whole function of noble houses, be they European or exotic, implies a fusion of categories which elsewhere are held to be in correlation with and opposition to each other, but here are henceforth treated as interchangeable: descent can substitute for affinity and affinity for descent. From then on, exchange ceases to be the origin of a cleft whose edges only culture can mend. It too finds its principle of continuity in the natural order, and nothing prevents the substitution of affinity for blood ties whenever the need arises. (Lévi-Strauss 1983a: 187)

What more vivid ablation of distinctions between descent and affinity could be imagined than intensely incestuous twins? Such symbols, moreover, transfer the burden of descent/affinity distinctions to cross/parallel gender. They seem almost deliberately to convey a palpable sense of difference from systems of balanced regulations that interrelate descent through affinity, such as the circulating connubium (MBD marriage) of Indonesia, the Dravidian terminologies of south South Asia, and so forth. Balinese culture displays an aura of transgressivity. Bali's historical situation between analytically separable complexes of value illuminates excesses of both exchange systems and hierarchies in touch with Indo-European ideology; the latter include Bali's odd variant of Hindu-Buddhism, Hinduism proper (!), and European heterodoxies. Perhaps any culture must tacitly recognize that it commits what various other cultures are obliged to prohibit. Without this subliminal awareness across cultural extremes, there could be no comparison and consequently— recalling our opening comment from Hocart—no explanation.

Chapter Six
Indo-European Affinities:
Ritual-rhetorics of "Love" Across Courtly
Cultures, Contexts, and Times

The connection between desire and figurative language is nowhere more apparent than in the *Leys D'Amors,* a manual of rhetoric and love . . . presented by a highly ambiguous genealogy occasioned by a series of mock-epic wars between the kings of linguistic vice (Barbarism, Solecism, and Allebolus) and the three queens of rectitude (Diction, Oration, and Sentence). After much fighting, hostilities are finally ended by Lady Rhetoric who arranges marriages between the three kings and the sisters of the three queens. . . . From the offspring of the three couples begins the genesis of the entire range of rhetorical figures: "Allebolus had with his wife Trope [sister of Sentence] thirteen daughters: Metaphor, Catachresis, Metalepsis, Metonymy, Autonomasia, Epithet, Synecdoche, Onomatopoeia, Periphrasis, Hyperbaton, Hyperbole, Allegory, Omozeuxis. . . . Allegory wed Alexis, which means 'foreign language,' and they had seven daughters: Irony, Antiphrasis, Enigma, Sarcasm. . . . Omozeuxis married Clarity from whom came three daughters: Icon [Image], Parable, and Paradigm. And since Allebolus was always on good terms with his wife Trope . . . , Lady Rhetoric blessed some of their daughters and granddaughters with the flowers [of rhetoric] of diverse colors gathered in her garden."

. . . The lineage of rhetoric, in defiance of all genealogical probability, consists entirely of females. . . . The use of poetic figure works to detach language from fixed meaning, its fixation in the proper, and thus to mobilize—through the very kind of alliances contained in the *Leys D'Amors*—its playful potential.

—R. Howard Bloch (1983) translating and interpreting French medieval, movable (*meubles*) signs.

Chapter 5 presented Hindu-Balinese courts and houses whose textual and ritual devices include images of brother-sister incest tied to marriage ideals of house endogamy, alliances between houses, and unions not constrained by group affiliation, although still hypergamous. In Siwaic rituals the bride becomes an icon combining the desirability of the nymph with the continuity of the ancestress; her make-up and costumes allude to both Sita and ideals of incestuous twinship.

This chapter explores affinities between Balinese culture and other cases of *courtoisie,* whose activities of beautification encompassed kings, corpses, suitors, combative courtiers, and unallowed brides.[1] One such case is European "chivalry," developed in contexts of rivalrous houses, serio-ludic liturgy and festivals, and a cult of youthful prowess (Duby 1977: chap. 7). The rhetoric and vernacularized literature of Europe included counterorthodox positions inflected toward a female side of ritual and textual genders:

> How many paths through the history of the medieval West lead to Woman! The history of heresies is in many respects a history of woman in society and religion. If there is one innovation in the area of sensibility with which the Middle Ages are generally credited, it has to be courtly love. (Le Goff 1980: 230)

My approach takes its cue from Indo-European themes of idealized suitors who win ordinarily forbidden, socially superior ladyloves by trial. So-called *svayamvara* (*sayembara* in Bali's "Archipelago Sanskrit") is most familiar from the *Mahabharata,* where it is opposed to two other Ksatriya modes of marriage: the *raksasa,* or abduction by force alone, and the *gandharva,* or attraction by pure desire, *kama.* The *raksasa* and *gandharva* number among eight formal modes of marriage standard in Indic legal treatises (Dumézil 1979: 31–38). Indic narratives on the other hand depict a seemingly sublimated style of martial marriage, where a highborn woman chooses as spouse a champion who has proved his knightly valor with magical weapons. Dumézil summarizes *svayamvara,* "a combination of abduction [*enlèvement*] by the boy and of choice by the girl," as follows:

> In kidnap-marriage [*mariage par rapt*], *raksasa,* the girl's free choice has been blocked violently and they are forcefully obliged to leave their father's palace. Particularly notable is the doctrine articulated by Bhisma at the start of his undertaking: The best marriage is "forced" marriage. The current and classic doctrine, that he summons up in order to contest it, is altogether different: for ksatriyas at least, the best marriage is made by mutual consent, whether in secret (*gandharva*), or in the stylized solemnities of *svayamvara.* . . . In a *svayamvara* of the purest kind . . . the youth indeed stands forth as candidate, but . . . it is the girl who chooses him.
> The *gandharva* mode yields in practice to a more regulated form . . . : this is *svayamvara;* all the suitors [*prétendants*] assemble, and

at the appointed time the girl declares her choice not only to the win-
ner [*bénéficiaire*] but to all the others (1979: 68–69, 81, my trans;
see Boon 1977: 200; Lévi-Strauss 1969: 447; Boon and Schneider
1974: 812).

Motives of *svayamvara* marriage mark Indo-European genres of romance and
cultural and historical processes designated "chivalry"—whether in the
Middle Ages or in subsequent revivals of Renaissance courtly fashion and
later literary movements, including Romanticism (Elias 1982, 1983). In India, Europe, Southeast Asia, and elsewhere, *svayamvara* marriage, courtly
love, and chivalric codes have been associated with plural authorities of purity
and power and competitive displays among houses, where channels of desire
cut across ecclesiastical, military, and popular-festival domains mediated by
shifting conventions of kingship. In these contexts, ritual categories of gender
and status are relational. Gender and status differences alike may even be reversible in the semiotic extremes of troubadorial eroticism and esoteric/exo-
teric Tantrisms, two complexes of texts and rites that suggest equivalent heterodox positions, from the European and Indic sides respectively.

This chapter enlists insights about ritual reversibility from A. M. Hocart
(1952, 1970) and more recent studies of troubadors and courts. Works in comparative interpretations of history, mythology, institutions and literature lead
us into elusive realms of courtly love and Tantric allure. On the European
side, I do not equate or confuse medieval, Renaissance, and subsequent romantic formations of "love" or related topics. Rather I purposefully draw on
studies that have grappled with historical transformations of medieval *society,*
to early modern *courts,* to nineteenth- and twentieth-century commoditized
literature. Taken together, interpretations by G. Duby, N. Elias, J. Le Goff,
C. Geertz, R. H. Bloch, M. Eliade, D. de Rougement, J. W. Keane, C. Lévi-
Strauss, L. Dumont, and particularly M. Weber and G. Dumézil help us question history's very categories of "society," "court," and "literature," opening
them to issues in discourses and economies of desire and rhetorics of affinities/
separations.

Dumézil's panoramic working-notions of Indo-European ideology have
been advanced with increased precision by investigators of local "social
codes" in myths, epics, and tales. Recurrent "contraposition(s) of alliance and
descent" characterize specific historical transformations, from epics of feuding parties, to narratives celebrating political centralization, to styles of romance deflecting lines of authority (Oosten 1985: 161). Here we glimpse another important feature of "houses." As discussed in Chapter 5, a *maison* is a
kind of social order that is neither a lineage, nor a continually corporate
group, nor a kindred. The devices houses accumulate to blazon their worth
may reiterate archaized fragments of myth, epic, romance, and folkloric representations. Dumézil's followers have illuminated movements of Indo-
European genres from myth, to epic, to romance, to tales narrowly focused
on "conflicts in the nuclear family and problems of hypergamy. Mythology

has moved a long way from the great cosmic conflicts that determined the fate of the world" (Oosten 1985: 167). The vast compass of Dumézil's works (see Littleton 1983) has been narrowed to manageable distinctions among myth/epic/romance/folktale and equivalent divisions in the realm of social orders: feuding parties/nobles/kingship-centralization/bourgeois urbanization. I see "houses" as a context of, and for, interpretive activities that play with and across this kind of development, recapitulatively. Their ritual and rhetorical displays rekindle affinities and resonances between their own "domestic" policies and myth, epic, and romance.

One further preliminary. Because there is no question of addressing specific South Asian cases in my reading of Indo-European extremes, it may help to flag relevant aspects of "medieval India" underscored by Weber. Now, I am more skeptical than Weber was about any outright contrast between orgiastic and sublimated as a way to distinguish phases of history. Since Weber's day, we have become more wary of the countertypes through which evidence of past ritual practice has been filtered (see Chapters 2, 4); and modern ethnography has revealed so-called sublimated and orgiastic components coexisting in rituals marked by intricate differentiations and specialization. Nevertheless, Weber's assertions about the absence of unification in Sivaism point toward "oppositional" components of India vital to any fuller discussion of Indo-European history. His words are worth reading and rereading:

> The Brahmans succeeded in concealing the alcoholic and sexual-orgiastic character of the adoration of the phallus (*lingam* or *linga*) and transformed it into a pure ritualistic temple cult . . . [that] recognized as orthodox commands the interest of the masses through its very cheapness which is not to be underestimated. Water and flowers serve for the normal ceremonies [Balinists in particular can profit from this insight].
>
> Brahmanical theory thoroughly identified the spirit which the Linga possessed . . . with Shiva. Perhaps already in the *Mahabharata* . . . , the god was happy when the lingam remained chaste. The *tantra* literature consists almost completely, corresponding to its orgiastic origin, of dialogues between Shiva and his bride. Through compromises with both tendencies Shiva became the particular "orthodox" god of medieval Brahmanhood. In this very general sense Shivaism also encompassed great oppositions for it was in no way unified. (Weber 1967: 298).

That noted, medieval India and, temporarily, Weber now recede, so that Hindu-Bali and chivalric Europe may be dramatically juxtaposed.

Balinese Contexts of "Love":
Houses, Spouses, and Makeup Magic

Chapter 5 introduced Lévi-Strauss's (1979, 1984) notion of ranked "houses," whose estates include both material and immaterial wealth expressed in land, titles, heirlooms, and ritual valuables. Widespread examples include ethnographic cases from Oceania and Indonesia and historical cases from Carolingian and Merovingian Europe. Balinese ancestral houses are striking for the degree they may sponsor marriages between the children or grandchildren of brothers. House endogamy—the marriage of patriparallel cousins—is just one Balinese motive linking bride and groom; others include prearranged unions between allied houses and ritualized bride abduction in love-induced episodes of mock capture. Until recent national restrictions on polygyny, a prosperous Balinese often supported multiple wives; ascendant ancestor groups harbor all varieties of wives. Tales of *svayambara*-style matches such as *Jayaprana* portray legendary marriages as if they could consolidate the advantages of love matches, interhouse alliances, and cousin unions (Boon 1977: 193ff). With the reminder that the three marriage motives are *not* formal, indigenous categories but extrapolations from complex rules, norms, practices, and rationalizations, I here outline their features from the perspective of varieties of brides.

1. Again, an optimal bride and groom may descend from a pair of brothers. Notions of "primary wife" (*padmi*), complicated by qualified shadings of preference for different degrees of cousin, liken marriages between first cousins (*misan*) to sibling incest viewed positively in Hindu cosmology; second-cousin (*mindon*) marriages may be actually preferred, justified as less ritually charged or "hot" (Boon 1977: chap. 6). The relatively "stepped-back" preference for second over first cousin may be repeated as a preference for fourth over third cousin as well (Hobart 1980). M. Hobart speculates that numerological codes of odd/even numbers may structure relative preferences, again confirming that house-endogamy does not gear simply to genealogical distance (H. and C. Geertz 1975; Boon 1974; Gerdin 1982).

2. Through interhouse alliances two groups become witnesses to each other's temple ceremonies. Hypergamous unions link an elevated house to the party (*wargi*) of a bride classed as a secondary wife (*penawing*). Or alliances may be carefully balanced affairs between two relatively equal parties (Boon 1977 chap. 4, pt. 2; Geertz 1980; Hobart 1980). Nothing precludes marriages of cross-cousins which, too, may renew an alliance. Hobart (1980) remarks that because of repeated unions of patriparallel cousins, partners are often cross-cousins as well. I have suggested that house endogamy is ritually executed as an alliance that reintegrates fractious collaterals. Nevertheless, cross-relations are not the fulcrum for perpetuating alliances. Indeed, Balinese may formally discourage reciprocal or matrilateral cross-cousin matches (Boon 1977: chap. 6; see also Gerdin 1982). What Hobart calls the "latent bilateral model underlying Balinese kinship ideals" (1980: 78) suggests to me a general "field" of possibilities against which parallel-cousin marriages stand out as a cultural "figure."

3. Next comes "love," a ritually charged bond joining some Balinese brides and grooms—not a sentimental motive but a dimension that complements

both strategic alliances across houses and house-endogamy thought to be favored by ancestors. Although Hobart agrees that individual options "in the absence of coercive forms of exchange" are important in Bali, he has questioned labeling the third motive, conventionally associated with mock-capture marriage, "love":

> In emphasizing that romantic marriage is part of a cultural nexus of values which stress the ideal of love, Boon is forced to adopt the Indonesian term *cinta*. He gives no word in Balinese at all, for the simple reason that, as my enquiries suggest, the Balinese do not have a suitable term for this. The closest approximations tend to have different connotations, which range from pure sexual desire or lust, to *tresna*, which is love in the sense of loyalty, as felt by subjects for a king. While I would not wish to argue that ideas must necessarily be reflected in specialized terminology in any culture, there may be problems in seeing as a crucial cultural concept something which the indigenous people have no term to express. (1980: 160–61)

I shall stick by my guns. In resonating specific Balinese ambiguities with motives of "love," "affinities," and related terms of attraction/repulsion, I have sharply distinguished Bali's "romance" from any pining romanticism projected onto the island's culture (even Covarrubias makes this crucial distinction—1937: 140). Abundant Balinists—including J. Kersten, C. Hooykaas, and J. Hooykaas—have designated by "love" the also-abundant Balinese conventions in arts of attracting and vanquishing partners and enemies. Informants bilingual in Balinese and Indonesian readily gloss Balinese *tresna* with Indonesian *cinta*.

No one is suggesting a one-to-one correspondence between Indonesian *cinta*, Balinese *tresna*, Western "love," or any other kind of love, Sanskrit varieties included. Cultural terms do not index categories directly; for reasons both semiotic and dialectic, terms skew and conceal as much as label or reveal (Boon 1973; 1982a: chaps. 3–4). But polysemy and multivocality do not preclude comparative interpretations of more general categories. Indeed, Hobart effects a relative generalization when he alludes to Western love without specifying *agape, caritas, eros,* etc. (see De Rougement 1983; I. Singer 1984: 3ff.). This example bears on his misgivings in another way: Although British and American cultures have no "indigenous" term for *eros*, only a "borrowed" one (paralleling Hobart's point about Balinese culture and Indonesian *cinta* = love), would anyone deny eros's relevance to British or American life? Speaking of eros, I have argued (1982a: chap. 6) the importance of Sanskrit *kama* not just in Balinese texts but in institutions and practices. Hobart (1987) makes a similar point, thus admitting that this particular "borrowing" (*kama:* desire, lust?) looms large in Hindu-Balinese experience. Why not call it all "love," or something equally contradictory, open-ended, and resonant?[2]

A scintillating range of Balinese desires—from lust (*kama*) to loyalty-love (*tresna*) and *asih* (see below)—are mingled. "Love" implies an axis of affinities not necessarily linked to kinship or strategic interest, yet ritually fraught. The attraction need be neither idyllic nor reciprocal; nor, emphatically, need it entail ideological individualism or idealized personal will often traced to bourgeois values of romantic love and property (e.g., Tanner 1979). Rather, transformations in Bali's constellation of *tresna-kama-asih* (*cinta*) recall complex Indo-European configurations of "courtly love" and their various revivals through history. The dynamics of love in Bali have emerged over the precolonial, colonial, national, and commercialized periods that produced Balinese culture today, saturated with Indonesian language (including catchwords like *cinta*) along with Balinese, Kawi (Old Javanese), and so forth. A summary of some pertinent evidence follows.

Love pervades Balinese courtship, seduction potions, magical practice, mantras and Tantras, iconography, dance and drama. It also enters the "sense of event" propelling the *Ramayana,* escapades of capture, and related rituals and narratives. To thwart a lovematch is to court misfortune, even when no advantage of alliance or ancestor-pleasing endogamy obtains (Boon 1977: chap. 6; Gerdin 1982). Cosmologies of love gods and goddesses inform diverse activities.

C. Hooykaas's (1957) translation of "love in Lenka" from the Old Javanese *Ramayana* restores passages once omitted because of their eroticism; the episode remains "exotericized" in contemporary Balinese myth, ritual, and practices of marriage by capture (likened to Rakshasa-ish dalliance). Other dalliance is more sublimated:

> There in Lenka all the women were awakening, dishevelled,
>   languid . . . , jaded by their love-play. . . .
> Rapture passed, their senses regained. . . .
> Sang Hyang Kama (the God of Love) is very wonderful
>   indeed. . . .
> Ah! The God of Love has no equal in that which is difficult to
>   capture. . . .
>
>   (C. Hooykaas 1957: 281–82)

Popular shadow-theater genres, including special *wayang gender* pieces and *tetandakan* variations in *rebong,* celebrate romance and beautiful women (Zurbuchen 1981). In the arts of *teka asih* (come love) generic distinctions between refined-sweet versus rough-strong (*alus/kasar-keras*) are mediated by the realm of the seductive (*lehleh*).

Elsewhere C. Hooykaas (1980a) itemized a panoply of mantras, charms, icons, figures, devices, emblems, and symbolic weapons available in Balinese "magic." The fragmentariness of this study was regretted by Hooykaas himself because of his philological preference for definitive canonical texts. Yet fragments powerfully convey the imperfectly standardized ingredients of *Pangasih:* arts of bewitching enemies and inspiring love. Amulets (*tumal*) and

reversers (*tulak*) for arousing or inverting sympathy interrelate motives of seduction, conquest, cure, and aesthetic desirability. *Sikep,* Hooykaas states, "is
a word for weapon and *kawula sikep* are common soldiers, but *pasikepan*
(perhaps originally "armory") now means amulet and even "artistic quality"
(1980: 182; on *kawula* in general, see Geertz 1980: 252–54). One token of
four-around-the center mandalas, discussed in Chapter 4, is thought both to
control epidemics and to turn enemies into friends and devotees. The force of
Lulut Asih "inspires the love" of superiors and enemies alike. In such conventions, loyalty merges with love.

Hooykaas lists over 250 specific mantras, many designed to produce sexual
strength (as in an erect phallus) and, I suppose, "elective affinity." Where
words (spells) and mantras fail, Ayu Ratih, the Goddess of Love, can work
"love for those who are too tongue-tied to declare themselves" (Hooykaas
1980: 45). Sanskritic mantras in the repertoires of Brahmana priests (*pedanda*) have equivalents in devices employed by low-caste priests (*pemangku*) and exorcist priests (*sengguhu*). But it is Bali's right-hand and left-
hand magicians (*balian*) who try to monopolize charms, spells, images, and
inscriptions that affect the realm of what Hooykaas calls simultaneously
"sympathy, tenderness, love, infatuation"—a good working-translation of an
inherently elusive category.

Overlapping influences of *pangasih,* Lulut Asih, or Ayu Ratih pertain to
our third marriage motive, where these forces are reckoned along with ancestral wishes and strategic interests. Ritual and myth may deem such concerns
complementary. Furtively captured brides and prearranged outsider brides are
beautified in *masakapan* ceremonies to enhance their chances to reproduce
and to be buried and cremated by their offspring. Parallel-cousin brides too
are spiced with *asih* to make endogamy even more appealing to ancestors.
Any bride may thus be idealized as an alluring love-object destined to become
a human "heir-loom." In the enacted honorifics of ritual, both actual endogamous partners and as-if endogamous partners are outfitted as ultimate house
valuables: not just future wives/mothers but future ancestresses.

Ritual busywork crosses all ranks of Balinese society, in once courtly towns
and hinterland alike. Arts of costuming and makeup extend from brides and
maiden dancers to grooms and sublimated warriors, and from living bodies to
dead ones. Meticulous *maquillage* is an applied refinement less exclusive than
the scribal arts traditionally sponsored by courts. Makeup involves methods
of enticement, attraction, and repulsion that should not be isolated as "magic"
(see Berthier and Sweeny 1976). Makeup activates hosts of activities and
commodities fundamental to the popularization of courtly codes.[3]

The costume applied painstakingly to a wedding couple ushers them toward
the refined (*alus*) pole of values; this process pushes actual marriage toward
incest, just as made-up corpses push actual *dangerous* death toward controlled
ancestry. Both incestuous unions and ancestral reincarnation are idealizations
of the rather radical experiment with intensive endogamy represented by Ba-

linese culture and history (Boon 1977:224). The outfitted bride and groom become divine consorts: procreative wife and husband dressed as siblingesque look-alikes—a ritual device particularly important in ascendant houses. So refined, the bride and groom pay homage to ancestors during *masakapan*. Makeup that helps a bride and groom become twin-like also helps a corpse appear ancestor-like to its buriers and subsequent cremators. Festooned, both the wedding couple and the corpse exist in state; microcosmic, still, undisturbed by demonic agitation. Makeup and costume seem designed to close the gap between incest (nonmarriage) and ancestry (nondeath), a gap in actuality consisting of society's marital practices and cycles of descendants. To costume a bride is both to visualize her as her husband's ideal mate and to imagine her as an ancestress of the house, more likely, if beautified, to bear the descendants who will one day render her homage. Ritual often anticipates a future it claims to produce.

Optional public rites (*masakapan*) of the bride's transfer (whether to another house or to another collateral line of the same house) deck out spouses in godlike finery. Similarly, augmented cremation rites outfit exhumed corpses and transfer them, through fire, to proper ancestorhood. Both spouses (particularly brides) and corpses are subjected to *maquillage* to prevent their theft by demons that threaten any and every exchange. In a sense then, makeup wards off *mésalliance*. This principle is manifest equally in rituals of marriage, death, and politics: loci of courtly comportment and politesse, the place where refined commodities and manners are transacted. Cosmetic activity accompanies dance, drama, and other performances thought vulnerable to hostile influence. In precolonial, more militant Bali, before a Dutch-imposed *pax,* cosmetics were likely another side of courtly battle. Still today, *balians* employ charming finery as techniques of attack and defense as well as allure and cure. In identified realms of aesthetics and well-being, the arts of seduction, of war, and of healing (white magic?) are the same arts. Activities associated with *maquillage* produce and circulate goods that represent a material equivalent of values designatable as "love," where magic and beauty meet.

While Balinese makeup highlights and echoes endogamy, it also promotes circulation and exchange. A thorough investigation of relevant practices would combine a survey of *maquillage* commodities, a cultural analysis of cosmetics, and a detailed sociology of what the Dutch call *schoonheidsmiddel,* including the nuanced division of labor entailed in decorating brides, corpses, and dancers. Concerned clusters of casual and specialist observers dominated by women continually check and countercheck makeup and ritual regalia. Requisite products include oils, ointments, powders, dyes, spangles, petals, foodstuffs, clothstuffs, and other paraphernalia basic to Bali's flow of goods: from specialist to specialist, region to region, market to market, and "commercially."[4] Such stuffs, redistributed, help convert houses into rivalrous legendary realms.

In summary, Balinese "love" enacts techniques of allure (*tresna-asih-kama*) that enhance gender differences and accentuate differential bridehood. This hierarchical *société à maisons* transforms the charismatic "charge" of ritual exchange across interconnected arts of attraction, seduction, war, and cure (Boon 1978, 1986)—arts linking ambitious houses, courts, and local networks of heterodox practitioners who, along with their clientele, stretch across every sector of society. Balinese *masakapan* marriage ceremonies convert brides into valuables (*pusaka*), conceived as the procreative wealth of an ancestrally favored house. House rituals convert such brides into human heirlooms. Contrary to functionalist theories, the rituals of marriage and kinship do not simply charter or legitimate social needs; rather, they harness cultural desires: desires not met so much as made.

Reversible Opposites:
A Ritual Register of "Love"

Ritual constructions associated with *courtoisie* direct polar contrasts to hierarchical ends. Such contrasts have become familiar from anthropological accounts of tribal practices which divide the year into ceremonial/productive phases and cycle among social segments the roles of administering versus witnessing each other's rites (Boon 1982a: chaps. 3–4). When a given polar contrast—right/left, up/down, elder/younger, male/female—is repeatable, I designate it relational rather than substantive (Dumont 1980; Bateson 1958). A ritual distinction of male/female is relational in this sense when it again divides into male/female on either or both of its sides. Following the views of Marcel Mauss (1967), a categorical distinction reapplied to itself generates *mana*like power. Moreover, the male valence of a female side, or the female valence of a male side may exhibit special charisma or enchantedness, heightened affinities attached to the gift, magic, or love.

Recurrent reversals of ritual categories, including topsy-turviness of gender, characterize heterodox formations in India and Europe as well. To trace resonances between European courtly love and tantric aspects of Hindu-Bali, I shall revisit an anthropological framework attuned to, and perhaps partly inspired by, medieval hierarchy, complexity, duple authority, and multiple confessions.

The well-turned essays in A. M. Hocart's *Life-Giving Myth* (1952) declared ritual's function to be "life" or health (as in German *heil*), which contains those *dua ultima* of sacred fertility and material welfare, or grace and security. In *Social Origins* (1954), metaphors of "sacrament" orchestrate his concise survey of world-wide ritual and sacrificial complexes. Like Hocart's better-known *Kings and Councillors*, these casual-looking but meticulous chapters—only occasionally flawed by pseudo-developmental schemes—forefront rival authorities, decentralized polity, and revolving roles of administering/witnessing. This format characterizes both exchange relations and more hierarchical circumstances—variations represented by Hocart's own work in Fiji and then in Ceylon. His most characteristic general claims include: (1) the interplay of myth, ritual, and the history of institutions is dialectic; (2) the charged ambivalence (polyvalence?) of ritual exchange stems from the fact that two parties, even if unrelated, must act *as if* they stand in a cross-relation (party of mother's brother to party of sister's son); (3) kinship (and marriage) is religious in nature and not a distorted or camouflaged biology (Hocart 1952).

Hocart's often precocious insights have been saluted by leading anthropologists of different persuasions (e.g.;, Lévi-Strauss 1963b Dumont 1980, Needham 1970, Sahlins 1976, 1985, Geertz 1980). Hocart resisted genealogical models of kinship, pinpointed certain functionalist fallacies of "kinship extensions," and announced that "all our difficulties spring from a preconceived idea that kinship terms everywhere try to express the same thing as they do in Aryan and Semitic languages, and that in those languages they show the place on the family tree" (1952: 176; see Schneider 1972, 1980). "If," Hocart twinkled, "the users of classificatory systems can get on without pedigrees, surely the fieldworker can" (1952: 176). Distinguishing structure from sentiment or emotionalism, he deemed both ritual and science anti-emotionalist constructions. He championed ritual's intellection against cultic emotions and against reformist detractors who would "spurn all ritual because there are ritualists who weave wearisome subtleties" (1952: 63; cf. Douglas 1970). In his depiction of Fijian myth-making, Hocart (1952: 41) like Lévi-Strauss (1962), closed the circle between science and *pensée sauvage*. Hocart at times matched Weber in panoramic sweeps of diverse cases, such as those Homeric kings, Hebrew judges, Vedic sages, and Fijian chiefs embraced in a paragraph on the "germ of monotheism" (1952; on parallels between Hocart's and Weber's interest in ancient Judaism, see Boon 1982a: 268).

Hocart resisted notions of static replication between myth, ritual, and social organization: "We cannot define what is always changing, because we can never find a formula that will express all the varieties and include even opposites . . . ; *ritual may become the negation of ritual*" (1952: 64; emphasis added). This historical, dialectical bent distances Hocart from both utilitarian and functionalist assumptions, bringing his views nearer formulations associated with *L'Année sociologique,* as Needham (1970) has indicated. Hocart, for example, adduced the "religious origins" of coins, currency, and "trade surrounded by form and usages":

> I think we have found that beginning in the exchange of offerings. One group [in Fiji] makes offerings to the gods of their kinsmen—that is to say, the gods of their mothers. . . . The theory which I have outlined identifies the original form of money with the fee paid to the priest who performs a sacrifice. . . . The sacrificial fee is assigned to

a deity; it follows the sacrifice to the world of the gods, and thus creates a bond between the gods and the sacrificer. (1952: 100–104)

Thus exchange, or proto-trade, connects two parties that stand in a cross-like relation: a social other (another clan) or a cosmological other (a deity). Through history economic transactions retain some flavor of the reciprocity plus status difference compressed into the cross-relation, whether the bonds in question are reciprocal (Fijian group to mother's brother's group) or hierarchical (worshiper to Brahmin sacrificer).

Like Mauss, Lowie, and Lévi-Strauss, Hocart traced ambivalent values of mother's-brother/sister's-son configurations across cultures and through time. For example, in "customs connected with cross-cousinship" in Fiji: "Uterine nephews are representatives of the gods. . . . Now if a man is a representative of his mother's gods or ghosts, he is a god to his cross-cousins, and since the relationship is reciprocal, his cross-cousins are gods to him" (1952: 197). Similar attributes grace host-guest relations from Polynesia, to India, to the Mediterranean. "Some societies," Hocart suggests, "inaugurate cousinships very readily" (1952: 189). The potential cross-cousin-likeness of the stranger allows the host to receive him; this dimension explains "the origin of the guest's divinity." Or elsewhere, in Africa, "total strangers may think it to their mutual advantage to become opposites from being nothing. They proceed to function as opposites (i.e., as reciprocal). A common way is to celebrate nuptials between the two parties, who thenceforth intermarry" (1952: 188; see Lévi-Strauss 1969). Even blood brotherhood operates similarly, according to Hocart: "The two parties must belong to different lines" which serve as principal and ministrant in each other's rites. In fact "the bloodbrotherhood is no brotherhood [and no cult]. It is just a covenant in which blood is used, and covenants are nothing but two-party rituals used . . . for *the sake of the alliance*" (1952: 186, 189; emphasis added).

Dramatic ambiguities—the kind eclipsed by increasingly centralized, state-level authority and forces of bureaucratic control—are most conspicuous in gender reversals. For Hocart gender codes, too, exist for "the sake of the alliance." Ritual irreducibly requires two, classified relationally as male/female:

A complete ritual requires two parties, male and female. These need not be a man and a woman, for the two parties come together as god and goddess, and a god and goddess may be represented otherwise than by a man and a woman. In modern India a male and a female idol may be bedded together, in Vedic India a dead stallion and the queen. . . . The male and female principals may even be represented by two men. In Vedic mythology two gods pair. . . . The male members of intermarrying parties, if they are of the same generation, are cross-cousins . . . ; a male's male cross-cousin is his male wife. . . .

> Among some hill tribes of Fiji a man calls his male cross-cousin "my
> cohabitor," though it is only a manner of speech. (1952: 191)

"Gender" attaches neither to men and women nor to actual sexuality, but *to
the ritual alliance*. This fact underscores what Hocart called "the religious
character" of kinship customs, when he boldly surmised that "nine-tenths of
them are religious in origin, and . . . the key to them will be found in reincarnation" (1952: 198).

The relevance of Hocart's insights to Hindu-Balinese hierarchy and history
is apparent from courtly texts characterized by ambivalences of "love" and
gender which were inadequately assessed in conventional philology (e.g.
Swellengrebel [1977]). For example, the *Korawasrama*, a sequel to the *Mahabharata* performed in Balinese and Javanese shadow-puppet theater, presents a flip-flop cosmology devoted to the Korawa culprits rather than the
Pandawa heroes celebrated in orthodox narratives. The tale contains Yudis-
tira's account (a story within the story) of how Wisnu and Brahma (here styled
as elder/younger brothers) changed shape in order to attain a jewel, actually
an incarnation of Parameswara. Along the adventurous way, Wisnu encounters a virgin and Brahma meets the heavenly Taya. In Swellengrebel's reading,
"Parameswara is the embodiment of high and low; Wisnu is the embodiment
of woman (literally: the beautiful); Brahma is the embodiment of Taya" (1977:
91–92). Brahma as heaven (*langit*) and Wisnu as earth (*pretiwi*) are traced to
other sources and a standard polar set is posed: (1) older brother, woman, low,
earth or underworld (demon), left, Wisnu; (2) younger brother, man, high,
heavens (god), right, Brahma. Swellengrebel finds this series entirely consistent with the general classification system of Java (and Bali). Consequently,
when he finds another variant of the story (called *Bomakawya*) with gender
code reversed, he infers a "misconception" or "misunderstanding" somewhere
along the line of textual transmission. I have room only to cite his conclusions:

> It is easy to see [*Bomakawya*] as the expression of a moiety opposi-
> tion. A woman of the earth moiety marries. Her son belongs to his
> mother's moiety; he is provided for by a member of the earth moiety
> (Brahma) who is not tolerated in the heavens; once full-grown, he
> fights his father, an expression of the familiar moiety rivalry, since
> the father does not belong to the same moiety as the mother. Accord-
> ing to this interpretation, Brahma is associated with earth-woman-
> demon, and Wisnu with heaven-man-god. . . . Thus, the classifica-
> tion found here fits with the four/five division. It is perhaps justifiable
> to assume that the Tripurusa story in the *Korawasrama* arose from a
> misunderstanding of the representation of marriage and moiety rela-
> tionships in *Boma-kawya* II (or a similar story). A misconception of
> this kind could also have influenced other stories and concepts re-
> lated to Brahma and Wisnu. (1977: 93)

The kinds of reversals that Swellengrebel found exceptional actually riddle both esoteric and daily cosmologies of Bali, as we saw in Chapter 4. And they conform to Hocart's "dialectics." In the *Korawasrama* and *Bomakawya* variations, for example, Wisnu-female becomes Wisnu-male as other valences shift. To infer (with Swellengrebel) some "misunderstanding" in an irretrievable past of transmission neglects another possibility: that such schemes and codes are fundamentally out of kilter. Even the orthodox *Mahabharata* performed in the (in this case Javanese) shadow theater contains a kink in its left/right lineup of protagonists: "The *wayang* grouping also accords with the division into an Elder and a Younger Line. . . . The Left-hand group corresponds to the Older Line, and the Right-hand group to the Younger. The Korawas are genealogically older than the Pandawas; Dasamuka (Rawana, the demon king) is older than Rama. The rulers are descended from the Younger Line, the Right-hand group, the Pandawas" (Pigeaud 1977: 77).

Episodes of the *Ramayana* and *Mahabharata* performed in Balinese ritual contexts locate reversibility and dialectical dislocations in marriage values and gender codes. Like courtly institutions over the Indo-European historical and geographic expanse, Balinese *puri* and ambitious houses sponsored exceptional practices that harness contradictions and transgressions. Marriages linking inferior males to highborn females could be made proper, although not normative, provided ritual measures insulated the infraction. Moreover, Indic courtly literature contains Tantric values contrapuntal to such special "proprieties" as *swayamvara* marriage—itself a hypogamous infraction of ordinary rules, acceptable only in carefully ceremonialized circumstances. This multiplying of resistant positions—hypergamy countered by hypogamy (*swayamvara*) and both in turn countered by Tantric excess—recalls semiotic principles of "texts" stressed in Chapters 3–4 above. In such tales as *Angling Darma,* Tantri's "Tantric words" envision the end of a cycle, whereupon the court collapses into a supercharged, overfertile phase set in an active-*sakti* female ritual register. Too-copious, exaggerated reversals thus enter the argument of contradictory values of status and authority balanced by courts in theatricalized honorifics, codes of etiquette, and ritualized rivalry.

Toward Comparative History

Earlier chapters sampled the formulaic descriptions of Hindu-Balinese practices that have appeared in European sources since the early sixteenth century. Ideas and countertypings of Bali have filtered through changing representations and standards of translation. Since the early nineteenth century parallels have often been drawn between Bali and specific aspects of Indic, Oceanic, and Indo-European configurations, including the feudal era of Europe and tributary states of South Asia. C. Geertz (1980) has reviewed the "pseudo-feudalization" produced in Bali when Dutch colonial policies transformed locally competitive loyalties into more centralized, territorial affairs.

Any such historical analogies remain entangled in the structures of control—
whether colonialist, nationalist, internationalist, commoditized, or otherwise
academic—that they help rationalize, legitimate, or subvert. The present
book is no exception.

Although Bali's infrastructures have perhaps never been "feudal," the island's history of status rivalries recalls features of three stages of "symbolic
ritual" scholars now associate with European vassalage. Le Goff outlines the
European case thusly: (1) subordination (vassal's homage to his lord); (2)
equality (*osculum* of mutual fidelity); (3) reciprocity that incorporates the inequality (Le Goff 1982: 237ff.). Le Goff summarizes *Annales* interpretations
of vassalage as a kinship ideal or a "family model," rather than an economic
or a political model. He outlines a style of statecraft not unlike that of precolonial Southeast Asia (Gesick 1983). Like Geertz (1980) on Bali's *negara*,
Le Goff stresses public spectators in ceremonies of loyalty (*karya* in the Balinese case); he distinguishes these political bonds from straightforward
patron-client relationships. In both Geertz's *Negara* and Le Goff's account of
vassalage, although bonds are hierarchical and inegalitarian, "the role of the
spectators, by contrast, is to reaffirm the reciprocity of the system" (Le Goff
1980: 274–275).

Economic and power relations in the Middle Ages are caught in a protracted
tension between an outright "potlatch system" of gift/countergift and a standard contract system (of the kind that existed in Roman property or later developed with more rationalized markets and capitalism). Many Balinese en-
terprises too, even today, seem neither potlatch nor contract, staged in
liturgical formats that couch social, political, and often economic transactions
in temple ceremonies and festival dramas beset by rival deities and demons.
Over Balinese history these formats have encouraged accommodations among
high Brahmana orthodoxies in league with courtly elites, lower local ortho-
praxies of commoner priests, and varied heterodoxies in the form of upstart
houses and white/black magicians, each sector given ritual auspices.

Vassalage, or its underpinnings, is doubtless too specific an institution to
bridge Bali and the Middle Ages. A more promising parallel is the tripartite
system of authority and power familiar from Dumézil's (1966–71) work on
"Indo-European ideology" (see also Duby 1984; Guermonprez 1984, Boon
1977:238; 1982a). Le Goff argues that the three familiar orders of clergy, warriors, and workers—corresponding to Dumézil's ritual, political, and maintenance functions—became jointly sacrosanct during Europe's twelfth century. Moreover, he opposes the "emerging class of knights within the lay
aristocracy" not just to clergy and laborers (including peasants and craftsmen)
but to the "king" as well:

> the appearance, between the ninth and twelfth centuries, of *bella-*
> *tores* in the tripartite schema corresponded to the formation of a new

nobility and, during a time when military technique was undergoing profound transformation, to the preponderance of the warrior function in this new aristocracy. As for the king of the *bellatores*, he was primarily a military chief and had the same ambivalence to the warrior order as the "feudal" king, being head of this military aristocracy and at the same time placed outside and above it. (Le Goff 1982: 55–56)

In Bali the kingly sector corresponds to parties claiming Majapahit-Javanese origins and superiority to local Balinese overlords. The "order" it represents is knightlike in its sacramental prowess; but it is also not-knight insofar as it is linked both to clergy who guarantee ritual purity, and to laborers (specialist artisans, even agriculturalists) who assure prosperity. Similarly, medieval kingship was "the beneficiary of the tripartite scheme"; it both arbitrated the three orders and foreshadowed their eclipse, after more centralized markets and land-based territories began working to monarchy's advantage during early modern commercial and agrarian developments. Beforehand, however, in the Europe Le Goff depicts, "the three orders constituted the social structure of the state, which would collapse if the equilibrium among the three groups, each of which stood in need of the two others, were not respected. The equilibrium could only be guaranteed by a chief, an arbiter. This arbiter was, of course, the king" (1980: 57).

Depicted in this way, the medieval case recalls Bali's nervous, dynamic equilibrium among priests (*pedandas*), rajas (*per Dewa*) warriors (*per Gusti*), and ritually charged specialists in artisanal and agricultural labor. A complementary tension among such sectors characterizes both Indo-European-style "orders" and the imperfectly centralizable courts of *negara* (C. Geertz 1973: chap. 12; 1980; Boon 1977: 227–28).

As vassalage is too specific, principles of Indo-European ideology may be too general a hinge for comparison. I turn, then, to more precise dimensions of religious and ritual specializations and classifications that both accommodate and deflect forces of central control. The European case eventuated in Renaissance and Reformation early modern economy; the Balinese case has eventuated in partial religious rationalization, increased colonial and post-colonial standardization, and strategies of response to an Islam-oriented nation. Other suggestive parallels include Bali's failure to institutionalize monastic authority as its "dominant confession" (Boon 1982a: chap. 6) and medieval Europe's inclination to trifunctional order rather than a leadership exclusively "ascetic in tone" (Davis 1984: 33).

Both Hindu-Buddhist Bali and medieval Europe accentuated scholastic-like casuistry plus convoluted categories of licit/illicit tasks indexed in ritually reversible codes of purity/impurity. Both, moreover, reserved prestige for exceptional specialists, including "goldsmiths, ironsmiths, and, especially, sword makers" (Le Goff: 58ff., 62). These resemblances have long been stressed by Western scholars attracted to Bali, Java, Indianized Southeast Asia, and other "archaic" traditional orders; whether area specialists such as W. H. R. Rassers (1959) or comparatists such as M. Eliade (1978).

A still deeper affinity may join Balinese culture and European *courtoisie.* Le Goff reviews Europe's ebbs and flows of what Van Gennep called "folklorized liturgical festivals"; in Europe they flourished in twelfth-century liturgy (like all liturgy, syncretist) and resurged in fifteenth-century popular festivals, where dragons, to take one handy example, signified both episcopal legitimacy and folk resistance, or at least ambivalence. Le Goff captures the play between rival ecclesiastic, knightly, and kingly authority plus popular "folkloric" undercurrents, occasionally combined in uneasy images of plural identity; again, the telltale dragon:

> The clerical dragon in stone (symbol of the church's victory over sin) and the folkloric dragon in wicker (ambivalently celebrated in carnival processions by rural workers and town artisans) are contemporaries. One revolves around the other as defying it, but no attempt is made to force the doors of the sanctuary guarded by the latter (Le Goff 1980: 185–86).

Readers of Balinese ethnology know that Bali too sports "dragons," both *nagas* and friendlier *barongs* (dragony lions in endless war with Rangda-widow-witches). A welter of paradoxical symbols and ambiguous protagonists counterpose priest, king, warrior, and producer (the rice cult, the sacred-dangerous crafts), along with peripheral parties of part resistance and part compliance— all joined in a heady array of courtly plus vernacular idioms.

Le Goff stresses local vernacular tales versus legends written into the more literate (and Latin) histories of high cultural circles: rising knights espouse fairy forces to counteract powers of the clergy's saints. We can compare Bali's priests who construe the cosmos in Hindu deities versus plural elites imagining their heroes ascending through more magical, less central, less Sanskritized power. I have called "romance" the multivocal vernacular-tapping dimensions of Balinese cultural processes and ritual arts contrasted to what could have become a more singular aristocratic "epic" of king allied with Brahmana (the Majapahit view), but did not.

Courts styled themselves to appear permanent, consolidating disparate authorities as best they could (see Geertz 1980). But upwardly mobile *arrivistes*—the "active middling families and locales" (Boon 1977:5)—have time and again aggravated the interplay of orthodox-literate-elite and vernacular-performed-popular. (This convenient analytic set is, of course, too polar to characterize adequately either Balinese or medieval complexity). In good *Annales* fashion Le Goff also peers beyond the royal cum ecclesiastic sphere. The ultimate heroic dimension of medieval folktales is not royal: "We are not dealing here with the king's son. We are looking instead at the world of the small to middling aristocracy, the knights or *milites,* sometimes designated as *nobles.* . . . Indeed, they are ambitious *milites,* eager to push back the bound-aries of their little seigneuries. The fairy (and not the deity or the saint) is the instrument of their ambition" (1980: 220).

Over Balinese history, middling challengers have continually enriched the repertoire of devices to extend their little seigneuries, their little "houses." This repertoire has included *courteoisie* and courtly love, among other sym-bols attuned to military-erotic values, hierarchical upheavals, status reversals, and deflections of power along alternative (often female-mediated) relation-ships. Such middling forces include ambitious ancestor groups, localities up-grading temple systems, and rajas (or now district heads, *bupati*) too, insofar as their authority was inherently insecure. It is not disadvantageous for such sectors to keep symbolic codes reversible, making this very quality something of a virtuosity.

But what about marriage institutions? Here, of course, the comparison with Bali pertains not to the contents of marriage types and motives but to the degree of differentiation and kinds of contradiction ordered by the institution of marriage. Medieval European marriage was gradually transformed into a peculiarly in-between sacrament. Unlike baptism, the Eucharist, and pen-ance, marriage in Europe had lacked definite liturgical form. As Duby (1983) demonstrates, marriage occupied a key position in lay rituals developed ac-cording to ecclesiastical models. Unlike ordination, marriage was deemed not life-giving but only prophylactic; even after inclusion among the seven sacra-ments of the church, marriage remained "tinged by vestiges of anxiety and repulsion" concerning sexuality (Duby 1983: 184–85). Duby shows that the twelfth century introduced more mobility and flexibility, indeed liquidity in the economic sense. Beforehand, the gradual sacralization of marriage coor-dinated tensions and rivalries between a church celebrating celibacy and a knightly class that, unlike Indic Ksatryas, never adopted polygyny; the knightly sector eventually "crystallized into great families clinging to the land—and to the right to rule, punish, and exploit the peasants" (p. 283).

The process of sacralizing marriage had been foreshadowed by the sacrali-zation of kingship at the shifting intersection of Dumézil's "three orders" (clergy/military/agricultural) devoted to sanctifying, protecting, and produc-ing. By the mid-twelfth century marriage had "come to be sacralized without being disincarnated" (Duby 1983: 35, 185). Over this historical destination of sacramentalization, European marriage increasingly mediates structural am-biguities linking values of reproduction and various contradictions and oppo-sitions. They include matrimonial moralities of priest/warrior; inequality/*ca-ritas;* chastity/wedlock versus wedlock/fornication; and asceticism versus "softened aversion to the institution of marriage." Related issues are the extol-ling of secular culture; arranged abductions for various motives of property; marriage versus concubinage versus secondary marriage, which differentiate ranks of heirs; male prowess/female virginity; procreation/sublimation; and the duple ritual register of grave betrothals/festive nuptials (Duby 1983: 29).

The church, moreover, preferred that the aristocracy make property-dispersing exogamous marriages, contrary to the aristocracy's own preference for endogamous marriages:

> The main preoccupation of the aristocracy, the handing down of an-cestral valor through the male line, made it essential for a man to be able to dismiss a wife who was slow to produce sons. . . . When it came to the mingling of two bloods, this same concern was imposed on the choice of a partner: the man should take his wife from among his near relations, provided she did not come within the third degree of consanguinity [deemed incestuous]. (p. 48)

In this centuries-long confrontation and accommodation of bishops and archbishops versus kings and noblemen, church views of abstinence pene-trated the court. Descent strategies were limited and lineage-building re-strained. The cult of asceticism vied with the cult of prowess: military, patri-monial, and sexual. Marriage, then, was the most paradoxical locus for playing out these contradictions. Studies of genealogies and priestly inquisi-tions were established to guard against incestuous marriages. Bold contrasts between sacred renunciation and reproduction by fornication had been trans-formed into finer, convoluted distinctions throughout the eleventh century. Eventually it was argued that "marriage, the remedy against lustfulness, kept men from sinning. Here, we see marriage on the verge of becoming a sacra-ment" (Duby 1983: 68).

Europe's twelfth century introduced fresh resonances of contradictions, with the new emphasis on "youth in aristocratic society" (Duby 1978: chap. 7). Maurice Keen has reviewed institutional contexts of vernacular literatures where the amorous culture of troubadours and the chivalrous narratives about martial episodes were "yoked together so that an old kind of story could be woven around a new axis of interest" (1984: 91). Martial adventure and amo-rous dedication became the dominant "twinned themes of narrative" (p. 116). The new ethic of courtly love "makes a powerful foil . . . to the primary loyalty to the king" in secular chivalric orders "consecrated" to upholding the honor of noble womankind (pp. 185–86). In Duby's summary account:

> What . . . the love songs of the second half of the twelfth century suggest is a new kind of erotic relationship, better suited to the posi-tion of the *juvenes*—that husbands should no longer pay court to ladies, and that they should no longer prevent their wives from re-ceiving "youth" and accepting their services of love. For the triangle "husband-wife-married lover," the poets of the "youthful band" wanted to substitute another triangle, "husband-lady-young courtly servant." They wanted to break into the erotic circle to the advantage of "youth." We know how well this ideal theme succeeded. (1977: 122)

This axis of "love"—set in contradistinction to reproduction and property transmission, "thematized" in ideals of enamored yet unrequited champions and European variations on *svayamvara* marriage—becomes congruent with the realm of "literature," or oppositional, vernacular literature, itself. It is this convergence and collision of "love" with alternative values of attraction/repulsion in the sphere of marriage that provides my parallel with Hindu-Bali, among other Hinduisms and Indo-Europeanisms.

Scholars of diverse persuasions have illuminated Europe's literary transgressions of the property and propriety of singular lines of authority. De Rougemont himself, for example, arguing in a partly idealizing mode, trenchantly compared courtesy's own ideal "love" to Indic Tantrism:

> The theme of submission to the lady leads to that of the test she imposes on her suitor. . . . This test, *assay* or *asaq,* would become in the thirteenth century . . . the heroic trial of chastity "in bed," *nudus cum nuda,* whose modalities in Tantrism have been described by Mircea Eliade. The *asaq* appears then as a kind of technique of *joy,* or the *joy* becomes the erotic game par excellence, . . . pleasure without procreation. (1983: 350)

Morcover, the West's ongoing transformation of that "emotional setting" of sublimated love prompted N. Elias's sweeping survey of courtly institutions and insights into an economic ethics of desire:

> Accordingly it is only the relation of a socially inferior and dependent man to a woman of higher rank that leads to the restraint, renunciation and the consequent transformation of drives. . . . Not as exceptions but in a socially institutionalized form . . . which make[s] the woman unattainable or attainable only with difficulty . . . and . . . particularly desirable. This is the . . . emotional setting of *minnesang* in which henceforth down the centuries lovers recognize something of their own feelings. (1982: 82–83)

It may require a combined attention to medieval texts and contexts, ideals and institutions, and ritual and rhetoric to appreciate heterodox vantages implicit in discursive formations. R. H. Bloch, for example, building on Duby, discloses a medieval model for contesting the authority of the noble lineage (*lignée*) tucked into the differences that characterize epic versus chronicle:

> In the genealogical history, family and story line coincide to such a degree that the uninterrupted sequence of ancestors compels the uninterrupted transcription of the tale. . . . Then too, there is in the chronicles discussed by Duby a definite sense that an order of consanguineal relations—a primogenital series—determines the order of narrative sequence . . . that a linear and continuous model of inheritance serves to define a linear textual mode. In the epic, however, the straight narrative economy that is equivalent to, and even synonymous with, lineage is problematized; and this is primarily through repetition. (1983: 102–3)

Bloch argues that the epic *chanson de geste* "represents from its inception the disruption of an essentially continuous past" (p. 107), and that the later courtly novel (romance) is a variegated form that both exaggerates and exposes tensions between patrimony and matrimony (pp. 107, 17). (For parallel suggestions about Balinese epic/romance, see Boon 1977: intr.). This emergent literary economy—which, like the money it emulates, is transgressive of land-wealth—provides a contraposition to "both the *canso* and the epic whose traits it shares" (p. 179). The female-inflected liquidity of love shares money's subversiveness; the new literary mode's mixed form becomes an "antigenealogical narrative," both an affirmation and "a contestation of the principles of genealogy and of noble property" (pp. 179, 178). Pushed to the extreme point of ludic resistance, antigenealogical narrative may be imagined as an exclusively female chain of figural reproduction, as this chapter's opening epigraph reveals (see p. 116).

This is not the place to track Bloch's accelerating readings through the lyrics, *chantefables,* and grail cycles produced in and as the ritualized rhetoric of courtly love in the French Middle Ages, a rhetoric entailing contradiction, fragmentariness, and dislocations from *lignée*-like propriety. It is, however, worth noting a "similarity of locus" between his study and this book's chapters on diverse destinations of Hindu-Bali, East Indies, and Indo-Europe. Both address "the mediatory semiotic fields of heraldry, patronymics, the plastic [and performing] arts, and historical narrative" (p. 76).

Bloch and other "new literary historians" see literature as part of the "practice of signs" emerging as a vernacular "when the noble family of the twelfth century became conscious of itself as a sign-producing organism" (p. 75). Legal frameworks, marriage strategies, the history of sacramentalization, and the production of texts are indissociable:

> [Feudal] marriage represented, above all, a treaty (*pactum conjugale*) to be negotiated between families; and it has often been said that the chivalric houses of twelfth-century France were so closely connected through common ancestry, matrimony, and collateral relation (not to mention fictive forms of kinship like adoption and participation in certain sacraments) that the nobles of the realm must have seemed like one big family. So complex a web of kinship depended upon careful surveillance of marital ties. (p. 70)

Bloch is apparently distracted by his references to Derrida from considering more seriously Lévi-Strauss's insights into complexes of texts, narratives, institutions, and marriage.[6] Yet Bloch's salient contexts of literary production parallel dimensions of *sociétés à maisons* stressed by Lévi-Strauss (1979, 1984) for many cases, including medieval Europe. To wit:

> These early armorial examples also show that the family insignia, like its land, was, from about 1150 on, transmitted lineally; and in this it constituted an integral part of the primogenital patrimoine.

First used for military purposes, in tournaments and battles, and first
connected only loosely to individuals, certain banners and pennants
came to belong exclusively to certain families and to represent, as
Duby notes, "a memory of common agnatic origin". . . . The inher-
ited heraldic sign was an important expression of the continuity of
lineage—of its origin in property, attachment to a distinct locus, and
to logos that was the sign of place. And if, as we have seen, rhetoric
is the science of *topoi,* or of proper places from which to speak,
heraldry constituted the rhetoric of aristocratic possession—a differential system of signs guaranteeing the propriety (discreteness) of the
family in relation to similar groups, in relation to its land, and even
in relation to its separate subbranches. (Bloch 1983: 77)

Moreover, as Bloch shows, and as we know from other *sociétés à maisons,*
conventions of *located* property and propriety contain the conditions for their
own undoing, a dialectics of doubting lineally transmitted privilege that rhetoric, or its figurative desires and desirability, can never forget. Rhetoric's
tropes of desire remind her "readers" that patrimony is never divorceable from
matrimony or descent from alliance; the ambiguities tropes "introduce" are
there from the start. Histories of presumed sequence like to tell a story of
decline from, or progress toward, intact property-cum-propriety, as if deflective difference were a marginal condition: either prior or lapsed. But these
narratives forget the foundational dialectics of exchange (Lévi-Strauss, 1969;
chap. 5) inherently deflected toward diverse destinations (Mauss 1967; Boon
1982a: chaps. 5, 7).

Hindu-Balinese ritual and rhetoric contrasts vividly with medieval European contents of institutions and virtuosities. Balinese houses have promoted
polygyny, positive endogamy, and ideals of sibling incest conspicuously,
while these particular valences remained confined to borderlands of Western
societies, dynasties, and polities, which forefronted other transgressions.
Nevertheless both cases (Hindu-Bali and the European side of Indo-Europe)
display an air of courtliness-redolent-of-multiple-reversals marked as "love"
and often in a female register of gender. Both also have enacted a discourse
that simultaneously sustains houses and deflects their claims to control. For
lack of a better word to "translate" such resonances across distant variations
and removals through time, might we call their resemblance a *Wahlverwand-
shaft?*

Reverberations

Louis Dumont has contrasted Tantrism to both Brahmanism and Buddhism
in a succinct formulation: Tantrism replaces orthodox renunciation with reversal (1980: 281). Hindu Tantric traditions make the very reversibility of ritual
categories, including male/female, categorically female: *sakti*. Reserving this
issue for subsequent chapters, I conclude with a few suggestions about

counter-androcentric reverses in the history of European chivalric love and eroticism (Nelli 1963).

In the broad reach of Indo-European courts and popular cultures—with their multiple confessions, uncentralized polities, and complex play among heterodoxies and rival orthodoxies—forms of ritual and literature have repeatedly enacted reversibility itself as "woman," or the inachievable love of her. Storied European examples of beautified or beatified females who "figure" inversions and reversings of status distinctions include an eleventh-century Virgin Mary emerging as the subject and object of an ecclesiastical cult, subsequent Melusina legends interrelating elite and folk sectors of society, and Saint Joan consolidating a proto-national identity (Le Goff 1980: chap. 5). Later, counterecclesiastical Renaissance courts would shape politics as a chivalric revival around Catherine de Medici, Elizabeth I, and so on—prelude to an errant history of chivalric re-revivals and medieval re-idealizings ever since.

To revisit "courtly love" as a comparative, historical topic is not to resuscitate roseate "allegories of love" that prettify a sanitized past.[5] No one today could imagine that fictions of beautification or rituals of allure can be harmonious. Within every poetics seethes a politics (and vice versa); "love" suffers inequalities and produces victims; and ritual celebrations play uncertainly across priests and knights, courts and peripheries, and popular festivities and resistances. Indeed, values of idealized ladyship and beautified femaleness were attacked unforgettably, with characteristic ideological overkill, by Horkheimer and Adorno: "Ever since the stunted jester, to whose gambolling and cap-and-bells the melancholy lot of broken nature once clung, made his escape from the service of kings, woman has been made the caretaker of all things beautiful" (1972: 249). Paradoxically, their intense objections to idealizing woman, or anything else, as aestheticized and later commoditized objects echo views of Schopenhauer, whose now notorious misogyny may (or may not) have been at base a rejection of courteous gallantry:

> Schopenhauer is not primarily interested in condemning women or putting them in their place as the *sexus sequior,* the second sex. What he really wishes to attack is the concept of "the lady." Schopenhauer is particularly revolted by Western notions of gallantry or adoration of the female, and in general what he calls "our preposterous system of reverence—that highest product of Teutonico-Christian stupidity." Above all, he wants to abolish the social consequences of medieval courtly love. . . . [which] elevates a few women of the upper classes at the expense of the great majority . . . (I. Singer 1984: vol. 2, 457).

Between Schopenhauer and Horkheimer-Adorno came Nietzsche; and after all of them, deconstruction. Today any reverential idealizing has come under attack, and gallantry too declared as dead as God.

Ironically, scholars combative of nostalgia may wind up nostalgic for gallantrylessness, another utopian ideal. In the history of commentary on and critique of "courtly love," Max Weber's works best sensed such an inevitability. Weber's prophetic insights extended to quandaries of escaping one idealization only to fall into an antithetical one. It is, indeed, Weber's sometimes ironic reading of the comparative history of eroticism and love that have provided one woof of the present chapter.

Weber's earliest discussions of religious motivations oscillate creatively across overlapping "spheres": economic, political, aesthetic, erotic, and intellectual. His rubric of the "erotic" conjoins the political-aesthetic and the intellectual, both in ideal and practice (Green 1988). Weber turns to chivalry after discussing the "exclusively masculine" character (erotics included) of Hellenic "democracy," where the boy was the cult-object of love and any eroticizing of "life-fate" with women would have appeared "almost sophomoric and sentimental" (1946: 345). Weber continues his unsettling comparative quest through "erotically sublimated sexual relations":

> The troubadour love of the Christian Middle Ages is known to have been an erotic service of vassals. It was not oriented toward girls, but towards the wives of other men; it involved (in theory!) abstentious love knights and a casuistic code of duties. Therewith began the "probation" of the man, not before his equals but in the face of the erotic interest of the "lady" . . . constituted solely and precisely by virtue of her judging function. (pp. 345–46; exclamation Weber's)

He next poses the Renaissance, which had "cast off the asceticism of Christian knighthood," as a transition to the nonmilitary intellectualism of *salon* culture; he continues:

> *Salon* culture rested upon the conviction that inter-sexual conversation is valuable as a creative power. The overt or latent erotic sensation and the agonistic probation of the cavalier before the lady became an indispensable means of stimulating this conversation. Since the *Lettres Portugaises,* the actual love problems of women became a specific intellectual market value, and feminine love correspondence became "literature." (p. 346)

I find it increasingly difficult to catch up to Weber; scholarship may be losing ground—such is entropy (Boon 1982a: chap. 3). Nevertheless, this book will conclude (Chapter 7 and Conclusions) by ushering Hindu-Balinese *courtoisie* and Tantrism into Weber's endlessly disturbing lights and shadows. To close this chapter's comments on courtly love, let it suffice to recall that a basic icon of Indic Tantrism, part of the history of Indo-European heterodoxies, is Sati, the self-immolated and dismembered consort of Siva. Sati's *Liebestod*-like myth is sometimes tied to Siva's mutual mutilation (castration). Moreover, Sati's fate is "strongly reminiscent of the tale of Isis and Osiris" (O'Flaherty 1975: 249), whose motifs recur through the history of European eroticism and heterodoxies (Hyde 1982). Bali's most visible embodiment, or avatar, of Sati is widow-immolation (*satya*), a ritual format that occupied a sensational, ambiguous place among court-sponsored cremation rites, as we saw in Chapters 2 and 4. Remember, too, that Balinese culture became "Kawified"—emblematized by selections of its most poignant Sanskritized texts—in colonialist representations that compared not only Hindu-Bali versus Islamic Java and Sumatra's Rejang, but implicitly opposed different schools of European policy in doing so. Over hybrid-history, the generative contradictions and ritual reversals of Balinese "love" have registered tragically in the contrast between Siwa's spouse and Rama's: Sati/Sita. Here we encounter figures who have sustained the hierarchical arts of refinement by becoming victims of their own desirability. Sati/Sita remind us, along with Weber, that cultures and their meanings—both enacted and attributed—materialize out of comparative pasts that are sometimes sinister, often unlovely, and always sad: *Mitleid*.[7]

Chapter Seven
Oppositionally Hindoo: Heterodoxies and Reformisms Dispersed

Snapshot taken from a public street in a neighborhood of Bali's provincial capital, Den Pasar, 1981. It shows a mosque bracketed by and entered through a Hindu split-gate. The structure existed then (and possibly now). The juxtaposition is "theirs"; it does not derive from a tricky camera angle or lens-distorted distance. That the tip of the onion dome viewed through the architectural fragment sports an Islamic insignia set sidewise rather than full-face, and thus obscured, is doubtless an artifact of this composite representation (a photo-framing of a Hindu-framing of Islam).

"**W**hy is Indian folklore different from all other folklores," wonders Wendy O'Flaherty in *Tales of Sex and Violence* (1985). Her half-rhetorical question could extend to "Hinduized" ritual and social forms in Southeast Asian populations as remote from India as Bali, or even Java's forty thousand Tengger. The latter case has recently been treated in Robert Hefner's *Hindu Javanese* (1987), which documents a counter-Islamic ethnic identity attached to "folklorized" Hindu myths and a transforming cult of Hindu-Buddhist priestly practitioners.

O'Flaherty's study of the tenth-century *Jaiminīya Brāhmana* continues her provocative rereadings of Vedic, Puranic, and epic materials—both central sources and odd-texts-out from India's complex pasts. Hefner's account mulls the cultural and historical circumstances of an odd-minority-out in the highlands of Java's eastern salient. Read together and played off against each other, O'Flaherty's scintillating corpus and Hefner's solid book provide fresh evidence for the comparative anthropology of hierarchy and the dialectics of Indicized myth, ritual, and social and economic arrangements. Once more I will interject Bali as a kind of third position, this time between all-India and tiny Tengger. I continue construing as destinations, rather than filiations, demarcations and labels like "Hindoo" which trail along a colonial, postcolonial, and precolonial history whose future is still in progress.

Jaiminīya

O'Flaherty's *Tales of Sex and Violence* addresses select episodes translated from a ribald Sanskrit composition dating from around 900 A.D. These seamy narratives have proved troublesome to past philologists who projected their own frowning standards of propriety onto philosophical, literary, and religious texts. O'Flaherty's professed enthusiasm for an unconventional *Brāhmana* stems in part from scholarly motives:

> Now, many of the stories mentioned in the *Rg Veda* are told in great detail in the *Jaiminīya;* and many of these are retold, in much the same detail, in the *Mahabharata*. . . . It seems that the *Jaiminīya*, combining as it does the priestly and the folk traditions, the sacred and the profane, and coming as it does almost precisely halfway between the Vedic and the Epic recensions, provided a kind of stepping-stone, a halfway house for the folk tradition to touch down for a moment in the Sanskrit world before leaping back into the vernacular culture that had always sustained it and would continue to do so for many centuries. (p. 117)

Her pungent commentaries stretch these domestic comedies in many directions, which she niftily outlines as follows: "Backwards" to priestly, sacrificial Vedas; "forwards" to bardic, courtly Hindu epics; "sideways" to more seemly Brahmanas; "upward" to standard index-motifs of world folklore; and "downward" to "deep meaning" in the "human heart" (pp. 29–30). She willingly leaps across history, philosophy, and cultural and psychological contexts.

O'Flaherty wishes to free such tales from overelaborate apparatuses in hermeneutics or structuralism and to disburden them of the disputatious arts of recension. These elliptical, convoluted, embedded Indic stories should, she feels, appeal with immediacy to any open-minded enthusiast. An academic iconoclast, she invites every "common reader" to become an authority in her or his own right by dint of human experience. One can acknowledge the valor of O'Flaherty's efforts to bypass interpretations that are too doctrinal, asterisk-laden, or kinshippish yet retain misgivings when she claims the tale can speak directly to the selves of readers.

O'Flaherty highlights critical transformations from sacrificial rites (philosophically glossed) toward vernacularized voices and transpositions of high ritual tonalities into low-narrative ones. She insightfully tags the *Jaiminīya's* tales "shadows of the sacrifice," Vedic tragedies turned into "stories with happy endings" (p. 16). We learn, moreover, that codes of reversal (many of them "Tantric") can in turn be absorbed into revised canonical doctrines.

Some presumably straitlaced predecessors, including W. I. Whitney and Max Müller, are chided for perpetrating prettified revisions in their established scholarship. Yet O'Flaherty insufficiently addresses the intricate and ambivalent history of British Indology that formed them—whether the early patronage of Brahmans' learning by Hastings or those first direct Sanskrit-English translations by Wilkins, who was declared "Sanskrit-mad" in 1788 by Henry Colebock. Even misguided and inaccurate responses by these figures were nevertheless weighty assessments of Muslim, Hindu, and once-Buddhist South Asia. Scholarly interests were interwoven with transforming motives—picturesque/exotic/romantic/sublime—for embracing, controlling, and merchandizing different aspects of India, including the textual, the pictorial, the archaeological, and the ethnographic (see Schwab 1950, Archer and Lightbown 1982, Willson 1964; Cohn 1985). Responses to the *Jaiminīya* have thus included stodgy scruples and now fresh Bohemian approval, among other extremes and compromises. All of these motives deserve being assessed within the fuller patterns of attraction and avoidance in the discourse of Indology (see above, Chapter 2). Omitting this background risks committing against past scholars errors similar to ones they committed against the *Jaiminīya*. O'Flaherty's dismissals of Whitney and Müller's offhanded dismissals of certain texts are themselves a bit offhanded.

The book's nonrandom assortment of excerpts is justified as follows: "I selected the stories that I selected, and grouped them as I grouped them, because of certain ideas about patterns of human emotion that I learned from reading Freud" (p. 23). This unblushing bias leads her at times to conjure up vague emotions "accessible to understanding across cultural barriers," emotions she explains by "conflicts within the nuclear family, fears of danger from sexual contact, and the primacy of images of the body" (p. 23). Her casual invocations of "the family context" here sidestep historical and cultural intricacies of alliance relations, marriage structures, ritual division of labor, polygyny, and related matters. Yet these dynamics and dialectics extend not just to courtly texts but to resistant ("folklorized") tales that accentuate domestic and popular affairs, norms of comportment, and quasimoralized messages.

In *Dreams, Illusions, and Other Realities* (1984) O'Flaherty mentions contradictory values of dynastic/monastic, courtly/local, renunciation/reproduction in Brahmanic, Buddhistic, and Hindu ideologies. Yet even that study, with its reflexive interpretations of the hyper-embedded *Yogavasistha*, generalizes a standardized "domestic" context of emotion. Her assumptions that "dream" implies private and "myth" implies public reinforces a universalizing and individualizing psychologism that diminishes the sense of shifting multiforms that prevailed in *The Erotic Aesthetic,* the founding work of O'Flaherty's corpus (1973). That study better seizes the continual play of rival orthodoxies, heterodox responses, and complex accommodations—the very things, I suspect, that make Indic folklore, and indeed history, seemingly different from all the rest. This difference may result in part from the fact that "all the rest" have been even more thoroughly reformed, revisioned, and expurgated along lines of ethicized propriety.

It may be advisable to read O'Flaherty's corpus as nonrandomly as she reads the *Jaiminīya,* selecting excerpts from her commentaries on the *Rg Veda* (1982) and other parts alert to counterreformisms accumulated in and as Indic (and Indicized) texts and rites. The historical drift of polyreformist Hinduism was earlier appreciated by A. M. Hocart, who drew memorable and controversial parallels:

> The Brahmanas are vastly earlier [than the *Ramayana*], and therefore, in the absence of definite evidence to the contrary, must be taken to represent an earlier point of view. They were written in the heyday of the old cult, when it had been developed in such detail and had become so burdensome that a reaction was sure to come. The reaction did come in the shape of Buddhism, which is to India what Puritanism was to England. Ceremonial and myth were discredited, and ethics became the absorbing interest. The *Ramayana* is doubtless based on traditions older than Buddhism, but it was not written down until after the ethical movement had broken up the old religion, and the remains of that religion had been revived by infusing them with a new spirit. We might as well go to the writings of the Oxford Movement for first hand information about Medieval Christianity, as to the *Ramayana* for a true account of pre-Buddhistic Brahmanism. Everything then is in favor of the *Brahmana*'s claim to represent the original most closely. The final verdict, however, must be left to the *Rig-Veda,* which is universally allowed to be the expression of the most archaic known form of Indian belief. Unfortunately the hymns, as

usual, are merely allusive, and all we can do is to collect the allusions
and see which view of the myth they fit best, the ritual or the epic.
(1950: 218–19).

Although Hocart retained that thematic sense of Buddhist doctrine once popularized in the West by Schopenhauer's philosophical parallels, he here seems
on the verge of withdrawal from a quest for origins, almost resigned to fragments and allusions. His remarks characterize the *Ramayana* returning towards the Brahmanas in a way that once countered Buddhism and, we can
add, continues countering other ethicized movements today.

Similar intricacies of Indic reformisms were powerfully summarized by
Weber. He, however, implied that explicit intentions and overt cultic hostilities were the driving force of change:

> Below the level of those seeking Brahmanical gnosis there was a
> scorned substratum of disreputable magicians preoccupied with the
> problem of folk religiosity. However, in the interests of their power
> position, the Brahmans could not completely ignore the influence of
> this magic and the need for rationalizing it. . . . In *tantra* magic folk
> ecstasy made its entrance into Brahmanical literature, and the *tantra*-
> writings were viewed by many as the "fifth Veda." (Weber 1967: 295)

Weber's overbold panorama may be phrased more cautiously, again along
lines suggested by Hocart: So-called Tantrism has "counter-countered" ethi-
cisms that developed subsequent to Buddhism, including devotionalist and
rationalist ones. Devices of this resistance have likely been less direct than
Weber conveys—more like the convoluted codings clarified by O'Flaherty's
readings of the *Jaiminīya,* part of the evidence of Hinduism's dispersal into
diverse destinations.

In *Sex and Violence,* more than in O'Flaherty's earlier works, the tale's the
thing. Narratives of Bhrgu's journey reveal complex varieties of oblations,
including material stuff, voice, and mental image. Metaphors of connection
and interrelationship differentiate between unmediated eating (by thumb) and
utensil-mediated eating (by spoon). Spoon-eating is a microcosmic resemblance of the macrocosmic mediation of ritual sacrifice. O'Flaherty reviews
Brahmanic conventions fundamental to hierarchic rites: "All human food consists of divine leftovers" (she adds distracting hunches that "the thumb may
be symbolic of the nourishing breast"—p. 38). She poses a vital distinction
between nonmoralizing tales (I call these "myths" in the more technical
sense—see Chapter 5) versus "suddenly ethicized" tales. From here she
adroitly surveys successive eras and genres, much as her other studies cover
variant visions-within-texts-within-visions:

> the things that Bhrgu sees in the other world could also be interpreted
> as a vision of the next life in *this* world . . . [thus making the tale] a
> very early fore-shadowing of the doctrine of reincarnation, which

first appears explicitly in the Upanisads. . . . Indeed, Bhrgu's experience in the other world set the pattern for what was to become an
important set piece in Puranic literature; the interlocutor of the Pur-
ana is presented with a lurid picture of the tortures in various hells,
to which, he is assured, he will be sent because of his karma. (p. 41)

These breathtaking leaps help O'Flaherty isolate a key device in the Brahmanic cosmology, central to the *Jaiminīya*:

First, the general categories of gods and men are narrowed; the result
is a cycle of tales about a particular god—Indra in opposition to a
particular human enemy, often an unwilling worshiper. In the second
stage, this enemy is identified as Indra's son, Kutsa. And, finally, the
conflict between a human father and son is presented without a theological frame, though such a frame may perhaps always be implicit.
(p. 57)

Similar stages, it might be noted, punctuate abundant Western works, ranging
from Aeschylus's *Oresteia* to Wagner's *Ring* (the latter modeled explicitly on
the former), plus innumerable texts and traditions that reticulate with these.
An Indo-European pattern of "narrowingly cosmological cycles" is a virtual
model of cosmology-become-history. Again, however, I suspect that these
frames and cycles pertain to cultures' and history's play of genres and not
necessarily to any psychological universals of the kind O'Flaherty's more recent works have saluted.

It is, moreover, her insights into generic play and reversal of categories that
provide the richest moments of her commentary. She traces the *Jaiminīya*'s
domestic/divine/demonic planes of interconnections and positive/negative
values of sacrifice and its varied sublimations. She modulates from thematic
fear of the father to fear of wives and demidemonic women (no psychology
need be implied); these fears culminate in the polygenital tales of Long-
tongue (here the text's Tantrism is unadulterated!). Stories weave together details of oblations of curds (a kind of parody of Brahmanical dairy proprieties?)
and equate them with the utter defilement of bitch-licked god-food. Issues of
status-inversion possibly echo Tantric conventions of purity attained through
sacralizing defilement. Narrative episodes involving Brahmans' wives portray
the villain as "sexuality in any form, female or male" (p. 109). O'Flaherty's
chapters pivot around the relevance of these details to sacrifice:

Explicitly, the only danger that [women pose] is the danger to the
sacrifice—the danger to the fire, which is needed to cook not only
the sacred oblations but all profane food. These two types of cooking
belong to the wife as well as the domestic fire; it is she who cooks
the everyday meals and makes it possible (by her presence at the
ritual) for her husband to offer the oblations. But the sexual fire is the
indirect sign of the demoness, who directly threatens the sacrificer,

not by rendering him impotent, but by rendering impotent the sacrificial fire and hence the sacrifice itself. . . .

Women threaten the sacrifice in two ways in the Brahmanas: evil
women (demonesses) threaten to destroy the sacrifice (and the sacrificer), while good women (wives) pose a danger to the sacrificer
through the likelihood that they will be seduced. For the sacrificer
had to be a married man, and his wife was essential to his ritual
completeness. (pp. 84–85)

(This pattern, by the way, extends to the *pedanda* and *istri pedanda* roles of
Balinese Brahmana priests.)

Although O'Flaherty's book goes far in these respects, it pulls up short of
the dialectics of different oblations, such as Brahmanical-dairy versus Tantric-
grains (see Conclusions). She alerts us to the *Jaiminīya*'s intricacies, which I
see as possible parodies of Brahmanical controls and their sacrificial style of
attracting the attention of gods whose potential indifference must be counter-
acted. Yet the *Jaiminīya*'s female-focused countering of Brahmanical orthodoxy is left in the air. Hemmed in by limitations of her source materials or
possibly distracted by Freud, O'Flaherty does not compare this mode of resistance to related ones: setting king off against priest, contrasting varieties of
priests and noble/royal lifeways, counterposing rival hierarchical authorities.
Instead she interjects psychologistic morals.

Contexts of tactical authority-countering have been undergoing intensive
reassessment in many disciplines. Examples already mentioned include wom-
en's studies; *Annales* historians' studies of indirect subversiveness in European "folkloric" pasts; work on Renaissance and early modern heterodoxies
inspired by Frances Yates and by the New Historicism; readings of literary
history attuned to Bakhtin's views of hybrid satire deflective of centralized
control. Findings from any of these approaches, which all rely on anthropological insights into rituals' polyvocality, could improve O'Flaherty's bare
mention of issues of property transfer, cumulative estates, aspects of alliance
and exchange, and status conflicts and reversals. More systematic attention to
issues of institutions and contexts, however, could impede accelerated readings across many texts reflecting "the competing concerns of sacrificial ritual
and folk narrative."

In short, O'Flaherty's readings of late (1988) have slipped around dynastic,
courtly, and local conflicts that remain at least indirectly pertinent to domestic
narratives. It may be true that in the history of Indo-European genres, compared to myth and epic, the "social code" of fairy tales is relatively restricted:

Kinship relations are simple, and confined mainly to the nuclear family. . . . Hypergamy solves everything. The poor boy or the poor girl
marries the rich prince or princess. . . . These hypergamous marriages do not raise complex dynastic problems. . . . Mythology has
moved a long way from the great cosmic conflict that determined the
fate of the world. (Oosten 1985: 162, 166)

Yet even folklorized tales which rework mythic and epic fragments, recontextualize traces of cosmic contrasts, alliance strategies, and partisan argument and opposition (Le Goff 1980: pt. 3). Any reading that muffles affinities with past extremes tends to "folklorize" our own interpretation of folklore, indeed to domesticate those very differences that O'Flaherty's work has often so boldly exposed.

O'Flaherty professes *Tales* to be an awkward entry in her corpus (p. 31)—one resembling her Penguin translation of *Hindu Myth* and the *Rg Veda,* yet hinting at her work about Hindu theodicy, women, and multiform mythic variants of Sivaic and Tantric formulations. A promised study of the horse, another of her professed passions, will likely offer something between vibrant reinterpretations of Vedic-sacrifice-becoming-Hindu-chivalry and a kind of *Equus*-East. Such is O'Flaherty's project. She seeks a reinvigorated philology of spicy translations and commentary, a more timely Indology, and a rehabilitated sense of the human side of texts she champions. Her wit is matched by willingness to question, spar, titillate, and now and then outrage. Like Indic folklore itself—different from all the rest—her shining works defy indifference.

Tengger

Hindu myths and associated ritual current among Java's 40,000 Tengger are far tamer than either the tales of the *Jaiminīya* or O'Flaherty's reading of them, and for interesting comparative reasons. Robert Hefner's sober study helps lay conclusively to rest lingering assumptions that remote populations of Indonesia may have dodged history. *Hindu Javanese* (1987) joins a growing body of anthropological works on mainland and island Southeast Asia—a classic one is E. Leach's *Political Systems of Highland Burma* (1964), a recent one is R. Rosaldo's *Ilongot Headhunters* (1984), a comparative one is S. Tambiah's corpus (1976, 1984)—that document processes linking less assimilated groups with lowland forces of control. Hefner thus advances the ethnography and ethnohistory of localities (in Java, Sumatra, Sulawesi, Lombok, Bali, etc.) characterized by only partial, often episodic centralization (see Wolters 1982).

The Tennger case has much in common with so-called Bali Aga, who contrast with Bali's Hindu majority much as Tengger contrast with Islamic Java. Noncremating groups in Bali are low on hierarchy and etiquette; their reputation has long figured in distinctions between rustic and Hinduized, part of the play of avoidances in Bali's status-caste distinctions (see Bateson 1937; Boon 1977; Geertz 1980; Guermonprez 1984). Recent studies of Bali Aga include official Indonesian researches linked to developing tourist sites (*Sejarah Desa Trunyan* 1976) and works by both Indonesian and foreign scholars who take for granted the venerability of upland rites (Danandjaya 1980; Lansing 1983). Because such researches by governmental and military officials accentuate separatist identities, or may be construed to, these studies themselves have become factors in reinforcing motives of ritual unorthodoxy among upland minorities—in this case, so-called Bali Aga eschewing Hindu cremation. (A parallel in Tengger is the avoidance of Islamic circumcision.)

Hefner's study achieves critical leverage on processes of demarcating ethnic divides. Although his book is restricted to long-term fluctuations in the "invention" of Tengger tradition (Hobsbawm and Ranger 1985), its questioning of historical fables of isolation illuminates more general motives (both "internal" and "external" ones) in stories of origins and ritual enactments of contrastive religious identities.

Today's Tengger are increasingly self-conscious "Hindus" through the efforts of Parisada Hindu Dharma, a Bali-based organization for consolidating an interisland ethicized Hindu order:

> The meaning of these [*japa-mantra*] prayers for priests or other Tengger cannot be defined in terms of the comparative or philological data an outside analyst might bring to their reading. For Tengger priests in particular, these prayers were not experienced as "Indic" or "Hindu" prior to the emergence of the Hindu reform movement in the Tengger region. . . . Historical evidence in Tengger indicates that over the past century there have been important changes in the "intellectual technology" . . . involved in the transmission of the priestly liturgy. These have complicated the priest's task of understanding the liturgy, and, in some instances may have compromised its resilience in the face of an Islamizing countryside. (p. 204)

Having once opposed both colonialist and Muslim formations and codes and now resisting standard-national ones, these "Buda folk" assert ties to fourteenth-century Majapahit Java and to contemporary Bali. Tengger tales depicting their trickster-hero Aji counter several identities, including Islam:

> Although nominally under Mohammad's command, Aji is an unreliable messenger of the word because he is, quite simply, too committed to Javanese ways. In building a place of worship, he thus constructs a sanggar rather than an Islamic langgar. For scripture, he uses a Javanese *primbon* rather than the Koran. Yet he never proclaims his independence from Mohammad. It should come therefore as little surprise that, in communities below Tengger, there exists a final chapter on Aji's fate. I recorded this oral addendum to the tale in a recently Islamized community to the south of Tengger. My informant explained that Ajisaka was a good king, but a lousy religious teacher. Neither Indic nor Islamic, nor even just Javanese, Aji is all of these at once—a fitting figure for the turbulent terrain of nineteenth- and early twentieth-century East Java. (pp. 136, 138)

Hefner fills out this turbulent history of unhierarchical highlanders still engaged in parrying usurpation of their lands and proletarianization of their labors.

Residents of the twenty-eight contemporary Tengger village units sustain the cult of Mount Bromo in settlements clustered below the mountain's crater. They possibly date from an outpost in the Majapahit network of widely dispersed brokers and craft specialists that circulated rice, spices, metals, and cloth as far as India and China. By the seventeenth century, now-Islamic courts of central Java extended conflicts into the eastern salient:

> In the 1680s, Madurese and Makassar rebels associated with the Trunajaya rebellion against the Mataram Court . . . were pursued by Dutch forces into the Tengger mountains, shortly after the Dutch had committed their forces to the side of the imperiled Mataram ruler. . . . The incident marked the beginning of almost a century of political violence around the Tengger region, as rebels used the mountain area as a staging ground for attacks on Mataram and their Dutch allies. (p. 29)

Depopulation ensued; Dutch plantation crops were introduced; a "coffee-line" altitude separated Islamic cultivators from Tengger withdrawn above. Entangled bureaucratic measures and Islamic policies included efforts to impose circumcision, regulate marriage offices, propagate peasant rebellions, and suppress amalgamations of "Buda" and Islam. This latter kind of composite ritual practice is what purist-reformists call "syncretism" or the equivalent. Tengger folk—or so goes the history Hefner collected—accentuated ancestry and localism over and against universalist doctrines.

Although he contrasts Tengger heterodoxy to Javanese and Madurese communities, the book disconcertingly retains a "village study" style of generalization with its undertones of consensus. Ethnographic chapters cover priestly liturgy, village concepts, and ritual forms. Repetitive descriptions are framed against allusions and references to Bali; he emphasizes Tengger's absence of clans, castes, irrigation, and ceremonial splendor: "Tengger villages have no temples, statues, shrines, or other structures that might announce to an outsider the non-Islamic faith of the community. . . . The ubiquitous aestheticism of Hindu Bali finds no counterpart in these villages" (pp. 53, 65–66). Only the Mount Bromo rituals mobilize region-wide exchanges and reciprocal service (p. 49). Tengger identity thus appears oppositional in the sense of retrenched, forged by a cult awaiting the restoration of "Buda" religion in a kind of muted messianism.

Tengger illustrates Southeast Asia's familiar highland ideology that poses generational cohorts of equals. Hefner designates the "Tengger way" as nonexclusive and familial, and he calls any trace of rank that can be detected "disruptive." Although he mentions systematic exchanges, he treats ritual not as a material flow (attuned to forces of replenishment as well as disbursement) but as items of expenditure taxing the resources of households (pp. 78, 81; chap. 10). Hefner reviews distinctions between rotary reciprocal labor (*getenan*) and festival labor (*sayan*). He stipulates that Tengger *sayan*—a style of

public generosity enlivened by conspicuous (ostensible) disregard of calcu-
lated costs—contrasts with *bowan* patronage with its self-conscious alloca-
tion of favors. Yet internal contradictions, softer inequalities, and possible
tinges of hierarchy in Tengger categories of exchange go unnoticed.

A discussion of "ritual reproduction" broaches the major issue of centralization: "Since Indonesian independence the continuing investment of wealthy
villagers in traditional ritual consumption has set in motion a process of ritual
inflation that threatens to diminish ritual sponsorship among the less affluent"
(p. 217). Reserving the equally central issue of "commercialization" for a
future work on economics, Hefner deems Tengger's blend of hierarchy and
what he calls egalitarianism—familiar enough where ritual exchange meets
market organizations—a "curious mix" (p. 222).

Any lack of consensus on the part of Tengger (which should not be surpris-
ing) is called "perplexing" and left at that. Hefner mentions discrepancies
between cosmology and economic practice—"ritual faith and social experience"—as if classic social theories had ignored the prevalence or even necessity of ideal/actual, ideal/ideal, and actual/actual contradictions. Passing mention of Durkheim and Weber (pp. 159, 162) makes their theories of
differentiation and specialization sound like a simple consensualism and a
monolithic model of traditional-becoming-rational, neither of which is accurate (Boon 1982a: chap 3; 1977: chap. 9)).

The book faults recent approaches for assumptions about "core symbols"
and a tendency to interpret rituals as "essential centers" or to analyze "symbolic structures alone" (p. 139). Naming few names, Hefner leaves readers to
guess at his opponents. Pierre Bourdieu taught him that cultural traditions are
not undivided property and Dan Sperber that cultural knowledge is tacit: "We
cannot assume here an easy correspondence between action-in-the-world and
meaning in actors' minds, as at least some interpretive approaches do" (p.
187). Yet his book retains shades of functionalist assumptions that ritual
change results from external forces. He has not yet presented local Tengger
rites as dialectical unto themselves with divided practitioners, or as complex
performances whose "internal" audience may be multiple. The oppositional
quality of both the politics and semantics of rituals (even when they appear
relatively consensual and reformed)—is an insight available from both structuralist and hermeneutic approaches. Tengger ritual can be seen in this light
either from these theoretical vantages or from the actual vantages of its storied
Hindu neighbors.

Tengger/Bali

To discern the style of reformism possibly represented by Tengger's retrenched Hinduism, I shall contrast Bali's ritual multiplicity, adding a few
illustrations from fieldwork in 1981 concerning responses by ancestral houses
to commercial developments and policies of state centralization affecting rit-

ual. Again, Tengger practice a kind of "dry Hinduism," a relatively homogeneous liturgy of Rsi priests focused on Mount Bromo. Here villages clustered above the old coffee-plantation line, retreating as Islam advanced throughout the Dutch colonial period. In contrast, what we might call Bali's "wet Hinduism" articulates elaborate controls and negotiations of irrigation; its array of rituals enlist sundry specialists across all caste-statuses who deploy diverse types of ritual knowledge, literacy, and styles of allure and cure.

In an appendix Hefner isolates the demon-banishing rites of Bali's *rsi bujangga* and draws the parallel with Tengger's central cult. But to compare Tengger and Bali means crossing from the former's relatively generalized Rsi liturgy to Bali's complex of rival or complementary specialists, in which the *rsi bujangga* is just one position. This interpretive maneuver (which runs contrary to a direction of change from the so-called traditional to the so-called reformed) requires acknowledging ritual's own (textlike) dialectics.

Compared to Tengger, Bali's Hinduism is even "wetter" than their respective subsistence modes and degrees of differentiating specialists suggest. Besides irrigation, another practice that "wet" Bali-Hindus emphatically *do* and dry Tengger Hindus do *not* do is cremate, although Tengger *do* reverse burial direction vis-à-vis Muslims (p. 68). Hefner once alludes to Balinese cremation, but he makes no mention of the issue (or of suppressing it) when discussing the impact on Tengger of Bali's Hindu reform movement (Parisada Hindu Dharma). Tengger's postmortem ritual (*entas-entas*) would, I think, strike any Balinese or Balinist as a kind of truncated cremation: pale parallels of Balinese formats for recalling, festooning, and sending-off the shades and deities. Even increasing state reforms of Balinese death ritual since 1979 have not eliminated double distinctions of first-burial, then-cremation. Mortuary practices remain a locus of ritual multiplicity and overlapping, shifting oppositions.

In their tales and legends as well, uncremating Tengger appear "ethicized" and "folklorized" by Hindu-Balinese standards, even given the reformist trends in Bali now advanced in Parisada Hindu Dharma programs and nationalist school curricula. One basic Tengger ritual narrative reported by Hefner reads like an enclave tale, a minority myth rather than a play across rival orthodoxies and heterodoxies in both courts and locales. Hefner designates the Tengger Kasada story "a moral tale that legitimates tradition by linking it to founding ancestors," making the Tengger themselves sound like good functionalists. He reports Tengger interpreting Dewa Kusuma's act as a melodrama of ancestral self-sacrifice: "This ancestor gave his life for his descendants." Yet Hefner might underestimate traces of contradictions that evade being moralized away. In the story he relates, Kusuma, a renouncer, has no descendants; it is his siblings who procreate, not he. Indeed, Dewa Kusuma is not precisely "the ancestor" Hefner calls him but an ascetic brother attached to another brother and sister. Such complementary ties between renunciation and procreation across coprotagonists possibly retain faint residues—mur-

murs, dispersals—of generic contradictions in Hindu narratives of cyclic authority. The signs of this cyclicity establish that field of Siwaic-Tantric values
visited in Chapters 4–5.

In the Tengger tale interpreted by Hefner's informants, generic contradictions between ancestry and renunciation have lapsed, if they ever emerged.
Regardless, *their* reading, as reported by Hefner, is not only reformist but
devotional. Hefner's study conveys a tone of Tengger devotionalism that may
resonate with his own expectations about devices of legitimation. Any such
devotionalism (registered, for example, in the gloss for Kusuma's founding
sacrifice) contrasts sharply with Siwaic-Tantric tonalities.

A comparison of the Tengger/Bali contrast might be phrased as follows,
taking a cue from the way rituals can compress and exaggerate affinities and
extremes: Hindu Javanese (Tengger) may be unlike Muslim Javanese in both
resisting circumcision and burying in an opposed direction, but they are like
certain Muslims in interpreting their folklorized tales devotionally. It is this
accommodation to Islam that contrasts with the style of resistance of much
Hindu-Balinese ritual. Nor do Tengger cremate. By accentuating this extreme
representation of contrastive ritual, I am resisting watering down differences
to "ethnicity." Ethnicity is really the nations's controlling view of differences,
differences whose more radical expression as ritual escapes detection in analyses geared to a narrow model of political economy. In the perspective of
rituals' own dialectics, Tengger and Bali contrast as two peculiar Hinduisms,
or Hindooisms, each "different from all the rest."

Hindu-Bali-Bali

My comparison of Bali with Tengger and the *Jaiminīya* turns on evidence
of Hindu ritual-cum-rhetoric posed both with and against reformism. I select
details of concrete Balinese developments at points of resistance to the influence of Parisada Hindu Dharma, centralized pedagogy, and Indonesian formats for nationalist hero-making and forging solidarity. These examples recall
this book's earlier discussion of the textlike nature of radical multiplicity (in
Barthes' sense); they include (1) Bali's legacy of court-sponsored arts, ceremonies, and wealth-circulation that intertwine localities and rival centers; (2)
reformist trends that become reencompassed by rituals transposed to different
registers of multilingual, intertextual forms. "Tantric" counterrites sustained
both through and against the Siwaic death-rite complex—imperfectly consolidated in different kingdoms (now districts) of precolonial, Dutch colonial,
and Indonesian Bali—will be addressed later.

A Legacy of Negaras

Balinese courts maneuvered many modes of authority in spheres of ceremony, judiciary, matrimony, wet-rice, artisanal activities, and textual expertise; they linked productive localities through specialized arts and services that

included militia and slave-trade (Geertz 1980). This protostate pattern need not have precluded ties among localities unmediated by courts. Indeed, diverse interpretations of affiliations among temples possibly sustained flexible interlocal connections as courts rose and fell and patronage shifted (Boon 1977: chaps. 4–5; see also Milner 1982). Renegotiations of temple-mediated relationships may go undeposited in court-sponsored evidence; chronicles conventionally weed the past they are cultivating (on specific gaps in *babad*, see Worsley 1972, 1984; Vickers 1987). If we judge from ethnography, some interlocal relations may have been clandestine.

We have, moreover, sampled the plethora of devices available to rivalrous Balinese houses for mobilizing their members and pleasing their ancestors. A repertoire of rites, temple-building, marriage strategies, text-producing, and performance-sponsoring assures that the record left will be one of gaps and partial positions, without center or closure (Boon 1977: 227–28). While the same may be true of any "history," it becomes extravagantly so in societies whose very modes of argumentation counterpose diverse authority. Although Balinese houses participate in a long-term pervasively literate culture, some of them have expressed their prominence by means other than written chronicles or compiled genealogies (*silsilah*). In these circumstances a kind of "mottled literacy" has predominated: hybrid translations and partial glosses across plural languages and esoteric/exoteric rituals, texts, and topoi. Diverse values of both comprehension and miscomprehension play across audiences and varieties of experts alike (see Chapter 4; Zurbuchen 1987; and especially A. Sweeney 1988). Knowledge "itself" remains radically pluralized in Barthes' sense: un-uniformed, but not for that reason unknowable or unauthorized.

Reformisms Remultiply

Several events from Bali during 1981 help illustrate how reformism may contain seeds of renewed oppositioning.

Item A. Reproliferating Temples. The Parisada Hindu Dharma bureaucracy has formulated taxonomies of temple functions and outlined ethicized rationalizations for worship. Typical frameworks regularly reported in *Bali Post*'s Indonesian journalism represent Hindu Bali as a community (like an *umat*), with sacred spots, gods (*para dewa*), male/female deities (*bhatara/ bhatari*), and God Almighty (*sanghyang Widi Wasa,* parenthetically *Tuhan yang Maha Esa*). Standard conventions include consolidating doctrinal dimensions of mercy-begging (*memohon anugerah*), ancestral and provincial-government commemorations (*monumen peringatan*), social action, religious education, and tranquility, said to console one's mind and heart alike. Tendencies toward devotional piety conform to the trend Geertz called "internal conversion" (1973: chap. 7; Boon 1977: chap. 9).

One typical *Bali Post* article (1981) made over sacrificial ritual cosmology into a quasiuniversalist ethical order suited to doctrinal propagation. Yet at the same time it renewed ritual distinctions and diverse temple types. Old colonialist schemes of state shrines (an earlier formalization) are hitched to repeated dichotomies of general/special (*umum/khusus*). It is stipulated that a "complete" locality would reveal a full gamut of ancestor temples: *paibon, panti, dadia, dadia agung, merajaan, merajaan agung.* This development fosters status rivalry among ancestor groups, including those represented as metalsmiths (Pande), low-caste high priests of the chthonic powers (*sengguhu*), and particularly elevated local administrators (Pasek). In 1981, for example, in the district of Tabanan, local differences among Pasek (including those disparaged by some as "new Pasek") were growing aggravated, despite the fact that an earlier motive for consolidating Pasek identity after 1965—namely, to weaken the power of the nationalist party (PNI) in order to consolidate the hold of the government-controlled functional groups (Golkar)—had long since been absorbed into Golkar's success during the Suharto era (see Boon 1977: chap. 7).

Item B. Ununiform Reform.   Before 1979, when the Eka Dasa Rudra purifications were celebrated in a Buddhist register of ritual exorcism, a government-backed regulation required that all corpses be exhumed and cremated (see Lansing 1983; Lueras 1987). Since then efforts to restrict and level cremation practices have continued. Although Eka Dasa Rudra was depicted as a unifying rite expressive of pan-Balinese values, its implementation could produce division rather than consensus. In 1981, many parties viewed the 1979 policy as an imposition that reduced poor families to relying on state-handout *banten.* Certain ancestor groups split into factions favoring or resenting what they perceived as governmental aid or interference, respectively. Death rites thus continue to provide provocative bones of contention for regular cultural arguments (Boon 1977: chaps. 4, 9).

Item C. A Repeated Success Story.   An ordinary Balinese bloke—the *topoi*-laden story translates—fell ill. A not-unenvious teller relates that a *balian* healer routinely diagnosed that the afflicted party had forgotten his origins and neglected his ancestors. Directed to search for two talismanic stones in upland Penebel, the victim received from a priest consecrated water (*tirtha*) which, sprinkled, induced health: *Yang sakit, cepat sembuh.* Wealth, too, soon ensued when he became an agent selling land near his home village. Well-heeled visitors to Bali today know the area as Nusa Dua, the new center of rich-and-famous international tourism. This explains, the story concludes, the freshly rebuilt splendor—promised in his heart to his ancestors, if well-being returned—of a temple in Penebel, more than 100 k. distant from Nusa Dua.

Item D. A Politico's Quick Cremation.   Scene: A village area in eastern Bali (beyond Klungkung), designated a "National Hero *desa*," commemorating local resistance to both Japanese occupation during World War II and the brief restoration of Dutch control afterwards, before independence. Hero-places and styles of speech-making (*pidato*) have multiplied in the rhetorics of nationalist Indonesia (C. Geertz 1973: chaps. 9–10; H. Geertz n.d.). Here an enterprising, fat-cat leader of Gusti title had convinced a neighbor Brah-mana pedanda to affirm his right for immediate cremation without provisional burial. (This once exclusive raja's prerogative has been increasingly opened to negotiation, although efforts to standardize practices have intensified since 1981; similarly cockfight wagers have again been uniformly, and ineffectually, outlawed.) Three days after the Gusti's death, funeral rites were inflected to-ward political and commercial interests along with sumptuary codes. Loud-speakered speeches, extolling the deceased's achievements, resonated through the village roads. Busloads of Balinese students and two vans of foreigners demonstrated the ancestor group's extensive networks in the educational bu-reaucracy and tourist industries. These onlookers enhanced the desirable ritual quality of bustle (*ramai*). The body was borne to the cremation ground by tearful kinfolk, thick with emotion because, exceptionally, the death was so recent. The corpse ignited propitiously, hastened by the flames of a burner leased from a *sekaha butane*. Gongs played, kinfolk mourned, villagers mulled, outsiders watched; the ashes were gathered, placed in their stylized receptacle (a small palanquin, but not "for a baby," as anxious-to-please guides told curious tourists), and thrown into the river to be returned to Siwa's sea.

So proceeded a hyperreformed cremation, which remains nonetheless and therefore Hindu-Balinese. The rite's margins, however, were less directly governed or intentionally controlled. One of the dispersed onlookers—neither bereaved descendant, loyal neighbor, enlisted schoolchild, tourist, nor eth-nographer—was heard mumbling Indonesian words that sounded familiar. Subsequently queried, he avowed he was a penniless dropout from religious-education courses in Bali's capital city. The sounds I had recognized were words from *Upadeça,* the manual of Balinese religious instruction standard-ized by Parisada Hindu Dharma. Pages were intoned from memory. Their speaker in his poverty had virtually restored to presumed ritual efficacy the neutralized literacy of a rationalist tract.

Thus, a fresh layer of "mantras" (or nearly that), now in Indonesian, joined the already copious ritual languages ingredient to Balinese death. I do not want to put too fine a point on an incidental anecdote from a field encounter. Yet, we would be remiss to ignore hints of "heterology" reemerging, paradox-ically, from the organization for doctrinal reform. An unintended consequence of Parisada Hindu Dharma may be a scattering of fresh ritual specialists—*balian Upadeça?*—into the abundant rites and rhetorics oppositioned into that cultural-historical formation called "Balinese."

Concluding Destinations:
Tantric Fragments, Extremest Extremes

"Buddha and Brahma"

. . . .

The Rajah pondered long, with darkened features,
As though in doubt increasing. Then he said: . . .
"Your Master, Sakya Muni, Gautama,
Is, like myself and you, a Kshatriya,
And in our youths we both, like you, rebelled
Against the priesthood and their laws of caste.
We sought new paths, desperate to find escape. . . .
Gautama found a path . . . I could not. . . .
Had I thrown down my sword, and fled my throne,
Not all the hermits, priests, and saints of Ind,
Buddhist or Brahman, could have saved our heads
From rolling in the dirt; for Rajahs know
A quicker than the Eight-fold Noble Way
to help their scholars to attain the End.
Renounce I could not and could not reform.

. . . .

. . . Thought
Travelling in constant circles, round and round
Must ever pass through endless contradictions,
Returning on itself at last, till lost
In silence. . . ."

—Henry Adams, 1895; meditating upon an Indic anecdote in Max Müller's *Natural Religion*, read by Adams in the tower library of Ceylon's Temple of the Tooth. The stanzas were mailed to John Hay with the blandishment, "They are yours. Do not let them go further" (Adams 1983).

The decisive form of the unclassical but orthodox Brahmanical reception of worship of feminine fertility goddesses is illustrated by the customarily designated "Sakta" sect. Important parts of *tantristic*, magical-esoteric literature. . . . formed its literary expression. Brahmans who sought to rationalize *tantrism* and thereby serve the popular Sakti-goddesses . . . sought . . . *maya*, which they conceived monistically as the original material, or dualistically as the feminine principle in opposition to masculinity, represented through Brahma as world creator.
(Weber 1967: 297)

Chapter 7 explored two examples of destinations of "Hindoo differences" and added evidence from Bali as a third extreme. O'Flaherty's corpus has pursued Indic Sivaic myths and texts backwards, forwards, upwards, and down. Hefner's book describes the recent intensification of Tengger's Hindu identity, part of a long history of relative retrenchment. His account of a uniform minority enclave in Java provided a foil for contrasting styles of resurgent polyforms characteristic of Balinese Hinduism, whose devices recall such "counter-Brahmana" texts as the *Jaiminīya* and related heterodoxies.

This study has compared ritual, social, and textual forms, tied in Hindu-Balinese history to wet-rice irrigation and insistent cremation, among other devices. Rhetorically charged representations—whether Pigafetta's paragraphs, A. R. Wallace's science, colonialist histories, Hindu-Balinese practice, or expanses of Indic and Indo-European configurations—have been approached as discourses and textlike "systems without closure." These representations are marked over time by dislocations, shifts, and reversals, even when they appear triumphant; that is part of their durability.

Each chapter has hinted or proclaimed that countercanonical history is a promising place for anthropology, literary theory, and area studies to meet. And indeed for "history" to meet too—again I employ Bakhtin's "cheerfully irreverent" rather than "piously stylized" quotation marks (1981: 55, 61). That conviction has influenced the selection of affinities and extremes documented, analyzed, and adumbrated; that hope has motivated my peculiar assemblage and style of interweaving texts, contexts, and Tantras. The sign of "Tantrism," then, has been beckoning, indeed welling up, throughout.

Like "totemism," "Tantrism" is a nineteenth-century European coinage based on an "exotic" term. The "ism" part makes shifting fields of oppositions, differentiations, and plural relations sound substantive, doctrinaire, and uniform (Lévi-Strauss 1963a; Boon 1989b). As Padoux reminds us: "There is no word in Sanskrit for Tantrism. There are texts called Tantras ("warp," "loom") (1987: 273). Nevertheless, the West's felt need for a term to token "doctrines and practices different from those of Brahmanism and classical

Hinduism" (Padoux 1987: 273) recognizes the negative play of Tantric persuasions across various orthodoxies and sects.

Western philologists have demonstrated ambivalence vis-à-vis Tantrism even as they translated, with frequent expurgations, its texts. A. S. Geden, for example, appreciated the Tantras' rejection of caste or sex distinctions and the forbidding of *suttee*. Yet he felt obliged to add that their diagrams (*yantras*), sacred circles (*srichakra*), spells, charms, amulets (*kavacha*), and crossing of the fingers (*mudra*) appeared "meaningless and puerile" (1922). More recently Tantric accents on sexuality and female-active power have been sympathetically construed by Sanskritists, historians of religion, and other scholars, both Western and South Asian, including those working in the wake of canonicity devised for Indic materials during colonialism and its aftermath.

Insofar as the Tantras (texts depicting dialogues between Siva's bride and Siva) cohere, they revolve around sexual desire (*kama*) put in the service of liberation (Biardeau 1981). Tantric texts may contest Brahmanical ranks, or their "Machineries" may reinscribe status differences. For example, by some Tantric standards Tantras are classified as highest female-among-peers, their Sivaic wisdom like a high-born woman, while the Vedas, Sastras, and Puranas are like a common woman.

Tantric texts and rites stress the *kama* component of complexes which oppose, whether agonistically or complementarily, priestly duty (*dharma*), inworldly power (*artha*), and sexual force (*kama*). *Kama* seems to resist patent consolidation into either a separate sociocosmic function (for Hinduism) or alternate "path" of liberation (for Buddhism). I have argued that the third extreme of Indic values of tripartition (dharma/artha/kama) remains disaggregated into matrixes of counterencompassment in Bali—again recalling "Tantrism" (Boon 1982a; chap. 6).

The dialectics of "transcendent sexuality," as clarified by J. Varenne, allow South Asian Tantrism to serve as a common accusation lodged by Buddhism and Hinduism against each other. This kind of mediating-negative thus deflects, or is deflected from, several orthodoxies:

> Tantric practitioners have the lively feeling that they are completely removed from the community (*samgha,* the Buddhist "Church"), even though integral to it, and their adversaries, agreeable to separating them from the regular faithful, conclude from that that they are heretics and therefore condemnable. In the extreme, the clergy is not far from thinking that Tantrism is a different religion, nearer Brahmanism than Buddhism. Orthodox Hindus moreover have a similar attitude and hold Tantrics to be Buddhists—"disguised" or not! Both of them cannot be mistaken, and Tantrism certainly contains in itself specific properties that give its adherents the feeling of belonging to an elite and its enemies the framework for rejecting this foreign body. (Varenne 1977: 121–22; my trans.)

Max Weber, as well as anyone before or since, appreciated the historical importance of Tantric discriminations: the "fifth Veda," the five "M"s, the substitution of blood sacrifice (the Vedic offering celebrated in sublimated form by Brahmans) with rituals about rice and its residues. As always Weber drew haunting parallels:

> In tantra magic folk ecstasy made its entrance into Brahmanical literature, and the tantra-writings were viewed by many as the "fifth Veda." While in India, as in the Occident, the systematic rationalization of magical art, namely, alchemy and nerve physiology for ecstatic purpose, formed the anticipations of rational empirical science . . . Tantra-magic . . . called forth . . . indulgence of the five nukara . . . : madia, alcohol; mamsa, meat; matsya, fish; maithura, sexual intercourse; mudra, holy finger gestures. . . . (1967: 295; see also Eliade 1978)

Extremes . . .

These Conclusions, mindful of Weber's comparative typologies and of Dumont's which build on them, will signal two specific Tantric variations in the destinations of Indo-European heterodoxies: (1) A realization of Tantric positions in seventh-to-twelfth-century Bengal, where they may have become, passingly, a concerted protest against Brahmanical orthodoxy; 2) Hindu-Bali, where Tantric positions have been less a polarized opposition than pervasively dispersed throughout many modes of control and ongoing styles of Malayo-Polynesian order.

Historical evidence of India's Tantric ritual practices has been deposited in that kind of discourse of gaps and expurgations emphasized throughout this book. So-called Tantrism apparently first flourished during the ebbing of urban Buddhism in South Asia. R. Thapar (1968), among many scholars, has reviewed this period of decline in commerce with China and Arab traders. Coinage and commercial regulations lapsed; wealth reverted to a local-land-base. Control of labor was consolidated by an alliance of royalty and Brahman priests who promoted plough agriculture and techniques of parboiling that made rice suitable for long-term storage and delayed redistribution. This economy of production eventually supported the *jajmani* system of redistribution, regulated by the dominant (land-owning) caste (Dumont 1980).

These vast developments, reminiscent of feudalization in Western Europe, have been concretely assessed in a stimulating paper by S. Lindenbaum (n.d.). Although she uses a Marxian notion of "mystification," Lindenbaum appreciates the obliqueness of representations; she implies that the "mystifiers"—if mystification it be—are mystified too, and that analytic models of domination/suppression miss crucial nuances in systems of inequalities (see also Lindenbaum 1987). Lindenbaum, moreover, addresses ritual, gender, and values of consumption as well as issues in the economy of production.

Tantric practices apparently bridged virtuosities of hunters, fishermen, horticulturalists, and artisans and small merchants. The "swidden look" of the five M's stands opposed to the dairy cult's sacred products of milk, curd, ghee, dung, and urine. Tantric alternatives of multiple crops and small-scale gift-expenditures occupied the breaches between Brahmanism and receding Buddhism as well as the borderlands beyond the advance of plough agriculture. Tantrism countered bovine symbols of Brahmanic propriety by celebrating "something meat-fish-alcohol-parched grain-like in their ritualized sexual intercourse" (p. 11). Lindenbaum calls such resistance to state-like power a code of ritual reciprocities among "equals" (I would say "complements"). This ritual resistance, of course, was counterresisted by incorporating Tantric elements in the Puranas (see O'Flaherty 1985, 1980; see above, Chap. 7).

Lindenbaum may be overdrawing the schism between what she calls a "grab-bag" of protest positions and caste exclusiveness, even for seventh- to twelfth-century Bengal, if then, as now, Tantric rites linked curing practices and artisanal specializations unamenable to centralized control. Relations between royal-Brahmanic "hierarchies of dependence" and Tantric "reciprocities" could entail the former crediting power to the latter and even acknowledging limitations to their own rituals of relative purity. As previous chapters implied, this kind of courtly value of its margins and partial dependency on ritual reversal make models of cultural "imperialism" questionable. Hierarchies operate differently from simple taxonomies of exclusion; and it is misleading to reduce them to the political catchword "hegemony."

Lindenbaum's analysis clarifies a range of affinities harnessed in the Tantric extreme, possibly consolidated as a polarized protest against intensive agrarian ideology:

> The historic debate we have been following has taken the form of a contest between two kinds of socio-religious organization, between the followers of Siva on the one hand, and the Tantric devotees of the goddess Manasa/Durga on the other, between restraint and enjoyment, between asceticism and eroticism, between cows and snakes, and between calories of orthodoxy and subversion. The most parsimonious expression of the debate takes the form of an opposition between milk and blood, where milk is understood as an agent of nourishing dependence, and blood a substance of shared reciprocities. . . . For humans, as the Tantrics knew, milk means bondage. (p. 17)

Her vivid formulation has decided advantages for the present study: it suggests a way to oppose one extreme among Tantric extremes to an opposed Tantric extreme: Hindu-Bali. In Southeast Asia there was no milk, and therefore no dairy cult to resist; nor did a technique of parboiled rice become dominant. Modes of bondage, and of reciprocities, there were; but they were otherwise (Reid 1983). Yet in Bali—this variant of Southeast Asian cultural formations within the old Malayo-Polynesian expanse—Tantric rites and texts have flourished, along with ritual rhetorics and poly-forms of the kind sampled in Chapters 4 and 7. One could almost say that Tantric rites became Bali's "dominant confession," except for the fact that dominance/submission may be one of the very polarities that Tantrisms resist.

A vague historical background of Tantric cultic components in Bali has long been acknowledged in Dutch philology and iconology (see J. Hooykaas 1957, 1960b). Bali's Tantric array includes those rites and texts of high transgression (overfertility) mentioned in Chapter 6. Courtly emphasis falls on interrelations of artisans patronized. Palmleaf manuscripts (*lontar*) of such texts as *Tantu Panggelaran, Usana Jawa,* and *Niti Praja* narrate mythic origins of court-backed specializations in carpentry, architecture, and sculpture, and cotton-weaving skills bestowed by the goddess Angga Ratih on a retinue of women. This high-side of Tantrism may render bodily symbolism more refined and "right-handed" by accentuating the four upper orifices (*chakra* or *padma*) and deemphasizing the three earthier orifices. More extreme are the famous Rangda exorcisms and *Chalonarang* dramas under the sign of Durga, whose demonic graveyard antics pertain to wedding stories and themes of widowhood (De Zoete and Spies 1939: 96–97, 273, 277). Most extravagant are curative practices whose arts of attracting/repelling diverse influences extend across techniques linking the fuller left-hand spectrum with right-hand ingredients as well (Boon 1982a: 185–204, 277).

The darker half of Balinese Tantrism has been coming gradually to light as research moved away from "proper" philology to rites and texts it once avoided (see Berthier and Sweeny 1976; C. Hooykaas 1980a). B. Lovric recently investigated magical practices of literate healers (*balian*), whose countertechniques constitute a virtual ethnosemiotics of lettered and unlettered devices (1987a, 1987b). I should stress that neither work on peripheral specialists nor interpretations of Tantric dimensions of court-sponsored arts (Ramseyer 1977; Worsley 1984) indicates a full-fledged philosophical doctrine, or even counterdoctrine, devoted to topsy-turvy ingestion of female juices and consorts' semen. Rather Tantric features are dispersed across the conversation of cycles in Balinese rituals. These materials include not just the wedding stories and widowhood of Rangda, Chalonarang, and Durga; but ribald servant scenes of *wayang,* images of lusty demons and "squatting female hobgoblins," ceremonies of public copulation between Siwa and Dewi Sri, and those unsublimated icons of the Linggodbhawa, called by Ramseyer "an enormous, erect penis with the grimacing face of a demon" (1977: 105). (This kind of gloss was not emphasized by C. Hooykaas [1964] in a slightly sanitized book on Siwaism: *Agama Tirtha.*) What should we call such Tantric positions: values? signs? valences? Yes.

Tantric terms for periodic hyperfertility—ideally controllable, inevitably escaping control—govern appetites of foodstuffs and of sexuality. The ritual register is feminine. This may be in a positive, even partly reformist mode: Sita victorious over the flames testing her loyalty; Saraswati in the vanguard of nationalist education reform; Dewi Sri as the focal power of elaborately ritualized wet-rice subsistence. Yet the encompassing female power (*sakti*) also tilts images, arts, and texts toward Tantric extremes upsetting to any androcentric orthodoxy. Such values, of course, are unmonastic, yet coupled with Siwaism they can incorporate components of ascetism and renunciation stages as well, in styles of reversal and ritual excess by means of rice-wine inebriations and other "grains" of exaggeration.

Lovric's study of Balinese male and female curers takes on added interest because it concentrates on Sanur, a locale that abuts an extensive touristic area, where property has been converted to hotel sites and commercial beachfronts. The density of magical specialists may form a prophylactic around Sanur itself, insulating the area from foreign influences and attracting clients from the entire island, and further. Historically this is one of Bali's most hybrid places—crisscrossed by local, provincial, colonialist, nationalist, and internationalist forces. And here we find the richest interweaving of alternative medico-magical practices.

Lovric deems the *balians'* techniques "a matter of confronting virulence with virulence, that is, like with like" (1987a: 425). Needless to repeat, precisely this kind of historical practice has been least likely to be deposited in evidence from the past. Lovric states the paradox of Tantrism, and why it can only be interpreted indirectly, in a fittingly dramatic way:

> The twin themes of horror and hilarity, of the lurid and the ludic, of invoking extremes and of dialectical reversals, demonstrable features of the Balinese magico-medical tradition, are all characteristic of Tantric rites. . . . In the case of Bali, the Tantric element in religion and magic is certainly an unexplored area of investigation. In view of the reformist efforts to define Balinese religion in terms of Hindu orthodoxy and to bring it into line with Islamic and Christian philosophers, one might suspect a deliberate neglect or even denial of the strong Tantric orientations. . . . (1987a: 426)

. . . And Affinities

Louis Dumont has stressed the significance of Tantric ambiguities and counterpositions in the long history of Indian religious differences. He calls the Tantras a "truly fundamental variant of Hinduism," an alternative to renunciation's antithesis to "caste" (1980: 281). Tantrism's dialectics include a tendency over time to be reincorporated into the very orthodoxies of world-disparaging renunciation resisted in its heightened sexuality. One might compare Europe's often agonistic complementarity of orthodoxy/heterodoxy or its dynamics of establishment, reformation, counterreformation. Dumont accentuates related paradoxes:

> There is also a large branch of Hinduism [that shows] the rejection of ascetic renunciation. . . . This is Tantrism . . . the sacramental enjoyment of all that is forbidden or despised in ordinary life: meat and fish, alcohol, sexual intercourse. . . .
>
> The rejection of asceticism is expressed in the rehabilitation of enjoyment, *bhoga*. But it is characteristic that yoga, or the discipline of liberation, is preserved at the same time, and that the doctrine claims to transcend the opposition of yoga, discipline, and bhoga, enjoyment. . . . We see that while rejecting renunciation, Tantrism accepts ideas which derive from it. . . . The [*Kula*] text . . . admirably shows the heterogeneity of Kula Tantrism and how it transcends . . . the opposition between transmigration and liberation. (p. 280)

Dumont notes that Tantrism "itself" is not so much a sect as a tendency affecting all movements (p. 280). It develops distinctions of right-hand/left-hand persuasions; but it should not be mistaken for anything corporate; and it may best be characterized by its extremes:

> I have referred to what is often called the extreme form of Tantrism, which the Indians call left-hand Tantrism to distinguish it from the more conformist right-hand Tantrism. . . . But the left-hand form is for us the pure one. It is true that there are attenuations, substitutions, and sublimations; it is true that the left-hand practices appear . . . increasingly through the centuries, mixed and combined with right-hand practices to produce a system finally in which right-hand forms predominate, but which preserves nevertheless its distinctiveness. (p. 280)

Taken to its limit, this approach poses Tantrism as a name for a polymorphous reservoir of ritual possibilities, continuously flirted with by orthodoxies yet also the basis of countering them. Again, a Western parallel is that range of hermetic heterodoxies, a murmur of Gnostic, Neoplatonist, crypto-liturgical positions: from freemasons to Bohemians, from counterculture to *poètes maudits*. Against the murmur of resistance more orthodox positions and transformations become shaped and motivated, or rather "motived."

From the perspective of the pool of Tantric possibilities, we may better appreciate the hybrid nature of "Hindu history." (By now I hope it is clear that any demarcated "history," or "culture," would do.) Critically construed, certain notions of history may at base be Indo-European—part of the chain of cosmology-become-chronicle developed in Sanskritic and Latinate traditions. Some nationalist projections are obviously a European invention, a distinctly local clothing of Clio (Bann 1984). Other notions of history are Islamic. "Hindu history"—in contact with many ideological slants on knowing, narrating, or discoursing the past—has been fashioned countercanonically in a way that unsettles any insider/outsider distinction. One might retrospectively pose the thrusts and shape of this invention as follows.

"Brahmanism" designates what written texts became labeled when Vedic ritual values were consolidated both to deflect and to accommodate the challenges of universalistic Buddhism and other sects. In Puranic variations, Brahmanism most explicitly assimilated Tantric terms that helped to counter reform movements. "Hinduism" names a subsequent reincorporation of Vedic-Brahmanic materials when Islam, among other forces, became adversarial. "India" betokens a consolidated Vedic-Brahmanic-Hindu complex that both resisted and succumbed to European controls across economics, politics, and diverse systems of knowledge. That the "Indian Archipelago" and such inventions as Shrivijaya Sumatra, Majapahit Java, retrenched Tengger, and Hindu-Bali were woven into and beyond these destinations intensifies and displaces the constant countering. Of course the things countered—Islam, Europe, etc.—are themselves counterformations as well, a fact displayed concretely in Chapter 3.

In an oppositioning process called Hindu history, frameworks of political, textual, and philosophical traditions have assumed contrastive proportions. Scriptively, Vedas become transformed to Brahmanas, to Upanishads, to Puranas; performatively, "ritual" is transformed to "myth," to "history," to "politics." (These labels trail dated periodizings of genres from colonialist standards.) Thus, formations of "Hinduism" and Hinduizations are not unstructured (to phrase the matter gently), yet they keep reopening. Might we say again that Tantrism denominates a dispersing and dialectical murmur beneath this very process, a field of possibilities from which more orthodox persuasions have been precipitated?

Chapter 2 concluded with a long list of sobriquets for Bali. We are now in a position to add another: "The land of Tantrism," *minus* any cultic complex—conjoining dairy products, plough agriculture, and parboiled rice—for its Tantrism to resist. The texts that Hindu-Balinese *tantras* have been texts-between are otherwise: Islam, nationalist standardizations, provincial or even district conformities (bureaucratically imposed). Balinese representations, shifting and reopening over time, have opposed different "others": the Dutch, Jakarta, the Ministry of Religions, tourists, ancestor-forgetting renunciation, Bali's "own" title-caste distinctions, and that "Kawified" image still lingering from the colonialist countertypes traced in the opening chapters. Tantric-Bali consists of affinities and extremes connecting rice production, rival houses, intense artisanal specializations, inter-regional temple networks, contrasts of hamlet/village/paddy organizations, and principles of allure and cure cycled, competitively and complementarily, among "functions" of priestly, political, and agricultural powers, along with waves of reformism, and commercial, governmental, and military developments. Because of the often hidden history of Tantric differences, their occurrence in places such as Bali becomes all the more beguiling.

It is safe to assume that every ritual process entails conflicts, occasional consensus, much difference, victimage, violence with its suffering, some generosity, and several kinds of tears and laughter. In the episodes selected for this book, I have tried neither to silence nor to privilege any of these intertwined tonalities. Nor have I shunned structures or, if that term offends, moments of structuration. My first work on colonialist constructions was prompted by the examples of C. Geertz's *The Social History of an Indonesian Town* and *Peddlers and Princes*, and L. Dumont's *Homo hierarchicus*, which began by rejecting British and American theories of caste that had domesticated hierarchy into a garden variety stratification (Boon 1977: pt. 1). Building upon a key allusion to *homo oeconomicus* in Mauss's *The Gift*, Dumont went on to scrutinize extreme values of ideological individualism implicit in the European categories of economic agency that underlie modernism (1977, 1982). It is "modernism" in this sense—associated with an individualist ideology of political economy—that is the strangest of all "Others" in Dumont's extensive comparative corpus (Boon 1982a: chap. 5).[1]

Dumont's (1977) critique of Western categories of political economy has implicated Adam Smith, John Locke, and Karl Marx, among all "us moderns." He has also compared the double apex of Hindu hierarchy (priest/king) to the peculiar historical circumstances fostering Christianity's pre-modern distinction between temporal and ecclesiastical (1982). As mentioned above, within the South Asian context Dumont places caste values amid undercurrent Tantrism, antithetical renunciation, and a historical conflux of centralizing polities and uncentralized exchange relations most apparent from the Indo-European/Dravidian divide. Sectarian movements are integral to this historical field of opposed values; yet each one, including Buddhism and Sikhism, like Brahmanism, considers its own position overarching. Dumont treats neither sects nor Tantric tendencies as simply reactionary to an inherent and intact cultural logic embodied in varna categories or ritual relationships of pure/impure relations. He is structuralist enough to consider resistance, too, prefigured; this fact alone makes it communicable. Nor does Dumont suggest that some rarified idea of holism tipped India's ideology toward Brahmans. Rather, history's engagements did so. Dumont makes just this point when summarizing developments of "Power and Territory" under Moghul controls (and later European ones—see Dumont 1980: 157). These historical circumstances stymied Rajas, checked their persuasiveness, and left the political (or ritual-rhetorical) field, so to speak, open for a relative ascendancy of Brahmans:

> In particular, much must have depended on the Brahmanic settlement, on the variety or varieties of Brahmans present—and earlier

on the extent of the popularity attained by Jainism and Buddhism. Similarly, it must be thought that in the "little kingdom" the king or chief would have been able to enjoy considerable power, patronage, and influence as against the Brahmans. Think of the commensality among the castes allied to the holders of power in a Malwa village. This can help to explain how the features of the royal way of life (meat diet, polygyny), although devalued in relation to the Brahman-ical model, have been able to survive and set an example to some castes for so long. By contrast, the disappearance of the king from vast regions under the Muslim domination must, as various authors have supposed, have increased the Brahman's influence, which then would have lacked any counter-balancing opposition. (1980: 155)

I mention these circumstances in conclusion because of parallels with con-texts of rivalrous authority discussed in this study: Bali's hybrid history, as well as medieval European society, early modern European courts, and Ro-mantic Europe's "kingdom of letters." In light of these specific cases, Chapter 6 recommended reading one era's "society" against a subsequent era's "court" against another era's "literature," to and fro. Transformations of our sense of the very boundary between text/context are required in fully dialectical com-parisons—both across times and between places, even ones like Tengger and Hindu-Bali that appear doctrinally linked. In all these examples—Indic Brah-manism, medieval chivalric society, Renaissance courts, Romantic literari-ness, Bali-not-Tengger (versus asymmetric houses of Eastern Indonesia)—the play of power seems too contradictory and multiple to fit snugly under any rubric of direct control or singular surveillance.

Scholar-critics today are understandably wary of the complicity of anthro-pology, area studies, literary theory, comparative history and philology, the media, and every variety of power-knowledge in colonialism and its after-maths. These misgivings have led many of us to advocate alternative demar-cations. To take just one example: "Third World Studies." But whether this fresh turf, or any other, can escape history's tangle of expropriations is doubt-ful (consider the source of the category "Third World"—see also Jameson 1986, Ahmad 1987). Lest we end by restoring an old-new dichotomy between "Third World Studies" and everything else, it may be worth accumulating an ever-shifting array—"Third World" among its constituents—rather than simply purging the despised past so to proclaim a clean slate.

It is in this spirit that I tolerate dated or outmoded hybrid boundaries such as "Malayo-Polynesian" or, some would add, "Indo-European." These con-structions, of course, have properly designated nothing more substantive than linguistic affinities, as do such successors as "Austronesian." They are partic-ularly ill-suited to convey "racial" identities, whatever those might be (if they existed). Such rubrics take on political value only positionally, commendable insofar as they oppose interests of old-colonialist, new-nationalist, and "X-world" standardizations as well. Taken alone, any one of them can be bogusly essentialized. The case of Indo-European, misconstrued as a supreme "Aryan" heritage, is just the most notorious example (Poliakov 1974). Any identity that starts isolating itself requires fracturing across cultures, epistemes, and areas, and their shifting relationships through time. Thus, the worth of a "monster" like Dumézil's "Indo-European ideology" is not to effect a synthesis but to keep overturning pat distinctions between Europe and Asia, Orient/ Occident, or any separating-off of places Indianized or Europeanized. A similar advantage attaches to Tantrism in the field of comparative ritual and textual heterodoxies that extend across East and West.

Instead of opting for a new demarcation, my readings—wary of purging relational holism, routing "systems," or banishing "structures"—have proceeded multiplyingly, often by threes or tripartites, as any Balinist or Indo-European might. Again I echo the late Roland Barthes, winkingly, at a nexus where he happens to be echoing (winkingly?) his own odd trio of Loyola, Fourier, and Sade:

> . . . Excess is not corrected by a return to balance, but according to a more careful physics, by a countermeasure: an oscillating instrument, the scale does not come to rest in perfect balance save through the interplay of a plus and a minus. . . .
>
> So replaced in the history of the sign, the Fourierist construction posits the rights of a baroque semantics, i.e., open to the proliferation of the signifier, infinite and yet structured. . . .
>
> It appears that the separation of languages is respected in every society, as though each one were a chemical substance and could not come into contact with a supposedly contrary language without producing a social conflagration. Sade spends his time producing these explosive metonymies. . . . Culture cannot be overthrown by a verbal coup; it can only be ruined—leave on the new field of language a few moments despoiled of their context and their superb past, and yet still possessing the highly elaborate grace, the delicious patina, the necessary distance which centuries of rhetorical courtesy have given them. This method of destruction (by the ill-timed citation of token throwbacks) constitutes Sade's *irony*. (1976: 74, 99, 148–49)

Which extreme—among faith (call it Brahma), utopics (call it Wisnu), and licentiousness or libertinage—does Barthes choose? Yes. Barthes' readings, moreover, were every bit as *lingam*-like as Siwa's disseminations. His intense combination of dispersal/retention could, ironically, be named nothing less than Tantric.

This book has hitched to heterodox rituals and texts ideas of reading and rhetoric drawn from Barthes and Kenneth Burke and companionable scholars. Some of my sources have been charged by their critics with overly structuralist inclinations (e.g., Dumont, Lévi-Strauss, even Hocart), or with consensualism in their leanings toward meanings (e.g., Geertz, even Weber). Yet these very figures, among the many frequently cited in these pages, have engendered in this reader half-hopes that the anthropology and history of things Indic, or Hinduized, or Europeanized (including the Indo-European, and parts of Indonesia) may keep tactically slipping past or out from under any national, historical, scholarly or academic "hegemony" (I mean domination)—each local, all-too-local, in its own right.

In this unlikely quest—if a quest be still allowed us occupants of Postmodernity—we cannot rest content simply to invoke universal order or to dream of optimum, healthy human solidarity—coeval, coequal, coauthoring, conversationalist, consociate (as in Fabian 1982). Comparative studies of the kind pursued in this book aspire instead, more realistically I profess, to a trickster-like status perhaps reminiscent of the Tengger's own composite Aji, encountered in Hefner's fine study of *Hindu Javanese*: a good king (which in *my* book means authored-by-subjects), indeed, but a lousy religious teacher.

Toward that serioludic end, these chapters and the icons of their title pages have crisscrossed not just Hindooisms and what they oppose, but times and texts, colonialisms and nationalisms, and Indonesian and Indo-European houses—impishly implicating themselves (chapters and icons and titles) in the parodoxes that research may more adequately specify but never solve. And never escape.

Since Chapter 1, that "totemism" discovered to be plotted unwittingly in A. R. Wallace's Western discourse on the Malay Archipelago has gradually given way to extreme "Tantrisms" transgressive of Hinduisms, Buddhisms, Western Hermetics, and anything gendered or age-graded. Tantrism is a ritual rhythm and rhetoric that the present text admires and would interpretively emulate. Yet so-called totemism and Tantrism are both nicknames after a fashion—European words coined from others' words, in part to subjugate exotic practices, but in part also (the part worth repeating) to query what is extra-orthodox in the very fact of cross-cultural encounters. *This very fact* is replete with struggles, deprivations, mysteries, recognitions, dominations, gifts, translations, and allure. Here may be enacted histories alternative to proprieties—*le propre*—read from any isolable affiliation. In this place (*topos*), never at rest, meaning-making remains polymorphous in its oppositionings, and bittersweet: a Tantric taste.

Postlude
Mead's Mediations:
Some Separations from the Sepik, by way of Bateson, on to Bali, . . . and Beyond

Not an engraver, I have traced, with apologies to Thurber, the representation of C. H. Wadding-ton's famous photograph of Margaret Mead (left) and Gregory Bateson (right), precisely as re-produced on p. 248 of the Pocket Book edition of *Blackberry Winter* (1975). The tracing, here reversed, nevertheless shows relative proportions accurately. A sign for separation is added.

Proprietary rights in photographs have inhibited my including an "original," the age of me-chanical (electronic) reproduction notwithstanding. Space did not permit illustrating the stature of New Zealander Reo Fortune, a third extreme.

That the icon next to this caption derives from a snapshot and not from the subjects themselves suggests affinities with visual emblems encountered earlier. Were either the outline or silhouette of the present author juxtaposed here, it would be immeasurably smaller and more featureless still.

Personally eschewing autobiography, I nevertheless salute Margaret Mead's medley of writings on her own life and the cultures it crossed. She became a destination of Hindu-Bali and, with Bateson, a particularly fit subject for rereading.

I was always glad that I was a girl. I cannot remember ever wanting to be a
boy.—Margaret Mead, inimitably (1975:265)

Semiology, in the wake of Saussure, stresses the mediatedness of all
codes, the open-ended systematics implicit in the communicability
(*langue*) of any emitted message (*parole*), and the principles behind the
processes of culture as performed. Strong stuff, highly debatable. Semiotics,
following upon Peirce, insists that knowledge happens as communicative
acts, thanks to selective symbolic substitutions of somethings-for-someones.
Any truth that is shared, any cultural truth, is received and thus transformable.
(Mertz and Parmentier 1985, M. Singer 1984). For Peirce there was no unmediated epistemological certainty: a stance resonant with antipositivism. So
where do we go from here?

One possible path is to push to extremes our sense of how intensely mediated matters can become. To this end this postlude uncorks an ethnological
nexus (plexus? sexus?) where everything appears intertwined—New Guinea,
Bali, Margaret Mead's marriages, Ruth Benedict's book, anthropology's future, respectability and deviance, *usw.* Yet by the same token and at the same
time, everything promises, praise be, to unravel.

Like Literature, Like Culture

However different their origins and ultimate implications, semiotics and
semiology join forces to accentuate complexity, prefiguredness, and multi-
determinacies, even indeterminacy, of every perception, every conception,
and (needless to say) every comparison. In literary theory and textual criticism Jonathan Culler has pursued a worthy policy of appeasement between
Saussure and Peirce: "Despite their different points of departure, Saussure and
Peirce agree that the task of semiotics is to describe those conventions that
underlie even the most 'natural' modes of behavior and representation"
(1981:24). He compares semioticians to Cassirer: they help us "think of our
social and cultural world as a series of sign systems, comparable with language" (1981:25).

Culler discerns common ground between semiotics and some high-critical
approaches often thought hostile: poststructuralist deconstruction, *rezeptions-
soziologie,* and other varieties of dialectic and/or transgression. There are certain costs to his consolidation. First, he opposes endeavors he calls semiotic
to "interpretation," a bogey-term in deconstruction's arsenal aimed against lo-
gocentrism. The artificiality of this tactic becomes apparent if we consider
scholars who restore nonabsolutist interpretation in the name of semiotics
(e.g. Geertz 1973, 1983; Steiner 1975) or who manage to merge hermeneutic
spurts with more fragmentary decodings (e.g., Ricoeur 1979; Frye 1981).
Second, Culler, again for commendable reasons, tends to isolate and monu-

mentalize literature, not, of course as a thing in itself (that would be both essentialist and logocentric), but as the sign system of, so to speak, sign systems. He underscores that "most complex of sign systems, *literature*" as "the most interesting case of semiosis" (1981:35). Culler echoes de Man, who deems literature "the only form of language free from the fallacy of unmediated expression (de Man 1971:17). Their reasons recall Lévi-Strauss's declaring "myth" the purest case of signification, freed from external constraints. For Lévi-Strauss (1964) myth "signifies signification," and for Culler "literature is itself a continual exploration of and reflection upon signification in all its forms" (1981:35). But we should recall that Lévi-Strauss admitted sundry ethnographic, ritual, and material orders into the domain he calls "myth," eventually posing four mega-orders of signification: myth, math, music, and language (1971). Although Lévi-Strauss once drew a line between myth and kinship or marriage systems (whose function of social solidarity he lodged in extrastructural constraints [Boon and Schneider 1974]), his concerted approach to "communications" of spouses, goods, and messages has facilitated dismantling false boundaries between domains of kinship and marriage, economy, and ecology, as well as myth, literature, and anything else cultural (everything that signifies is!).

To the nonsemiotic critic no literary fact seems more natural, direct, or unmediated than "reading a text." Similarly, to the nonsemiotic ethnographer no anthropological fact seems more natural, direct, or unmediated than "crossing a culture." Frowning on such naiveté, semioticians avow that texts are never read and cultures are never crossed innocently. Thus, literary semiotics can expose loaded expectations (or overextended textual strategies) in previous literary theory: for example, "the New Criticism's dream of a self-contained encounter between innocent reader and autonomous text is a bizarre fiction" (Culler 1981:11). Similarly, anthropological semiotics can reveal that functionalism helped produce and sustain the bizarre fiction of self-contained encounters between an innocent observer and an autonomous culture. To spotlight this fiction is not necessarily to purge it, but to recognize it as one among many possible other fictions (Boon 1982a: chaps. 1, 7).

In these respects then, culture is no different (or rather no less *différant*) than literature. This is not to suggest that culture is "merely literary," because thanks to the pursuits in literary theory that Culler handily reviews, the "merely" has definitively been taken out of *literaturnost* (it must be serious, it's Russian). Moreover, the kind of indeterminacy that characterizes "literariness" with its paradoxical play of specificities, rules, effacement, and intertextuality is culture's achievement as well. I would willingly proclaim anthropology's proper terrain to be inherent interculturality. Just as many critical theorists predict the restitution of literary history, I have implied that anthropology's future promises a renewed cultural history, precisely because, as Culler suggests for literature, "The historical perspective enables one to recognize the transience of any interpretation [present company self-included],

which will always be succeeded by other interpretations, and to take as object
of reflection the series of interpretive acts by which traditions are constituted
and meaning produced" (1981:13; see Boon 1977: pt. 1; 1982: chaps. 2,
5, 7).

Finally, the metaphor of reading, so vital to intertextual approaches, informs cultures as well. Geertz (1973), for example, has deftly read over the
shoulders of Balinese subjects reading their own cultural performances "as
texts" (on reading anthropological theories "as texts," see Boon 1972:11).
Culler summarizes relevant principles of intertextuality: "To read is always to
read in relation to other texts, in relation to the codes that are the products of
those texts and go to make up a culture" (1981:12). His statement applies
exponentially to observers crossing cultures, reading each culture as texts in
relation to other texts, each reader in turn a text to other readers in his or her
own culture and the cultures crossed: like Margaret Mead and her future husband and future ex-, all "reading" both New Guinea and Ruth Benedict to
understand the cultures they were encountering and each other (and each others' cultures) in the act of encountering them and each other. Our heightened
semiotic example offers a larger-than-life case—there were giants on the earth
in those days (1932)—which nevertheless typifies any and all crossing of cultures, however we protagonists (we readers) conspire to disguise the fact.

There is so much to read into the mediations here assembled, because the
wonder that was Margaret Mead wrote. She wrote incisively, yet repetitiously,
almost always in duplicate, almost always in duplicate, and often all over
again, whether soon after or years later. And she published what conventional
ethnographers ordinarily conceal. Thanks to Mead's rewriting and republish-
ing, particularly in *Blackberry Winter* (1975), we have at our disposal a storied ethnological episode in the form of an episodic story. Like every other
ethnological episode—even Derek Freeman researching Samoa (in order to
defame Mead?), while believing devoutly in Karl Popper—nothing is unmediated, however much displeasure this fact causes positivists. Margaret Mead,
above all ethnographers, deserves posthumously to be neither canonized
(*American Anthropologist* 1980) nor tarred and feathered (Freeman 1983).[1]
Her writing was too gutsy to be ennobled, too intricate to be formalized, and
too important to be dismissed. Rather we might embrace the odd *écriture* of
published letters, ethnography, journalism, and autobiography she has be-
queathed, so better to savor the semiosis at play whenever members of any
culture imagine and document (i.e., "read") any others. This much we readers
owe Mead's memory, embodied in her vibrant texts and the many other texts
and cultures hers touched.

My readers should note that in what follows I am unconcerned with Mead's
private side; such matters can be discussed best by those once intimate with
her. I employ nothing but her published materials; part of my topic is what *she*
found fitting to publicize, to commit to public print, to reveal to a readership.
While opinions on Mead's research vary dramatically (I personally admire

much of her work, including much of it on Bali), a suitable response to her host of *publications* can only be, on the surface, irreverent. This chapter is a comic piece and doubtless falls short as such, since I feel compelled to say so. I comically read Mead (plus Bateson and Fortune) very seriously. I find in their works a multivocal complexity worthy of the cultures they investigated.

All right always already (to invoke Derrida's eventless deconstruction), give us the facts: who, when, where, what, how (to invoke Kenneth Burke's dramatism of acts, actors, scenes, means, and motives). The story is well known, oft retold, indeed rewritten, albeit with variations (to invoke Lévi-Strauss's methodological *mythologiques*). The story: three anthropologists and the cultures they either knew or would soon know met at last; and in a peculiar, perhaps a dialectical way, they communicated, they exchanged, they "happened." Round about Christmas, 1932, upon the banks of the Sepik, Margaret Mead and Gregory Bateson, saturated with experiences of New Guinea, upon reading Ruth Benedict, devised one mediating theory (both cross-cultural and interpersonal) to compare surrounding societies, to antici-pate the contrastive ethos of Bali, and to rationalize Mead's eventual divorce from Reo Fortune and marriage to his rival Bateson. A full dramatistic inter-pretation (à la Burke) would pursue, ironically, the gamut of whos, whats, wheres, whens, and hows ("how": there's the thorn in semiotics' side). This brief chapter can barely scratch the semiotic surface. Still, I hope to demon-strate that one reason ethnographic description is so "thick" (to invoke Geertz invoking Ryle) is that it is unavoidably and multiply mediated, as are descrip-tions of those descriptions (like this one).[2]

Who Did What to Whom . . .

1. Margaret Mead
I suppose the perfect anthropologist is as cynical as a newspaper reporter.
—Gregory Bateson (Lipset 1980:132)

Mead was soon to become (to cite the newsreel narrator from *Citizen Kane*) "twice married, twice divorced," then to remarry; more anon.

2. Reo Fortune
When *Sorcerers of Dobu,* beautifully produced in England, finally reached us [in New Guinea], Reo looked at the book sadly and said, "that's the last book I'll ever write alone. You'll be in all the others."
—Margaret Mead (1975:217)

Fortune was Mead's second husband and her co-worker in New Guinea. His earlier six months of fieldwork in Melanesia resulted in a classic Mali-nowskian monograph, *Sorcerers of Dobu* (1963). Hints of rivalry with Bate-son dated from their work at Cambridge with A. C. Haddon:

Then professionally envious, Fortune suspected that Bateson was favored there for hereditary reasons. "Haddon is very kind to me," he
had written Margaret, "but he gave Gregory Bateson his mosquito
net." Fortune had also been highly critical of Bateson's first Iatmul
articles in *Oceania* and demanded to know why he had not been
given the opportunity to work in the most splendid culture along the
Sepik River. (Lipset 1980:135–36)

Fortune's own subsequent article in *Oceania* (1933) conceptualized cross-
cousin marriage rules as liens on the offspring of a partner-group. Later Mead
would manage simultaneously to praise Fortune (slightly), allusively to dis-
parage either Radcliffe-Brown's work on Australia or Lévi-Strauss's *The Elementary Structures of Kinship* (1969), and to appropriate still another major
development in anthropology—all in one artful reminiscence and editorial
remark: "Little notice was taken of his analysis, although twenty years later,
it was the kind of thing on which a man could found his career. But that
afternoon in Tchambuli we felt it was a triumph" (Mead 1975:235).

Fortune combined his precocious model of systematic marriage exchange
with an advanced view of incest in dialectic with specific social usages (not
just a crime against nature or standard stigma of abnormality). His entry in
Encyclopedia of the Social Sciences (1932) likened incestuous relations of
subjects to morganatic marriages of rulers: both the commoner who cohabits
chez lui and the king who weds a commoner and fathers disinherited offspring
fail "to produce an expected alliance between social groups." In tribute to
Fortune, and to demonstrate that my remarks on Mead in the preceding paragraph are intended as no slur, I now commit an equivalent act of self-centered
retrospection (unavoidable in both careers and autobiography) by placing
"Boon" at a critical juncture in anthropology, much as Mead placed herself.
Here goes: Had Fortune's ideas been immediately taken to Bali and investigated in light of that island's social structure and multivalent values of incest,
the conclusions of a later anthropologist (Boon 1977:140) might well have
arisen more than a generation earlier. However, neither Fortune nor his ideas
accompanied Mead to Bali (so much for Boon's bit of *Blackberry*). But Bateson did.

3. Gregory Bateson

Naven literally had been put together from bits and pieces, fragments of
myth and ceremony, recorded in the field as they happened, or as an informant thought to mention them. . . . To all these vicissitudes Bali presented
an extraordinary contrast. Bali was beautiful.

—Margaret Mead (1975:249)

Gregory Bateson: theoretician and fieldworker, *bricoleur* avant la lettre,
toujours précoce, and tall, very tall (Patagonian to Mead's *petite,* Great Dane
to her dachshund in an oft-published photo of this outlandish duo taken in
Ireland in 1934 [see Mead 1975:248; or Lipset 1980]). Here, however, we are

concerned less with Bateson's *taille* than his text (anyway, Fortune wasn't much shorter). In 1932 Bateson was an ethnographer with much disconnected data only eventually patched into *Naven* (1958).

Considerably more than a decade of devotedly assigning Bateson's *bizarrerie* to all ranks of readers has persuaded me it finally defeats any nutshell; *Naven*'s arguments recall nothing so much as Grandville's *Voyages en Zigzag*. Still, Lipset makes a noble effort at condensation:

> The book took its title from the name of an Iatmul congratulatory ritual which occurred in order to laud a sister's child for having performed some specified adult deed for the first time. At its most ornate, the ceremony involved transvestitism and ritualized homosexuality. The mother's brother of the initiate, dressed in bedraggled skirts, would offer his buttocks to the sister's son, and would also simulate the female role in mock copulation with his wife. (1980:140–141)

Bateson revised his own summary of matters in a renowned second epilogue:

> The *naven* ceremonial, which is an exaggerated caricature of a complementary sexual relationship between *wau* [mother's brother] and *laua* [sister's son], is in fact set off by overweening symmetrical behavior. When *laua* boasts in the presence of *wau*, the latter has recourse to *naven* behavior. . . . Contexts in which *wau* uses *naven* to control that breach of good manners of which *laua* is guilty when he presumes to be in a symmetrical relationship with *wau* [include] . . . when *laua* is a baby and is being held in *wau*'s lap, if the baby urinates, the *wau* will threaten *naven*. (Bateson 1958:289–90)

Naven ties ritual theatrics to the specialized roles and social differentiation evident in Iatmul's regularized "sense of paradox, a sense of direct dualism—that everything has a sibling—and a sense of diagonal dualism—that everything has a symmetrical counterpart" (Lipset 1980:141).

In 1932, before *Naven*, Bateson showed Mead that there was something basically in-between about the Iatmul and their Tchambuli neighbors (today called the Chambri—see Gewertz 1983). In a letter of 1933 Mead perceptively opposed such high Sepik societies to the agonistic Mundugumor, with their dearth of regularized rivalries and conspicuous eruptions of outright hostility:

> Now in Tchambuli we have the opposite kind of society, one which knows all about euphoria and all the rules of avoiding conflict. Dual organization and cross-cousin marriage, and the two wives of a man always come from the same clan, if possible, which means there are not two opposed kin groups back of half-brothers. (1977:143–44)

She and Bateson were alert to historical upheavals along the Sepik (recently reviewed by Gewertz [1983] and others); for example:

> There were three divisions of the Tchambuli that once had been cere-
> monially and socially separate. In the past they had exchanged their
> criminals and delinquents to be executed as first-kills by the boys of
> the other groups. About twenty years earlier, the Iatmul had chased
> the Tchambuli away and had appropriated their land; each of the di-
> visions had run away to a different set of trade friends. They had been
> able to return, under government protection, only a few years be-
> fore. . . . Exhilarated by their success, they built a string of beautiful
> new men's houses all along the lake shore. . . . Even now the three
> divisions were exceedingly rivalrous. (Mead 1972:232–33)

Mead, Fortune, and Bateson thus focused on ritual divisions, seeking systematic underpinnings in both social organization and ethos of whatever cultural
arrangements endured.

Certain Sepik societies seemed to institutionalize "indecision" between en-
acting conflict openly and suppressing conflict through regularized alliance
and both symmetrical and complementary exchange. The Iatmul in particular
combined ritual and social options elsewhere antithetical. Although *Naven* has
mystified two generations of readers, today the book provides an almost eerie
prognosis of current insights into the repertory of forms selectively distributed
over New Guinea space and through New Guinea time. Shirley Lindenbaum,
to take one exceptional scholar, ties the ludic ambiguities of *naven* to transformations between: (1) ritualized male homosexuality (more precisely, male-to-
male semen transmission), where men exchange both sisters and sperm in
ultra-direct cycles; and (2) ceremonial exchange of shell, feather, and pig valuables in long cycles of more "proper" economies, marked by bride-price
rather than sister-exchange. Lindenbaum (1987) reviews the work of Bateson,
Tuzin (1977), Handelman (1979), and much controversial New Guinea material. She suggests that the Iatmul illustrated a transition (whether inherently
fleeting or potentially long-term) between (1) a system of nervous equality,
implemented as sister-exchange plus homosexuality, and (2) a future of nervous inequality, geared to bride-price and incipient commodity-wealth, with
superior wife-giver creditors. The fascinating cultural variations revolving
around semen/blood now impressively documented for New Guinea seem
concentrated into the play of *Naven:* fading sister-exchange between moieties,
vestiges of semen-exchange between male affines, anticipations of complementary ranked rivalries based on bride-price. In Lindenbaum's analysis *naven*'s "curiosity" pervades the whole of New Guinea's "gender-inflected universe":

> This is a curious homosexual relationship, since the male of a senior
> generation acts as a "wife" to a junior. However, the message is not
> one of direct dominance, but of switched-circuit dominance, for the
> Wau [mother's brother] offers his buttocks in a burlesque manner.
> Naven behavior is ironic, and is thus only apparently self-depreca-
> tory. . . . As a ludic ritual of reversal, it is a twisted reassertion of a

dominance order of the general homosexual pattern, a communication the Laua [sister's son] recognizes, for he hurries to present the Wau with a gift of compensating valuables. (1987:234)

Bateson's fractured book about a fractured ceremony (and society?) becomes a case study in vicissitudes between passing systems of immediate gratifications and an emergent system of economic "delay." How perfectly *Naven* has come to suit what we now think we know about *naven,* about Iatmul rivalries, and about the social and political transformations in the history of New Guinea cultures.

Naven's composite fragments retrospectively seem suited as well to the theoretical and professional posture of Bateson himself: always in-between. He was never quite functionalist in Malinowski's way nor even quite structural-functionalist in the fashion of Radcliffe-Brown. Rather, through a sense of cybernetics, Bateson converted his views of Iatmul gender and social structure into a studiously abnormal career, celebrated in *Steps to an Ecology of Mind* (1972):

> If functional analysis stressed the unity of societies, Bateson was interested in creating a language for the analysis of dynamic—yet synchronic—processes of sustained differentiation. . . . Bateson's was a view of observable social relations oscillating or perhaps vibrating, during which a process of intensification of role occurs. . . . ["Schismogenesis"] stood for processes of disintegration or of increased differentiation. He further distinguished between two fundamental patterns of "schismogenesis": complementary patterns in which two roles differ but coincide [*in extremis,* schism], as in dominance-submission, exhibitionism-spectatorship, feebleness-succorance, master-apprentice, and various classes of feudal hierarchy; and symmetrical patterns in which both sides exhibit competitively similar behavior [*in extremis,* heresy], as in boasting, armaments races, and wars. In the complementary cases, a dominant person or group in an interacting pair will become more assertive while the submissive one becomes more passive. . . . In the symmetrical case, progressive change will occur as each actor [party] reacts identically but increases the degree of reaction [i.e., ups the ante]. (Lipset 1980:144)

Naven documented the conjunction of complementary and symmetrical schismogenesis and their ritual control through ceremonial short-circuits. Moreover, the book possibly smacks of the schismogenesis Bateson had lived out when encountering Fortune and Mead. Mead was probably, as usual, right: after all that fragmentary fieldwork and personal stress experienced along the Sepik (described later), she and Bateson needed something whole, less fraught with vicissitude, even beautiful. They needed Bali, or what they thought Bali would be: not New Guinea. Or rather they needed to think something was not New Guinea, whether or not it was not.

Bateson later formulated (in 1949) the stressless circumstances they had needed to imagine (in 1932) and to find in Bali (in 1936). He devised a model of the steady state and "nonprogressive change":

> The next step toward making our model resemble Balinese society more closely is clearly to postulate in the character structure of the individuals and/or in the contexts of their daily life those factors which will motivate them toward maintenance of the steady state not only when they speak in council, but also in their other interpersonal relations. . . . Balinese society is nonschismogenic. . . . The Balinese child learns to avoid cumulative interaction. . . . The social organization and contexts of daily life are so construed as to preclude competitive interaction. . . . The Balinese ethos [values] . . . the clear and static definition of status and spatial orientation, and of balance and such movement as will conduce to balance. (Bateson 1972:125)

Although Bateson documented institutions and myths indicative of Balinese cumulative change (Boon 1977:55), in the realm of interaction he beknighted Bali as "balanced"—albeit in the best of his work, precariously balanced ("equilibrated"), but balanced nonetheless. To understand how Bateson's influential part-truth about Bali's nonschismogenesis arose from the Sepik requires returning to Mead's darkest and strangest of texts (inexplicably called by the *Washington Post* "brilliantly clear"!): *Blackberry Winter.*

Across Cultures and Husbands

> I was thirty-four and Gregory was thirty-one. I had what amounted to a lifetime of completed work behind me; Gregory had a lifetime of work he wanted to do, and felt he had not yet done, ahead of him. We looked about the same age—a little younger than we were. But in many ways there was a tremendous age difference between us. I had grown up at eleven.
> —Margaret Mead (1972:246)

There'll never be another Mead. As a graduate student attending meetings of the British Association for the Advancement of Science in Toronto, she had quickly noticed a basic "fiction" in the claims to authority by comparative scholars: "Everyone there had a 'people' to whom he referred in his discussion. . . . I too wanted to have a 'people' on whom I could base my own intellectual life" (1975:135). She outdid herself. By the time of our renowned episode, she had accumulated Samoa, Manus (Admiralty Islands), the Omaha, and two New Guinea cultures: the "mountain Arapesh" and the Mundugumor. Moreover, her "crash of illuminations" (1975:244) was beginning among the Tchambuli; and with Bateson she would add the Iatmul and finally Bali to this impressive list.

We catch up with Mead and Fortune among the Mundugumor. The psychology of the ethnographers is beginning to match the cultures they report in petty envy and territorialism sufficient to shame a stickleback:

> While we [Mead and Fortune] were still in Arapesh we had received the issues of *Oceania* in which Gregory Bateson's short report on the Iatmul was published, and neither of us thought it was very good. Reo still felt, as he had earlier, that Gregory had been overpreferred simply because he came out of the Cambridge tradition. . . . We knew that Gregory was back on the Sepik—and why, Reo demanded, should he, and not we, have that magnificent culture? . . . So when we decided to go to the Sepik, I concentrated on making sure that we would not invade Gregory's territory. I insisted that we, Reo and I, go somewhere where no one else had done any work. (1975:220–22)

So they bypassed the middle Sepik, proceeding to the recently pacified and therefore dispirited Mundugumor, whose ritual gender segregation had atrophied under government restrictions. Mundugumor culture offered little to Mead's theory of contrasting sex styles:

> Fierce possessive men and women were the preferred type; warm and cherishing men and women were culturally disallowed. . . . As in Arapesh, both men and women were expected to conform to a single type: the idea of behavioral styles that differentiated men and women was wholly alien. As far as my central problem was concerned, I felt completely stalemated. (Mead 1975:224)

But no setback hampered Mead for long. Mundugumor's mismatch to her expectations itself yielded the distended framework of *Sex and Temperament* (1963), her triumphant escape from seeming stalemate:

> I found three tribes all conveniently within a hundred mile area. In one, both men and women act as we expect women to act—in a mild parental responsible way; in the second, both act as we expect men to act—in a fierce initiating fashion; and in the third, the men act according to our stereotype for women—are catty, wear curls and go shopping, while the women are energetic, managerial, unadorned partners. (1963:i)

In her preface of 1952 Mead acknowledges that many readers felt the scheme was "too pretty. I must have found what I was looking for." She then charges them with misunderstanding how anthropology works; she defends her results empirically, yet retains passages that almost imply an invisible hand guiding her (Fortune fading) from Arapesh, to Mundugumor, and then to Tchambuli's paler variation on Iatmul splendor:

> But when it is realized that whereas the Arapesh have standardized the personality of both men and women in a mould that, out of our traditional bias, we should describe as maternal, womanly, unmas-

culine, the Mundugumor have gone to the opposite extreme and, again ignoring sex as a basis for the establishment of personality differences, have standardized the behavior of both men and women as actively masculine, virile, and without any of the softening and mellowing characteristics that we are accustomed to believe are inalienably womanly—then the historical accident that led us to study [the Mundugumor] rather than some other people is the more remarkable. (1963:132)

Meanwhile, back in *Blackberry Winter,* still fearing stalemate in 1932 (as recalled in 1973), she and Fortune turned their backs on the malignant mothers of Mundugumor and returned toward the middle Sepik, Bateson's scene.

This stretch of the Sepik is wide and deep with fens that stretch far back from both banks, and only here and there, on slightly rising land, tall trees make a dark green splash against the sky. We sailed past Tambunam, deep in shade, the most impressive village on the Sepik and one of the most beautiful villages in New Guinea with its great dwelling houses that have rattan faces woven into the gables and its great double-peaked men's house set in a green plaza planted with crotons. Again Reo and I responded with a pang of envy. This was a culture we would like to have studied. (Mead 1975:226)

The landscape is evoked otherwise in Mead's less lush letter of 1933 (published in 1977): "The Sepik itself is a wide, monotonous and rather dirty yellow river, remarkable only for its varying load of drifting islands which have detached themselves from the half-submerged fen lands and have drifted out through some waterway and finally will float out to sea" (1977:138–39). But *Blackberry Winter* is not a letter; it is a psychocultural, a spiritual, voyage, whose style and organization conform to Mead's idea of her own personal navigation: always (retrospectively) on course, even-keeled, never just floating anywhere, much less out to sea.

Here beginneth the first line of the sixteenth chapter of *Blackberry Winter* (1975):

Late in the afternoon the launch pulled in at Kankanamun, the Iatmul village where Gregory Bateson was working. (p. 227)

This is our principal text, dissected to facilitate commentary on the mediations at work. I aim to "unread" these pages, to detect what makes them "written," if only to belie the *Washington Post*'s claim, unfair to Mead's prose, that they are "utterly readable," an affirmation semiotics doubts for any text or any culture, which must be multiply mediated, and often darkeningly.

Mead recalls that Bateson's soothing, sympathetic words contrasted to Fortune's fierceness (directed against both his own illnesses and Mead's), much as middle Sepik landscapes and cultures contrasted to Mundugumor scenes and lives. Her palpable relief is understandable:

> Gregory was floundering methodologically; we were feeling starved
> for theoretical relevance. And for a year none of us had met anyone
> with whom we could talk about what we were doing. In addition, I
> felt wonderfully released from prison—the prison of that Arapesh
> mountaintop, where I had not been able to take a step outside the
> village for seven and a half months, and the nightmare prison of the
> disintegrating, hostile, and mosquito-ridden village. (p. 229)

All three pains—the dearth of conversation, the starving for theory, and the
suffering under both Fortune's and the Mundugumor's psychological at-
tacks—are assuaged during their reconnaisance with the Washkuk. In this dis-
mal episode Mead's own bent toward embittered analytics persists forty years
later:

> Reo woke to hear Gregory and me talking. There is much to be said
> for the suggestion that the true oedipal situation is not the primal
> scene but parents talking to each other in words the child does not
> understand. And by then Gregory and I had already established a
> kind of communication in which Reo did not share. (p. 230)

Here Fortune is juvenilized with respect to Mead and Bateson; above we saw
Bateson later suffering the same fate with respect to Mead alone. Her writing
often remembers herself as unnaturally (unchronologically) senior to some
male or even to other females, insofar as mature motherhood moved her ahead
of girlish infertility (see below). That night on the Sepik, fearing a Washkuk
attack, Mead began communicating with one rival to excommunicate another;
then came the morning after:

> The situation was made more difficult the next day when we began to
> climb the Washkuk mountain. I was walking barefoot because that is
> the only way I can climb a New Guinea mountain. On the way Greg-
> ory proposed that we have a swim, assuming, with the Bohemian
> standards of his university youth, that we would all swim in the
> nude—a suggestion that horrified Reo. Gregory came out of a world
> in which multiple and complex love affairs were commonplace; Reo
> came from a world [New Zealand] in which the sternest Victorian
> values still obtained. It had been hard for him to cope with the fact
> that I had, after all, been married before and that when he married
> me, he was, in his own view, taking another man's wife. And it was
> always hard for him to cope with rivalry at any level. The fact that he
> himself was enjoying Gregory's company as much as I was did not
> help at all. (p. 230)

The plot thickens; the semiotic quickens. What rightly wary reader could say
whether the "scene" appropriate to such reminiscence and insinuation is the
Sepik or Vienna? Does tacky recollection warrant tacky interpretation? What
mediated Mead's own sense of rivalry at the time and/or forty years later?
Regardless, it is important to note that her absorbing writing both stems from

and engenders suspicious readings. *Blackberry Winter* is compelling because
it invites sly decipherings and smoking-gun explanations, yet never quite de-
livers them. And this is the book *Newsweek* called "warmly captivating"!

The "complex reversals" occurring in Fortune's, Bateson's, and Mead's relationships gain ascendancy in a pivotal nexus in Anglo-American anthropology, represented in a sequence of rapid fades: one paragraph signaling *Naven*'s
masculine-feminine contrast; three paragraphs of "falling in love"; a salute to
Benedict (plus Jung and Mendel); finally, a scheme of New Guinea cultural
variations with Bali ushered onstage as New Guinea's antithesis (or antidote).
Coupled with Mead's play of writing-remembrance, this "passage" comprises
a perhaps unwitting dialectics woven through a seamless text that deserves
resolute unstitching.

1. Naven. "Mother's brothers . . . mimed a grotesque femininity, while
father's sisters, decked out in male finery . . . noisily grated their husband's
serrated lime sticks in and out of their lime gourds. . . . [in] a type of
masculine-feminine contrast that was quite familiar to the Euro-American
world" (Mead 1975:236).

2. The "triangular situation." Mead initiates a litany of wonder questions:

> What if . . . other kinds of innate differences . . . cut across sex
> lines? And what if a society . . . could place its emphasis on one
> type of temperament, as among the Arapesh and the Mundugumor,
> or could, instead, emphasize a special complementarity between the
> sexes, as the Iatmul and the Tchambuli did? And what if the expec-
> tations about male-female differences, so characteristic of Euro-
> American cultures, could be reversed [here her rhetorical excitement
> intensifies], as they seemed to be in Tchambuli [i.e., brisk women,
> catty men]? (1975:236)

Few humans (all too human) could have avoided the obvious interpretive
transgression while "cooped up together in the tiny eight-by-eight foot mosquito room." Mead reports neither regret nor shame that "we moved back and
forth between analyzing ourselves and each other, as individuals, and the cultures that we knew and were studying, as anthropologists must." Then the
earthshaking *aperçu:* "Gregory and I were close together in temperament—
represented, in fact, a male and a female version of a temperamental type that
was in strong contrast to the one represented by Reo" (Mead 1975:237). By
this account Mead and Bateson conceived of themselves as a gender system at
the personality level like the Arapesh at the cultural level: male-female, both
sympathetic (but neither any more "feminine" than an Arapesh man was maternal; rather, a gender distinction *within* a temperamental type). Fortune is
thus isolated in his fierce Mundugumor-likeness, with no opposite-gender
equivalent: the odd man, now out. During this outrageous, this naive

"struggle to arrive at a new formulation" (the news of which would be immediately wired to Boas, so thrilled were its discoverers), the inevitable, as is its wont, happens: "Gregory and I were falling in love. . . ." Not to worry, however: ". . . but this was kept firmly under control [!] while all three of us tried to translate the intensity of our feeling into better and more perceptive field work" (Mead 1975:237). Such are the wonders of the scientific method. Ultimately their sense of "cultural differences between Arapesh, Mundugumor, Tchambuli, and Iatmul" becomes the model for "differences in temperamental emphases in the three English-speaking cultures—American, New Zealand, and English—that we represented" (1975:237). Shine on, shine on Sepik moon.

3. Benedict's book. Mead affirms Benedict's Sapirian sense of cultures that select "only certain human traits to emphasize"; but she notes Benedict's failure systematically to relate "culturally patterned types of personality" (1975:237–38). She corrected this deficiency with Jung's fourfold psychological typology.

4. The necessity of Bali. Her wedding of Benedict and Jung produces a scheme of complementarity either within or across different cultures' gender differences: Dominant Iatmul men complement (are temperamentally opposite from) submissive Iatmul women; likewise Tchambuli men complement Tchambuli women (with the traits reversed); Mundugumor men and women together complement Arapesh men and women together (no temperamental contrast by gender characterizes either). The scheme sports one more axis, the oddest: Manus men and women also are not distinguished from each other by temperament: both are (we must infer from the scheme) somewhat schismogenic, to borrow Bateson's term. This slot leads to the complement (temperamental opposite) of Manus: no gender difference, and *not* schismogenic; and this is the slot labeled "Missing: no culture in which both men and women belonged to fit here." Presto, Bali:

> We came to the conclusion that there must be one kind of culture of which we had no good example. I made a guess that Bali would exemplify that missing type. When at last we went to Bali, it turned out that my guess had been an accurate one. (Mead 1975:238)

In Mead's recall of her own prefigurings of what was foreordained to fulfill the scheme, readers can never be sure whether she is invoking science, fate, or both.

"Here endeth the lesson" of Chapter 16—to invoke Mead's first husband, Luther, an Episcopalian priest, her partner in a "student marriage, out of which neither a book nor a child had come" (Mead 1975:316). Mead nevertheless remained Episcopalian, and in fact later in life helped preserve parts of the traditional Anglican *Book of Common Prayer* (with this move I am totally sympathetic). What a woman: an irresistible persona! Her writing merited and merits all the attention we can muster.

"Meadiations"

I can't find any carbon, so I don't know whether I told you that the Mundugumor proved a most perfect study in the pathology of incest.
                                         —Margaret Mead, letter of 1933 (1977)

As we have seen, Margaret Mead was a fieldworker-writer who always climbed a New Guinea mountain barefoot because that's the only way she could climb one, even when deciding that Washkuk was not the place she and Fortune wanted to work. Here, moreover, was a writer who seldom lacked carbon, but when she did confessed even that. Indeed, with apologies to Gertrude Stein (at last invoked), Margaret Mead was a fieldworker-writer who was always glad she was a girl and, judging from her written recall, was almost always sure she would be a mother and always glad that she was afterwards—at least so she remembered, or writes that she did, decades later in *Blackberry Winter* in a chapter exultantly titled (following the account of her miscarriage in Tchambuli) "On Having a Baby." The bald identification of professional world and intimate life manifest in Mead's correspondence, journalism, autobiography, and even ethnography is a thing apart: it is what makes her work both courageous and somehow "American." She employed the oldest rhetorical device (and a good one) in autobiography: amalgamating the vantages of subject reminiscing and self reminisced. Mead thereby heightened the drama of her resolve and her ethnological calling:

I took pride in being unlike other children and in living in a household that was itself unique. But at the same time I longed to share in every culturally normal experience. . . . I longed to live out every bit of it. But I also wanted to be very sure that I would always be recognized as myself. (1975:18–19)

If being American is having it both ways—(1) normal self, (2) unlike all the others—then Mead was, according to her recollection, virtually fated to become Ms. American *anthropologiste*.

But how could Mead's self-presence be both authoritatively "at home" and exotically "abroad"? She managed to have her self/other both ways through a play of deviance so convoluted it wound up straight and narrow. Mead deviated from then-normal American womanhood by wanting a career; she deviated from normal careeerwomanhood by wanting a baby. End to end the two deviations consolidated into a woman with a child (normal-looking motherhood), but with a difference (fieldwork plus publications). Mead achieved a double-barreled deviance: like two wrongs that do too make a right. It was this knack that she recalled sharing with Bateson:

> Both Gregory and I felt that we were, to some extent, deviants, each
> within our own culture. Many of the forms of aggressive male behav-
> ior that were standardized in English culture did not appeal to him.
> My own interest in children did not fit the stereotype of the American
> career woman or, for that matter the stereotype of the possessive,
> managing American woman and mother. It was exciting to strip off
> the layers of culturally attributed expected behavior and to feel that
> one knew at last who one was. However, Reo did not have as great a
> sense of revelation about himself. (Mead 1975:240)

(That Fortune just *refused* to strip.) Such exaggeration of roles and reversals
is enough to make an Iatmul *laua* blush. Mead writes how she contrived to
transcend Momism while achieving motherhood and how Bateson surpassed
the mere man's man. Together they would produce an alternative family-life
style. Their alliance would be a marriage of misfits that paradoxically would
uplift the standard norms of the cultures that produced them. The scheme's
Naven-like reversals declare Bateson counter-British and Mead counter-
American, despite the advantages their respective indigenous backgrounds afford, which dictate where they should reside. Always, whether advocating
breastfeeding or opposing (given the chance) circumcision—the arch-couple
meant to apply exotic field wisdom to homelife:

> We had already decided that if the baby were a boy, we would make
> our home in England, because the English did a better job of bringing
> up a boy; but if it were a girl, we would live in the United States,
> where girls are better off [there's objectivity]. . . . We had also dis-
> cussed circumcision, which Gregory disapproved of, but the ques-
> tion was left unresolved. When the cable was sent, "Mary Catherine
> Bateson, born December 8th," Gregory started to cable, in a return
> message, "Don't circumcise," and then, remembering he had a
> daughter, cabled instead, "Don't christen." (Mead 1975:280–281)

Again, the *wau* out*wau*ed.

So Mead remembered and/or wrote; actually, so she wrote remembering (to
invoke *Tristes Tropiques*).[3] Mead also wrote that she married Fortune when
she temporarily anticipated a future without children, only to arrive amongst
Mundugumor men and women, whose unparentlike temperament held a
"strange kind of fascination for Reo" but renewed her resolve to prove her
doctors wrong, to produce an offspring, and to raise her right: "Perhaps after
all I could have a child; perhaps I could manage it" (1975:268). One subplot
threading its way through *Blackberry Winter* is Mead's fecundity versus her
fieldwork: could they harmonize and who would accompany her in either or
both? With Bateson Mead achieves fieldwork *cum* fecundity. But the child's
ultimate significance *in the book* is that she is the mother of Mead's grandmother's great-great-grand-daughter.

Either gender of offspring would have distinguished Mead from certain female colleagues, particularly Ruth Benedict, who remained barren: "A few friends . . . objected to any discussion [by Mead in *An Anthropologist at Work* (1959)] of the way Ruth had felt about her childlessness. But this she had written about at length and over many years' time in her [private] diaries and journals" (Mead 1975:313). By Mead's standards Benedict was barren of full-fledged fieldwork too, another flaw worth publicizing. Mead portrays Benedict near the end of her life (1948), suddenly given a chance to visit several European cultures about which she had theorized during World War II:

> Should she go? Should she, in the middle of the project, take the risk? She intensely wanted to go. All the war years of trying to see through other peoples' eyes, without fieldwork, had built up a great accumulated passion to find out for herself whether these patterns so laboriously worked out at a distance were actually related to a reality she could observe with her own senses. So we said, "Go! If this is what you want to do, do it." For this was what she had said to us during her teaching years. (1959:437)

Even during the many generous moments of this moving account, Mead somehow portrays herself as more successful than Benedict in practicing what the latter preached. Moreover, whatever she is writing-remembering, the mark of Mead is candor—incessant, relentless (one is here tempted to say ruthless) candor: about herself (or so we are to assume) and about those she deemed her others, whether Bateson, Benedict, Manus, Tchambuli. . . . A signal difference between Margaret Mead and Ruth Benedict is that the following is something that Mead could (and did) write: "I was always glad that I was a girl. I never wanted to be a boy" (1975:265); while it is something that Benedict didn't (and doubtless couldn't) write. That Mead could and did, without apology, without self-subversion, write remarks like that represents her own excess, her own scandal, her own deviance, but not the one she recognized in print.

Blackberry Winter identifies Mead's dual fruit of research and offspring. It confesses a life and work that is "closely interwoven" but never discloses that this is so because they are *written*. Mead selectively orders her marriages and fieldworks so to orchestrate a continuity of wisdom stretching from her own grandmother to her own granddaughter (Mead's "own" remains, as always, the central connection). The book's implicit plot-pattern reminds this reader of Balinese intrafamilial transmigration (rebirth in Balinese beliefs occurs within an ancestor group)—but with a matrilineal, yea a matriarchal, inflection. No detail fails to mesh Mead's career with her descent: "I discovered when I had a child of my own that I had become a biased observer of small children" (1975:308). Luckily, this bias postdated her intensive field studies of early socialization. Thus, not just her fecundity but her *delayed* fecundity gains sanctification through retrospect.

Many of us, like lesser Goethes or retroactive Rousseaus, from time to time

review life's passages as though they concealed a *bildungs* format. "Autobiography" implies writing a life and its work into some sort of religious and/or
literary shape. It is Mead's apparent absence of irony (in our day and age!)
toward the traditional devices of this genre (although I am not altogether convinced that her narrative voice was perfectly straight) that makes much of
her work so extreme, even monumental. Mead's Americanesque quasi-
straightforwardness is, to paraphrase Lévi-Strauss's comment about the "exotic" tropics, not so much "domestic" as out-of-date. Through ethnography
she accomplished the restoration of an old-fashioned style of story: a purpose-
ful life-career. By so doing she vastly augmented anthropology's public, for
which achievement both her profession and her readership should be grateful.

   Less out-of-date than *Blackberry Winter,* equally fascinating, and at times
more *Naven*esque is Mead's commentary on Benedict "at work" (1959).
Mead's exquisite phrases capture Benedict's "gentle, wraithlike figure, her
hair going prematurely grey and never staying in place, dressed with a kind of
studied indifference, just deaf enough to miss a great deal of what was being
said before others recognized it, and painfully shy—the beauty of which had
been hers as a young girl misted over by uncertainty and awkwardness"
(1959:9). Mead nearly confesses her own feelings of rivalry, almost suggests
they were reciprocal, and occasionally conveys the ambivalence in this kind
of student-teacher relationship. One example comes when Benedict, who sent
Mead earmarked passages from Nietzsche to help improve her shipboard
cramming, passed aloof, if not condescending, judgment on Mead's aesthetic
acumen:

> One of the most violent disagreements she and I ever had was over
> the ceiling of the Sistine Chapel—whose outsized demigods repelled
> me and delighted her—as she [Benedict] smiled mischievously, say-
> ing, "I knew you wouldn't like it." (Mead 1959:85)

Here Mead—whose writings are nurture to us all—perhaps approached a
self-directed wink. But if her texts concealed any irony, it was that of a parent—preserving the necessary mysteries (Santa Claus and so forth), but only
for the children's sake. She sympathized with Benedict's plight and cited
many of Edward Sapir's quiet love letters (reciprocated) to unhappily married
Benedict, including this perception: "There is something cruel, Ruth, in your
mad love of psychic irregularities. Do you not feel that you extract your loveliness from a mutely resisting Nature who will have her terrible revenge?"
(Sapir, cited in Mead 1959:85). Yet Mead's final response to her teacher's
poetic flickerings was to document them. There remained her own steady
flame of character that she assumed should illuminate the road to professional
anthropology's future. This fact explains the advice she wrote Benedict about
simplifying *Patterns* by cutting out its "scraps" of Boas and Lowie (Boon
1982a:106); she recommended Benedict make it a single-theme essay on three
peoples, like she herself was shortly to write in *Sex and Temperament.* Twenty

years later her highest praise for Benedict's classic on Japanese culture (1946) was that Benedict had at last followed her earlier instructions:

> In [*The Chrysanthemum and the Sword*] there were no ghosts of old-fashioned anthropological scholarship, no demands that predecessors who had not influenced her work must nevertheless be mentioned. There was no one whom she trusted more than herself to say what she should write or how she should write it. The work of her students and younger contemporaries had become so much a part of her thinking. (1959:425–26).

Patterns of Culture was mentioned briefly in *Sex and Temperament* (1963:284). Decades later *Blackberry Winter* expanded the acknowledgment by tracing highlights in Benedict's quest for an appreciation of deviance; here are the relevant fragments:

> When Ruth Benedict sent us a first draft of *Patterns of Culture*, Reo commented that it was not enough to say that cultures are different; the point was that they arc "incredibly different." . . . She had recognized, with a sense of revelation, the fundamental differences between those American Indian cultures that emphasize ecstasy . . . and those that emphasize moderation and balance. . . .
> Even earlier she had made the point that it is those individuals whose characteristics are too far removed from the norm of their culture who find their culture deeply uncongenial. . . . In *Coming of Age in Samoa* I wrote a chapter called "The Deviant," in which I described girls whose temperament—defined as an extra intensity of response . . . made them deviants from the expected Samoan personality. (Mead 1975:212–13)

Benedict's own extra intensity of response inclined her to long for a "really undiscovered country"; ironically, or perhaps consequently, she stayed home. Mead on the other hand may have always been glad she was a girl and almost always sure she would be a female mother; but, American enough to want it all, she apparently also always wanted to be a deviant, and not just to write about them in Samoa. We have seen how she managed to stake her claim in even this shaky territory: "It was clear to me that I was a deviant in the sense that I had a much greater interest in the kinds of things in which most women not committed to careers were interested" (1975:213). But this is to let so-called deviance in through the backest of back doors. While Mead displayed her own brand of "extra intensity of response," it was hardly "Benedictine." Still, she remained alert enough to Benedict's deeper riddles to publish them:

> And I puzzled about the contrasts between Ruth and myself, especially when she made what seemed to me contradictory remarks, such as that it was quite impossible to imagine me as a man and that "you'd make a better father than a mother." (1975:214)

Now what could shadowy Benedict possibly have meant, given that steadfast, unenigmatic Margaret was and always had been glad she was a girl?

Concluding Indeterminate Questions

The laua [sister's son] makes the symmetrical gesture [implying rivalry] and *wau* [mother's brother] responds not by overbearing complementary dominance [competitively] but by the reverse of this—exaggerated submission [a metaresponse that effectively places *laua*'s gesture in quotation marks]. *Or should we say the reverse of this reverse? Wau's* behavior is a caricature of submission [effectively placing itself in quotation marks?].
                                                    —Gregory Bateson (1958:250; my italics)

Blackberry Winter aggravates questions of the part played by *Patterns of Culture* in subsequent perceptions of its Sepikside readers, particularly Bateson. *Naven* salutes Benedict in both its foreword and its complex first epilogue:

> While we were all three of us working on the Sepik river, there arrived from America a part of the manuscript of Dr. Benedict's *Patterns of Culture,* and this event influenced my thinking very profoundly. (1958:x)

> The arrival of a part of the manuscript of Dr. Benedict's *Patterns of Culture,* an event already mentioned in the Foreword, together with conversations with Drs. Fortune and Margaret Mead, gave me a vague clue to what I wanted to do in anthropology, and in the last three months before I left New Guinea, I tried to follow this up. (1958:258)

Alas, the exact nature of this profound influence yet vague clue remains obscure. Perhaps Benedict's manuscript, a comparative study of ritual emphasis and excess, taught Bateson to play off extremes, either by systematically contrasting opposed cultures (e.g., Zuni/Kwakiutl) or by accentuating the exaggerated opposition of roles in ritual buffoonery, as in *wau*'s caricature (Boon 1982a: chaps. 1, 3). Or was it Mead, or the rivalry with Fortune, that catalyzed Bateson? Again, rival claims to this credit rival the rival claims of *naven* ceremonialists themselves.

Whatever Benedict indirectly communicated to Sepik studies is just one point in our semiotic nexus and must not be isolated: Semiotics keeps opening out rather than closing mediations, even in conclusion. Thus, in homage to Mead's litany of "And what if"'s (cited above) and to Bateson's reinterrogation in 1958 of his previous queries in *Naven* (1936)—"*Or should we say the reverse of this reverse?*"—we end by still asking what are not the answers but the questions (to invoke one last time Gertrude Stein, that other stolid figure within a "charmed circle," not unlike Mead later amidst the expatriot Bohemians of Bali).

And what if we traced the intertexuality *cum* interculturality of Sepik-not-Bali studies back to Benedict's own "influences"? When writing *Patterns* (1961), she was reading not just Nietzsche, among other Germans, but Virgina Woolf's *The Waves,* doubtless learning to compare cultures as one might contrast vulnerable character-types woven into wisps of interior monologue. *And what if,* following a cue from Modell (1983), we wondered whether some deep sympathy might have joined Bateson-Mead to Benedict? Discomforted by the too serene-seeming Apollonian Zuni, and dissatisfied with the too perfectly opposed Dionysian Kwakiutl, Benedict reached toward a third extreme—Fortune's paranoid Dobu—to animate her typology and turn its triangulation of Amerindia and Melanesia back on ourselves. Similarly, discomforted by the restricted varieties of schismogenesis represented by New Guinea cultures (those both with and without opposed temperaments by. gender), Bateson and Mead reached toward a last extreme, thereby inventing-discovering "balanced Bali." Might we say that their view of Bali—confirmed by select components of values and practice—resulted from semiotic forces similar to the ones that produced Chapter 5, the middle Dobuan extreme, of *Patterns of Culture?*

And what if these discoveries stemmed in part from Mead's capacity to tolerate (as a mother might) deviance. Harnessing her own double-barreled deviance, Mead ploughed on from one charmed circle to another—in New York, in New Guinea, in Bali—circles graced with fieldworker-writers more flawed (and faceted?) than herself. Her writing tagged many who had surrounded her, including husbands and colleagues, as part-deviant: barren, or insufficiently published, or homosexual, or short on fieldwork, or too bookish, poetic, or otherwise hypersensitive. She, the confirmed "careerwoman-mother," could abide any frailty, whether in the person of friends or in the world of cultures, but herself admitted no such shortcoming. Mead's autobiographical persona merges the gusto of youth with the wisdom of ages: like a granddaughter reincarnating her grandmother and reproducing a daughter (and a granddaughter) destined to do likewise: the manifest superplot of *Blackberry Winter.* Along the way cultures get crossed and presumably understood—maternalistically. But there are costs: the superplot finally marginalizes subtler contributors to Mead's story: those more delicate writers and less robust fieldworkers outdone by her professional example: like Benedict-reading-Woolf, or like Jane Belo, whose superb pre-Mead work in Bali and late tendency to restore a touch of transgression to Bateson's stereotype of "balanced Bali" could provide another installment to this semiotic study.[4] Still other installments would also help correct our overconcentration on Mead. Despite her stupendous professional and popular stature, we must be careful not to mistake her for the center of all mediations in which she figured. But neither should she, or her vital works, be neglected.

Semiotics—*Naven*ized interpretation—approaches everything as mediations: shifting selections of substitutables, communicating as well, sometimes inadvertently, the conditions of possibility of their own message-making. Thanks to such semiotic crossings, all odds, possibilities, doubts, and "what if"s are on. "Something further may follow of this masquerade" (to invoke in conclusion Melville's total, transgressive mediations to the verge of indeterminacy in *The Confidence Man*). Much indeed followed of the masquerading interplay of Iatmul, Tchambuli, Dobu, Manus, not-Bali, Radcliffe-Brown (via Bateson), Malinowski (via Fortune), Boas (via Mead), Benedict-reading, Mundugumor, and more: that panoply of motives concentrated into the "persons" of Mead, Bateson, and Fortune, all "cooped up together in the tiny eight-foot-by-eight-foot mosquito room." Thus transpired a risqué dos-à-dos of fuzzy cultures, books, and selves that "happened" one retrospectively enchanted night on the Sepik, fearing a Washkuk attack, sometime around Christmas, 1932.

P.S. de Résistance

Speaking still of Melville: when that exemplary reader was writing *Mardi,* he consolidated Malayo-Polynesian and Near Eastern terminologies into an embellished nomenclature more convincing than the real Marquesan and Tahitian terms he had heard on his visits. Can empirical studies, including fieldwork data and comparative history, be as persuasive as Melville's prose, yet answerable to evidence?

Mardi spun its distended traveler's tale, recapitulating all philosophies past, around Sir William Jones's influential fourfold division of stages in world mythology (Franklin 1963; see above, Chap. 2). Over the course of his corpus Melville authored a profoundly intertextual "world's language"; his salty seagoers establish for all nations a "*lingua franca* of the forecastle."

Along the way to *Mardi,* and beyond, Melville's resplendent parodies exposed the rhetoric of mid-nineteenth-century writing, including cosmopolitan treatises and ethnological tomes. The following example, called "How Teeth Were Regarded in Valapee," invites delivery in the style of a bad, a very bad, Shakespearean actor:

> Now human teeth, extracted, are reckoned among the most valuable ornaments in Mardi. So open wide thy strong box, Hohora, and show thy treasures. What a gallant array! standing shoulder to shoulder, without a hiatus between. . . . something farther needs be said concerning the light in which men's molars are regarded in Mardi.
>
> As in all lands, men smite their breasts, and tear their hair, when transported with grief; so, in some countries, teeth are stricken out under the sway of similar emotions. To a very great extent, this was once practiced in the Hawaiian Islands, ere idol and altar went down. Still living in Oahu, are many old chiefs, who were present at the famous obsequies of their royal old generalissimo, Tammahammaha, when there is no telling how many pounds of ivory were cast upon his grave.

Ah! had the regal white elephants of Siam been there, doubtless they had offered up their long, hooked tusks, whereon they impale the leopards, their foes; and the unicorn had surrendered that fixed bayonet in his forehead; and the imperial Cachalot-whale, the long chain of white towers in his jaw; yea, over that grim warrior's grave, the mooses, and elks, and stags, and fallow-deer had stacked their antlers, as soldiers their arms on the field.

Terrific shade of tattooed Tammahammaha! if, from a vile dragon's molars, rose mailed men, what heroes shall spring from the cannibal canines once pertaining to warriors themselves!—Am I the witch of Endor, that I conjure up this ghost? Or, King Saul, that I so quake at the sight? For, lo! roundabout me Tammahammaha's tattooing expands, till all the sky seems a tiger's skin. But now, the spotted phantom sweeps by; as a man-of-war's main-sail, cloud-like, blown far to leeward in a gale.

Banquo down, we return. . . .

From the high value ascribed to dentals throughout the archipelago of Mardi, and also from their convenient size, they are circulated as money; strings of teeth being regarded by these people very much as belts of wampum among the Winnebagoes of the North; or cowries, among the Bengalese. So, that in Valapee the very beggars are born with a snug investment in their mouths; too soon, however, to be appropriated by their lords; leaving them toothless for the rest of their days, and forcing them to diet on poee-pudding and banana blancmange. (Melville 1970:205–6)

Well-read in Pacific mythologies, well-listened to travelers' exaggerations, and oddly experienced in Marquesan, Tahitian, and Sandwich Islands adventures, Melville nevertheless changed Hawaii's Kammahammaha (Kamehameha) to *Mardi*'s Tammahammaha, apparently for the sake of alliteration and assonance: Tattooed Generalissimo Tammahammaha, or *MacBeth?* Who could say in a fictive world, realer than real, of *poee*-pudding and banana *blanc-mange,* where all cultures, histories, languages, and rhetorics theatrically, parodically, semiotically, and apocalyptically collide?

So Melville wrote; and so anthropology writes—not to the point of altering evidence for alliteration's sake, but still sometimes to the point of selecting evidence for alliteration's sake—just like cultures "themselves," from time to time. The very jargon of our textual and historical discipline recalls Melville's hybrid sailor-*sprache.* Our oft-derided technical parlance sustains (in the musical sense) motives of and for humankind's rarities and varieties in, if not a world language, then a worldly one, less provincial than "reason." Coinages accumulate: totem, taboo, *fétiche,* tattoo, hapu, mana, tantra, orenda, *raison,* amok, *dan lain lain;* taking care to preserve classical-sounding and even colonialism-engendered complements as well: *anima,* connubium, common sense, exogamy, "Indians," "Europeans," "the West," "the ~~Orient~~," "~~primitives~~," *et cetera.*

Like Melville's profuse intertextualities (Rogin 1983), against an expanding world-order (advancing toward uniformity of both the right and the left), comparative studies may champion heterodoxies. Melville's emblem (or *summa*) of this rhetorical possibility is any copious paragraph like this one:

> As among Chaucer's Canterbury pilgrims, or those oriental ones crossing the Red Sea towards Mecca in the festival month, there was no lack of variety. Natives of all sorts, and foreigners; men of business and men of pleasure; parlor men and backwoodsmen; farm-hunters and fame-hunters; heiress-hunters, gold-hunters, buffalo-hunters, bee-hunters, happiness-hunters, truth-hunters, and still keener hunters after all these hunters. Fine ladies in slippers, and moccasined squaws; Northern speculators and Eastern philosophers; English, Irish, German, Scotch, Danes, Santa Fe traders in striped blankets, and Broadway bucks in cravats of cloth of gold; fine-looking Kentucky boatmen, and Japanese-looking Mississippi cotton-planters; Quakers in full drab, and United States soldiers in full regimentals; slaves, black, mulatto, quadroon; modish young Spanish Creoles, and old-fashioned French Jews; Mormons and Papists; . . . jesters and mourners, . . . Sioux chiefs solemn as high-priests. In short, a piebald parliament, an Anacharsis Cloots congress of all kinds of that multiform pilgrim species. . . . [I have tried to omit more patently offensive tags rejected in public discourse since Melville; some, however have doubtless slipped through, as times and tastes keep changing.]
>   As pine, beech, birch, ash, hackmatack, hemlock, spruce, basswood, maple, interweave their foliage in the natural wood [no need to edit or expurgate names of trees]. . . . A Tartar-like picturesqueness; a sort of pagan abandonment and assurance. Here reigned the dashing and all-fusing spirit of the West, whose type is the Mississippi itself, which, uniting the streams of the most distant and opposite zones, pours them along, helter-skelter, in one cosmopolitan and confident tide. (Melville 1971:6; compare Wolf 1982:6)

But Melville was not really so "confident" about the all-fusing Spirit of the West. Other paragraphs undermine any smug certainty. And in that fragment called "The River,"—never added to *The Confidence Man*, but possibly portending its unwritten sequel—Melville's flirtation with apologia recovers darker doubts and contests History's seeming irreversible flow:

> As the word Abraham means the father of a great multitude of men so the word Mississippee means the father of a great multitude of waters. . . . Like a larger Susquehanah like a long-drawn bison herd he hurries on through the prairie, here and there expanding into archipelagoes cycladean in beauty, while fissured & verdant, a long China Wall, the bluffs sweep bluly away . . .
>   But at St. Louis [locus of *The Confidence Man*'s *topoi*], the course of this dream is run. Down on it like a Pawnee from ambush foams

the yellow-jacked Missouri. . . . The peace of the Upper River seems broken in the Lower, nor is it ever renewed.

The Missouri sends rather a hostile element than a filial flow. . . . Under the benign name Mississippi it is in short the Missouri that now rolls to the Gulf, . . . the Missouri that not a tributary but an invader enters the sea, long disdaining to yield its white wave to the blue. (Melville 1971:222–23)

All destination; no filiation. Melville, then, kept allegorizing recognitions of abundant ironies in his empathies. Yet how would his professed concerns for otherness differ from that view Melville parodied of Christian apologists who sought to reconcile exotic mythologies and theological orthodoxy?:

All things form but one whole; the universe a Judea, and God Jehova its head. . . . Away with our stares and grimaces. The New Zealand-er's tattooing is not a prodigy; nor the Chinaman's ways an enigma. No custom is strange; no creed is absurd; no foe, but who will in the end prove a friend. In heaven, at last. . . . (Melville [*Mardi*] 1970:12; see also Boon 1982a:150–51)

Or if not there, in Uttara Kurus? Might anthropologists and fellow/sister comparatists be emboldened explicitly to ask, both rhetorically and otherwise, a question that Melville, Menippean texts, and similar cultural performances perhaps implicitly ask of themselves? Are we—in our findings, our destinations (Bali and *Mardi!*)—the apologist or the parodist? And might we join a fractured, antiphonal, polyglot chorus, responding (to invoke Carlyle) ever-lastingly: YEA, and No, and yes, and . . . in an unstoppably reversing, *Na-vene*sque, low-comic equivalent to Siwa-Sati's dance across "Tantrized" cultures and times: flameful, laughing/weeping, cyclic, listy, and disbursed? *Peut-être:* The everlasting could-be.

Only one point remains—not quite a rhetorical commonplace—to be stipulated by an author to autonomous readers: Neither the European choruses (polyglot in their own right) nor the other choruses (as much or more so), nor practices and differences they enchant, would be there unless not only we/they but they/they (not to mention we/we) were. Both sides of every dichotomy, including hierarchical ones, contain the potential for multiplication and reversal, as does any mark of separation (/). This book's odd combination of ethnology and history has married affinities and extremes of entexted tote-misms and Tantrisms garnered from comparative evidence. It may now, then, be fitting to divorce ourselves from this process of reading. Bali-Hindu-Buddhistic styles of *jouissance*-pessimism require only that in so doing we anticipate further destinations, pending *oubli*.

Notes

Chapter 1

1. The term "ethnology" in this work refers to the general study of cultural differences, as distinct from ethnography, the intensive description of a particular people. Ethnology implies comparative contrast. For sixteenth-century materials "ethnology" accentuates the theme of sectarian differences worldwide; for nineteenth-century materials "ethnology," better than "anthropology," alludes to issues of language difference as much as physical difference. A central issue in the history of ethnological ideas has been whether languages or physicalities (if either) provide the salient model of human differences. See particularly Stocking (1987).

2. This view is confirmed by Dudley and Novak (1972); the volume's essays on "wild man" *topoi* from the Renaissance through Romanticism also address a longer history of Western discourses of self/other. The classic account of "The Great Chain of Being" is Lovejoy (1964 [1936]), the major source of Hodgen's discussion; over the years this idea has been treated in the *Journal of the History of Ideas* and other periodicals in a way that makes it seem more doctrinal and bounded than it ever need have been. Again, my interest is in fragmented recurrences of allusions to hierarchical order as a way to wrap arguments up or round texts off.

3. Pigafetta (1906 [1525]), 2: 71). I leave place names in this translation's spellings. Throughout this book place-names, deity-names, and other names will be less standardized than is customary in studies unconcerned with variations in the history of cross-cultural discourse. "Odorous Moluccas" is an epithet in Melville's *Moby-Dick* (see Boon 1982a: 149–53).

4. Bausani (1960) n.s. 11: 229–48; see also Echols (1978), 38: 11–24.

5. On symbolic dimensions in stereotypes of Patagonians and signs of kingship in such scribes as Pigafetta and compilers-commentators as Jacobean Samuel Purchas, see Boon (1982a: chap. 2, 5). For other sources and related issues see below, Chapter 3.

6. Hose's own books—especially a self-absorbed retrospective on his career and the unparalleled continuity of Sarawak's colonial administration (1927)—show that "nineteenth century" discourse could extend nearly three decades into our own. The "stars" of *Fifty Years of Romance and Research* include a native "Rob Roy of Sarawak," Hose's adoring wife Poppy, and a mispreserved giant orangutan head she valiantly delivered to Cambridge's Dr. Duckworth. (Readers are referred to this work to see just how innocently "degenerative" English life of the times could be—see Boon 1989a for more on Keith's passage and Hose; see also Pringle 1970).

7. The place of Wallace in evolutionary theory and his contributions to natural

selection are briefly reviewed in Oldroyd (1980). That study includes Wallace's account of his visionary flash concerning "the survival of the fittest," when he was ill and "prostrated . . . for several hours every day during the cold and succeeding hot fits" (p. 107). That Wallace persisted in viewing the human mind as "the only divine contribution to the history of life" (Gould 1977: 25) is as troubling to historians of biological sciences as it is pertinent to Wallace's ethnological imagery.

Additional background on Wallace's natural-history work in Indonesia and Sarawak on varieties (versus species) among human populations is given in Brooks (1984), an important source for any fuller reading of Wallace than the one attempted here. For comments on Wallace's "hard hyper-selectionist line," his optimism about humanity's eventual emancipation from suffering, and his "conventional Christian solution," see Gould (1982). Wallace's interest in spiritualism largely postdated his travels in the Malay Archipelago; relevant studies are too numerous to cite here.

8. For a summary of archaeological and historical evidence about the inhabitants of Aru (and of coastal Sumatra), see A. C. Milner, McKinnon, and Sinar (1978).

9. Lévi-Strauss traces such codes well beyond so-called primitive societies. After rethinking the history of anthropological interest in tribal totemisms, he suggests that to divide the world into totemic versus nontotemic populations is itself a kind of "totemism." Who, then, practices "totemism today" (*Le totemisme aujourd'hui*)? The West.

Chapter 2

1. Hall (1962) and Soedjatmoko (1965) contain essays on the background of these scholars; see particularly Bastin (1965a). Weatherbee (1978) raises important points about Raffles' sources. Of many biographies of Raffles, a recent example is Collis (1970). For Marsden's sources, see n. 4 below.

2. Following such works as Levin (1969), I use *topos* in the broad sense of "rhetorical set piece" repeated in compressed figures and conventions, such as "Once upon a time" as a "golden age" or "paradise" *topos*. Visual emblems also convey distinct *topoi* and may be read as more rhetorical representations than descriptive ones. On adapting E. Curtius's classic study of literary *topoi* and E. H. Gombrich's related notions of visual "matching" to evidence from the history of Balinese studies, see Boon (1977 chap. 1).

3. W. Godzich (1986: xx) has situated De Certeau's "heterological" countertraditions in "the complex, and properly textual, play of the other with the more overt, representational part of the discourse." He goes on: "This other, which forces discourses to take the meandering appearance that they have, is not a magical or a transcendental entity; it is the discourse's mode of relation to its own historicity in the moment of its utterance." Godzich contrasts De Certeau's "heterologies" to Foucault's idea of discourse: "De Certeau's conception of discourse, so different from Foucault's hegemonic one, recovers an agential dimension for us inasmuch as it recognizes that discursive activity is a form of social activity, an activity in which we attempt to apply the roles of the discourses that we assume. These may not be heroic roles, but they place us much more squarely in front of our responsibility as historical actors" (p. xxi). Nevertheless, Foucault's (1970) sense of murmur may have come closer to De Certeau's counterheroic model of reading-interpreting that he compares to tactics of bricolage and multiplied, indirect, uncentralized resistances (De Certeau 1984: chap. 3). For more on murmurs and heterodoxy, see Conclusions. De Certeau's way of reading-

remembering the past, cities, and so forth, in order to subvert heroic authority (including that of the state) seems compatible with positions taken by Barthes (see Chapter 3).

4. Marsden's possible sources are discussed in Wink (1924), Gonda (1939), and briefly in Bastin (1965a); research on this issue continues. The issue of indigenous written sources, particularly the place of court chronicles in colonialist scholars' histories, is a major topic in the current history of Southeast Asian historiography; for a provocative overview, see Wolters (1982). For my purposes here, it would be more relevant to trace *antecedents* (both Western and Islamic) of Marsden's genre than sources of his data; but this task lies beyond the scope of this essay and my expertise.

5. Such eighteenth-century schemes varied depending on the features selected. J. F. Blumenbach, for example, rejected Linnaeus's accounts of troglodytes or apemen; but his studies of craniology "taught that the four other races had resulted from the degeneration of the Caucasian in one direction through the American Indian to the Mongolian; and in the other through the Malay to the Ethiopian. The degeneration, he declared, was the effect of 'turning aside' of the 'formative force'" (J. G. Burke 1972).

6. On the history of Bali's and Lombok's trade and slave trade, see Schulte Nordholt (1981, 1980) and van der Kraan (1980, 1985). Questions about the meaning of "slavery" in nineteenth-century Bali are raised in C. Geertz (1980); tentative points about slaves and emblems of/for Bali are made in Boon (1977: 68). In Raffles' different works relevant terms shift; for example, debtor "slaves" resulting from marriage transactions described in Raffles (1816) are called "servants" in Raffles (1817). For recent general discussions about the history of slavery and/or servitude in Java, Bali, and elsewhere in Indonesia, see Kumar (1987) and relevant essays in Reid (1983).

7. A later 1844 edition of Raffles' illustrations flanks the Papuan with two new plates, one an unfinished, amateurish sketch of a Balinese maiden and "Brahmin"; the other "The Rajah of Bali Bliling, and a Regent of Java, in undress" (meaning unofficial attire). The intricate history of the actual production of plates in Raffles' *History*, including the points of the process of producing representations where "interventions" could alter their implied message, is the subject of recent stimulating research by A. Forge, Department of Anthropology, Australian National University. Here I am emphasizing the relation of an illustration *to the text* and the flavor of emblem retained.

8. The point I am raising is, of course, not to be confused with issues of philological accuracy or inaccuracy. For reviews of the place of actual Kawi texts in Balinese culture over time, see especially Robson (1972, 1983), as well as Worsley (1972), Zurbuchen (1987), and the sources they cite. Various ways to cut across anthropological and philological concerns, so to question pat distinctions between text/context, are broached in Boon (1977, 1982a).

9. I learned much about the historical depth of such practices in precolonial India from lectures by historian R. Thapar, of the University of Delhi. For a general discussion, see particularly Biardeau and Malamoud (1976). Some recent critics have tried to approach suttee in India (along with dowry, infant betrothal, etc.) exclusively with reference to colonialist domination of women, thus narrowing this much more venerable topic; see, for example, Spivak (1987).

10. For summaries of general approaches to rituals of animal sacrifice, human sacrifice, and plant sacrifice, see Herrenschmidt (1982) and Valeri (1985). These studies have the merit of comparing traditions as distinct as biblical, Indic, and Oceanic sacrifice, as did classic approaches by Hubert and Mauss and, of course, J. G. Frazer.

Valeri's "model of Hawaiian sacrifice" is particularly valuable for its critique of Girard's (1977) substantivist and moralizing commentary on sacrifice-as-violence. Girard's work, like many others, ends by isolating and indeed privileging violence as a kind of touchstone relevant issue. Valeri's objections are both theoretical and empirical:

> Girard believes it is possible to isolate a psychological process in its pure state, independent of the cultural order. He believes, therefore, that the cultural order is just a rationalization, a cover-up, of this very simple eternal process. . . . The excessive emphasis Girard puts on violence obfuscates the symbolic, figurative value of the victim's death or destruction. Sacrificial death and destruction are also images; they represent the passage from the visible to the invisible. . . . common both to blood sacrifice and to the sacrifice of vegetable offerings—which, of course, is not in the least accounted for by Girard's theory. In fact, the vegetable offerings that are simply abandoned on the altar rot and disappear exactly like the animals that are put to death. Decomposition, which marks the separation from the human and visible world, seems thus a more general and perhaps more important element than the violent act of killing, which is present only in animal and human sacrifices (1985: 68–69).

Valeri's comments can be extended to Sivaic, Tantric, and Hindu-Balinese themes of sacrifice, where the issue of substitutability of grains for animals for humans is fundamental (see O'Flaherty 1985; 1988; see below, Conclusions; see also Bloch and Parry 1982, and Mauss 1967: chaps. 1, 3).

11. This sample of examples is meant to be suggestive. For background on several of them, see Boon (1977: chaps. 1–3, 9). Some discussion of "Kecak" dances is provided in Bandem and de Boer (1981); the Bali-wide "Eka Dasa Rudra" exorcisms are addressed in Lansing (1983), among many other sources. Neither of these studies, however, sufficiently addresses "standardizing" and centralizing dimensions, both commercial and political ones, entailed in these formats for Balinese performance. For suggestions that C. Geertz's influential essay on Balinese cockfights (1973: chap. 15) was neither an essentialized nor an averaged analysis of Bali and that it dramatically displaced earlier "epitomes" (including temple ceremonies and Rangda performances) in a chain of necessarily exaggerated representations focussing and contrasting "Bali," see Boon (1977: 32–33). Recent critics (e.g., Crapanzano 1987) bent on refuting or deconstructing Geertz have overlooked contexts of Bali and Balinese studies alike.

12. Jones's famous thesis and his influential views of language and mythology are reviewed in Feldman and Richardson (1972). On implications for early Romanticism, see Willson (1964) and Boon (1982b: chap. 7).

13. Unable here to trace the reception of such works, I might suggest the special quality of narrative imagination in Maurice's study by noting its influence later on Herman Melville. Melville, parodist-pasticher par excellence of Romantic scholarship (following Thomas Carlyle), structures his romance of *Mardi* (1849) around William Jones's historical typology of world mythologies. Melville's two works that continue *Mardi*'s parody-quest are *Moby Dick* (1851) and *The Confidence Man* (1857), each patterned in part on the rhythm of mythic avatars that Maurice, following Jones, drew from India to organize a "history" of "Hindostan" itself. On the doubly ambiguous Egyptian-Hindu mythic undercurrents in Melville, see Franklin (1963) and Kulkarni (1970), which stresses Melville's encounter with Maurice's illustrations. For a sense

of the dense layering throughout Melville's political-minded corpus, see especially Rogin (1983) and also Beaver (1973), Herbert (1982), Blair (1982) and Reynolds (1988). For an illustration of the effects of Melville's inspiration, see Postlude.

Chapter 3

1. The suitability of an Erasmian and/or Bakhtinian sensitivity for Balinese materials was suggested in Boon (1984a), part of which is adapted here. To get a fuller sense of what "Erasmian" may imply for Erasmus's and Rabelais' own era (sixteenth century) and for ours, see Kott (1987), Febvre (1982), Frye (1976), McLuhan (1962), and particularly M. Green (1972) and T. More (1517/1972). I hope to develop this perspective elsewhere in a different genre or composite genre.

2. Wherever possible, I put the theoretical accent on reading or rereading—whether applied to "their" activity and interpretation, "our" activity and interpretation, or an epistemological locus that questions this dichotomy. For fresh senses of interdisciplinary "reading" which cut through more recondite formulations of sources that have inspired them, see particularly Darnton (1984), Eco (1979), De Certeau (1984), LaCapra (1982) and the fine summary of theoretical issues in "reading and performance" in Wadlington (1987). Wadlington's work combines literary, anthropological, and historical perspectives and advises against equating any interpretive turn to rhetoric and reading with that "best-advertised current variant" of deconstruction (p. 224). He then sides with Kenneth Burke's (1966) dialectics. Wadlington makes important distinctions between approaches to reading by structuralists and C. Geertz, emphasizing the latter's relation to K. Burke (see Boon 1982a: chap. 4). Wadlington underestimates the length of time—just "over a decade," he suggests—that Burke has been of interest to anthropologists. As early as the late 1940s C. Kluckhohn was saluting Burke; the interest accelerated with Geertz's work. J. Peacock was assigning Burke's *Grammar of Motives* and *Rhetoric of Motives* in anthropology courses in 1965. During the same period, Dell Hymes and others insisted on the importance of Bible criticism for anthropological approaches (see also Leach 1987). I mention all this not to stake out claims of priority but to offer something of a counterpoint to recent marketing of high critical moves. There are multiple rhythms to even short-term advances in theory and method, just as there are multiple *durées* to Braudel's long-term history.

3. My sense of texts and contexts of early modern Europe and of continued counterpositions to centralized state control relies on a range of sources, including Skinner (1978) Davis (1975), P. Burke (1978, 1987), Greenblatt (1980, 1988); see also sources for Chapter 6, and Boon (1982a: chap. 5).

4. The distinctiveness and concrete virtuosities of Southeast Asian polities and spheres of exchange are now being assessed in approaches that do not reduce ritual to a compensatory disguise and that address issues in economies of desire as well as labor-production. See, for example Gesick (1983) and the general overview in Wolters (1982). The details and palpable practices (in Braudel's sense) of Southeast Asian commerce and cross-religious transactions are the subject of major work by A. Reid (1988). Like D. Lach before him, Reid notes such "peculiar" practices as the ones I am stressing (circumcision and bells), but, again like Lach, he does not turn the issue back on the values of the observers (or on historians like himself building on their documents); he does not rise (some would say stoop) to reflexivity; I think we should, but not only to that.

5. Extraordinary insights into mystical Jewish circumcision and metaphors of Midrash interpretation are provided in Wolfson (1988). One Renaissance text devoted to rethinking the place of circumcision as a diacritical in Christianity was G. Biel's, *The Circumcision of the Lord* (1966). A recent book by M. Bloch considers the ideology of circumcision amongst the Merina of Madagascar (1986). But for me to mention in one note such studies as if their *topos*—circumcision—were an isolable issue (attaching, say, to men or sons or to a particular style of control or expropriation) is a questionable procedure.

The most recent information on Javanese circumcision, including daughters, is Carpenter (1987); most important for this study, she notes occurrences of "double circumcision" which "seat newly circumcised opposite-sex siblings together as brides and grooms" (p. 78). Here, then, Javanese Islamic circumcision rites, recently revitalized, trail traces of courtly conventions of marriageable twins (see below, chap. 5; Boon 1977: chaps. 6, 9). I hope to pursue issues of sixteenth-century secrecy and circumcision and its aftermath—extending to Freud's *Moses and Monotheism*—in another essay.

6. The term "Baliology" is used half-winkingly, but not sarcastically, in Boon (1977) to designate a phase in the history of Balinese studies since the 1920s, following "Balipedia" (mid-ninteenth to early twentieth century), and earlier idealizations and miniaturizations of the island in European (particularly Dutch) representations. Today the Indonesian term *Baliologi* is an official designation for Balinese studies, competing for national and international resources with Javanese studies and other regional specializations.

7. Many sources on Bali are mentioned in subsequent chapters. Much of the ongoing work at various levels of formality and informality is tracked in *Balinese Arts and Culture*, a newsletter edited by F. de Boer at Wesleyan University. Other journals with frequent items on Bali in English include *Review of Indonesian and Malaysian Affairs, Indonesia, Indonesian Circle, Bijdragen tot der Taal-, Land- en Volkenkunde*, and *l'Archipel*. The most representative translation of Dutch colonialist research in Bali remains Swellengrebel (1960, 1969). A prime mover in coordinating contemporary local, Indonesian, and international work on Bali is Professor I Gusti Ngurah Bagus. For extensive bibliographies, see Stuart-Fox (1979), Bandem and de Boer (1981), Belo (1970), Boon (1977), C. Geertz (1980), H. Geertz (n.d.), Lovric (1987a), Ramseyer (1977), and Vickers (1986). The "basics" offered here forefront aspects of performance, rituals, discourse, reading-interpreting, and social contexts of rivalrous houses in a history of institutional complexity and multiple resistances to be emphasized later.

Chapter 4

1. A recent study by G. Robinson of state and society in Bali, concentrates on political conflicts of 1945–46; following the example of Anderson (1972), he isolates a cohort of youth ("bellicose, armed *pemuda*") as potential prime movers of liberation. Robinson says that this revolutionary faction could have mobilized locals and for that reason offended and threatened the Dewa Agung and the anti-Republican royalist status quo. His study has characteristic drawbacks resulting from abstracting *pemuda* from their own social statuses, as if they were *pemuda* first and foremost and nothing else, fated to spearhead revolution. Generalizing his arguments well beyond 1945–46,

war, and Japanese/Dutch occupation, Robinson reduces Balinese regional and district politics to "three structural types of *puri* [court] rivalry—dispersed, polarized, and hegemonic" (p. 18). He stipulates that Badung, Buleleng, and Tabanan kingdom-districts showed a pattern of *dispersed* rivalry, while a clear ideological hegemony or "*hegemonic* pattern" existed in Klungkung and most of Gianyar. This claim overlooks much that was mottled in actual interrelations of kingdom-districts and their modalities of power. For example, Tabanan's power structure (which Robinson calls dispersed) included houses transferred from Klungkung (which he calls hegemonic); the houses continued tracing their links there and developed complex ties on the border with Jembrana (a kingdom-district he calls polarized) (Boon 1977: chaps. 4–9). Little is made of Karangasem district—which also conspicuously explodes such distinctions.

Robinson's state-oriented view of power does not seem to reckon marriage alliance as a viable strategy or ritual as part of the field of resistance. Contrary to Geertz (1980), he makes politics in Bali a matter of "local states." He perhaps follows in the vein of Anderson's (1983) efforts to set Geertz's "Old Societies and New States" on its head ("Old State, New Society"). It strikes me that what needs dispersing is this very polemic of polar head-setting. Analyses that impose narrow standards of political seriousness (the state, the military, crisis-conflict) can imply that resistance occurs as a knee-jerk reaction to hegemony and that dispersed/polar/hegemonic forms can be neatly separated out. For a contrasting sense of Bali, see below, Chapter 7 and Conclusions.

2. In a later work Hobart (1986) distances himself from Bloch and, for different reasons, from Geertz and the present author, among others. He echoes scruples about the inadequacy of any translation or comparison now prevalent in R. Needham's (1981) essays. It is not clear how Hobart's own description (based, of course, on his translation) intends to overcome the classic dilemma of "translation-betrayal"—whose difficulties no one I know would deny. For some responses to particulars in this turn in Hobart's accounts of Bali, see Chapter 6, n. 2.

3. This may be the place to stress that Balinese ritual forms include "visualized" codes. Formalist mandalas are employed not just by high priests and courtly cosmographers but by local curers; indeed spatialization enters many aspects of local, regional, and island-wide representations. Any effort to read the history of both Balinese forms and discourse about Bali must take into account the visual-distancing component of Hindu aesthetics and politics. This is the point overlooked, I think, by Fabian (1982), when he suggests that Boon (1977) fails to emancipate its interpretations from visualized distancing (although he applauds my relating the "arts of memory" to ritual and spatial forms and *topoi*.) Regardless, Fabian's important work seriously underestimates formalist schemata beyond those of Western regimented controls. For example, when he decries the coercively-visual as Western, Fabian is building on the insights of W. Ong. Yet Ong himself accentuates not just Western manuscript and print media but Chinese characters and other scripts so "visual" as not to "represent" speech's flow of phonemes at all. When Fabian's book becomes politically programmatic, it tends to reverse congratulate the West as the arch-visualizer-gazer. I question so melodramatic a representation of the history of dominance and resistance (see Boon 1982a: app. C).

4. Just to convey the range of Menippean possibilities, let me add: More's *Utopia;* Erasmus, Rabelais, *Don Quixote;* Burton's *Anatomy of Melancholy; Tristram Shandy;* Hoffmann's *Kater Muur;* Grandville's *Un Autre Monde;* Carlyle's *Sartor Resartus;* perhaps Henry Adam's *Education,* offered as the meditations of a "second Teufels-

dröckh"; Melville's *Mardi, Moby Dick, Pierre,* and *The Confidence Man;* Multatuli's (alias Edward Douwes Dekker) *Max Havelaar;* Flaubert's *Bouvard et Pécuchet;* Twain's *Connecticut Yankee;* Nabokov's *Lolita* (indeed, his *oeuvre*); plus much more modern literature and antiliterature in the wake of Joyce (have I left out Kierkegaard?).

Chapter 5

1. I wish to dedicate this chapter—especially its refusal to assume genealogy to be the constant foundation of kinship and marriage—to David Schneider, an incomparable teacher. His insistence on the cultural constitution of various systems of social solidarity and difference, including unbounded units and open-ended transformations, has motivated much of my research on Balinese kinship and marriage. See particularly Schneider (1976, 1980, 1984).

2. For a parallel study of South Asia that contrasts North and South Indian images of brides, wedding observations, and marriage practices, see Kolenda (1984).

3. Lévi-Strauss's formulation qualifies his earlier models, more social-organizational in character, that assumed societies are ideally bounded and, directly or indirectly, cohesive. A functionalist residue in his work on elementary structures produced blind spots to aspects of parallel cousin marriage and inhibited addressing so-called complex systems (see Boon and Schneider 1974). Following Schneider, I question classifications of kinship and marriage that assume social coherence to be what they are "all about"; such assumptions make Balinese houses, among others, appear anomalous (see Geertz and Geertz 1975: conclusion). I employ the "maisons" notion not to produce another reified category of societal type but to contest the typologies that let houses "slip through" or go unnoticed. The model of "maisons," moreover, does not simply reintroduce the distinction between kin-based and contract-based societies and polities. Rather, houses muddle conventional analytic distinctions of clan, lineage, guild, warna, jati, party, etc. Nor do criteria of birth versus voluntarism get us very far into the meanings, hierarchies, exchanges, and various options of houses. Paramount is the fact that "house" can relate to "house," even across presumed boundaries of language, society, nation, or other construction. One might, then, want to think of "houses" and any construction of boundable "society" in some kind of dialectical tension, neither actualizable. This possibility is developed below.

For another case that calls into question the isolability of cross-cousin systems, see Carter's summary of evidence from Maharashtrian Brahmans who "do not distinguish parallel cousins from cross cousins. . . . What is involved are not rules enjoining or forbidding cross-cousin marriage, but a series of considerations revolving around ritual status. Wife-givers are inferior in ritual status to wife-takers, and younger persons are inferior to their elders" (1984: 93–94).

4. Compare Traube (1980b, 1986) on the categorical femininity of the Mambai (Timor) house. Similarly, the entrenched Balinese house (ritually Siwaic) contrasts to more active "masculine" (Wisnuvaic) challengers moving in and up from the peripheries (Boon 1977: 203–5).

On what we might call *maison*-like attributes fundamental to Balinese statecraft, see C. Geertz (1980). Another advantage of "house societies" as a guiding category of comparative interpretation is this: it avoids rigid distinctions between court and commoner, accentuating instead many dimensions of rank, economy, historical narrative, ritual performance, etc. The notion, suited to historical contexts of medieval and early modern Europe (see Chapter 6), should also facilitate cross-*cultural* analyses of Bali, Java, Bugis, Dyak, Battak, Toraja, and so forth, thus advancing H. Geertz's (1963) seminal article on comparative Indonesian social structures.

5. More practical aspects of houses, marriages, and weddings are discussed in Boon (1977: chaps. 4–8), with information about high-titled commoner houses engaged in social mobility (e.g., Pasek). Options of dowering daughters, meticulous adjustments of titles of spouses and offspring ("immaterial wealth"), and strategies of prearranged alliances remain important today; colonial Dutch scholarship on these dimensions was summarized in Korn (1932). C. Geertz (1980) outlines the marriage alliance system (*wargi*) from the court's vantage. H. and C. Geertz (1975) review dowry negotiations when "gentry" houses are tied to noble ones. For additional details and interesting case studies, see Hobart (1980), Gerdin (1981, 1982), Guermonprez (1984), and articles in H. Geertz (n.d.).

A few additional details on twins among the Balinese of Lombok have recently appeared in Duff-Cooper (1986), who notes that opposite-sex twins may both be called *nengah,* implying a canceling of birth-order codes. For some banter about twins that may echo a kind of teasing among Balinese, see Hobart (1974) and Tjokrosudarmo (1975).

6. For analyses employing a notion of "valence" rather than "social relation," that refines Lévi-Strauss's approach to marriage structures, see Héritier (1979). I thank Stephen Headley for suggestions on this point.

7. I hope my treatment of incest conveys the importance of seeing the woman not just as wife to her husband but as sister to her brother; indeed the sister-spouse image accentuates the tie brotherward. Much more is made of the relation between twins and incest in Boon 1977, 1983a, 1989b. Although sympathetic to Errington's (1989) work on Sulawesi, I am less inclined than Errington (1987) to see incest (even of twins) as a symbol of unity or of reunification of opposites (in the early Romantic tradition). Errington draws on many studies of "house societies," twinship, and marriage relations, including a version of this chapter. Her important points contain some positions I would modify. She twice calls relative exogamy of houses "in a sense imperialistic" (pp. 407, 421), when such "expansion" into distant kin is inseparably part of the dialectic of endogamy/exogamy. She states that in Indonesia's "centrist Archipelago," brothers-sisters are icons of "primordial unity"; she adds that, as in New Guinea, "to collapse sex difference is to return to it the primordial unity from whence it came" (pp. 407, 429). I have argued that polyvalent dimensions of twins-separated-then-reunited preclude a gloss of symbolic unity.

Errington's approach to contradictions (perhaps reflecting the values of Luwu nobility) is thus more functionalist than the dialectics stressed here. She sometimes implies that hierarchies seek to escape (rather than to harness) contradictory marriage strategies; she observes that "in Bali, the gods married their twins; in Luwu, twins separated" (p. 407), as though these outcomes were mutually exclusive, when the two fates of twins are imagined as complementary in the ideology of Bali's ancestral houses, a key case in Errington's comparative survey.

When emphasizing inherent contradiction trailing through narrative and ritual devices of twins-separated-then-married, I follow L. Dumont and A. M. Hocart in detecting counter-centrist aspects of hierarchical forms. Unlike bureaucratic rank orders (and some "Great Chains of Being"), hierarchies need not add up to a singular taxonomic stratification. I keep scrutinizing the relation of incest (and twins) to signs of extremest social and political difference—irreconcilable, transposable difference.

8. Themes of fertility, plus renunciation and eclipses between exchange and hierarchy in realms of religion and discourse, are developed in Boon (1982a: pt. 3). Upon mention of exchange, I should note that the tripartite conclusions to this chapter are modeled after the same device in M. Mauss's *Essai sur le don* (1925/1967). Only now Mauss's three varieties of conclusion can be folded back over the work of Lévi-Strauss that succeeded his and was inspired by it; see also Boon 1989b.

9. For a review of objections, often citing the feminist position of Rubin (1975), to Lévi-Strauss's occasional comments on "men exchanging women," see Peletz (1987). Peletz's article—based on the author's extensive work on Ngeri Sembilan, a classic Malay case of a *société à maisons*—can stand for the many critiques of Lévi-Srauss on this issue. Now, Lévi-Strauss was wrong here, and he has qualified these remarks since 1949, as Peletz reports. But neither Peletz nor most scholars he cites want to let Lévi-Strauss off the hook. My disappointment with this body of criticism concerns its failure to grasp the major force of exchange theories like Lévi-Strauss's: refuting the ideology of individualism and individualist theories of the production of value. Certainly, Lévi-Strauss should have insisted only that members of alliance units exchange spouse relations. "Men exchanging women" (or vice versa) cannot be brought to bear on marriage systems at the level he addresses them (called formalist by Pelezt and others, a misleading label). But the point that much feminist theory (including Rubin's) misses, is that anything "exchanged" (including spouses), in gift-transactions of the kind disclosed by Mauss and Lévi-Strauss, is not a commodity, much less chattel. Rather, exchange-items are "signs," productions-for-exchange, valueless if retained (see Boon 1982a: chap. 3). Even Lévi-Strauss's unfortunate formulation of "men exchanging women" (a matter which he elsewhere stipulates can only be addressed empirically, with regard to practices of decision and structures of authority) does not make women into objects, in the sense of depersonalized objectifications. Critics' insensitivity to this issue in so-called alliance theory may indicate their own uncritical participation in that "practical reason" that takes for granted individualized value and production-economies of scarcity (see Sahlins 1976). Finally, a model of "exchange" need not sanitize politics, victimage, and so forth. Rather, it explores alternative modes of counterobligations, sacrifices, and death in the destinations of value-making (see, e.g., Lederman 1986, Strathern 1988, Lindenbaum 1987, Weiner 1976, Hyde 1982).

Chapter 6

1. It may be worth reiterating that "Balinese culture" here implies a contrastive construction: not Java, not the eastern Lesser Sundas, not India, etc., but related to them. As stressed above, it is enacted variably across title-castes and localities, and it is continually transforming. Chapter 7 will add details that illustrate Balinese developments during the 1980s. Part of my interest in a "courtly love" notion concerns its relevance to increasingly commercialized and commoditized sectors of contemporary Bali. This chapter, moreover, explores parallels between Bali and sociopolitical dimensions other than the "distinctively modern idea of the State as a form of public power separate from both the ruler and the ruled, and constituting the supreme political authority within a certain defined territory" (Skinner 1978, 2: 353).

2. Hobart (1987) returns to these issues in a very different tone, one he said (personal communication) was urged upon him by the series' editor-in-chief and not to be taken too seriously. This piece directs against me the reprimand that Hooykaas (1976a) had leveled against Geertz for calling something "sacred" (Hooykaas apparently presumed that this analytic term implied "holy" rather than "set apart" in Durkheim's sense; Hobart implausibly suggests that Geertz could be unaware of nuances in meanings of Balinese *suci*). Hobart again ignores my distinction between Romance and romantic and adds that Boon (1982a) "calls Balinese Eastern Romantics," when I actually compare early Romantic philosopher-linguist Sanskritists to Balinese Brahmana literati—two cases of distanced involvement with Indic matters. Later in the article, Hobart concurs with this point.

The piece is instructive because Hobart no longer sides with Maurice Bloch; rather Bloch is found guilty of an equal and opposite fault: "Bloch objects to the absence, in cultural accounts such as Geertz's or Boon's, of any way of explaining much of the practical action and political manipulation recorded in the Balinese ethnography . . . but . . . Bloch's vision of human nature looks remarkably like Utilitarian Man writ large and it is just as cultural in another sense as is Geertz's. . . . In place of thinker and thespian, we are given shopkeeper or mercenary" (p. 147). Hobart deems Geertz's thespian metaphors, my literary genres, and Bloch's "universal model" essentialist and Western, yet offers his own evidence as "Balinese views" (omitting to explain why he laces the essay with insights from European thinkers, theorists, and texts). Here Hobart makes it appear as if symbolics "run out" not at gravity or at true-undisguised-relations-of-production (see Chap. 4), but at context. He simply keeps interjecting caveats about inadequacies of translation, as if *their context* could ultimately be coincided with; as if meaning were not fundamentally transposed, converted, substituted; as if comparison occurs only after description, and secondarily. Taken to its limit, this view can only become atomistic (see Boon 1982a: chaps. 3–4).

Hobart's approach and that of the present study both question notions of fixed patterns and essentialist models of social organization (Boon 1973; 1977: chap. 3, Conclusions). However, my sense of "culture" as multiple constructions that are *at base* contrastive questions Hobart's occasional recourse to an empiricist zero-degree (this analytic locus should be radically distinguished from the local as variation [Geertz 1959, 1983]). For example, at one point Hobart authorizes his account in this way: "A *caveat* obviously applies to my use of terms like 'culture' and 'the Balinese.' I do not wish to suggest there is any essential Balinese culture. There are only the myriad statements and actions in which people living on the island of Bali, and calling themselves Balinese, engage. In speaking of 'the Balinese' I am really referring to those in the settlement of Tengahpadang, North Gianyar, where I did field research; they include both men and women of high and low castes, unless otherwise stated. How far usage varies between communities in Bali is an empirical issue and is still far from clear. Rather than hypostatize an entity called 'Balinese society' and postulate its structural principles, I shall look instead primarily at how the people in one area set about interpreting their own collective representations" (p. 152). Now, these scruples simply back standard concerns about comparative representations to the infralocal. Hobart cannot escape problems of representation, typology, and contrastive generalization if he has ever selected or been selected by an informant or if he has ever generalized about his field research settlement; and he has. Indeed, every paragraph (not to mention the title) of his article commits the very hypostatization that Hobart tends more readily to recognize in the work of others. Finally, I would again stress that "the Balinese" hypostatize themselves (and others) too. To fail to keep this fact uppermost in mind is to reinscribe the fallacy of we-interpreters/them-interpreted. Typology cannot be escaped; it can, however, be multiplied and cross-contested.

3. In 1944 Lévi-Strauss discussed his own work on "Indian cosmetics" compared to tatooing, etc.; he distinguished masks that constitute a pantheon from those that constitute an ancestry (1963b: 269, 259). As usual, Balinese culture does both, playing with or between the difference. Much feminist literature shows that cosmetics and fashion are a crucial link between commoditized culture and whatever preceded it (e.g., Bowlby 1985). Fresh work on this topic is being pursued by J. Goldstein, following an incisive piece on consumer culture (1987).

4. I learned many facts about this issue at a Wenner-Gren conference on "Cloth and the Organization of Human Experience" organized by Annette Weiner and Jane Schneider.

5. Sustained controversy about "courtly love" has centered on C. S. Lewis's *Allegory of Love* (1938). On chivalry in depth, see especially Duby (1978) and the intriguing semiotic and typological study by Meylakh (1975). For further insights into medieval semiotics, see, for example, Gellrich (1985), many books by U. Eco (e.g., 1986), Ladner (1979), Vance (1979), Uitti (1973).

6. R. H. Bloch's introduction boards the bandwagon of critics echoing Derrida's (1967) charge that Lévi-Strauss is naive about the politics of *écriture* and wistful for an unfallen presence of speech. If we read *Tristes tropiques*'s ironies with the same intensiveness that Bloch does *Tristan*'s (p. 182), we find that the "writing lesson" given notoriety by Derrida figures in *Tristes tropiques*'s text as a hackneyed philosophical chestnut resorted to by the narrator to fight insomnia. It enters into the *histoire* as fevered trope, not as anything *hors-texte*.

7. In this context, to sound the note of *Mitleid* recalls Weberian *verstehen*. For other resonances of *Mitleid* with empathy and *pitié* compressed into the comparative discourse of Rousseau, Lévi-Strauss, and Schopenhauer's pessimism, see Boon 1972: 154; 1989b). For an incisive critique of confusing *Mitleid*, compassion, or *pitié* with "purely emotional" phenomena, see Valeri (1985: 80–81), who assesses the cultural importance of "identification" with animals, gods, or other others in forms of sacrifice (versus just totemism).

Conclusions

1. Certain critics of Dumont have equated his "holistic" accounts with politically nefarious totalization. Recently, A. Appadurai, rightly on guard against India's being tagged as inherently fated to caste, has even accused Dumont of essentialized "Orientalism," in the sense of disempowering-feminizing projection of the Other, made routine by Edward Said (Appadurai 1986, somewhat softened in Appadurai 1987). Now, to confuse Dumont's relational wholes (hierarchicus/oeconomicus) with Said's wholesale brand of Orientalism (coined to echo accusations of racism, sexism, etc.) overlooks the thrust of Dumont's corpus. Dumont criticizes ideas of individualistic agency and isolable "good" that triumphed in the West's utilitarian economism; he has himself exposed state totalitarianism as a form of rampant individualism; he has pinpointed colonialist errors produced by projecting individualistic assumptions onto multiplex relations of hierarchy, as if any hierarchy were a "stratification" or an outright hege-

mony. For Appadurai to elide "holistic" with totalized also looks past possible "mystifications" tucked into critical positions such as Said's (see Boon 1982a: 280; Clifford 1988: 271). For example, Said occasionally evokes a future human condition (in recent lectures on "Imperialism," he called it a "brotherhood"), transcending differences of generation and gender and thwarting differentiations of deferred return on what is produced and exchanged. The pipedream of communitarian differencelessness—like-minded, gratified, like-hearted individuals, unhampered and uninhibited by deferral— keeps returning, despite, or because of, its proved impracticability.

Postlude

1. I wish to stress that this essay's writing predated two biographies of Mead by C. Bateson and J. Howard that in part exposed her privacy. My topic was and remains, I think, as profound: the semiotic intricacy of Mead's "publicity." I had not read those biographies in 1983, when this postlude was composed (its first version was published in 1985). I was struck then, as now, by what could be really read from Mead's publications; that topic seems to me still crucial, even increasingly so today. History keeps winking.

2. On Derrida's famous/notorious "always already," see the introductions in Derrida (1976, 1978); a quick way into Kenneth Burke's dramatism is Burke (1966), particularly the opening essays. Lévi-Strauss's commitment to endless plays of variation is stressed in Boon (1972, 1982a, 1989b); the Geertz allusion is to "thick description" (1973: chap. 1). There is, of course, no question of synthesizing these scholars or their approaches.

3. On relevant dimensions of Lévi-Strauss's *Tristes tropiques,* see Boon (1972: chap. 6,; 1982a, 1985a, 1986, 1989b). It would, parenthetically, be difficult to invent a fact that better undermines any developmental or "progressive" history of autobiographical-ethnological discourse (or any other discourse) than this one: *Blackberry Winter* was written after *Tristes tropiques.*

4. I have pursued the Belo story, and companion stories, in Boon (1986). Neither there, here, nor any place, could "I" adopt Mead's mode of autobiography, when she imagined that everything she discovered was fated, in the stars. Elsewhere lie my affinities, contrarily occur my coincidences; otherwise are my preferred extremes (Boon 1989a, 1989b). Yet, gifted was Mead at oscillating in and out of a discourse of the personal. Either to execute or to ironize first-person discourse is, as we all know, risky business.

Bibliography

Adams, H.
1947 [1893   *Tahiti: Memoirs of Arii Taimai e Marama of Eimeo. . . .* R. E.
1901]   Spiller, ed. and intro. New York: Scholars' Facsimiles.

1959 [1904]   *Mont-Saint-Michel and Chartres.* R. A. Cram, intro. New York:
              Doubleday.

1961 [1907]   *The Education of Henry Adams.* D. W. Brogan, intro. New York:
              Houghton Mifflin.

1983   *Novels. Mont-Saint-Michel. The Education.* E. and J. Samuels,
              eds. The Library of America.

1986   *History of the United States of America . . .* 2 vols. New York:
[1889–91]   The Library of America.
Adams, M. J.
1980   Structural Aspects of East Sumbanese Art. In Fox (1980a).
Ahmad, A.
1987   Jameson's Rhetoric of Otherness and the "National Allegory." *So-
              cial Text* 17: 3–27.

Alter, R., and
F. Kermode
1987   *The Literary Guide to the Bible.* Cambridge: The Belknap Press
              of Harvard University Press.

*American
Anthropologist*
1980   In Memoriam, Margaret Mead 82(2): 262–373.
Anderson,
B. R. O'G.
1965   *Mythology and the Tolerance of the Javanese.* Data Paper 27. Ith-
              aca: Cornell University Southeast Asia Program.

1972   *Java in a Time of Revolution.* Ithaca: Cornell University Press.

1983   Old State, New Society: Indonesia's New Order in Comparative
              Historical Perspective. *Journal of Asian Studies,* 42(3): 477–96.

Appadurai, A.
1986   *Is Homo Hierarchicus? American Ethnologist* 13(4): 745–61.

1988   Putting Hierarchy in Its Place. *Cultural Anthropology* 3(1): 36–
              49.

Archer, M., and
R. Lightbown
1984   *India Observed: India as Viewed by British Artists, 1760–1860. Victoria and Albert Museum.* London: Faber and Faber.

Archipel
1978   Satu Windu "Archipel." *Archipel* 16: 3–5.

Babcock, B., ed.
1978   *The Reversible World.* Ithaca: Cornell University Press.

Bakhtin, M.
1968   *Rabelais and His World.* H. Iswolsky, trans. Cambridge: M.I.T. Press.

1981   *The Dialogic Imagination.* M. Holquist, ed. C. Emerson and M. Holquist, trans. Austin: University of Texas Press.

Bali Post
1981   Mengenal Pura Kawitan/Padharman dan Pura Panyungsungan Jagat. June 8, 1981, p. 1.

Bandem, I Made,
and F. E. De Boer
1981   *Kaja and Kelod: Balinese Dance in Transition.* Kuala Lumpur: Oxford University Press.

Bann, S
1984   *The Clothing of Clio: A Study of the Representation of History in 19th Century Britain.* Cambridge: Cambridge University Press.

Barthes, R.
1976   *Sade/Fourier/Loyola.* R. Miller, trans. New York: Farrar, Strauss, and Giroux.

1977   *Image, Music, Text.* S. Heath, trans. New York: Hill and Wang.

Bastin, J.
1965a   English Sources for the Modern Period of Indonesian History. In Soedjatmoko (1965).

1965b   Introduction to Raffles (1817 [1965]).

Bataille, G.
1989   *Theory of Religion.* R. Hurley, trans. New York: Zone Books.

Bateson, G.
1937   An Old Temple and a New Myth. In Belo (1970).

1958   *Naven: A Survey of the Problems Suggested by a Composite Picture of the Culture of a New Guinea Tribe Drawn from Three Points of View.* Stanford: Stanford University Press.

1972   *Steps to an Ecology of Mind.* New York: Ballantine Books.

Bateson, G., and
M. Mead
1942   *Balinese Character.* Special Publication, 2. New York Academy of Sciences.

Bausani, A.
1960   The First Italian-Malay Vocabulary by Antonio Pigafetta. *East and West,* n.s. 11, 229–48.

Beaver, H.
1973   Introduction and Notes. *Moby Dick*. H. Melville. London: Pen-
                guin Books.
Beck, B.
1982   *The Three Twins: The Telling of a South Indian Folk Epic*. Bloom-
                ington: Indiana University Press.
Becker, A. L.
1979   Text-building, Epistemology, and Aesthetics in Javanese Shadow
                Theater. In *The Imagination of Reality*. A. L. Becker and A. Yen-
                goyan, eds., pp. 211–43. Norwood, N.J.: Ablex.
Belo, J.
1935   A Study of Customs Pertaining To Twins in Bali. In Belo (1970).

1936   A Study of A Balinese Family. *American Anthropologist* 38(1),
                12–31.

1949   *Bali: Rangda and Barong*. Monographs of the American Ethnol-
                ogical Society. Seattle: University of Washington Press.

1953   *Bali: Temple Festival*. Monographs of the American Ethnological
                Society. Seattle: University of Washington Press.

1960   *Trance in Bali*. New York: Columbia University Press.
Belo, J., ed.
1970   *Traditional Balinese Culture*. New York: Columbia University
                Press.
Benedict, R.
1946   *The Chrysanthemum and the Sword*. Boston: Houghton Mifflin.

1961 [1934]   *Patterns of Culture*. Boston: Houghton Mifflin.
Berthe, L.
1972   Parenté, pouvoir et mode de production: Éléments pour une typol-
                ogie des sociétés agricoles de l'Indonésie. In *Echanges et com-
                munications*. J. Pouillon et P. Maranda, eds. The Hague, Mouton.
Berthier, M-T.,
and J-T. Sweeney
1976   *Bali: L'Art de la magie*. Paris: Librairie Armand Colin.
Bhadra, I. W.
1969   Nonconformity in Villages of Northern Bali. In Swellengrebel
                (1969).
Biardeau, M.
1981   *L'hindouisme: Anthropologie d'une civilisation*. Paris.
Biardeau, M.,
and C. Malamoud
1976   *Le Sacrifice dans L'Inde ancienne*. Paris: Presses Universitaires de
                France.
Bickmore, A. S.
1869   *Travels in the East Indian Archipelago*. New York: Appleton.
Biel, G.
1966   The Circumcision of the Lord. In *Forerunners of the Reformation*.
                H. A. Oberman, ed. New York.

216   *Bibliography*

Blair, R.
1982   Perspectives of Form and Meaning in Melville's Prose Narratives.
                  Ph.D. Dissertation. Cornell University.
Blau, H.
1982   *Take up the Bodies: Theater at the Vanishing Point.* Urbana: Uni-
                  versity of Illinois Press.
Bloch, Marc
1961   *Feudal Society.* 2 vols. Chicago: University of Chicago Press.
Bloch, Maurice
1987   *From Blessing to Violence.* Cambridge: Cambridge University
                  Press.
Bloch, M., and
J. Perry, eds.
1982   *Death and the Regeneration of Life.* Cambridge: Cambridge Uni-
                  versity Press.
Bloch, R. H.
1983   *Etymologies and Genealogies: A Literary Anthropology of the
                  French Middle Ages.* Chicago: University of Chicago Press.
Boon, J. A.
1972   *From Symbolism to Structuralism: Lévi-Strauss in a Literary Tra-
                  dition.* New York: Harper and Row.

1973   Further Operations of "Culture" in Anthropology: A Synthesis of
                  and for Debate. In *The Idea of Culture in the Social Sciences.* L.
                  Schneider and C. Bonjean, eds. New York: Cambridge University
                  Press.

1974   The Progress of the Ancestors in a Balinese Temple Group, pre-
                  1906–1972. In *Journal of Asian Studies* 34: 7–25.

1977   *The Anthropological Romance of Bali, 1597–1972: Dynamic Per-
                  spectives in Marriage and Caste, Politics and Religion.* New
                  York: Cambridge University Press.

1978   The Shift to Meaning. In *American Ethnologist* 5(2): 361–67.

1982a   *Other Tribes, Other Scribes: Symbolic Anthropology in the Com-
                  parative Study of Cultures, Histories, Religions, and Texts.* New
                  York: Cambridge University Press.

1982b   Incest Recaptured: Some Contraries of Karma in Balinese Sym-
                  bology. In *Karma: An Anthropological Inquiry.* C. F. Keyes and
                  E. V. Daniel, eds., pp. 185–222. Berkeley: University of Califor-
                  nia Press.

1982c   Introduction to *Between Belief and Transgression.* M. Izard and P.
                  Smith, eds. Chicago: University of Chicago Press.

1982d   Review of J. Fox, ed., *The Flow of Life.* In *American Anthropol-
                  ogist* 84(1): 218–20.

1983a   Functionalists Write Too: Frazer/Malinowski, and the Semiotics
                  of the Monograph. In *Semiotica* (issue on "Signs in the Field." M.
                  Herzfeld, ed.).

1983b	America: Fringe Benefits. In *Raritan* (Spring): 97–121.
1984a	Folly, Bali and Anthropology, or Satire Across Cultures. In *Text, Play, and Story*. E. Bruner, ed. Washington, D.C.: Proceedings of the American Ethnological Society for 1983.
1984b	Structuralism Routinized, Structuralism Fractured. In *American Ethnologist* 11(4): 807–12.
1985a	Claude Lévi-Strauss. In *The Return of Grand Theory*. Q. Skinner, ed. Cambridge: Cambridge University Press.
1985b	Mead's Mediations: Some Semiotics from the Sepik, by way of Bateson, on to Bali. In *Semiotic Mediations*. B. Mertz and R. Parmentier, eds. New York: Academic Press.
1986	Between-the-wars Bali: Rereading the Relics. In Malinowski, Rivers, Benedict, et al. *History of Anthropology*, vol. 4. George Stocking, ed. Madison: University of Wisconsin Press.
1986b	Symbols, Sylphs, and Siwa. In Turner and Bruner (1986).
1987	Anthropology, Ethnology, and Religion. In *Encyclopedia of Religion*, vol. 1. Mircea Eliade, ed. New York: Macmillan.
1989a	Against Coping Across Cultures: The Semiotics of Self-Help Rebuffed. In *Semiotics, Self, and Society. Essays in Honor of Milton Singer*. G. Urban and B. Lee, eds. Mouton.
1989b	Lévi-Strauss, Wagner, Romanticism: A Reading-Back. In *History of Anthropology*, vol. 6, Romantic Motives. G. W. Stocking, ed. Madison: University of Wisconsin Press.
1990	Cosmopolitan Moments: Echoey Confessions of an Ethnographer-Tourist. Manuscript.

Boon, J. A., and
D. M. Schneider

1974	Kinship vis-à-vis Myth: Contrasts in Lévi-Strauss's Approaches to Cross-Cultural Comparison. *American Anthropologist* 76(4): 799–817.

Bowlby, R.

1985	*Just Looking: Consumer Culture in Dreiser, Gissing, and Zola*. New York: Methuen.

Brady, I.

1982	The Myth-Eating Man. Review Article on W. Arens, *The Man-eating Myth*. *American Anthropologist* 84, 595–611.
1984	Introduction to review articles on M. Mead and D. Freeman. *American Anthropologist* 86.

Brandon, J.

1970	*On Thrones of Gold: Three Javanese Shadow Plays*. Cambridge: Harvard University Press.

Brooks, J. L.

1984	*Just before the Origin: Alfred Russel Wallace's Theory of Evolution*. New York: Columbia University Press.

Bruner, E., ed.
  1984   *Text, Play, and Story.* Proceedings of the American Ethnological
                         Society. Washington, D.C.
Burke, J. G.
  1972   The Wild Man's Pedigree: Scientific Method and Racial Anthro-
                         pology. In Dudley and Novak (1972).
Burke, K.
  1962   *A Grammar of Motives and a Rhetoric of Motives.* New York:
                         Meridian Books.

  1966   *Language as Symbolic Action.* Berkeley: University of California
                         Press.

  1970   *The Rhetoric of Religion: Studies in Logology.* Berkeley: Univer-
                         sity of California Press.

Burke, P.
  1978   *Popular Culture in Early Modern Europe.* New York University
                         Press.

  1987   *The Historical Anthropology of Early Modern Italy.* Cambridge:
                         Cambridge University Press.

Carpenter, C.
  1987   Brides and Bride-Dressers in Contemporary Java. Doctoral Dis-
                         sertation. Cornell University.

Carter, A. T.
  1984   Kintype Classification and Concepts of Relatedness in South Asia.
                         American Ethnologist 11(1): 81–97.

Cave, T. C.
  1979   *The Cornucopian Text. Problems of Writing in the French Renais-
                         sance.* Oxford: Clarendon Press.

Chamberlin, J.E.,
and S. L. Gilman,
eds.
  1985   *Degeneration: The Dark Side of Progress.* New York: Columbia
                         University Press.

Chase, C.
  1986   *Decomposing Figures: Rhetorical Readings in the Romantic Tra-
                         dition.* Baltimore: Johns Hopkins University Press.

Clifford, J.
  1981   On Ethnographic Surrealism. *Comparative Studies in Society and
                         History* 23(4), 539–64.

  1986   On Ethnographic Allegory. In Clifford and Marcus (1986).

  1988   *The Predicament of Culture.* Cambridge: Harvard University
                         Press.

Clifford, J., and
G. Marcus, eds.
  1986   *Writing Culture: The Poetics and Politics of Ethnography.* Berke-
                         ley: University of California Press.

Coedès, H.
1968   *The Indianized States of Southeast Asia.* Honolulu: East-West
                Center Press.

Cohn, B.
1985   Representing Authority in Victorian India. In Hobsbawm and
                Ranger (1985)

Collis, M.
1970   *Raffles.* London: Faber and Faber.

Covarubbias, M.
1937   *Island of Bali.* New York: Alfred A. Knopf.

Crapanzano, V.
1987   Hermes' Dilemma: The Masking of Subversion in Ethnographic
                Description. In Clifford and Marcus (1987), 51–77.

Crawfurd, J.
1816   An Inscription from the Kawi, or ancient Javanese Language. *Ver-*
                handelingen van het Bataviaasch Genootschap der Kunsten en
                Wetenschappen, VIII Deel.

1820   *History of the Indian Archipelago, Containing an Account of the*
                Manners, Arts, Languages, Religions, Institutions, and Com-
                merce of its Inhabitants. 3 vols. London: Frank Cass (reprinted
                1967).

1856   *A Descriptive Dictionary of the Indian Islands and Adjacent*
                Countries. London (reprinted 1971).

Culler, J.
1981   *In Pursuit of Signs: Semiotics, Post-Structuralism, Literature.* Ith-
                aca: Cornell University Press.

Curtius, E.
1953   *European Literature and the Latin Middle Ages.* Princeton:
                Princeton University Press.

Danandjaya, J.
1980   *Kebudayaan Petani Desa Trunyan di Bali.* Jakarta: Pustaka Jaya.

Darnton, R.
1984   *The Great Cat Massacre, and Other Episodes in French Cultural*
                History. New York: Vintage Books.

Davis, N. Z.
1975   *Society and Culture in Early Modern France.* Stanford: Stanford
                University Press.

1984   Revolution and Revelation. Review of Duby (1984). *New York*
                Review of Books 31(1): 32–34.

Day, A.
1983   Islam and Literature in South-East Asia: Some Pre-modern,
                Mainly Javanese Perspectives. In *Islam in South-East Asia.* M. B.
                Hooker, ed. Leiden: E. J. Brill.

De Casparis, J. G.
1962   Historical Writing on Indonesia (Early Period). In Hall (1962).

De Certeau, M.
1984   *The Practice of Everyday Life.* S. F. Rendall, trans. Berkeley: University of California Press.

1986   *Heterologies: Discourse on the Other.* B. Massumi, trans. Minneapolis: University of Minnesota Press.

De Man, P.
1971   *Blindness and Insight: Essays in the Rhetoric of Contemporary Criticism.* New York: Oxford University Press.

1979   *Allegories of Reading: Figural Language in Rousseau, Neitzsche, Rilke, and Proust.* New Haven: Yale University Press.

Dening, G.
1980   *Islands and Beaches: Discourse on a Silent Land; Marquesas, 1774–1880.* Honolulu: University Press of Hawaii.

1986   Possessing Tahiti. *Archaeol. Oceania* 21, 103–18.

1988   *History's Anthropology: The Death of William Gooch.* Association for Social Anthropology in Oceania. New York: University Press of America.

De Rougemont, D.
1963   *Love Declared.* New York: Pantheon.

1983   *Love in the Western World.* Third Ed. Princeton: Princeton University Press.

Derrida, J.
1976   *Of Grammatology.* G. C. Spivak, trans. Baltimore: Johns Hopkins University Press.

1978   *Writing and Difference.* A. Bass, trans. Chicago: University of Chicago Press.

Detienne, M.
1979   *Dionysos Slain.* M. and L. Muellner, trans. Baltimore: Johns Hopkins University Press.

1982   Rethinking Mythology. In Izard and Smith (1982).

Douglas, M.
1970   *Natural Symbols.* New York: Vintage Books.

Duby, G.
1977   *The Chivalrous Society.* C. Postan, trans. Berkeley: University of California Press.

1983   *The Knight, The Lady, and the Priest.* B. Bray, trans. New York: Pantheon.

1984   *The Three Orders: Feudal Society Imagined.* A. Goldhammer, trans. Chicago: University of Chicago Press.

Dudley, E., and
M. E. Novak, eds.
1972   *The Wild Man Within: An Image in Western Thought from the Renaissance to Romanticism.* Pittsburgh: University of Pittsburgh Press.

Duff-Cooper, A.
1986   Twins and Transvestites: Two Aspects of the Totality of the Ba-
               linese Form of Life in Western Lombok. *Zeitschrift für Ethnologie*
               111(2).

Dumézil, G.
1966–1971   *Mythe et épopée*. Three vols. Paris: Gallimard.

1979   *Mariages Indo-Européens*. Paris: Payot.

Dumont, L.
1975   Understanding Non-Modern Civilizations. *Daedalus* 104 (2):
               153–72.

1977   *From Mandeville to Marx*. Chicago: University of Chicago Press.

1980   *Homo Hierarchicus: The Caste System and Its Implications*. Rev.
               ed. Chicago: University of Chicago Press.

1982   A Modified View of Our Origins: The Christian Beginnings of
               Modern Individualism. *Religion* 12, 1–27.

1986   *Essays on Individualism: Modern Ideology in Anthropological
               Perspective*. Chicago: University of Chicago Press.

Echols, J. M.
1978   Presidential Address: Dictionaries and Dictionary Making: Malay
               and Indonesian. *Journal of Asian Studies* 38, 11–14.

Eco, U.
1979   *The Role of the Reader: Explorations in the Semiotics of Texts*.
               Indiana University Press.

1986   *Travels in Hyperreality*. London: Picador.

Eisenstein, E.
1979   *The Printing Press as an Agent of Change: Communication and
               Cultural Transformation in Early Modern Europe*. Cambridge:
               Cambridge University Press.

Eksteins, M.
1985   History and Degeneration: Of Birds and Cages. In Chamberlin and
               Gilman (1985).

Eliade, M.
1978   *The Forge and the Crucible*. Second ed. Chicago: University of
               Chicago Press.

Elias, N.
1982   *Power and Civility*. New York: Pantheon.

1983   *The Court Society*. New York: Pantheon.

Eliot, T. S.
1965 [1922]   The Waste Land. In *The Oxford Anthology of English Literature*,
               vol. 2. F. Kermode and J. Hollander, eds. Oxford: Oxford Uni-
               versity Press.

Emigh, J.
1982   Playing with the Past: Visitation and Illusion in the Mask Theatre
               of Bali. *The Drama Review/* T82, 11–36.

Emigh, J., and
I. M. Bandem,
trans.
  1982   Jelantik Goes to Blambangan: A Topeng Pajegan Performance by
                I Nyoman Kakul. *The Drama Review/* T 82, 37–48.
Emmerson, D. K.
  1980   A Maritime Perspective on Southeast Asia. *Journal of Southeast
                Asian Studies* 40 (1): 130–45.
Erasmus, D.
  1941 [1511]   *The Praise of Folly.* H. H. Hudson, trans. Princeton: Princeton
                University Press.
Errington, S.
  1987   Incestuous Twins and the House Societies of Insular Southeast
                Asia. *Cultural Anthropology* 2(4): 403–45.
  1989   *Meaning and Power in a Southeast Asian Realm.* Princeton:
                Princeton University Press.
Fabian, J.
  1982   *Time and the Other.* New York: Columbia University Press.
Febvre, L.
  1982 [1942]   *The Problem of Unbelief in the Sixteenth Century: The Religion of
                Rabelais.* B. Gottlieb, trans. Cambridge: Harvard University
                Press.
Feldman, B., and
R. D. Richardson,
eds.
  1972   *The Rise of Modern Mythology, 1680–1860.* Bloomington: Indi-
                ana University Press.
Forge, A.
  1980   Balinese Religion and Indonesian Identity. In Fox (1980b).
Fortune, R.
  1932   Incest. In *Encyclopaedia of the Social Sciences,* vol. 7. New York:
                Macmillan.
  1933   A Note on Some Forms of Kinship Structure. *Oceania* 4 (1): 1–9.
  1963 [1932]   *Sorcerers of Dobu.* New York: Dutton.
Foucault, M.
  1970   *The Order of Things: An Archaeology of the Human Sciences.*
                New York: Random House.
  1977   *Discipline and Punish: The Birth of the Prison.* A. Sheridan,
                trans. New York: Random House.
  1984   *The Foucault Reader.* P. Rabinow, ed. New York: Pantheon.
Fox, J. J., ed.
  1980a   *The Flow of Life: Essays on Eastern Indonesia.* Cambridge: Har-
                vard University Press.
  1980b   *Indonesia: The Making of a Culture.* Canberra: Research School
                of Pacific Studies. Australia National University.

Franklin, H. B.
1963   *The Wake of the Gods: Melville's Mythology.* Stanford: Stanford
                University Press.
Frazer, J. G.
1920   *The Magical Origin of Kings.* London: Macmillan.
Freeman, D.
1983   *Margaret Mead and Samoa: The Making and Unmaking of an An-
                thropological Myth.* Cambridge: Harvard University Press.
Frye, N.
1957   *Anatomy of Criticism.* Princeton: Princeton University Press.

1976   *Spiritus Mundi.* Bloomington: Indiana University Press.

1981   *The Great Code: The Bible and Literature.* New York: Harcourt
                Brace Jovanovich.

Geden, A. S.
1922   Tantrism. *Encyclopedia of Religion and Ethics.* Vol. 12.
Geertz, C.
1959   Form and Variation in Balinese Village Structure. *American An-
                thropologist* 61, 94–108.

1960   *The Religion of Java.* New York: The Free Press.

1963   *Peddlers and Princes.* Chicago: University of Chicago Press.

1965   *The Social History of an Indonesian Town.* Cambridge: The
                M.I.T. Press.

1968   *Islam Observed.* New Haven: Yale University Press.

1973   *The Interpretation of Cultures.* New York: Basic Books.

1976   Reply to Hooykaas. *Archipel* 12, 219–25.

1980   *Negara: The Theater State in Nineteenth Century Bali.* Princeton:
                Princeton University Press.

1983   *Local Knowledge.* New York: Basic Books.

1984a   *Bali: l'Interpretation d'une culture.* Paris.

1984b   Culture and Social Change: The Indonesian Case. *Man* 19, 511–
                32.

Geertz, H.
1959   The Balinese Village. In *Local, Ethnic, and National Loyalties in
                Village Indonesia.* G. W. Skinner, ed. New Haven: Yale Univer-
                sity Southeast Asia Studies, pp. 24–33.

1963   Indonesian Cultures and Communities. In *Indonesia.* R. T.
                McVey, ed. New Haven: HRAF Press.

N.d., ed.   *Balinese State and Society.* Volume from the 1984 Conference,
                Leiden, KITLV.

Geertz, H., and
C. Geertz
1975   *Kinship in Bali.* Chicago: University of Chicago Press.

Gellrich, J. M.
1985   *The Idea of the Book in the Middle Ages: Language, Theory, My-
               thology, and Fiction.* Ithaca: Cornell University Press.
Gerdin, I.
1981   The Balinese Sidikara: Ancestors, Kinship, and Rank. *Bijdragen
               tot der Taal-, Land-, en Volkenkunde* 137 (1): 17–36.

1982   *The Unknown Balinese: Land, Labor, and Inequality in Lombok.*
               Gothenburg: Studies in Social Anthropology.
Gesick, L., ed.
1983   *Centers, Symbols, and Hierarchies: Essays on the Classical States
               of Southeast Asia.* Yale University Southeast Asia Monograph No.
               26.
Gewertz, D. B.
1983   *Sepik River Societies: A Historical Ethnography of the Chambri
               and Their Neighbors.* New Haven: Yale University Press.
Girard, R.
1977   *Violence and the Sacred.* P. Gregory, trans. Baltimore: Johns Hop-
               kins University Press.
Godzich, W.
1986   Introduction to De Certeau (1986).
Goethe, J. W. von
1962   *Elective Affinities: A Novel.* F. Ungar, intro. New York: Ungar.

1971   *Elective Affinities.* R. J. Hollingdale, trans. New York: Penguin.
Goldstein, J.
1987   Lifestyles of the Rich and Tyrannical. *The American Scholar*
               56(2): 235–47.

Gombrich, E.
1969   *Art and Illusion.* Princeton: Princeton University Press.
Gonda, J.
1939   William Marsden als Beoefenaar der Taalwetenschap. *Bijdragen
               tot de Taal-, Land- en Volkenkunde* 98, 517–28.

1975   The Indian Religions in Pre-Islamic Indonesia and Their Survival
               in Bali. *Handbuch der Orientalistik,* 3(1): 1–54.
Goody, J.
1987   *The Interface Between the Written and the Oral.* Cambridge: Cam-
               bridge University Press.
Gossman, L.
1984   Basle and Bachofen. *Journal of the Warburg and Courtauld Insti-
               tute* 47: 136–85.
Gould, S. J.
1977   *Ever Since Darwin.* New York: W. W. Norton.
1982   *The Panda's Thumb.* New York: W. W. Norton.
Green, M.
1972   *Cities of Light and Sons of the Morning.* Boston: Little, Brown.

1979   *Dreams of Adventure, Deeds of Empire.* New York: Basic Books.

1987   *The English Novel in the Twentieth Century: The Doom of Empire.*
                Pennsylvania State University Press.

1988   *The Von Richthofen Sisters.* University of New Mexico Press.

Greenblatt, S., .ed.
1980   *Renaissance Self-Fashioning.* Chicago: University of Chicago
                Press.

1988   *Representing the English Renaissance.* Berkeley: University of
                California Press.

Greenwood, D.
1984   *The Taming of Evolution.* Cornell: Cornell University Press.

Guermonprez, J-F.
1984   Les Pande de Bali. Mémoire pour le Doctorat de Troisième Cycle.
                Paris: École des Hautes Études en Sciences Sociales.

1985   Rois divins et rois guerriers. *L'Homme* 25:39–70.

Hall, D. G. E., ed.
1962   *Historians of South East Asia.* London: Oxford University Press.

Handelman, D.
1979   Is Naven Ludic? Paradox and the Communication of Identity. *So-
                cial Analysis* 1:177–91.

Hanna, W.
1976   *Bali Profile.* New York: Whitman Press.

1978   Toward a History of Bali. In *Spectrum: Essays Presented to Sutan
                Takdir Alisjahbana.* S. Udin, ed. Jakarta: Dian Rakyat.

Harpham, G. G.
1982   *On the Grotesque: Strategies of Contradiction in Art and Litera-
                ture.* Princeton: Princeton University Press.

Harrison, B.
1961   English Historians of the "Indian Archipelago": Crawfurd and
                St.John. In Hall (1962).

Headley, S.
1983   Le Lit-grenier et la Déesse de la fécondité à Java: Rites nuptiaux?
                Dialogue 82, 77–86.

Hefner, R.
1987   *Hindu Javanese.* Princeton: Princeton University Press.

Held, G. J.
1935   *The Mahabharata: An Ethnological Study.* London: Kegan Paul,
                Trench, Trubner.

Herbert, T. W.
1982   *Marquesan Encounters.* Cambridge: Harvard University Press.

Héritier, F.
1979   Symbolique de l'inceste et sa prohibition. In *La Fonction symbo-
                lique.* M. Izard et Pierre Smith, eds. Paris: Gallimard.

Herrenschmidt, O.
1979   Sacrifice: Symbolic or Effective? In Izard and Smith (1982), 24–
                43.

Hinzler, H. I. R.
1986   *Catalogue of Balinese Manuscripts*. Part Two. Leiden: E. J. Brill,
               Leiden University Press.
Hobart, M.
1974   Some Balinese Uses of Animal Symbolism: Are Aristocrats Pigs?
               Indonesia Circle 5: 18–20.

1978   The Path of the Soul: The Legitimacy of Nature in Balinese Con-
               ceptions of Space. In *Natural Symbols in Southast Asia*. G. B.
               Milner, ed. London: School of Oriental and African Studies, pp.
               5–28.

1980   *Ideas of Identity: The Interpretation of Kinship in Bali*. Den Pasar:
               Universitas Udayana, Jurusan Anthropologi Budaya.

1986   Thinker, Thespian, Soldier, Slave? Assumptions about Human
               Nature in the Study of Balinese Society. In *Context, Meaning, and
               Power in Southeast Asia*. M. Hobart and R. H. Taylor, eds. Ith-
               aca, New York.

Hobsbawm, E.,
and T. Ranger, eds.
1985   *The Invention of Tradition*. Cambridge: Cambridge University
               Press.
Hocart, A. M.
1950 [1927]   *Kingship*. London: Oxford University Press.

1952   *The Life-Giving Myth*. London: Methuen.

1954   *Social Origins*. London: Watts.

1970 [1936]   *Kings and Councillors*. R. Needham, intro. Chicago: University
               of Chicago Press.

1987   *Imagination and Proof*. R. Needham, ed. University of Arizona
               Press.
Hodgen, M.
1964   *Early Anthropology in the Sixteenth and Seventeenth Centuries*.
               Philadelphia: University of Pennsylvania Press.
Holmberg, D.
1989   *Order in Paradox: Myth, Ritual, and Exchange Among Nepal's
               Tamang*. Ithaca: Cornell University Press.
Hooykaas, C.
1957   Love in Lenka. *Bijdragen tot de Taal-, Land- en Volkenkunde* 113,
               274–89.

1964   Agama Tirtha: Five Studies in Balinese Religion. *Verhandelingen
               der Koninklijke Nederlandse Akademie van Wetenschappen, Afd.
               Letterkunde* 70.

1970   The Treasure of Bali. In *R. C. Majumdar Felicitation Volume*.
               H. B. Sarker, ed. Calcutta: K. L. Mukhopadhyay.

1973a   *Religion in Bali*. Leiden, E. J. Brill.

| 1973b | Balinese Bauddha Brahmans. *Verhandelingen der Koninklijke Nederlandse Akademie van Wetenschappen* 80. Amsterdam: North Holland. |

1973c   *Kama and Kala: Materials for the Study of Shadow Theater in Bali.* Amsterdam: North Holland.

1976a   Social Anthropology, A "Discipline" of Theories and Hearsay? *Archipel* 11, 237–43.

1976b   The Dukuh as a Balinese Priest: A Sociological Problem. *South East Asian Review* 1, 91.

1980a   *Drawings of Balinese Sorcery.* Leiden: E. J. Brill.

1980b   *Tovenarij op Bali.* Amsterdam: Meulenhoff.

Hooykaas, J.
1957   De Godsdienstige Ondergrond van het Praemuslimse Huwelijk op Java en Bali. *Indonesië* 10(2): 109–36.

1960a   Changeling in Balinese Folklore and Religion. *Bijdragen tot de Taal-, Land-, en Volkenkunde* 116.

1960b   The Myth of the Young Cowherd and the Little Girl. *Bijdragen tot de Taal-, Land-, en Volkenkunde* 117(2).

Horkheimer, M., and T. W. Adorno
1972   *Dialectic of Enlightenment.* J. Cumming, trans. New York: Seabury.

Hose, C.
1927   *Fifty Years of Romance and Research, or a Jungle Wallah at Large.* London: Hutchinson.

Huntington, R., and P. Metcalf
1979   *Celebrations of Death.* Cambridge: Cambridge University Press.

Hyde, L.
1982   *The Gift: Imagination and the Erotic Life of Property.* New York: Vintage.

Izard, M. and P. Smith, eds.
1982   *Between Belief and Transgression.* J. Leavitt, trans. Chicago: University of Chicago Press.

Jameson, F.
1986   Third-World Literature in the Age of Multinational Capital. *Social Text* 15: 65–88.

Jay, M.
1982   Should Intellectual History Take a Linguistic Turn? In LaCapra and Kaplan (1972), 86–110.

Jenkins, R.
1980   The Holy Humor of Bali's Clowns. *Asia* 3(2), 28–35.

Josselin de Jong,
J. B. P. de
1977 [1952]   Lévi-Strauss's Theory of Kinship. In *Structural Anthropology in the Netherlands.* P. E. de Josselin de Jong, ed. The Hague: Nijhoff.

Kapferer, B.
1983   *A Celebration of Demons.* Bloomington: Indiana University Press.

Keeler, W.
1987   *Javanese Shadow Plays, Javanese Selves.* Princeton: Princeton University Press.

Keen, M.
1984   *Chivalry.* New Haven: Yale University Press.

Keith, A. B.
1917   *Mythology of All Races,* vol. 6. Boston: Marshall Jones.

Kenner, H.
1962   *The Stoic Comedians.* Berkeley: University of California Press.

Kermode, F.
1987   The Canon. In Alter and Kermode (1987), 600–611.

Kolenda, P.
1984   Woman as Tribute, Woman as Flower: Images of "Woman" in Weddings in North and South India. *American Ethnologist* 11(1): 98–117.

Korn, V. E.
1932   *Het Adatrecht van Bali.* Second edition. The Hague.

Kott, J.
1987   *The Bottom Translation.* Evanston: Northwestern University Press.

Kristeva, J.
1980   *Desire in Language.* L. S. Roudiez, ed. New York: Columbia University Press.

Kulkarni, H. B.
1970   *Moby-Dick: A Hindu Avatar.* Logan: Utah State University Press, Monograph Series 18.

Kumar, A.
1987   Literary Approaches to Slavery and the Indies Enlightenment: Vaan Hogendorp's Kraspoekol. *Indonesia* 43, 43–44.

LaCapra, D.
1982   Rethinking Intellectual History and Reading Texts. In LaCapra and Kaplan (1982).

LaCapra, D. and
S. Kaplan, eds.
1982   *Modern European Intellectual History: Reappraisals and New Perspectives.* Ithaca: Cornell University Press.

Lach, D. F.
1967   *Asia in the Making of Europe.* Vol. I, bk. 1. *The Century of Discovery.* Chicago: University of Chicago Press.

1965   *Southeast Asia in the Eyes of Europe*. Chicago: University of Chicago Press.

Ladner, G.
1979   Medieval and Modern Understanding of Symbolism: A Comparison. *Speculum* 54 (2).

Lansing, S.
1983   *The Three Worlds of Bali*. New York: Praeger.

Leach, E. R.
1964   *Political Systems of Highland Burma*. Boston: Beacon Press.

1987   Fishing for Men on the Edge of the Wilderness. In Alter and Kermode (1987), 579–600.

Lederman, R.
1986   *What Gifts Engender*. Cambridge: Cambridge University Press.

Le Goff, Jacques
1980   *Time, Work, and Culture in the Middle Ages*. A. Goldhammer, trans. Chicago: University of Chicago Press.

Levin, H.
1969   *The Myth of the Golden Age in the Renaissance*. New York: Oxford University Press.

Lévi-Strauss, C.
1962   *La Pensée sauvage*. Paris: Plon.

1963a   *Totemism*. R. Needham, trans. Boston: Beacon Press.

1963b   *Structural Anthropology*. C. Jacobson and B. Grundfest Schoepf, trans. New York: Doubleday.

1964   *Le Cru et le cuit*. Paris: Plon.

1969   *The Elementary Structures of Kinship*. R. Needham, ed. Boston: Beacon Press.

1971   *L'Homme nu*. Paris: Plon.

1973a   *From Honey to Ashes*. J. and D. Weightman, trans. New York: Harper and Row.

1973b   *L'Anthropologie structurale deux*. Paris: Plon.

1979   Nobles sauvages. In *Culture, Science, et Développement*. Toulouse: Privat.

1983a   *The Way of the Masks*. Second edition. S. Modelski, trans. London: Jonathan Cape.

1983b   *Le Regard éloigné*. Paris: Plon.

1984   *Paroles données*. Paris: Plon.

Lewis, C. S.
1938   *The Allegory of Love*. London: Oxford University Press.

Lindenbaum, S.
1987   The Mystification of Female Labors. In *Gender and Kinship*. J. Collier and S. Yanagisako, eds. Stanford: Stanford University Press.

n.d.   Understanding Siva: An Anthropological Analysis. Unpublished
                     paper.
Lipset, D.
1980   *Gregory Bateson: The Legacy of a Scientist.* Englewood Cliffs:
                     Prentice-Hall.
Littleton, C. S.
1983   *The New Comparative Mythology: An Anthropological Assessment
                     of the Theories of Georges Dumézil.* Berkeley: University of Cali-
                     fornia Press.
Lovejoy, A. O.
1964 [1936]   *The Great Chain of Being: A Study of the History of an Idea.*
                     Cambridge: Harvard University Press.
Lovric, B.
1987a   Rhetoric and Reality: The Hidden Nightmare. Ph.D. Dissertation.
                     University of Sidney.

1987b   Bali: Myth, Magic and Morbidity. In *Death and Disease in South-
                     east Asia.* N. Owen, ed. Singapore: Oxford University Press.
Lowie, R. H.
1961 [1920]   *Primitive Society.* New York: Harper and Row.
Lueras, L.
1987   *Bali: The Ultimate Island.* Photog. R. I. Lloyd. New York: St.
                     Martin's Press.
Lyons, J. D.
1983   In the Folds of the Renaissance Text. Review of Cave (1979).
                     Diacritics, Fall.
McLuhan, M.
1962   *The Gutenberg Galaxy.* Toronto: University of Toronto Press.
McPhee, C.
1966   *Music in Bali.* New Haven: Yale University Press.
McVey, R.
1986   The *Wayang* Controversy in Indonesian Communism. In *Context,
                     Meaning and Power in Southeast Asia.* M. Hobart and R. H. Tay-
                     lor, eds. Ithaca, N.Y.
Marsden, W.
1783   *The History of Sumatra,* Third Edition, 1811. London.
Maurice, T.
1795–98   *The History of Hindostan.* London.
Mauss, M.
1967   *The Gift.* I. Cunnison, trans. New York: Norton.
Mauss, M., and
H. Hubert
1972   *A General Theory of Magic.* Boston.
Mead, M.
1959   *An Anthropologist at Work: Writings of Ruth Benedict.* Boston:
                     Houghton Mifflin.

1963 [1935]   *Sex and Temperament in Three Primitive Societies.* New York:
                     Morrow.

1975 [1972]   *Blackberry Winter: My Earlier Years*. New York: Morrow, Pocketbook edition.

1977   *Letters from the Field, 1925–1975*. New York: Harper and Row.
Melville, H.
1970 [1849]   *Mardi and a Voyage Thither*. Evanston: Northwestern University Press and the Newberry Library.

1971 [1857]   *The Confidence Man*. H. Parker, ed. New York: Norton Critical Edition.

1973 [1851]   *Moby Dick*. London: Penguin Books.
Merleau-Ponty, M.
1964   *Signs*. R. C. McLeary, trans. Evanston: Northwestern University Press.

1973   *Adventures of the Dialectic*. J. Bien, trans. Evanston: Northwestern University Press.

Mertz, E., and
R. Parmentier, eds.
1985   *Semiotic Mediations*. Orlando: Academic Press.
Meyer, H. M. J.
1985   *Fragments of Reading: The Malay Hikayat Merong Mahawangsa*. Proefschrift, Rijksuniversiteit te Leiden.

Meylakh, M.
1975   The Structure of the Courtly Universe of the Troubadours. *Semiotica* 14 (1): 61–80.

Milner, A.
1982   *Kerajaan: Malay Political Culture on the Eve of Colonial Rule*. University of Arizona Press.

Milner, A. C.,
E. McKinnon, and
T. L. Sinar S. H.
1978   A Note on Aru and Kota Cian. Indonesia 26, 1–42.
Modell, J. S.
1983   *Ruth Benedict: Patterns of Life*. Philadelphia: University of Philadelphia Press.

More, T.
1975   *Utopia*. R. Adams, ed. New York: Norton Critical Editions.
[1516–18]
Mrazek, R.
1983   *Bali: The Split Gate to Heaven*. London: Orbis Books.
Mullaney, Steven
1988   Strange Things, Gross Terms, Curious Customs: The Rehearsal of Cultures in the Late Renaissance. In Greenblatt (1988).

Multatuli
[E. D. Dekker]
1967 [1860]   *Max Havelaar*. Roy Edwards, trans. London: Heinemann.
Mulyono, I. S.
1978a   *Wayang: Asal-usul, Filsafat dan Masa Depannya*. Jakarta: Gunung Agung.

1978b	*Wayang dan Karakter Wanita.* Jakarta: Gunung Agung.
1979a	*Wayang dan Karakter Manusia.* Jakarta: Gunung Agung.
1979b	*Simbolisme dan Mistikisme dalam Wayang.* Jakarta: Gunung Agung.

Napier, A. D.
1986   *Masks, Transformation, and Paradox.* Berkeley: University of California Press.

Needham, R.
1970   Introduction to Hocart (1970).

1981   *Circumstantial Deliveries.* Berkeley: University of California Press.

1985   *Exemplars.* Berkeley: University of California Press.

Nelli, R.
1963   *L'Erotisme des troubadours.* Toulouse: E. Privat.

Obeyesekere, G.
1984   *The Cult of the Goddess Pattini.* Chicago: University of Chicago Press.

O'Connor, S. J.
1985   Metallurgy and Immortality at Candi Sukuh, Central Java. *Indonesia* 39: 53–70.

O'Flaherty, W. D.
1973   *Asceticism and Eroticism in the Mythology of Siva.* Oxford.

1975   *Hindu Myths.* Baltimore: Penguin Books.

1980   *Women, Androgynes, and Other Mythical Beasts.* Chicago: University of Chicago Press.

1984   *Dreams, Illusions, and Other Realities.* Chicago: University of Chicago Press.

1985   *Tales of Sex and Violence: Folklore, Sacrifice, and Danger in the Jaiminīya Brāhmana.* Chicago: University of Chicago Press.

1988   *Other Peoples' Myths.* New York: Macmillan.

O'Keefe, D. L.
1983   *Stolen Lightning: The Social Theory of Magic.* New York: Vintage Books.

Oldroyd, D. R.
1980   *Darwinian Impacts.* Atlantic Highlands: Humanities Press.

Ong, W. J.
1967   *The Presence of the Word.* New Haven: Yale University Press.

1977   *Interfaces of the Word.* Ithaca: Cornell University Press.

1982   *Orality and Literacy.* London: Methuen.

1983   *Ramus, Method and the Decay of Dialogue.* Cambridge: Harvard University Press.

Oosten, J. G.
1985   *The War of the Gods: The Social Code in Indo-European Mythology.* London: Routledge and Kegan Paul.

Ortner, S.
1977   *Sherpas Through Their Rituals*. Cambridge: Cambridge University Press.
Padoux, A.
1987   Tantrism: An Overview; and Hindu Tantrism. In *Encyclopedia of Religion*. M. Eliade, ed. New York: Macmillan.
Paul, R.
1982   *The Tibetan Symbolic World:* Chicago: University of Chicago Press.
Payne, F. A.
1981   *Chaucer and Menippean Satire*. Madison: University of Wisconsin Press.
Peacock, J. L.
1968   *Rites of Modernization*. Chicago: University of Chicago Press.
1973   *Indonesia: An Anthropological Perspective*. Pacific Palisades: Goodyear.
1978   *Muslim Puritans: Reformist Psychology in Southeast Asian Islam*. Berkeley: University of California Press.
1987   *The Anthropological Lens*. New York: Cambridge University Press.
Peirce, C. S.
1955   *Philosophical Writings*. J. Cuchler, ed. New York: Dover.
Peletz, M. G.
1987   The Exchange of Men in 19th-Century Negeri Sembilan (Malaya). *American Ethnologist* 14(3); 449–69.
Pelras, C.
1978   Indonesian Studies in France: Retrospect, Situation, and Prospects. *Archipel* 16, 17–21.
Pigafetta, A.
1906   *Magellan's Voyage Around the World. The Original Text of the Ambrosian MS*. 2 vols. J. A. Robertson, trans. Cleveland: A. H. Clerk.
Pigeaud, T.
1967–70   *The Literature of Java*. 3 vols. The Hague: Martinus Nijhoff.
1977 [1928] In *Structural Anthropology in the Netherlands*. P. E. de Josselin de Jong, ed. The Hague: Nijhoff.
Poliakov, L.
1974   *The Aryan Myth: A History of Racist and Nationalist Ideas in Europe*. New York: Basic Books.
Pope, A.
1960 [1712] *The Rape of the Lock*. New York: Dover.
Prichard, J. C.
1843   *The Natural History of Man*. London.
Pringle, R.
1970   *Rajahs and Rebels: The Ibans of Sarawak under Brooke Rule, 1841–1941*. Ithaca: Cornell University Press.

Pucci, I.
1986   *The Epic of Life: A Balinese Journey of the Soul.* New York:
               Alfred van der Marck.
Rabinow, P., and
W. M. Sullivan.
1979   *Interpretive Social Science: A Reader.* Berkeley: University of
               California Press.
Radin, P.
1972   *The Trickster.* S. Diamond, intro. New York: Schocken Books.
Rafferty, E.
1984   Languages of the Chinese of Java. *The Journal of Asian Studies*
               43: 247–72.
Raffles, T. S.
1816   Discourse of the Honorable the President Tho. Stamford Raffles.
               Verhandelingen van het Bataviaasch Genootschap der Kunsten en
               Wetenschappen, 8 Deel.

1817   *The History of Java.* Kuala Lumpur: Oxford University Press.
               (Oxford in Asia Historical Reprints, 1965).
Ramseyer, U.
1977   *The Art and Culture of Bali.* New York: Oxford University Press.
Rassers, W. H. R.
1959   *Panji, the Culture Hero.* The Hague: Martinus Nijhoff.
Reid, A.
1983, ed.   *Slavery, Bondage and Dependency in Southeast Asia.* St. Lucia:
               University of Queensland Press.

1988   *Southeast Asia in the Age of Commerce, 1450–1680:* Vol. 1. New
               Haven: Yale University Press.
Reynolds, D. S.
1988   *Beneath the American Renaissance.* New York: Knopf.
Ricklefs, M. C.
1971   Foreword to Crawfurd (1856).
Ricoeur, P.
1979   The Model of the Text: Meaningful Action Considered as a Text.
               In Rabinow and Sullivan (1979).
Robinson, G.
1988   State, Society, and Political Conflict in Bali, 1945–1946. *Indone-*
               sia 45: 1–48.
Robson, S. O.
1972   The Kawi Classics in Bali. *Bijdragen tot de Taal-, Land- en Volk-*
               enkunde 128 (2–3), 307–29.

1983   Kakawin Reconsidered: Toward a Theory of Old Javanese Poetics.
               Bijdragen tot de Taal-, Land- en Volkenkunde 139 (2–3), 291–
               319.
Rogin, M. P.
1983   *Subversive Genealogy: The Politics and Art of Herman Melville.*
               Berkeley: University of California Press.

Rosaldo, R.
1984   *Ilongot Headhunting*. Stanford: Stanford University Press.
Rosenthal, J. T.
1985   Kings, Courts, and the Manipulation of Late Medieval Culture and
                Literature. *Comparative Studies in Society and History* 27(3):
                486–93.
Rubin, G.
1975   The Traffic in Women. In *Toward an Anthropology of Women*. R.
                Reiter, ed. New York: Monthly Review Press, 157–210.
Sahlins, M.
1976   *Culture and Practical Reason*. Chicago: University of Chicago
                Press.

1981   *Historical Metaphors and Mythical Realities: Structure in the
                Early History of the Sandwich Islands Kingdom*. Association for
                Social Anthropology in Oceania. Ann Arbor: University of Mich-
                igan Press.

1985   *Islands of History*. Chicago: University of Chicago Press.
Said, E.
1978   *Orientalism*. New York: Pantheon Books.
Santoso, S., ed.
1973   *Lilaracana-Ramayana*. Yogyakarta: Gadjah Mada University
                Press.

Saussure, F. de
1966   *Course in General Linguistics*. W. Baskin, trans. New York:
                McGraw Hill.

Schechner, R.
1986   *Between Theater and Anthropology*. Philadelphia: University of
                Pennsylvania Press.

Schneider, D. M.
1972   What Is Kinship All About? In *Kinship Studies in the Morgan
                Centennial Year*. P. Reining, ed. Washington, D.C.

1976   The Meaning of Incest. *Journal of the Polynesian Society*. 85(2):
                149–69.

1980   *American Kinship: A Cultural Account*. Second edition. Chicago:
                University of Chicago Press.

1984   *A Critique of the Study of Kinship*. Ann Arbor: University of
                Michigan Press.
Schulte Nordholt,
H.
1980   Macht, Mensen en Middelen: Patronen van Dynamiek in de Bal-
                ische Politiek, 1700–1840. MA Thesis. Free University of Am-
                sterdam.

1981   The Mads Lange Connection: A Danish Trader on Bali in the
                Middle of the Nineteenth Century. *Indonesia* 32, 17–47.
Schwab, R.
1950   *La renaissance orientale*. Paris: Payot.

Sejarah Desa
Trunyan
    1976   [History of Trunyan Village]. Bangli: Daerah Kepolisian 15, Nusa
                     Tenggara, sertu Klungkung.
Serres, M.
    1982   *The Parasite*. L. Schehr, trans. Baltimore: Johns Hopkins Univer-
                     sity Press.
Singer, I.
    1984   *The Nature of Love*. Vol. 2. *Courtly and Romantic*. Chicago: Uni-
                     versity of Chicago Press.
Singer, M.
    1972   *When a Great Tradition Modernizes: An Anthropological Ap-
                     proach to Indian Civilization*. New York: Praeger.

    1984   *Man's Glassy Essence: Explorations in Semiotic Anthropology*.
                     Bloomington: Indiana University Press.
Skinner, Q.
    1978   *The Foundations of Modern Political Thought*. 2 vols. Cambridge:
                     Cambridge University Press.
Soedjatmoko, ed.
    1965   *An Introduction to Indonesian Historiography*. Ithaca: Cornell
                     University Press.
Spence, J.
    1985   *The Memory Palace of Matteo Ricci*. New York: Viking.
Spiller, R. E.
    1947   Introduction in H. Adams (1947).
Spivak, G.
    1987   *In Other Worlds: Essays in Cultural Politics*. New York: Methuen.
Stallybrass, P.,
and A. White.
    1986   *The Politics and Poetics of Transgression*. Ithaca: Cornell Univer-
                     sity Press.
Steinberg, L.
    1983   *The Sexuality of Christ in Renaissance Art and in Modern Obliv-
                     ion*. New York: Pantheon/*October*.
Steiner, G.
    1975   *After Babel*. New York: Oxford University Press.
St. John, H.
    1853   *The Indian Archipelago: Its History and Present State*. 2 vols.
                     London: Longman.
Stocking, G.
    1978   Anthropology as *Kulturkampf*: Science and Politics in the Career
                     of Franz Boas. In *Anthropology and the Public*. W. Goldschmidt,
                     ed. Washington, D.C.

    1987   *Victorian Anthropology*. New York: The Free Press.
Strathern, M.
    1988   *The Gender of the Gift*. Berkeley: University of California Press.

Stuart-Fox, D. J.
1979   *Bibliography of Balinese Culture and Religion*. Jakarta: KITLV
                and Lembaga Ilmu Pengetahuan Indonesia.
Sweeney, A.
1988   *A Full Hearing: Orality and Literacy in the Malay World*. Berke-
                ley: University of California Press.
Swellengrebel,
J. L.
1977 [1936]   Some Characteristic Features of the *Korawasrama* Story. In *Struc-
                tural Anthropology in the Netherlands*. P. E. de Josselin de Jong,
                ed. The Hague: M. Nijhoff.
Swellengrebel,
J. L., ed.
1960   Bali: Some General Information. In *Bali: Studies in Life,
                Thought, Ritual*, pp. 3–76. The Hague: W. van Hoeve.

1969   *Bali: Further Studies in Life, Thought, Ritual*. The Hague: W. van
                Hoeve.
Tambiah, S.
1976   *World Conqueror and World Renouncer*. Cambridge: Cambridge
                University Press.

1984   *The Buddhist Saints of the Forest and the Cult of Amulets*. Cam-
                bridge: Cambridge University Press.
Tan, R. Y. D.
1960   The Domestic Architecture of South Bali. *Bijdragen tot de Taal-,
                Land- en Volkenkunde* 116:442–75.
Tanner, T.
1979   *Adultery in the Novel: Contract and Transgression*. Baltimore:
                Johns Hopkins University Press.
Tedlock, B.
1984   The Beautiful and the Dangerous: Zuni Ritual and Cosmology as
                an Aesthetic System. *Conjunctions* 6: 246–65.
Tedlock, D.
1983   *The Spoken Word and the Work of Interpretation*. Philadelphia:
                University of Pennsylvania Press.
Thapar, R.
1968   *A History of India*. London: Penguin.
Tjokrosudarmo, S.
1975   Are There Aristocrats Among Pigs? *Indonesia Circle* 6: 11–12.
Todorov, T.
1984   *The Conquest of America: The Question of the Other*. R. Howard,
                trans. New York: Harper and Row.
Traube, E.
1980a   Mambai Rituals of Black and White. In Fox (1980a).

1980b   Affines and the Dead: Mambai Rituals of Alliance. *Bijdragen tot
                de Taal-, Land- en Volkenkunde* 136: 90–116.

1986   *Cosmology and Social Life: Ritual Exchange Among the Mambai of East Timor.* Chicago: University of Chicago Press.

Turner, V.
1974   *Dramas, Fields, and Metaphors,* Ithaca: Cornell University Press.

Turner, V., and
E. Bruner, eds.
1986   *The Anthropology of Experience.* University of Illinois Press.

Tuzin, D.
1977   *The Ilahita Arapesh.* Berkeley: University of California Press.

Tyler, S.
1986   Post-modern Ethnography: From document of the Occult to Occult Document. In Clifford and Marcus (1986).

Uitti, K.
1973   *Story, Myth, and Celebration in Old French Narrative Poetry.* Princeton: Princeton University Press.

Valeri, V.
1980   Notes on the Meaning of Marriage Prestations Among the Huaulu of Seram. In Fox (1980a).

1982   The Transformation of a Transformation: A Structural Essay on an Aspect of Hawaiian History (1809–1819). *Social Analysis* 10, 3–41.

1985   *Kingship and Sacrifice.* Chicago: University of Chicago Press.

Vance, E.
1979   Mervelous Signals: Poetics, Sign Theory, and Politics in Chaucer's Troilus. *New Literary History* 10, 293–338.

Van der Kraan, A.
1980   *Lombok: Conquest, Colonization, and Underdevelopment, 1870–1940.* Singapore: Heinemann.

1985   Human Sacrifice in Bali: Sources, Notes, and Commentary. *Indonesia* 40, 89–121.

Varenne, J.
1977   *Le Tantrisme: la sexualité transcendée.* Paris: Retz.

Verne, J.
1957   *The Mysterious Island.* Cleveland: World.

Vickers, A.
1982   A Balinese Illustrated Manuscript of the Siwaratrikalpa. *Bijdragen tot der Taal-, Land- en Volkenkunde* 138.

1984   Ritual and Representation in Nineteenth Century Bali. *Review of Indonesian and Malaysian Affairs* 18: 1–35.

1986   The Desiring Prince: A Study of the Kidung Malat as Text. Ph.D. Thesis. University of Sydney.

1987   Hinduism and Islam in Indonesia: Bali and the Pasisir World. *Indonesia* 44: 31–58.

Wadlington, W.
1987   *Reading Faulknerian Tragedy.* Ithaca: Cornell University Press.

Wallace, A. R.
1869   *The Malay Archipelago.* New York: Harper and Brothers.

1870   *Insulinde: Het Land van den Orang-Oetan en den Paradijsvogel.*
                P. J. Veth, trans. Amsterdam: Pn N. Van Kampen.
Ward, D.
1968   *The Divine Twins.* Berkeley: University of California Press.
Weatherbee, D. E.
1978   Raffles' Sources for Traditional Javanese Historiography and the
                Mackensie Collections. *Indonesia* 26: 63–93.
Weber, M.
1946   *From Max Weber.* H. Gerth and C. Wright Mills, eds. New York:
                Oxford.

1967   *The Religion of India.* H. Gerth and D. Martindale, trans. New
                York: The Free Press.
Weck, W.
1937   *Heilkunde und Volkstum auf Bali.* Stuttgart: F. Enke.
Weiner, A.
1976   *Women of Value, Men of Renown.* Austin: University of Texas
                Press.
White, A.
1982   Pigs and Pierrots: The Politics of Transgression in Modern Fic-
                tion. *Raritan* 2(2), 51–70.
Willson, A. L.
1964   *A Mythical Image: The Ideal of India in German Romanticism.*
                Durham: Duke University Press.
Wink, P.
1924   De Bronnen van Maarsden's Adatbeschrijving van Sumatra. *Bijdr-
                agen tot de Taal-, Land- en Volkenkunde* 80, 1–10.
Wolf, E.
1982   *Europe and the People without History.* Berkeley: University of
                California Press.
Wolfson, E.
1988   Circumcision, Vision of God, and Textual Interpretation. *History
                of Religions* 27(2): 189–215.
Wolters, O. W.
1982   *History, Culture, and Region in Southeast Asian Perspectives.*
                Singapore: Institute of Southeast Asian Studies.
Worsley, P.
1972   *Babad Buleleng: A Balinese Dynastic Genealogy.* The Hague:
                Martinus Nijhoff.

1984   E 74168 (An Analysis of a Balinese Painting of a Ramayana Epi-
                sode). *Review of Indonesian and Malaysian Affairs* 18: 64–109.
Yates, F.
1971   *Theater of the World.* Chicago: University of Chicago Press.

1972   *The Rosicrucian Enlightenment.* London: Routledge and Kegan
                Paul.

1979   *Print Culture.* Encounter 52(4), 59–64.

Young, E. F.
1982   The Tale of Erlangga: Text Translation of a Village Drama Per-
                      formance in Bali. *Bijdragen tot de Taal-, Land- en Volkenkunde*
                      138(4), 470–91.
De Zoete, B.,
and W. Spies.
1939   *Dance and Drama in Bali.* New York: Harper's Magazine Press.
Zurbuchen, M.
1987   *The Language of Balinese Shadow Thater.* Princeton: Princeton
                      University Press.
De Zwaan, J. P. K.
1919   Denkbeelden der Inlanders van den Indischen Archipel omtrent de
                      Geboorte van Tweelingen. *Tijdschrift van het Koninklijk Neder-
                      landsche Aardrijkskundig Genootschap* 36.

INDEX